FROM BUTLER TO BUFFETT

FROM BUTLER TO BUFFETT

THE STORY BEHIND THE *Buffalo News*

MURRAY B. LIGHT

FOREWORD BY WARREN E. BUFFETT

59 John Glenn Drive
Amherst, New York 14228-2197

The publisher gratefully acknowledges
Butler Family Papers courtesy of E. H. Butler Library Archives,
Buffalo State College
Buffalo and Erie County Historical Society Archives, C67–6,
Alfred H. Kirchhofer Papers

Published 2004 by Prometheus Books

Inquiries should be addressed to
Prometheus Books
59 John Glenn Drive
Amherst, New York 14228–2197
VOICE: 716–691–0133, ext. 207
FAX: 716–564–2711
WWW.PROMETHEUSBOOKS.COM

08 07 06 05 04 5 4 3 2 1

Library of Congress Cataloging-in-Publication Data

Light, Murray B.
From Butler to Buffett : the story behind the Buffalo news / Murray B. Light.
p. cm.
Includes bibliographical references.
ISBN 1–59102–180–4 (hardcover)
1. Buffalo news (Buffalo, N.Y. : Daily) I. Title.

PN4899.B9165B845 2004
071'.4797—dc22

2004001574

Printed in Canada on acid-free paper

For my daughter Lee

We cannot know how much we learn
From those who never will return,
Until a flash of unforeseen
Remembrance falls on what has been

—*Edwin Arlington Robinson*, Flammonde

CONTENTS

Foreword

I'll never forget 1977.

Early that year Blue Chip Stamps (later to be merged into Berkshire Hathaway) purchased the *Buffalo Evening News*. The *News* had more than double the daily circulation of the *Courier-Express*, its morning rival, but it had forsaken Sunday publication. The *Courier-Express* reigned supreme and uncontested on that day, which, then as now, was by far the favorite for advertisers.

That was a mortal threat to the *News*: throughout the country, one major daily after another had failed when competing with rivals who initially had trailed badly on weekdays but were dominant on Sunday. There were no exceptions to this rule.

My partner, Charlie Munger, and I therefore knew we had to launch a Sunday edition, no matter what the cost. And we promptly did so.

The *Courier-Express* responded with a lawsuit and found a friendly judge, Charles L. Brieant. He quickly laid down harsh terms for publication that crippled the introduction of our Sunday edition. His actions also devastated the morale of our 1,100 employees. Many had not been happy with our decision to enter the Sunday field—their routine had been uncomplicated before Charlie and I had come to Buffalo—and now they found their beloved paper under attack from all sides. Understandably, most were beginning to rue the day that the *News* had been sold.

Murray Light was the exception. And he was the one we needed—a brilliant and tireless editor who had to infuse life into a Sunday product that was maimed at birth by the court and sent out to compete with a product that over fifty-seven years had become a deeply entrenched habit for Buffalo citizens.

Murray's instructions were to put out a first-class Sunday edition, no matter how scarce the ads and how dispirited his troops. Our survival depended on his ability to do so. And Murray pulled it off. The outstanding product he delivered established a solid base of subscribers.

Then after fifteen months, the U.S. Second Circuit Court of Appeals ruled unanimously that Judge Brieant's decision had been "infected with legal and factual error" and reversed his order. Circulation subsequently began to climb slowly and eventually the better product carried the day.

The *News* recently recorded its 125th anniversary. It's a birthday we wouldn't be celebrating if Murray Light had not been our editor in 1977.

Warren E. Buffett
Berkshire Hathaway Inc.

INTRODUCTION

I had just gotten back to my office at the *Buffalo News* when Warren E. Buffett, my friend and boss since 1977, walked into my office. We both had just come from a luncheon in my honor given by the executives of the *News*. It was early in September 1999 and my retirement had been set for September 19, fifty years to the day that I started at the paper as a reporter.

Buffett said he had an idea and wondered if I would be interested in pursuing it. He asked if I had any interest in researching and writing a history of the newspaper. I immediately said yes, explaining that it would fill the void I had been dreading since I decided a year earlier to retire. I told him that I had continued working until I was seventy-three because I still enjoyed what I was doing and was concerned about what I would do in retirement since I had neither the time nor the desire to develop any hobbies.

Some time before this meeting with Buffett, I had reached an agreement with Stanford Lipsey that in retirement I would write a weekly Sunday column to express my opinions on a wide variety of topics. But I didn't feel that the column would be enough to occupy me fully. The Buffett proposal was ideal.

Alfred H. Kirchhofer, one of my predecessors as editor of the *Buffalo News*, had undertaken the task of writing the history of the paper and had spent more than a decade on the endeavor prior to his death in 1985 at the age of ninety-three. He never completed the task but numerous typed chapters are on file in the *Buffalo News* archives at Buffalo State College. An ardent student of western New York politics, the completed chapters go into detail of countless political campaigns through the years, including those for committee persons and other minor party positions. He obviously became bogged down in tracking politics at even the most local levels. The archives include countless memos Kirchhofer exchanged with his assistant, Wayne Jordan, who conducted the research and wrote all of the completed chapters. Kirchhofer would then make corrections, additions, and deletions to Jordan's work. Kirchhofer's passion for politics became the dominant theme of his "history" of the *News*. The completed chapters appeared to lose sight of the book's original objective. Nevertheless, it is a treasure trove of information, trivial and otherwise, of the political machinations of his time as editor. Unfortunately the chapters are not footnoted so it is difficult to trace any of the information to its original source.

Buffett had suggested that I could utilize the services of any *News* staffer to assist me in my research for the book. I had two reasons for deciding early on not to take advantage of this generous offer of assistance. First, I did not want to upset any of my former editors by pulling one or more of their people from their assigned duties. Second, I felt that I would find it more beneficial to view all the available historical material directly and make the judgments on what should be used rather than obtaining the information indirectly through an assistant.

Most of my research was in the archives of Buffalo State College. Thanks to the wonderful cooperation of archivist Mary Delmont and her very capable assistant, Margaret Hatfield, my seven or more months of working there four or five days a week was a highly productive and pleasant experience. In reviewing the memoranda of Edward H. Butler Sr., I was surprised to learn that many of his concerns, going back to the start of the *Sunday News* in 1873 and continuing through his stewardship over the *Buffalo Evening News* from 1880 to 1914, were the same as I had during my period of overseeing the *News* from 1969 to 1999. He counseled his editors and reporters about the necessity of keeping their material tightly written by excluding peripheral material. He stressed the need to present all sides of controversial subjects, to keep the writer's opinions out of news stories, to avoid the use of adjectives that could be considered prejudicial, and to write simple, declarative sentences that would be easily understood. These and many other bits of advice were the same as those I strongly emphasized to my editors and staffers many years later. Only recently did I come to realize that the founder of the newspaper had advocated them himself.

It is unfortunate, in my opinion, that many of these precepts are being violated today to a greater degree than ever before. The proliferation of local columnists and even staffers who are supposed to be dealing in facts, but instead express their opinions, has readers confused about who or what the newspaper supports. The proliferation of opinion also substantially minimizes the thrust of the editorial page, which is supposed to present the official position of the newspaper.

E. H. Butler's strong objection to overly long stories appears to have been totally set aside despite repeated studies that have shown through the years that readers' attention will not focus on stories that run on and on. Of course there is the need for an occasional complex story to occupy several columns of space, but these should be the exception rather than the rule. The Butler desire to control the length of stories was reinforced numerous times in memos by Kirchhofer and myself but they were heeded for a short time and then forgotten.

Among its many shortcomings, this book can be criticized for omitting the names and achievements of the hundreds of men and women who contributed to the success of the *News* through the years in departments other than the newsroom. I would never underestimate the importance of their roles but I decided early in this undertaking that to include them would increase the size of this volume beyond reasonable limits. Their activities and exploits are worthy of another book. My fifty years at the *News* were all in the newsroom and these were the people and events that I could best describe. While I certainly had involvement with the principals in other departments, I do not feel comfortable attempting to portray them here. This book, then, concentrates on the reporters, editors, and other newsroom people as well as the publishers of the *News*. Failure to cite William Goodspeed, Clayton Underhill, Edgar Steeb, Dick Feather, and the dozens of others from the business office who contributed mightily to the *News* from its beginnings and continuing today, is not to diminish their roles in any way.

I feel compelled to admit that in my thirty years of newsroom oversight I failed to achieve one objective I long sought. I never did manage to integrate the staff so that it truly represented the community. I was successful in adding a significant number of women to the staff and promoting some to positions of responsibility. But I never succeeded in my quest to add to the numbers of African Americans. The basic problem was my determination not to hire a minority person just for the sake of adding to the numbers of minorities on the payroll. My concern was to hire only those who had a good chance of doing well. Adding minority staffers who would fail to perform well would, I felt strongly, only reinforce the feelings of some staffers that minority people could not perform as well. Adding to the problem was the reality that a good many of the fine minorities we did hire and who performed so well, departed after a time for jobs in papers such as the *Los Angeles Times*, the *Philadelphia Inquirer*, *Newsday*, and the *Boston Globe*. Fortunately, we did not lose all of our talented minority people but the numbers were less than satisfactory.

In addition to the wonderful cooperation I received from the Buffalo State College archives, I also spent several months doing research at the Buffalo and Erie County Historical Society, whose staffs were extremely cooperative and attentive. Other invaluable sources were the master's degree thesis on Edward H. Butler by Jerry Goldberg, editorial-page editor of the *News*, and the superlative special sections of the *News* published October 12, 1980, marking the one-hundredth anniversary of the paper; May 12, 1982, covering Buffalo history from 1832 to 1982; and January 1, 2000, Buffalo history from 1900 to 2000.

Last, but certainly not least, I have to credit my wife and children for the enormous support and assistance they provided through the three years I spent writing this book. Most particularly, I doubt if I would have continued my research and writing without the constant support and encouragement of my wife, Joan. When my attention flagged, she pushed me to continue working. When I had problems with my computer, and there were many, she worked them out so I could continue. When I made numerous corrections in the manuscript, she entered them in the computer. And she also undertook the arduous task of compiling all the footnotes, a task made most difficult by the mass of notes I had and the disarray in which I left them. Many of the details in this book are from my experiences and recollections over the fifty years I worked at the *News*, thirty of them in management. These are not cited in the footnotes.

My three children also play a role in the production of this volume. My son, Jeff, deputy editor of the *Orange County (CA) Register*, spent days here in Buffalo editing my text with the assistance of his talented wife, Teri, also a *Register* staffer. And my daughter, Laura, came in from her home in Massachusetts to contribute to the editing process by utilizing her experience in producing several books. My eldest daughter, Lee, was always on the sidelines encouraging me to continue working and making some excellent suggestions. I owe all of them an enormous debt of gratitude. They were a fine support team that I needed and welcomed and without whom I likely would not have persevered to complete this project.

I would be remiss were I not to cite the dedicated and loyal support I received from my secretary, Jeanne Ray, for more than twenty-five years. She had a wonderful ability to satisfy the concerns of thousands of callers through the years, saving me countless hours on the telephone. Mary Muzyka, who replaced her in my last years as editor, was also someone I could always depend on to perform the many duties required in a difficult role.

Finally, I have to acknowledge the role of my very good friend and adviser, attorney Arnold Gardner, for his active and significant participation in working with Steven L. Mitchell, editor in chief of Prometheus Books, to shape and finally formulate the agreement forming the relationship that has resulted in the publication of this book. Gardner guided me through the legal complexities that had to be overcome and I am extremely grateful to him and Mitchell for their important roles in making this book a reality. My thanks, too, must go to Prometheus publisher Paul Kurtz for recognizing the merits of my book, and to Stanford Lipsey, publisher of the *Buffalo News*, for both his constant support and his efforts on my behalf.

1 BUFFALO AND THE NEW JOURNALISM

In the years after the Civil War, men like Butler, Joseph Pulitzer, Melville Stone and E. W. Scripps melded the idealistic spirit of earlier papers like Horace Greeley's New York Tribune *and the sensational methods of the ante bellum penny press to carve out a vital new role in civic life for newspapers. Cheap, broad, and accessible, the new journalism was predicated on political independence and civic leadership.*

—Michael J. Dillon*

In the decades following the Civil War the nation fell into a long recession. Along the muddy streets of Buffalo, New York, business was bad and unemployment high. But on Canal Street, between Main and Terrace, things were happening. This was "the wickedest street in the world," compared by seamen throughout the world to the Barbary Coast and the ports of Calcutta and Shanghai. On Buffalo's lakefront, Canal Street had ninety-three saloons, fifteen dance halls, and a goodly number of "sporting houses." The female talent a man could hire there was amazing. Area directories listed as many as

*From Michael J. Dillon, "From Populist to Patrician: Edward H. Butler's *Buffalo News* and the Crisis of Labor, 1877–1892," *American Journalism* 16, no. 1 (1999): 41–58. Reprinted by permission.

five hundred names under headings of cooks, laundresses, seamstresses, fortune-tellers, and maids.[1] A lonely seaman or canaller had no problem finding a companion. One reporter wrote that "The women of the district, their hair high on their heads and covered with wide-brimmed, feathery hats, were among the first to saunter onto Canal Street after dark, the rich colors of velvet and lace dresses mixing with the golden glow of the street lamps."[2]

The saloons were wild places. Police records of the era recorded numerous instances of finding bodies in the canal. Their investigations would show that visitors to saloons often were drugged, robbed, and then thrown through a trapdoor directly into the canal. The canal at daybreak often revealed quite a few bodies, which nobody came to identify and claim. The city, anxious to keep this disreputable conduct confined, assigned watchmen to keep depraved activity within the Canal Street boundaries so as not to affect the "innocent" society of the city.[3] The sheriff of Erie County in 1873 was Grover Cleveland, the future president, and his jail for a time during this period housed more prisoners than any other in the state.[4]

But sin was not Canal Street's only product. The minstrel show, a form of musical comedy featuring singing and gags, had the bawdy unconventionality that waterfront revelers loved. Edwin P. Christy, a singer, banjo player, and dancer, who always performed in blackface, became known throughout the world with hits like "Oh! Susanna" and "Buffalo Gals":

> Buffalo gals, can't you come out tonight?
> Can't you come out tonight? Can't you come out tonight?
> Buffalo gals, can't you come out tonight?
> and dance by de light ob de moon?[5]

These were the tunes hummed by a changing America. Immigrants were pouring in—Poles and Italians joining the Germans and Irish who had come years before. Between 1870 and 1890, America's population grew by 65 percent, and Buffalo grew even faster—nearly 120 percent, from 117,714 to 255,664.[6] In the neighborhoods of cities like Buffalo these immigrants formed a burgeoning class that would enjoy a remarkable era. In the next twenty years they would see the first telephones, the first electric lights, and the first automobiles.

The urbanization of America had begun, and with it the great era of American newspapers. Buffalo was one of the places in which this era was born. The city fared better than most during the postwar depression. It sat at the terminus of the Erie Canal, which at 363 miles was the longest artificial waterway in the Western Hemisphere.[7] Buffalo had been the final stop for American slaves on the Underground Railroad before reaching freedom in Canada. The community quickly became a center of free black life in America.[8]

The world's greatest breakwater along Lake Erie provided an excellent lake harbor.[9] The stockyards along William Street were growing into a nucleus of what would become the largest livestock-processing center in the nation outside of Chicago.[10]

The few wealthy families in the city almost all resided on the West Side. "Over there on the East Side [was] where the hard-faced men unknown to us all lived," was recorded in one Delaware Avenue memoir of the era. Another account published at the time claimed that "Our instinctive feeling toward the East Side was one of contempt."[11] Their Buffalo was "a sleepy old place" with "nine months [of] winter and three months [of] late fall."[12]

But by the 1870s, the city had still not progressed very far from Civil War days. A real-estate boom was only just beginning, but there were still cobblestone streets, and sidewalks made of wood. Much of Buffalo was still a frontier town with drifters who blew in and out on ships and canal barges and a great many Native Americans in traditional dress frequenting the downtown streets.[13] The real-estate boom was soon followed by what has been described as Buffalo's golden age of architecture, a period of time during which many of the city's most outstanding buildings were planned and constructed by architects who became world renowned.[14] Electric power from Niagara Falls helped make the city a manufacturing center.[15] The growing industries were bringing more young people into the community, including many with tremendous energy who decided to make Buffalo their home and were not affected by the earlier generation who were content with the status quo. They were committed to continued growth for the city.[16]

It was in this growing town of Buffalo that a young entrepreneur named Edward H. Butler arrived in 1873 to establish a Sunday newspaper in a community that seemed sleepy to some, bawdy to others. A town with hitching posts in front of its houses but electric power from Niagara Falls inside its factories. Buffalo was a place, like America, that was about to change.

There were ten newspapers in town when Butler arrived, but none were published on Sunday.[17] Religious organizations were bitterly opposed to such Sunday publications; the city's ministers and the daily newspapers attacked them saying that they degraded the Sabbath.[18]

But events had overpowered the protesters. The Civil War had stimulated the growth of Sunday editions throughout the country, and newspapers everywhere were becoming more popular, less expensive, and a bigger part of American life.[19]

In New York City, four papers reflecting the "new journalism" were launched between 1833 and 1860.[20] Joseph Pulitzer's two-cent *New York World* captured the attention of publishers nationwide and many rolled back their subscription prices to be competitive. Butler idolized James Gordon Bennett's *New York Herald*, a one-penny paper that arrived on the scene in 1835 and mixed society news, bloody murders, and explicit sex, and included the nation's first financial page.[21]

Most of the papers were started primarily by printers in both small communities and major cities. In 1836 the *Boston Daily Times* was established but ceased publication after twenty-three years. In Philadelphia, the *Public Ledger* was also launched in 1836, copying the New York penny papers. In Baltimore, the *Sun* was started in 1837. Horace Greeley established the *New York Tribune* in 1841, and the sole survivor, the *New York Times*, was founded in 1851. St. Louis had six daily papers by 1850 and Illinois had over four hundred papers. The *Chicago Daily Tribune*, forerunner of the *Chicago Tribune*, began publication in 1847. It went through a series of owners until Joseph Medill became part owner in 1855. Medill became one of the most admired journalists in newspaper history.[22] On a Sunday in May 1881, the *Tribune* published what it still considers to be one of the greatest scoops in history. It ran sixteen pages, without a single omission of chapter or verse, of the recently completed American Revised Version of the New Testament.[23]

By 1880, there were approximately seven thousand American newspapers, almost double the number published in 1870.[24] The invention of the typewriter (1867) and linotype typesetting (1886) helped make newspapers cheaper to operate. The expansion of literacy among the immigrant communities added to circulation. Amid the hunger for information about the new postwar society, illiteracy dropped from 20 percent to 10.7 percent between 1870 and 1900.[25]

While government and politics still remained paramount in newspaper coverage, the loosening of party loyalties had a salutary effect, allowing the papers to criticize government policies and leaders. Independent journalism was taking root in the nation.[26]

Edward Butler was just twenty-three years old when he arrived in Buffalo to begin his publishing career. After his death, Dr. Charles Elliott Fitch, a historian, wrote: "Mr. Butler had the distinction of being the most successful newspaper publisher in the United States, who was the founder, developer, sole proprietor, and editor of his paper, and who retained these relations from the beginning. No other man has built up so splendid a newspaper property all by himself."[27]

NOTES

1. George E. Condon, *Stars in the Water: The Story of the Erie Canal* (New York: Doubleday, 1974), p. 260.

2. Ibid., p. 261.

3. Ibid.

4. Jerry Goldberg, "Edward H. Butler and the Founding of the *Buffalo Evening News*: The Life and Times of One of the Last Publisher-editors" (master's thesis, State University of New York at Buffalo, 1997), p. 24.

5. Condon, *Stars in the Water*, pp. 265–69.

6. U.S. Bureau of the Census, "Nativity of the Population for Urban Places Ever Among the 50 Largest Urban Places Since 1870: 1850 to 1890," release date, March 9, 1999, www. Census.gov/population/www/documentation/twps0029/tab22/html (accessed January 8, 2003).

7. *A History of the City of Buffalo, Its Men and Institutions* (Buffalo, NY: Buffalo Evening News, 1908), p. 36.

8. Mark Goldman, *City on the Lake: The Challenge of Change in Buffalo, New York* (Amherst, NY: Prometheus Books, 1990), p. 15.

9. Edwin F. Rundell, rev. Charles W. Stein, *Buffalo: Your City* (Buffalo, NY: Henry Stewart, 1962), p. 108.

10. William H. Dolan, comp., *Our Police and Our City: The Official History of the Buffalo Police Department and a History of the City of Buffalo*, ed. Mark S. Hubbell (Buffalo, NY: Bensler & Wesley, 1893), p. 194.

11. Mark Goldman, *High Hopes: The Rise and Decline of Buffalo, New York* (Albany: State University of New York Press, 1983), p. 73.

12. Dolan, *Our Police and Our City*, quote from H. M. Kinne, p. 192.

13. Rundell, *Buffalo: Your City*, p. 111.

14. Introduction to *Buffalo Architecture: A Guide* (Cambridge, MA: MIT Press, 1996), p. 1.

15. *A History of the City of Buffalo*, p. 32.

16. Dolan, *Our Police and Our City*, p. 202.

17. Goldberg, "Edward H. Butler," pp. 25, 26.

18. Frank Luther Mott, *American Journalism, 1690–1940* (New York: Macmillan, 1941), p. 318.

19. Ibid., p. 397.

20. Goldberg, "Edward H. Butler," p. 9.

21. Mott, *American Journalism*, p. 235.

22. Ibid., pp. 238–85.

23. Alfred Kirchhofer files, Butler Family Papers, E. H. Butler Library Archives, State University College at Buffalo, box 1, "History," chap. 2, p. 8.

24. Mott, *American Journalism*, p. 411.

25. National Center for Education Statistics, "Literacy from 1870 to 1979, Illiteracy," necs.ed.gov/naal/historicaldata/illiteracy.asp (accessed January 8, 2003).

26. Mott, *American Journalism*, pp. 411–12.

27. Lance Zavits, "The Edward H. Butlers—Father and Son," an address presented at a meeting of the Le Roy Historical Society, August 16, 1958. It was reprinted in full in the *Le Roy Gazette-News* on August 21, 1958.

2 Family

Edward Hubert Butler was not from a wealthy family. His father, Dennis, an itinerant minister, was born in Wilkes-Barre, Pennsylvania, in 1812. His mother, Lucy M. Chaney, was born in Dublin, Ireland, in 1830. Married in Wilkes-Barre, Dennis and Lucy moved to Le Roy, New York, a few miles west of Rochester, where Dennis helped organize the Roman Catholic congregation and used his family home for Sunday services for some time. Their first home in Le Roy was a log cabin, where Edward was born on September 5, 1850. The family moved several times to different homes but never one that they owned. Edward Butler had three siblings: Anna Maria (b. 1846), Ambrose (b. 1853), and Dennis (b. 1855). His ties to his younger brother Ambrose were very close and the two continued a strong lifelong relationship of mutual understanding, trust, and affection. His father died in 1856 when Edward was only six years old. Lucy Butler was a widow at the age of twenty-six with four small children to support. She worked out of her home taking in washing to provide for her children.[1]

Edward Butler had little formal education but he was a bright and industrious young man with a deep love for his family. He attended Le Roy's public schools and also a parochial or private school in Buffalo for a short time. He did not attend college but he was a voracious reader as a youth. Reading, in fact, was his principal recreation in his early life and a good deal of what he read remained fixed in his memory. He had developed what is known today as a "photographic memory." According to his granddaughter, Marjorie Van Antwerp,

> The reason he was so great was [that] when he was a young lad he used to read to a blind man whose name, I think, was Webster. . . . I think he lived in Le Roy. Grandfather would read to him and he became so fascinated with books that he himself became an avid reader and because he had a photographic mind and a great memory he became a tremendous person. You could give him any word in the English language and he could give you a quotation and tell you where it came from. . . . He was a great friend of writers. Eugene Field was one of his favorites and Eugene Field came here one time to have dinner with him. He was asked to recite some of his poetry. He recited for all these people and grandfather corrected him three times. He said it was the greatest compliment he had ever had.[2]

Nobody in Butler's family had newspaper experience. He got his first job on the weekly *Le Roy Gazette* as a printer's devil or apprentice. He started at twenty-four cents a week folding papers as they came off the press. He delivered papers and sold subscriptions, earning one cent for each additional subscriber he procured. From time to time he would do some writing for the *Gazette*. He also performed some minor duties in the weekly's production and circulation departments.[3]

At the age of nineteen Butler left Le Roy for a full-time reporting job as the Pittston, Pennsylvania, correspondent for the *Scranton Times*. After a short stay there he joined the staff of the *Scranton Evening Democrat*, where he was a prolific writer, producing from eight to ten columns of local news each day. In 1872 he became an advertising salesman and one of four partners in the newly formed *Scranton Sunday Free Press*, where he became acquainted with J. B. Adams, a printer who later became his partner. The paper had a short life and eventually folded for lack of financial support.[4]

While in Pittston Edward met Mary Elizabeth Barber, who became his bride in 1872. Mary came from a well-to-do family and rumor had it that Edward received financial help from them at times. She was an educated young woman who was a cousin of Ralph Waldo Emerson. She was Edward's helpmate and companion and bore him four children. Unfortunately Mary died in 1893 at the young age of thirty-eight, leaving him a lonely man with young children to raise. Only two, Ada, thirteen, and Edward H. Jr., eleven, were alive when she died. The other two children did not survive infancy.[5]

Edward H. Butler Sr., editor, publisher, proprietor, and founder of the *Buffalo Sunday Morning News* in 1873 and the *Buffalo Evening News* in 1880. (Courtesy *Buffalo News*)

Mary Butler, a Presbyterian, was instrumental in getting her Catholic husband to convert to the Protestant faith. Her obituary in the *News* described her as an "earnest Christian and an active member of Westminster Church." According to the *Buffalo Express*, "Her disposition was for a quiet home life rather than for social success."[6]

Butler raised their two children and was a very devoted father throughout his life. He never remarried, although through the years many of his friends and newspaper colleagues encouraged him to do so. In 1907, in correspondence with his friend Clark Howell, editor of the *Atlanta Constitution*, he wrote, "I have been a widower fourteen years and now I begin to feel, as one after another of my household begin to marry away, that I will be left entirely alone. It is a horrible thought for there are some things that money cannot buy."[7]

He loved his family and was very generous with them but he had definite ideas about what he wanted for them. According to his granddaughter, Edward Butler was a domineering person and had a temper. He used to check up on his children constantly and even listened to their phone calls. His daughter, Ada, would go to a friend's house when she wanted to talk on the phone to avoid being overheard. When Ada married he bought a house for her as a wedding present, but it had to be a house he liked and it had to be placed in trust for her children. Even if she sold the house, the proceeds would be kept in trust for her children. He even specified in his will what school Ada's son would attend.[8]

Ada married Roscoe Mitchell and later wed Donald Lindsey. She had three children, but when she died April 1, 1934, at the age of fifty-four, only one, Marjorie, survived her. Marjorie married Kent McKinley and later Ted Van Antwerp. At the time of Ada's death, she owned a 40 percent interest in the *News* through a trust set up by her father, Edward, in his will. Ada's interest passed to her only living daughter, Marjorie McKinley.[9]

Edward also selected the woman his son was to marry. Edward H. Butler Jr. married Kate Maddox Robinson at his father's urging. The elder Butler met her on a trip to Atlanta while his son was a student at Yale. He thought she would make an ideal wife for his son and eventually they were married in 1909.[10] It turned out to be a difficult marriage. According to their daughter Kate, her father adored her mother but her mother was a very independent and egotistical woman who was hard on her husband.[11] A review of personal letters between the younger Edward and his wife reveals she spent a good deal of her time in South Carolina, the place of her birth, or in Paris, France.

Edward Butler Jr. and Kate had one surviving daughter, Kate, who had little freedom when she was growing up and was dominated by her parents just as Edward Sr. had dominated his children.[12] She married James H. Righter in 1943. Her mother resented the time Kate spent with her husband; especially travel time, because she wanted Kate to travel with her.[13] Kate and Jim had two children, Kate and Edward.[14] In "100 Years of Pride," Marsha Ackermann, a *Buffalo Courier-Express* reporter, said Edward had been groomed to take over the *News* but was forced by circumstances to relinquish his birthright.[15] The sale of the paper and the loss of influence of the Butler family heirs brought about his departure.

The daughter of young Edward and Kate Butler later married Bruce

Wallis and, following his death, she married Dr. Robert D. Wickham. The Wickhams reside in New York City and in Sarasota, Florida.

Edward Sr.'s brother Ambrose was one of his most trusted advisers. Ambrose served as business manager of the *Sunday Morning News* and the *Buffalo Evening News* until he retired in 1902 and returned to live in Le Roy.[16] The American Newspaper Publishers Association (ANPA) was his brainchild. In July 1886 he sent letters to the business managers of the nation's largest newspapers, asking their thoughts on forming an association. The reception was cool with only a few responding. Ambrose persisted and followed up with personal visits to many of the business managers. The effort paid off and ANPA was formed at a February 1887 meeting in Rochester, New York, with seventy in attendance. Ambrose served as secretary and vice president of ANPA and a director for two terms.[17] This information is at odds with other sources that claim the organization was launched in Detroit in 1887 and that W. H. Brearly of the *Detroit News* was the organizer and first secretary.[18] Years later Edward Butler Jr. was president of ANPA and a director for two terms.[19] ANPA merged with six other newspaper associations in 1992 to form the Newspaper Association of America. This association focuses on strategic problems that affect the newspaper industry from marketing to readership.

When Ambrose Butler died on October 2, 1909, at the age of fifty-six, Edward discovered his brother's body in a room at the Waldorf-Astoria Hotel in New York City. "His loss is all the more keenly felt because he was the last of my family and I have no one to sit down with and talk of olden times," Edward later told friends.[20]

Notes

1. Alfred Kirchhofer files, Butler Family Papers, E. H. Butler Library Archives, State University College at Buffalo, box 1; Jerry Goldberg, "Edward H. Butler and the Founding of the *Buffalo Evening News*: The Life and Times of One of the Last Publisher-editors" (master's thesis, State University of New York at Buffalo, 1997), p. 1.

2. Marjorie Van Antwerp, interview by Sister Martin Joseph Jones,

October 13, 1981, Butler Family Papers, p. 3; Goldberg, "Edward H. Butler," p. 19.

3. Kirchhofer files, Butler Family Papers, box 1; Goldberg, "Edward H. Butler," p. 20.

4. Goldberg, "Edward H. Butler," p. 24.

5. Kirchhofer files, Butler Family Papers, box 1; Goldberg, "Edward H. Butler," p. 23.

6. Ibid., p. 24.

7. Edward H. Butler Sr. files, Butler Family Papers, box 1; Goldberg, "Edward H. Butler," p. 115.

8. Van Antwerp, interview, p. 3; Goldberg, "Edward H. Butler," p. 97.

9. Kirchhofer files, Butler Family Papers, box 1.

10. Goldberg, "Edward H. Butler," p. 114.

11. Kate Wallis, interview by Sister Martin Joseph Jones, August 1981, Butler Family Papers, p. 5.

12. Ibid.

13. Kate Butler Wickham, interview by Murray Light, September 25, 2002.

14. Kate Robinson Butler files, Butler Family Papers, box 1.

15. The wife of Edward H. Butler Jr., *Buffalo Courier-Express*, October 1980.

16. Edward H. Butler Sr., Butler Family Papers, box 1.

17. Kirchhofer files, Butler Family Papers, box 3.

18. Frank Luther Mott, *American Journalism, 1690–1940* (New York: Macmillan, 1941), p. 490.

19. Kirchhofer files, Butler Family Papers, box 3.

20. Edward H. Butler Sr., Butler Family Papers, box 1; Goldberg, "Edward H. Butler," p. 115.

3 A Sunday Birth

When the four partners of the *Scranton Sunday Free Press* determined that their lack of adequate financial support meant that they must dissolve their business association, they did it with panache. They drove out to a grove in a rig they borrowed and ceremoniously tossed a penny. They agreed that the two partners who lost were to forfeit four hundred dollars each to the other two and the losers would leave town so as not to compete with the winners. Buffalo was chosen as their destination, leaving the promise of a more successful operation for those remaining in Scranton. The penny was tossed and Butler and Adams lost.[1]

Butler and Adams arrived in Buffalo in 1873 prepared to launch a Sunday paper and were fully aware that the history of Sunday papers in the city and the economy in general made the chances of success somewhat slim.[2] There were, however, pluses to encourage the new partners: the increasing acceptance of Sunday newspapers in the New York City market and the ever-increasing volume of advertising that newspapers were attracting.[3]

The ever-optimistic younger partner, Ed Butler could not be deterred from his objective of starting a new Sunday morning publication. Butler felt that any enterprise he was involved in could not fail.

His faith in himself proved to be right. So he and Adams, a much older and more experienced man, upon their arrival in Buffalo almost immediately started to make arrangements that could lead to their paper's startup.

They contracted for printing the newspaper with a local job printing company and opened an office at 200 Main Street.[4] Butler concentrated on determining what kind of newspaper they would be producing while Adams, who was experienced in dealing with politicians, spent much of his time contacting area public officials with the message about what the new publication would represent to the community.[5]

The coming of the *Buffalo Sunday News* was announced only in an advertisement in the *Buffalo Evening Post* on the day before its first edition hit the street on Sunday, December 7, 1873, a cloudy day with a mild winter temperature of forty-six degrees. The ad proclaimed it would be "a large, first-class Sunday morning paper containing all the latest telegraphic news up to the hour of going to press and all the local and general news of the day. It would be for sale everywhere for five cents." Only the *Buffalo Evening Post* carried a news item about the birth of the new paper. The brief story on page 5 simply said, "A new Sunday paper. The first number of the *Sunday News* will appear tomorrow."[6]

The *Buffalo Evening Post* in 1873 was one of five English-language dailies. In the Buffalo marketplace there were: the *Commercial Advertiser*, the leading paper in the city and a Republican Party paper; the *Buffalo Courier*, the Democrat Party paper; the *Buffalo Evening Courier and Republic*, an independent paper; the *Buffalo Express*, a Republican Party paper; and the *Evening Post*, a second independent paper. In addition, there were five German-language dailies and dozens of town and village papers and special subject publications in the Buffalo market. There was no Sunday paper and none had been published since the mid-1850s except a few that never survived infancy.[7]

Historian Roswell Phillips, in his book *The History of Scranton and Its People*, described Butler even in these very young years as inclined to be stocky "but a bundle of energy with a dynamic nature," qualities that never left him. Butler was well-read, ambitious, and inspired by the new ideas that fueled the Progressive Era. Adams was experienced, politically savvy, and largely self-educated. Phillips wrote that if like attracts like, this could explain the association of J. B. Adams and E. H. Butler. Adams was considerably older and more experienced, but Phillips says he was a "human dynamo, as ceaseless in his activity as the eternal sun. He was of chunky build, nervous, excitable and always on the move. He came to Scranton first as a tramp printer, one who moved from job to job, and liked the Lackawanna Valley. The records show he was a wanderer, like the tramp printers of the day, some of exceptional ability which led them to become newspaper editors or publishers."[8] Adams was described in the *Scranton Times* as "somewhat eccentric." E. H. Butler, on the other hand, was "stable and poised with his own peculiarities, to be sure, but he was not erratic."[9]

The two men were greatly encouraged by the 1873 Buffalo City Directory, which had just been published with the statement that "The future of Buffalo as a great manufacturing center and distributing point is assured beyond all doubt." If Butler needed any more assurance that this was the ideal city to start a new newspaper, this was it.[10]

In addition to writing editorials on the paper's philosophy, Butler developed a highly successful content formula. He successfully sought to create a politically independent newspaper that focused on events rather than ideology, which marked the competing dailies. The *Buffalo Sunday News* entertained its readers and also kept them informed with more serious news of all kinds. The paper carried stories on government, taxes, schools, and other matters of interest to the daily lives of readers, but at the same time it published articles on crimes and love affairs. The formula Butler stressed was aimed at providing information for everybody in the family.[11]

The Butler approach established the foundation for the *News* through the years and continues even today. He stressed the importance of governmental news but insisted upon carrying articles that would appeal to a wide spectrum of readers. His formula for a successful paper was an approach that worked well for the one hundred twenty-five years of the *News*'s existence.

An early issue of the paper carried a review in rhyme written by Meander Miles, whom many surmised was actually Edward H. Butler. The feature appeared for many years and became known for its witticisms and cynicism. Much more poetry was published in those days than now appears in newspapers. For example, on October 4, 1874, the *Buffalo Sunday Morning News* published Henry Longfellow's *The Hanging of the Crane*.[12]

The paper was never subtle or dull. Readers weren't expected to agree with it but the paper was direct so they knew where it stood. An early editorial stated that the purpose of the paper "was to fill that hiatus which has prevailed so long in our city, in which telegraphic and mail intelligence has been virtually at a standstill from the time of issuing the Saturday afternoon papers until Monday morning while so large a proportion of the business of the country and of the world goes steadily on and events transpire in political and social circles of a varied and interesting import as during the same hours of any other day."[13]

Butler also aimed to create a newspaper whose appeal would cut across class lines and attract the growing middle class of Buffalo, as well as the working class and the more affluent people in the community. The "History of the *Buffalo Evening News*," an unpublished volume written in 1945 by the paper's Albany political correspondent, Charles K. Armitage, quotes the opening editorial announcement of the paper:

> Today we issue the first number of the paper that has made so much confusion and stir in the newspaper circles of the city. We came here simply because we saw a vast field for an enterprise like ours and not for the purpose of producing ill feeling or assuming rights that legitimately belong to other and older citizens. The *News* will be so conducted as to commend itself to all classes.[14]

Butler never failed to stress to his staff the need to come up with "scoops." Highly competitive in nature, he wanted his paper to consistently beat the dailies on stories so that *News* readers would get the information first despite the fact that the paper was published only one day a week.[15]

The combination of the Butler editorials outlining the philosophy of the paper and the across-the-board appeal of the paper's content resulted in almost immediate circulation success. On April 5, 1874, the *Buffalo Sunday News* trumpeted this achievement with an editorial stating that "The circulation of the *Sunday News* is more than double the city circulation of any daily paper or weekly issued within the corporation [city] limits." The *News* at this point claimed a circulation of 6,150. Two months later a New York advertising agency claimed that the *News* circulation had reached 10,850.[16]

The *Sunday News* was off to a fine start with circulation ahead of all projections and advertising picking up steadily. With the initial eighteen months of publishing behind them, the partners' gamble on starting the newspaper appeared to have been justified. Always aware of competition from the daily newspapers being published in Buffalo, Butler continued his spate of editorials stressing the role he saw for his newspaper. One noted that it is the function of the *Sunday News*

> to endeavor, if possible, to awaken the spirit of reform which shall permeate the entire community and render our beautiful city as perfect in its municipal administration and as chaste in the moral sentiment of its people as it is commanding in situations and delightful in every physical feature as a place of residence. . . . We have endeavored to incite a spirit of inquiry and investigation by pointing out specific and existing abuses, and there it would be traced to individuals, insisting that they be compelled to wear the brand of wrongdoing or purge themselves by irrefragable evidence.[17]

This editorial was prompted by criticism that the *Sunday News* was getting from individuals and organizations who were targets of the investigative stories the paper had been publishing about conditions that Butler felt had to be corrected. The *News* was doing much more of this kind of reporting than the competing dailies and it quickly became known as a crusader on behalf of the city's underclass. It exposed the sale of diseased meat and tainted milk in 1874 and in 1876 published stories on patent-medicine frauds. Corruption in awarding city contracts was given ongoing exposure by the weekly paper as were constant calls for the expenditure of more dollars for education and improved conditions in the county jail.[18]

Butler's concern for the working class resulted in the startup of a labor column in May 1874, one of the first such newspaper columns in the nation.[19] And he followed this the next year by offering the unemployed free ads to assist them in their job search. Butler originated classified advertising in the *Sunday News*. At a charge of one cent per word, it was the start of classified advertising in Buffalo newspapers.[20]

As the publisher of a weekly newspaper, Butler was aware he could not compete with the city's dailies for timely presentation of spot news but could capture the attention of the community with a continuing series of exposés on conditions that his competitors for the most part ignored in their publications.

The dailies were not reluctant to take their shots at the *Sunday News*, and Butler was not bashful about responding with strong editorials, often laden with sarcasm. For example, in 1874 the *Commercial Advertiser* had made some negative editorial remarks about the *News*. In response, Butler penned this editorial:

> Mr. James Waneng of the *Commercial*, in speaking of the *Sunday News*, said he would usc it only for one purpose. If he does so for a few weeks, the preponderance of his business will not be in his head. It is a law of nature that any portion of his body can be educated by using the proper means.[21]

Butler's *News* often took positions that were not popular with some segments of the community. He had persevered in the paper's early confrontations with many of the city's ministers who had railed against the start of a Sunday publication, contending that publishing on that day of the week degraded the Sabbath. The city council sided with the clergy and for a time ordered the arrest of newsboys who hawked the *Sunday News* on the streets. Butler met these criticisms head-on. He wrote an editorial stating that "We do not intend to submit to any interference with the sale of our newspaper. The rumholes open at 5 AM and the *News* shall be sold at that hour. If these sleepy heads are disturbed at that hour let them stuff their ears with cotton before they go to bed Saturday night." In another tough editorial, Butler again lashed out at the critics of a Sunday newspaper. "The old fogies who held up their heads in holy terror at the idea of a Sunday paper being issued in Buffalo are going into their antediluvian holes, and some of them are drawing the hole in after them."[22]

In the fall of 1875 Butler launched a campaign against his daily competitors with a barrage of news stories and editorials designed to expose their partisanship. The *News*, he wrote in one strong editorial, filled a vacuum for independent news that "could not be supplied by our partisan contemporaries, as they are the veriest slaves of their respective political rings, and doubly hampered by that social and personal toadyism which at one time characterized the American press above all others."[23]

In a more philosophical vein, Butler addressed *Sunday News* readers with these words, "I regard the *News* as a business enterprise and I have not made it a political organ nor a reform organ but I have made it a clean newspaper. It is an independent newspaper. It is not under the domination of any political party."[24]

The *News* again upset some of the city's clergy with its stand on prostitution. Although it roared against the practice, the paper angered many with an editorial that called for the establishment of a red-light district, saying it is inevitable and needed. "The most the law can do toward the correction of such evils," the *News* said, "is to confine them by barriers, which if overstepped will lead them to sure punishment, and by keeping such women from daily contact with those who are pure, prevent the infection from spreading."[25]

One of the paper's major efforts in 1876 was an exposé of the poor working conditions and wages of contract sewing women.[26] The *News* built its circulation and influence in part as a strong advocate for the workers. In the 1877 rail strike the *News* defended the workers and condemned military intervention. It said the rail workers had every right to strike in the face of an unfair wage reduction and criticized New York's governor for allowing railroad management to call on the military to settle the strike. The *News* also criticized the soldiers and attributed the strike violence to the presence of the military. The paper strongly supported the workers' right to strike but also urged them to refrain from violence. At the same time, the *News* concluded that the workers were almost being forced to seek justice through violent means. Butler's paper applauded the men for striking but advised them to "strike at the ballot box and shake both parties."[27]

While there was no indication of any problems separating young Butler and Adams, on March 21, 1875, there was a change on the front page that astute observers had to notice. The usual masthead that listed Adams and Butler as editors and proprietors did not appear. There was no explanation but after a two-month absence, the old masthead was back in its usual place, only to disappear again in the June 20 issue. When the June 27 issue came out, the front-page masthead was in its usual place but only contained the name Edward H. Butler as editor and proprietor. Also on that front page was a farewell note to the readers from J. B. Adams. His valedictory made no mention of Butler, but took note of the paper's success and mentioned that "It is appointed unto all men once to die. An editor, in a professional way dies many times." In a front-page article under Adams's valedictory, Butler wrote, "I cannot refrain from bearing public testimony to the many admirable journalistic qualifications of my late partner. The *Sunday News* will remain substantially what it has been from its birth; the avowed enemy and fearless opponent of every species of wrongdoing, the independent champion of people's rights, the organ of the honest masses."[28]

Unbeknownst to Butler, Adams had inserted a notice on page 4 of that same issue under the header, "Mrs. J. B. Adams." It was a bitter diatribe against a woman who was "calling herself by my name for the past few years, persistently followed me, and in every way that human indignity can conceive, seeking opportunity to harass and injure me. She claims to be my wife. This I emphatically deny. She has no legal right to the use of my name." Adams wrote that "For hours she would indulge in the most profane language I have ever heard fall from human lips, in low vulgarity that would put to blush the vilest of her fallen sex, living and festering in the lowest depths of moral degradation and prostituted vice. She is a female tigress, devoid of human sympathy or feeling. . . ."[29]

Adams went on to say that she had him arrested for desertion and nonsupport but "she utterly failed to substantiate her charges. While she could not prove she was my legal wife, the impression was strongly felt that she had occupied a position no true woman would voluntarily accept." Told to leave the city, he wrote, she didn't. "She is spreading scandalous reports, unfounded, unjust and false, for the purpose of traducing my character and satisfying a disposition that would reflect upon a fiend incarnate." He went on to say that she shot at him in Scranton and that is why he left the city.[30]

> In July 1875 Butler, under a one-line heading "Personal" and his signature, wrote: Having unintentionally published with the last issue

> of the *Sunday News* a statement by my late partner, J. B. Adams, concerning his domestic affairs, and having incurred the criticism of many personal friends by so doing, I now, at the request of the lady involved publish in another column her statement of the case. I would prefer that the matter had never appeared in this paper, but as it did and the *Sunday News* has always espoused the cause of the oppressed, of which class the lady referred to claims to belong, I give her side of the story. It is a very painful duty.[31]

The reply of the woman who claimed to be Mrs. Adams filled two full columns in the *News*. She presented a text of the marriage certificate. She claimed that soon after their marriage she learned that Adams's first wife was living and confined to an institution. She said he assured her he was divorced but a suit against him charged him with bigamy. She admitted "that I used a pistol. That gun saved my life when he was crazy drunk."[32]

Butler later said he had no knowledge of the vitriolic message his partner Adams had prepared for publication in the *News*. But there was no doubt, given his reaction and the material he approved for use in the *News*, including her response, that he was concerned that the stories she was telling could negatively affect the paper. He also had concerns about a libel action by her. The whole series of events and the exchange of charges between his partner and the woman who claimed to be Adams's wife horrified Butler. The aftermath of the whole sordid episode that unfolded for the public in the relatively new Sunday newspaper was the termination of the Butler-Adams partnership with Butler buying his former partner's interest in the paper. The future of the *Sunday News* and later the *Buffalo Evening News* was established by this affair as Butler and his successors had acquired sole control of the direction and ownership of the enterprise.[33]

Following the breakup of his partnership with Butler, Adams opened a job printing shop, started another Sunday newspaper in Buffalo that ceased after one year, established still another Sunday paper in 1877 that also lasted about a year, and then finally moved south and out of the Buffalo picture entirely. Although Butler had stated that the departure of Adams would not change the *News*, a statement following the partnership breakup does indicate that the two did have some philosophical differences. He wrote in an editorial that "We as journalists, disapproved of and since coming into exclusive control of the paper, our untiring efforts have been to eliminate whatever there was objectionable in it." Here he was undoubtedly referring to the Adams affair. Although he did not spell out what he found objectionable in the paper, he did add that to change the tone of a newspaper "is a work that must be gradual, not abrupt."[34]

Butler had to face still another unhappy but fortunately short-lived situation not too long after Adams departed. William Gatchell joined the *News*, thinking he was taking over Adams's role in the operation. Gatchell filed a suit against Butler describing what he said was a partnership entered into with Butler after the Adams breakup. Gatchell claimed Butler bought out his partnership for six hundred dollars but never paid him. He charged Butler with fraud. It resulted in the arrest of Butler but it all ended quickly with dismissal of the suit and payment to Gatchell of six hundred dollars.[35]

With the departure of Adams and the Gatchell gadfly suit out of the way, Butler, not yet twenty-five, became much more aggressive in his approach, desiring to show his independence. He editorially blasted the other newspapers in town for being too partisan and stated that the *News* "filled a want for independent news that could not be supplied" by its contemporaries. In October 1875 the paper endorsed twenty-four candidates on the "People's Ticket" and fourteen won their races. The People's Ticket was a bipartisan selection of candidates for state, judiciary, county, and city offices. It was put together by the paper and run prominently on page 1 for several weeks. Readers were urged to be "honest voters" and support the ticket, thereby preventing any political party from dominating civic affairs.[36]

Butler demonstrated his love of family in many ways and was very sensitive concerning any talk at his *Sunday News* about the Butler family. He allowed no shoptalk about either his family or his early life in Le Roy. A bad situation arose when his brother Ambrose hired a man from Le Roy as a printer. This employee gossiped about the Butler family money problems after Butler was left fatherless at the age of six. The same employee also discussed with others at the *News* that Butler's mother had to take in washing to make ends meet. Butler felt this talk by an employee denigrated the Butler family and it so infuriated him that when he heard that a second person from the village had been hired by Ambrose, he told his brother not to give employment at the paper to any other resident of Le Roy. He was concerned that it could result in even more gossip.[37]

Ironically, Ed Scanlon, the second man Ambrose hired, was to become a trusted and loyal member of the editorial staff. Scanlon eventually became the Albany correspondent of the *Buffalo Evening News* and was utilized as Butler's personal emissary to the governor. He also was enormously successful later when he penned a local gossip column "Around the Town" for many years. Butler's initial reaction to the hiring of Scanlon by Ambrose was typical of him. He could act quickly and firmly but was always willing to reconsider an action when events proved that his initial reaction was too hasty.[38]

Butler's feelings about his birthplace and its residents eventually changed. He bought a house in Le Roy for his mother and built a summer home for himself there when his newspaper enterprise became successful. He utilized it on many a weekend for years and shared with his Le Roy friends the fruits and vegetables he grew on his land. In the village he was looked up to as a Horatio Alger hero, the native son who had achieved success in the largest neighboring city.[39]

From 1873 to 1879 the *Buffalo Sunday Morning News* grew and prospered. In 1874 Butler purchased a new press to accommodate the news he wanted in the paper, which was being squeezed out by the amount of advertising coming in. The May 24 issue was called "our mammoth sheet." It was approximately twenty-four by thirty inches with ten columns per page. The name of the paper was changed to accommodate the greater width. Instead of the *Buffalo Sunday News* it became the *Buffalo Sunday Morning News* though the paper continued to be referred to by its former name or as just the *News*. Butler also moved from the fourth floor to the second floor of 200 Main Street to have larger quarters. There were periods when he had financial difficulties and at times he even borrowed money from customers to pay bills, but by 1879 the paper was on a firm financial footing.[40]

The year 1879 was a significant one in the publishing life of Butler. The *News* was financially successful and its influence was growing both locally and beyond. The paper that year took a bold stand for labor, advocating the restriction of convict labor so that it would not compete with local free labor. The principle was adopted throughout the United States, becoming one that labor organizations insisted upon to protect their members' jobs. The *News* was credited with having established an important principle of national labor practice.[41]

Another effort that won strong labor support for the *News* was its vigorous and successful campaign for construction of a Bird Avenue sewer, an expensive but needed sanitary improvement. The low bid for the sewer was $250,000, an enormous sum at that time, making the project very controversial. The sewer project, in addition to its public health benefits, also provided employment for many local people and had the strong support of labor, although the *News* was the only media outlet to consistently fight for the project. The other papers were opposed to the project because of the cost. At the same time, the *News* launched a major campaign for the elimination of the Hamburg Canal, an open sewer that crossed Main Street just south of Terrace Street that was later converted to a covered drain. The *News* reprinted a report from a Lockport paper that said the smell from the canal was intolerable.[42]

Use of an article from another paper was not unusual. The *News*, like other newspapers throughout the country, would clip and reprint material from other publications, crediting the source. Copyright protection was not the major concern it is today, but the *News*, unlike some newspapers, always credited the source of material it lifted from others and expected its competitors to credit it when using *News* material. This was not always forthcoming and the *News* was not reluctant to let its readers know when this occurred.[43]

Sunday publication eventually became competitive as other papers entered the market. The *Sunday Courier* was started in 1875, followed by the *Buffalo Times* in 1879. Four years later, in 1883, the *Sunday Express* began competing for the city's weekend attention.[44]

Having successfully started a Sunday paper in Buffalo, the dynamic and ambitious Edward Butler made his next move into neighboring Pennsylvania. Lured by the oil boom in Bradford, he established the *Bradford Sunday News* with little fanfare. Its first issue came out on April 6, 1879. The four-page paper was sold for a nickel a copy and was very close in style and format to the *Buffalo Sunday Morning News*. Its circulation reached the five-thousand level not too long after its inception.[45]

Butler almost immediately launched an editorial attack against the powerful Standard Oil interests in the Bradford area, championing the cause of the local oil producers. Due to the lack of adequate transportation to move the oil out whether by tank wagon or pipeline, more oil was pumped than the market could absorb and as a result prices dropped. The distributor, the forerunner of Standard Oil, took advantage of the overproduction and kept the price it paid for the oil low. The *News* took up the cause of the producers against the low prices, which likely resulted in its excellent circulation results early on. Butler obviously enjoyed engaging the gigantic Standard Oil in battle and editorially noted that "When we started the *Bradford Sunday News* it was in the face of obstacles and the usual discouragement accompanying all new ventures with the additional assurance that the Standard Oil Company would do their best to crush us, but we felt equal to the self-imposed task. . . . The paper is a success. It already has a circulation of five thousand copies, wrung, too, from an area noted for journalistic failures. . . ."[46]

Butler, while enjoying his Bradford venture and its battle with a major corporation, sold the paper in November 1883. He had in 1880 established the *Buffalo Evening News*, a daily edition of the *Buffalo Sunday Morning News*. It was a major undertaking that was to keep him from continuing his presence in Bradford.[47]

Notes

1. Jerry Goldberg, "Edward H. Butler and the Founding of the *Buffalo Evening News*: The Life and Times of One of the Last Publisher-editors" (master's thesis, State University of New York at Buffalo, 1997), p. 3.
2. Ibid., p. 25.
3. Ibid., p. 29.
4. Ibid., p. 25.
5. Michael Dillon, "Private Life and Public Identity: Two Nineteenth Century Publishers Confront Scandal" (academic paper presented at the

Mid-Atlantic Popular Culture Association/American Culture Association, November 5, 1993), p. 7.

6. Alfred Kirchhofer files, Butler Family Papers, E. H. Butler Library Archives, State University College at Buffalo, box 1; Alfred H. Kirchhofer, "History of the *Buffalo Evening News*" (unpublished data, chap. 1), p. 21.

7. Goldberg, "Edward H. Butler," pp. 25, 26.

8. Kirchhofer, "History" (chap. EHB Sr.), p. 10; Goldberg, "Edward H. Butler," p. 25.

9. Goldberg, "Edward H. Butler," p. 25.

10. Kirchhofer files, Butler Family Papers, box 1; Goldberg, "Edward H. Butler," pp. 28, 29.

11. Goldberg, "Edward H. Butler," pp. 33, 34.

12. Kirchhofer, "History," chap. 4, p. 17.

13. Kirchhofer files, Butler Family Papers, box 2; Goldberg, "Edward H. Butler," p. 30; Warren Buffett made the same statement when the Sunday edition of the *News* was started on November 13, 1977.

14. Kirchhofer, "History," chap. 11, p. 1, quoting Charles Armitage in his "History of the *Buffalo Evening News*" written in 1945 (unpublished data); Goldberg, "Edward H. Butler," p. 30.

15. Kirchhofer, "History," chap. EHB Sr., p. 13; Goldberg, "Edward H. Butler," p. 32.

16. Kirchhofer, "History," chap. 4, p. 4; Goldberg "Edward H. Butler," p. 30.

17. Kirchhofer files, Butler Family Papers, box 2.

18. Michael Dillon, "From Populist to Patrician: Edward H. Butler's *Buffalo News* and the Crisis of Labor, 1877–1892," *American Journalism* 16, no. 1 (1999): 44.

19. Ibid.

20. Kirchhofer files, Butler Family Papers, 1870–1880, box 2; Goldberg, "Edward H. Butler," p. 59.

21. Kirchhofer files, Butler Family Papers, box 2.

22. *Buffalo Sunday News*, editorial, May 3, 1974, Kirchhofer files, Butler Family Papers, box 2.

23. Dillon, "From Populist to Patrician," p. 43.

24. Goldberg, "Edward H. Butler," p. 33.

25. Kirchhofer files, Butler Family Papers, box 2.

26. Ibid.; Michael J. Dillon, "From Populist to Patrician," p. 44.

27. Ibid., pp. 48, 49, 50.

28. Kirchhofer files, Butler Family Papers, J. B. Adams, box 2, pp. 1–13;

Goldberg, "Edward H. Butler," pp. 36–45; Michael Dillon, "Private Life and Public Identity," pp. 8–12.

29. Ibid.

30. Ibid.

31. Ibid.

32. Ibid.

33. Ibid.

34. Ibid.

35. Goldberg, "Edward H. Butler," pp. 45–46, Kirchhofer files, Butler Family Papers, story from *Buffalo Commercial Advertiser*, June 6, 1876.

36. Dillon, "From Populist to Patrician," p. 43; Goldberg, "Edward H. Butler," pp. 47, 48.

37. Goldberg, "Edward H. Butler," pp. 20–22.

38. Ibid.

39. Ibid.

40. Goldberg, "Edward H. Butler," p. 51; Kirchhofer files, Butler Family Papers, box 2, Circulation, pp. 11–14.

41. *A History of the City of Buffalo: Its Men and Institutions* (Buffalo, NY: Buffalo Evening News, 1908), p. 240.

42. Kirchhofer files, Butler Family Papers, 1879, box 2, p. 1.

43. Ibid., p. 13.

44. A. Gordon Bennett, *Buffalo Newspapers since 1870*, Adventures in Western New York History (Buffalo, NY: Buffalo News and Erie County Historical Society, 1974), pp. 6, 13, 18.

45. Goldberg, "Edward H. Butler," pp. 52–54; Kirchhofer files, Butler Family Papers, 1879, box 2, pp. 3–5.

46. Ibid.

47. Ibid.

4 The *Buffalo Evening News*

The Beginning

Circumstances for the publication of a new daily in Buffalo in 1880 were more favorable than they were in 1873 when the *Sunday News* was established. The population of Buffalo had increased in those early years to more than 155,000. The tonnage of vessels arriving and departing from the Port of Buffalo was growing rapidly. Shipments of anthracite coal into the port were up substantially and Buffalo was one of the largest cattle markets in the world.[1]

There were two morning papers, the *Courier*, the *Express*, and one afternoon paper called the *Commercial Advertiser*, selling for a nickel a copy.[2] Butler offered the *Buffalo Evening News* for a penny a copy and Buffalo's business community, anxious to get a larger audience for its ads, pledged support to Butler's venture before it got under way.[3] The *Telegraph*, a Scripps paper, followed Butler into the afternoon field. The *Enquirer* entered the afternoon field ten years later.[4]

Not yet thirty, Butler had all the enthusiasm of youth and the optimism that he had manifested for years, feeling that nothing he might undertake could fail. He had been thinking for about five years of the need for a daily newspaper that would give him a major voice in the community. Hastening his decision were the persistent reports in the newspaper industry that James E. Scripps of the *Detroit News* was preparing to launch the *Evening Telegraph* in Buffalo. Butler beat Scripps to the Buffalo newsstands by just three weeks on October 11, 1880.[5]

News editor Alfred H. Kirchhofer, many years later, in talking to his editorial department about the need to pay attention to every detail large or small, often cited an incident involving Edward Butler. On October 23, 1880, the young publisher suffered an attack of unknown origin and was ordered by his doctor to take a rest. He followed orders and went west, not returning until December. Because he had planned everything thoroughly for the start and operation of the daily paper, there were no problems resulting from his absence. His competent staff performed as planned.[6]

One potentially major problem did occur on October 11, the day the first edition of the *Buffalo Evening News* was scheduled to come out at 2 PM. That edition never made it to the newsstands. A lift in the *News* building malfunctioned and what would have been the four pages of that first edition that were on the elevator fell to the floor, scattering the type. However, the ingenuity of Butler and his new staff quickly recovered from the shock and the second edition, which in fact had become the first edition of the *Buffalo Evening News*, made its debut at 4 PM, a remarkably fast recovery from near disaster.[7]

Scripps's *Telegraph* started publication on October 30, 1880, as a penny paper. It made plain almost from the beginning that the management was out to get the *News*. The *Telegraph* printed direct attacks against Butler, calling him a coward and a publisher of willful falsehoods. The *Telegraph* also referred to Butler in its pages as "Walrus Blubber Butler." Butler's strategy was to ignore the *Telegraph*'s attacks on him and his newspaper. The battle ended on August 17, 1885, with victory for Butler as he announced that he had purchased the *Telegraph* and ended its publication.[8]

The initial issues of the *Evening News* contained four pages, six columns to a page, which measured fourteen by eighteen inches. The paper had twenty-four employees and was capitalized at $9,000.[9] Butler introduced the evening daily with an editorial that stated,

> We do not think it necessary to devote much space in introducing the *Evening News* to public notice; neither do we intend to indulge

Buffalo Sunday Morning Times

Buffalo, Sunday, Oct. 10, 1880.

"THE EVENING NEWS."

Mr. E. H. Butler, of the Sunday *News*, has just returned from New York and perfected his arrangements for starting The Evening *News*, which will make its first appearance to-morrow evening.

The editorial staff will be an exceptionally strong one, the managing editor being Mr. McIntosh, late of the New York *Star*.

The Evening *News* will be a penny sheet, and it is designed to furnish cheap reading for the million.

A cheap evening paper is a necessity long felt, and Mr. Butler, with his accustomed enterprise, is the first to fill the want. His success as a publisher is already established, and we have no doubt he will make this new enterprise a grand financial success, to all of which he is fully entitled.

Announcement in the *Buffalo Sunday Morning Times* of the first issue of the *Buffalo Evening News* on October 10, 1880. (Butler Family Papers, courtesy E. H. Butler Library Archives, Buffalo State College)

> in extravagant promises. . . . The *Evening News* will be all that industry and well-directed efforts can make it. It will be the organ of neither party nor clique. It owes nothing to either political organization, and occupying, as it will, an independent position, it will be enabled to expose wrong and point to errors without compromising allegiance. It has long been evident that a bright, cheap evening daily is a necessity in a city the size of Buffalo, where there are thousands of laboring men who cannot give time to wading through the larger journals and it is to supply a demand that is apparent to all that the *Evening News* is given to the public.
>
> If errors exist, we shall speak of them plainly and justly; if crime and immorality overstep the law and public safety, the *News* will be outspoken and bold in denunciations. . . . [10]

Nothing, it seemed, escaped the notice of the editor and publisher. Butler took his responsibilities very seriously and constantly strove to keep all his executives alert to any shortcomings he saw in the news product. Nor did he hesitate to make moves he felt would enable the *News* to increase its circulation.[11]

A year after the *Buffalo Evening News* made its debut Butler launched a major campaign on June 12, 1881, which was the paper's first effort to establish itself as a community newspaper. The kickoff to the series outlined conditions in Polish tenements in the city and followed up day after day in the news columns and on the editorial page with hard-hitting material about "Buffalo's Shame" with challenges to city officials and residents.[12] One editorial, typical of others in the campaign, raised the question of "What has become of Buffalo's boasted charity that poor immigrants are permitted to starve in our midst without efforts being made to alleviate their suffering? Is this right, just, or human? We put this question to every man in Buffalo that has a heart."[13] In one day the *News* carried five "Page One" stories on the plight of the city's Polish community where the people lived in overcrowded tenements with little food or medical care. Despite such intense effort, the *News* did not generate much public support for its crusade on behalf of the Poles in the Buffalo area. Union members were concerned that the Poles would compete for jobs, and many openly stated that they wished these foreigners had never come to the city. The other newspapers made no attempt to join the *News* in its efforts to better the lot of the Polish community. The mayor, Alexander Brush, told the paper, "I am very busy with pressing official business. I read the newspaper accounts very carefully but as I said before I am too busy to inquire into the matter."[14]

The *News* started to back off, modifying its tone and in effect terminated its community reform campaign on June 24. It addressed the health threat of existing conditions more than the plight of the Polish population and then called for the curb of immigration. "The city of Buffalo," the *News* said editorially at this point, "is the greatest sufferer now from the present system of immigration and should take the initiative to avert its growing evils." The *News* had bowed to public and political opinion although its campaign had indeed resulted in some reforms that improved the living conditions of the city's Polish inhabitants. Butler had the satisfaction of knowing that he fought for reform that others disdained.[15]

The first managing editor of the *Evening News* was William McIntosh, who had been the managing editor of the *New York Mail and Express*.[16] He was a short man with great energy who refused to use a typewriter or a wastebasket. His work area was a long table in the center of the newsroom that was always surrounded by crumpled and torn copy paper. McIntosh wrote the editorials in addition to directing the news operations. He was known as a man of humor and a battler. Once when confronting a group protesting a story in the paper, he is reputed to have said, "Don't you try to bluff us. We are bluffers ourselves." As managing editor for thirty years, he set a precedent at the *News* for using direct quotes from news sources. He also started "Everybody's Column," the letters to the editor feature.[17]

It is interesting to note that back in 1880 William McIntosh wrote all the editorials. And for the first seventy-six years of the paper's history, Edward H. Butler and later his son, Edward H. Butler Jr., would have each new editorial read to them. Traditionally, when these publishers said, "Let's hold that one for a while," it meant that editorial would never be published.[18]

The first person known to have worked full time as an editorial writer was James Cromley, a courtly gentleman in appearance and personality. His successor was William M. Cruttendon who became known as a "sledgehammer editorialist," a hard-hitter who pulled no punches. Away from his duties at the *News*, he was known as a man of humor with a delightful personality. Many who were the subjects of his editorials would not agree with such an appraisal.[19]

The first reporter luminary on the *Buffalo Evening News* was Frank Bloomer. A *News* reporter from the 1890s until his death in 1947, Bloomer was a favorite of editor-publisher Edward Butler Sr. Bloomer was a great reporter who had an uncanny ability to overcome obstacles that stood in the way of getting a story. A fantastically competitive man, Bloomer's exploits were the pride and joy of Butler and the cause of constant concern for his city editor, William O'Connell, who was never sure that the reckless Bloomer would end up with a story. Bloomer, soft-spoken, yet tenacious, invariably delivered the goods to his city editor's desk, who grudgingly praised his star reporter. Bloomer, without a doubt, was the first of a long line of fine *News* reporters.[20]

Ambrose Butler headed up the business department, assisted by William Goodspeed who became business manager.[21] The year 1892 saw the introduction of the first linotype machines in the *News* composing room, a major move in speeding up the production process from hand-set type to machine production. Ambrose devised a method for the linotype machines that kept the molds free of lead sediment or film and produced a printed letter that was as clean and clear-cut as anything printed from a steel plate.[22]

In addition to his talents as a journalist and administrator, Edward Butler Sr. also had the instincts of a showman. He was the first to bring the electric light to the city of Buffalo. In March of 1880, he studied the workings of a generator, made numerous adjustments, and then lit the exterior of the *News* building with a 20,000-candlepower light that could be seen for half a mile. The illuminated building became a tourist attraction, drawing thousands to the city and heightening the awareness of the *Buffalo Evening News*. Not only was he the first person to promote the electric light in Buffalo, he was among the first to use a phone for his business. There was a single wall phone in the editorial department, but Edward and Ambrose Butler, and William Goodspeed had phones on their desks.[23]

Eleven years after starting the daily newspaper, Butler was still making adjustments to the finished product. In 1891 he started a "Page One" summary of important news. He also introduced innovative headings over short items that included "The dark side of life," the "Doings of evil men, which marred the record of 1891," and "Nature's whims." Butler was a century or more ahead of editors and publishers who have come to value the use of short, pithy items in their pages.[24]

In 1892 the *News* purchased a new press and made the move from a four-page paper to a six-page paper. Butler at the same time introduced new typography featuring larger headlines and decks, the secondary headline on a story, which were smaller but heavier and easier to read. In the same year Butler opened the paper's first Washington bureau to concentrate on news pertaining to the Buffalo area. A few years later, in 1895, the paper published its first comic strip. In 1899 the *News* introduced photoengraving in its pages with its first use of halftones.[25] Photoengraving involved the making of a plate, usually a zinc plate, and using acid to etch the photograph instead of the carved-wood block formerly used. The most important improvement in printing pictures was the use of halftones that allowed a reproduction with gradations of tone.

Although a strong proponent of "hard news" and the need to get directly to the point in stories, Butler wanted his newspaper to include something of special interest to as many readers as possible. Toward this end, he started covering fashion news early on and, as the paper grew, he added a boys and girls page and even a magazine for juniors for a while. A weekly travel page, one of the first in any newspaper, was introduced around 1897 as well as a column of news and gossip about royalty called the "Courts of Europe."[26]

The dynamic young publisher was a dominant figure in every facet of the *News*. There are few, if any, publishers then or now who could say they are responsible for coming up with a new formula for their newspaper's ink. Butler, unhappy with the ink being used by the *News*, experimented with changes in the ink mixture. The manufacturer was finally convinced it was an improvement and started to produce it. Ambrose said the result was as handsome as book ink, "black and even brilliant."

Ambrose Butler, Edward's brother, who was his closest confidant and who worked with him until he retired in 1902. (Butler Family Papers, courtesy E. H. Butler Library Archives, Buffalo State College)

Furthermore, the ink dried instantly, giving Butler exactly what he was seeking.[27] Other newspapers ultimately adopted the ink formulated by Butler.

Shortly after the *Evening News* began publishing, Butler decided he was not pleased by the typeface being used for its headlines. Working with the American Type Founders, he helped to develop a new typeface, which was eventually cast and adopted by the *News*. This new type made the headlines strikingly prominent. "They do not ruin the appearance of the page or smite the reader with brutal coarseness," said Butler. "There are brains and art and good sense in the *News* headlines. The *New York Journal* has taken pointers on type from the *Buffalo Evening News*. I think it would be a good scheme for the *Cincinnati Enquirer*, the Scripps-McRae league, and other papers of that misguided headline school to study the *Buffalo Evening News* headlines."[28]

As editor and publisher of the *News*, Butler involved himself in every area of the enterprise; his enormous energy enabled him to immerse himself totally in circulation, advertising, production, and editorial. His brother Ambrose, the business manager of the paper, was a key member of his team and relieved Ed of many of the daily details of the business. There's no doubt that Ed Butler's first love was the paper's editorial content. That was manifested from the first day of its publication in 1880 until his death in 1914.[29]

The *News*'s circulation continued to increase through the years and Butler was not bashful about letting the community know about it. On March 22, 1897, seventeen years after its debut, the *News* carried a front-page story boasting, "The *News* has a larger circulation than the combined circulation of all the Buffalo dailies." This prompted an immediate attack from the *Enquirer*, accusing the *News* of "reprehensible lying" and adding, "No other Buffalo daily is so barren of the current news of the day or so disreputable in its financial and editorial management." It continued, "William J. Connors, publisher of the *Buffalo Enquirer* and the *Buffalo Record*, will deposit with a Buffalo bank $5,000 to be given to a charitable institution in the city if the statement in the *News* is true. The only condition attached is that the publisher of The *News* deposit $5,000 to be given to a charitable institution of the city if the statement is not true." The *Express* joined the chorus, "What is the use of growing excited over such an empty boast?"[30]

The *News* ignored the attacks. The fact is that the 1896 W. W. Alter Newspaper Directory showed the *News* circulation at 62,417 with the combined circulation of the other five dailies, based on their publisher statements, at 82,929. The closest competitor in circulation numbers was the *Evening Times* with 35,000.[31]

Butler never overlooked the role of marketing the newspaper. Modern-day publishers pride themselves on their advances in this area, but E. H. Butler was aggressively marketing the *News* in the early 1890s. For example, he ran a campaign to sell an American edition of the *Encyclopedia Britannica* with the first volume going for $1 and the others for $1.50 plus fifteen coupons from the *News*.[32]

Edward Butler Sr. was innovative and never lacked initiative. He was one of the pioneer publishers to offer incentives to newspaper carriers who could sign up new subscribers. In 1891 he hosted a dinner for 1,200 *News* carriers. Striving to reach a circulation base of 75,000 in 1897, he offered carriers bicycles for adding new customers. The paper bought and distributed thousands of bicycles and the effort brought circulation up to 71,000, an increase of about 8,000.[33]

There are numerous examples of Butler's love affair with the news content of the paper. For example, on December 14, 1900, the *News* apologized to its readers because "ads occupied a large portion of the space in the *News* on December 13. Merchants clamored so persistently for space in Thursday's paper that it became necessary to condense the dispatches and the local news. . . ." The statement ends with a reminder to readers that "if any reader feels the ads have overstepped their bounds, let him remember that lots of advertisements mean plenty of prosperity." It's likely that brother Ambrose convinced him to add that final sentence.[34]

In the early days of its publication, the *Evening News*, like other papers at the time, accepted some advertising for its front page. At one point, however, Butler felt the encroachment on news space on that page had gone too far. It brought a memo from the publisher's office with an order:

> Please do not accept more than three of the liner ads for the first page and then not more than two lines each and they must be put at bottom of the page. I want to keep the first page free and I don't care whether I loose [sic] money or not. I want to have as much of that page as possible to make it look like a newspaper. There will be no more of that [too many ads] on the front page.[35]

Butler made his presence felt constantly in the newsroom through an avalanche of memos that came from his office to the managing editor, the city editors, individual staffers, and the newsroom bulletin board. An ardent advocate of the *News*, always staying ahead of its competitors with any and all news, Butler posted the following in 1894: "Remember that a stickful of today's news when printed today is worth a page of the same thing printed tomorrow."[36]

One example of Butler's insistence on covering the news without delay is the Peter Otto execution. In May 1896 Peter Otto, wife murderer, was hanged at 10:26 AM. By 10:38 the first edition of the *News*, containing a full report of the execution and portrait cuts of Otto and the attorneys in the case, was on press and by 10:40 newsboys were hawking the paper. The story ran one-quarter of a column. The *News* had thirty-five printers at the time, twenty-one of which were used to get the story in print.[37]

Another bulletin board posting from the editor-publisher informed the staff, "We have a rule that any man, who writes anything that the mother or sister in any house in this city would blush to read, shall loose [sic] his job immediately." And still another along these same lines advised: "Print nothing in The *News* a child may not read."[38] Butler's sense of humor was manifested in a note to an editorial writer who he felt was too verbose: "You write well. You not only shoot a man but throw the gun after him. But remember that some day someone may pick up the gun and turn it on you."[39]

In 1894 a city editor was told by Butler to offer a cash award to the reporter who reported and/or suggested the largest number of local stories. Stories, he stressed, must be written concisely "with a bit of spice to enliven them."[40]

Consistent with his desire to outdo his competitors by the volume of news reported in his paper, in 1907 Butler wrote a note to every employee of the company: "You are hereby ordered to be a reporter on The *News* as well as advertising solicitor (or whatever). I wish to get a piece of news from everyone of my employees every day. I am going to try this method of making the paper better and newsier."[41]

The reaction of Butler's editors to his barrage of memos indicates the respect they had for their boss. Commenting on it, one of his early city editors said: "When another [paper] got a scoop on us, he saw it and he panned me and the reporter in whose territory it occurred. I thought then that he was the most artistic faultfinder I ever knew. But now I realize that it was necessary to keep the staff on its toes and keep the lead he had in the newspaper field."[42]

Still another *News* city editor in its early days, Benjamin Coe, recalled years later that "E. H. Butler set such a hot pace that it kept the whole organization on its toes. He swung the big stick pretty bad at times, but he had the greatest respect for any one who stood up and came back at him. Great-heartedness is the mark of the man and E. H. Butler certainly had it." He goes on to cite individual instances of Butler's "kindness and generous impulses" to employees who had come upon hard times.[43]

Another city editor, Henry Saunders, is not memorable in the history of the *News* but one incident he precipitated resulted in a *News* policy that remained in place for decades. Saunders was a pipe smoker. One day he emptied the ashes from his pipe into a wastebasket beside his desk. The papers in the basket ignited at the precise moment Butler walked into the editorial room. There was a scramble of several newsroom people to put the fire out and conceal what had happened. Butler turned and went back to his office without saying a word about the incident. But only minutes later, a messenger arrived in the newsroom with a memo dictated by Butler. He had acted quickly. The memo forbade all smoking in the editorial department, starting at once. The rule lasted for decades, much to the chagrin of the many staffers who then and in future years were smoking addicts. The only other American newspaper with the same no-smoking rule was the *Christian Science Monitor*.[44] The no-smoking edict was enforced until the late 1960s, after which it was more violated then observed until it was reintroduced in the 1990s when the entire *News* building became a nonsmoking environment with few exceptions.

Still another city editor serving Butler was Harold Balliett, who recalled Butler as "A man of keen insight, tremendous force, and a wonderful memory and knowledge of events. He could recite Shakespeare and other authors and could remember the lines of poetry and prose that he had written in the *News* years before. On several occasions he took me down to the bound files of the *News* early days and we looked up things he had written. They were word for word as he had given them to me in his private office."[45]

One of the early top reporters on the *News* staff, William Gorman, recalled, "Butler was as insistent upon accuracy to the last detail as he was eager for scoops. He had an aversion for quotations without attribution to the source. He wanted names and dates in every story."[46]

Butler was indeed a tough taskmaster who had definite ideas on what defined a good reporter. In an 1892 speech he set out these thoughts,

> No man is too well qualified for the profession which taxes a wider variety of intellectual qualities than any other, a reporter should have quick perception and sound judgement above all. He should be a good writer, too, and should be able to put his impressions in clear words. He should have keen insight into human nature to be able to know when he is being lied to and breadth enough to avoid being unduly censorious in his judgement of motive. A reporter should, of course, have as much education as he may be able to muster. But education will not take the place of natural abilities. It can only put an edge on a good metal.[47]

The Butler archives in the library of Buffalo State College indicate that Butler fired off hundreds of letters and memos through the years and that he was a deeply dedicated editor and publisher. Many were quite direct, with no punches pulled. For example, a memo to William McIntosh, his managing editor, on July 11, 1907, was right to the point. "I wish you would take the state news matter in hand at once and work a reform there or I shall be compelled to change the editor. . . . On July 9 we had no East Aurora news, no Fredonia, Westfield, Silver Creek and a list of others left out. . . . I want you to please take a hand in this and give it more than five minutes thought." Two days earlier, the publisher informed McIntosh that "Today's paper is about the punkiest I have seen around this office. We had four columns left over and yet we run a lot of ads for the office and things of that kind. Kindly instruct your men to look after this and have them govern themselves accordingly. I shall look for a better paper Friday than I got on Thursday."[48]

An indicator of how closely Butler observed all that went into the *News* can be seen in a brief memo to his city editor, Henry B. Saunders, on August 2, 1907. "See me personally every two or three days anyway. We can then go over things together and I will know what you are doing and you know what I like. Make it your business to find me when I am in the building. Please do not forget this."[49]

Showing his concern for mistakes and typographical errors, Butler on December 30, 1907, in a memo to his managing editor, wrote: "I cannot railroad any more editorial because it makes for errors and blunders. I would rather you hold it over until the day following if it cannot get in, in time, for the first edition because the proof readers fill our pages with blunders."[50]

In a letter to his managing editor on June 23, 1908, Butler wrote, "Please let the police officials alone so far as they are engaged in battling with the car robbers in the railroad yards. I want to uphold the police. I wish they could clean out the whole thieving, monstrous gang. We have been inclined too much to criticize the officials. Let us take another tack. . . . It is bad enough for the police to have to come in contact with these thieves and murderers without being disciplined by a newspaper. . . . You know you and I seldom disagree on policies but in my judgment the *News* has been wrong in this matter and I felt so every time I read what you wrote."[51]

Butler was not shy in expressing his desires to his editors and coming forth with story ideas. For example, on July 24, 1908, in a memo to city editor Charles Armitage, he wrote, "Get men to interview the heaviest taxpayers in Buffalo. Mr. Halliett or the assessors can give you the list. I want to show that the biggest taxpayers in Buffalo are in favor of a new Chippewa market. [A market where people of the city could obtain fresh produce brought in by farmers daily.] I want an interview with John Coleman, who is the business agent of the workmen of the city, who are compelled by reason of the high and fancy prices to go to a market where they may get things that they have to eat, cheaper."[52]

In another memo, dated November 11, 1908, Butler showed his aggressive nature. He suggested an interview and with heightened emphasis he wrote, "Now don't get scooped on this. Get it by all means, by hook or crook. Put a reporter on it, have him see [Seymour] Knox and tell him you heard he bought a building. Go after it, be persistent, follow him up. I want you to get this particular purchase above all things you do tomorrow."[53]

And then shifting his target to Armitage, Butler, in a July 16, 1909, memo, said, "If you cannot get a long article of news in the last edition, cut it down rather than leave it out. This is in reference to the very latest news. Don't be beaten by anyone. If you cannot get in ten lines then get in two lines. You can even put two or three lines in our Extra at the same time when it is important. Don't be beaten in anything. I shall watch for the very latest news."[54]

Butler the disciplinarian was manifested in a memo to the "counting room" force on January 14, 1910: "Visiting from one department to another had been forbidden in this office by my direction. The rule has been broken. All employees will be required to remain in their own department during business hours and visiting must be discontinued. Any violating this rule will be subject to suspension or dismissal."[55]

Butler did not neglect form in individual stories. For example, in an April 6, 1910, memo to Armitage, he comments, "The man who wrote the article on page seven of the *Sunday Morning News* did a good job and I am glad to see this. The dialogue form makes the matter interesting and the article understandable. I have spoken to you many times about breaking up that stiff way of telling the story and putting it into dialogue. Actual facts can appear in dialogue as well as the narrative form."[56]

Butler was direct and often gruff in his communications with the newsroom staff. He hammered away at the need to keep stories tightly written. "State the facts right off," he wrote in one of his memos to all reporters. "I want more dialogue and less Mother Hubbard stuff. You will come to the point at once without a long palavering of a quarter of a column. I want briefer articles and more thought given to the writing of them. We have not the space for long, needless stories."[57]

In a letter to a reader dated October 26, 1912, Butler wrote, "We do not run cartoons in The *News* except on very rare occasions because a number of newspapers, at the time President McKinley was killed, were of the firm belief that the assassin's mind had been affected by seeing and reading these cartoons, which made McKinley out [to be] everything but what a President of the United States ought to be."[58]

And on a matter that still is of continuing concern to editors, Butler told his managing editor, "I want to stop breaking over stories from one page to another. It is getting to be played out [overdone]. The best newspapers don't do it. We must get everything told in no more space than three quarters of a column."[59]

Butler never deviated in his dedication and devotion to his beloved *News*. Totally focused even though some physical ailments had become increasing annoyances as time passed, he remained open to new ideas but still dedicated to the basic principles he had laid down early in his career as a publisher. While he had changed through the years, as he became more successful and prosperous, he remained steadfastly loyal to his employees and obsessed with producing an outstanding product every day.

NOTES

1. *A History of the City of Buffalo, Its Men and Institutions* (Buffalo, NY: Buffalo Evening News, 1908), p. 31.

2. A. Gordon Bennett, *Buffalo Newspapers since 1870*, Adventures in Western New York History (Buffalo, NY: Buffalo News and Erie County Historical Society, 1974), pp. 4–11.

3. *Buffalo Evening News*, October 11, 1880, p. 1; Jerry Goldberg, "Edward H. Butler and the Founding of the *Buffalo Evening News*: The Life and Times of One of the Last Publisher-editors" (master's thesis, State University of New York at Buffalo, 1997), p. 49.

4. Alfred Kirchhofer files, Butler Family Papers, E. H. Butler Library Archives, State University College at Buffalo, box 2.

5. Kirchhofer files, Butler Family Papers, "History," chap. 1879, p. 3.

6. Ralph Dibble, "The *Buffalo Evening News* Is Born," *Buffalo News* centennial publication, October 12, 1980, p. H-2.

7. Kirchhofer files, Butler Family Papers, box 4, Charles Armitage, "History of *Buffalo Evening News*"; Goldberg, "Edward H. Butler," p. 50.

8. Ibid., p. 51.

9. Kirchhofer files, Butler Family Papers, box 3.

10. Goldberg, "Edward H. Butler," p. 52; Kirchhofer files, Butler Family Papers, "History," chap. 11, p. 1.

11. Goldberg, "Edward H. Butler," p. 53.

12. Ibid., p. 60.

13. Ibid., p. 62; Michael J. Dillon, "Anatomy of a Crusade: Reform Independent Politics and the *Buffalo Evening News'* Polish Crusade of 1881" (academic paper presented at the Mid-Atlantic Popular Culture Association/American Culture Association, October 28, 1994), p. 11.

14. Goldberg, "Edward H. Butler," p. 63.

15. Ibid., p. 66.

16. Kirchhofer files, Butler Family Papers, box 3.

17. "One Hundred Years," *Buffalo News*, October 12, 1980, p. H-5.

18. Ibid.

19. Ibid.

20. Ralph Dibble, "Bloomer Often Played Role in His Own Stories," *Buffalo News*, October 12, 1980, p. H-4.

21. Kirchhofer files, Butler Family Papers, box 3.

22. "History of the News," *Buffalo Evening News* Business Department (1901), p. 4.

23. Kirchhofer files, Butler Family Papers, box 4, "History," chap. EHB, p. 1D.

24. Kirchhofer files, Butler Family Papers, box 3.

25. Ibid.

26. Ibid.

27. Kirchhofer files, Butler Family Papers, "History," chap. EHB Sr., p. 1F; Goldberg, "Edward H. Butler," p. 61.

28. Ibid.

29. Goldberg, "Edward H. Butler," p. 53.

30. Kirchhofer files, Butler Family Papers, box 3.

31. Ibid.

32. Ibid.

33. Ibid.

34. Ibid.

35. Memo to Goodspeed from E. H. Butler, July 24, 1909; Goldberg, "Edward H. Butler," p. 62.

36. Kirchhofer files, Butler Family Papers, box 1, Kirchhofer, "History," chap. EHB Sr., p. 3F.

37. Kirchhofer files, Butler Family Papers, box 4.

38. Ibid.

39. Kirchhofer files, Butler Family Papers, box 1.

40. Kirchhofer files, Butler Family Papers, "History," chap. EHB Sr., p. 3F; Goldberg, "Edward H. Butler," p. 64.

41. Kirchhofer files, Butler Family Papers, box 2.

42. Goldberg, "Edward H. Butler," p. 63.

43. Kirchhofer files, Butler Family Papers, "History," chap. EHB Sr., p. 2F.

44. Kirchhofer files, Butler Family Papers, "History," chap. EHB Sr., p. 4F; Goldberg, "Edward H. Butler," p. 60.

45. Kirchhofer files, Butler Family Papers, "History," chap. EHB Sr., p. 5F.

46. Ibid., p. 6F.

47. Kirchhofer files, Butler Family Papers, box 3.

48. Memo to McIntosh from E. H. Butler, July 9, 1908.

49. Goldberg, "Edward H. Butler," p. 63.

50. Kirchhofer files, Butler Family Papers, box 4.

51. Ibid.

52. Ibid.

53. Ibid.

54. Ibid.

55. Ibid.

56. Goldberg, "Edward H. Butler," p. 64.

57. Kirchhofer files, Butler Family Papers, box 1.

58. Letter to Clark Ingham, E. H. Butler Sr. Correspondence, Butler Family Papers, box. 5.

59. Ibid., box 4.

5 Changing Years

Nobody can project how their philosophy and outlook on life might change with the passage of time and the circumstances with which they have been surrounded. Edward H. Butler, strong-willed and intelligent as he was, was not immune to this human characteristic. His outlook did change considerably from the time he started the *Buffalo Sunday Morning News* as a young man of twenty-three to the time of his growing affluence as the successful publisher of the *Buffalo Evening News*.

The *Buffalo Sunday Morning News* was published at 200 Main Street. When it became a daily several years later, Butler moved the operation in February 1880 to 214 Main Street to get needed additional space. In July 1886 the *News* moved to 218 Main Street, which was barely twenty feet wide. It had no electric lights and no running water; printer's devils took buckets to the nearest outdoor pump to bring in water.[1] In May 1897 the *News* moved into a new building at 216–218 Main Street. Butler was determined that this structure would be the most beautiful newspaper building in the nation and indeed, when it was completed, many of the professional publications in the newspaper industry gave it that designation.[2]

In the decades to follow, the newspaper purchased additional properties in the immediate vicinity and added facilities as the paper continued its growth pattern. News operations were centered at 216–218 Main Street for seventy-six years.[3]

Butler's lifestyle changed with the passage of time as did his attitude about politics and labor. The boy, who was brought up in a less than affluent environment and who had struggled financially to get his start in business in the 1870s, had become financially successful in the decades of the eighties and nineties. Not surprisingly, he now indulged in some of the luxuries he had dreamed about in the past but could not afford.

The *Commercial*, a rival newspaper in Buffalo, in August 1883 wrote that "Mr. E. H. Butler of the *Evening News* has one of the finest pair of chestnut roadsters in the city. They are of Louis Napoleon pedigree, very stylish and speedy, and when hitched to his new French Surrey present a natty appearance."[4]

Butler long held an obsession for horses and as his financial resources grew he continued to increase his ownership of them. By the late 1880s he owned twenty-five horses that were housed at his homes in Buffalo and Le Roy, New York, and Darlington, South Carolina. A horseman's publication in Chicago commented in March 1886, "Col. E. H. Butler, the well-known proprietor of the *Buffalo Evening News*, the newspaper that did so much to boom Grover Cleveland for governor and for president, holds the ribbons behind a natty span of roadsters. The colonel takes considerable interest in fine-blooded horses and nothing pleases him better than to take an occasional outing behind his fleeting team."[5] The Butler-owned horses were used for business as well as for his personal pleasure. Early on, many were utilized to haul the *News* lightweight delivery trucks that carried the papers from the printing plant to the distribution centers. Streetcars and trains serviced the more remote points.[6]

By the 1890s Butler lived like a country squire at his Le Roy summer retreat and his winter home in South Carolina.[7] According to Marjorie Van Antwerp, the house in Le Roy was a lovely home, which he gave to his mother, Lucy. Lucy lived there with his wife's mother until Lucy's death at the age of seventy in 1900.[8] While visiting Edward in Buffalo, she slipped on a banana peel in front of his newspaper building and fell, fracturing her hip. An embolism followed resulting in her death.[9]

In 1894 Butler left his brother Ambrose in charge of the *News* and departed for Europe with his two children, Ada and Edward. He needed a rest and was suffering from rheumatism. He remained in Europe for a year but kept in constant touch with the *News* office through a barrage of letters and cables. He had assigned his managing editor, William McIntosh, the responsibility of overseeing the paper's editorials and he was in constant communication with his city editor, Sherman Moss, on local news coverage, always a major concern of his.[10]

216–218 Main Street was the center of *Buffalo Evening News* operations for seventy-six years. (From Buffalo Evening News, *A History of the City of Buffalo: Its Men and Institutions*, 1908)

In April 1895 he cabled Ambrose from Europe that W. J. Conners, the owner of the morning *Courier* and the afternoon *Enquirer*, had contacted him with an offer to purchase the *News*. Butler said he had categorically rejected the offer, telling Connors that the *News* was not for sale at any price.[11] As the sole owner of the *News* he could reject this overture without consulting others. It was a historic advantage that Butler had over other publishers who had to consult with stockholders and/or family members in reaching such decisions.

A clipping from the *Scranton Republic* of October 4, 1904, quotes a *Los Angeles Times* article on Butler, describing him as "a man who could do in a minute what would take the other fellow an hour to accomplish." It goes on with what it claims the writer observed: "Mr. Butler is the only great editor whom I know with a genuine Turkish bath of the most elaborate type in his private office for his own exclusive use. It is built of marble and tiles and brass. It [his office] has a hot room and a steam room and a deep cold plunge and all the accessories. . . . A professional masseur is in attendance at all times. No Oriental potentate has quite the equal of this. Nero could not indulge in such luxury. He enjoys it as other wealthy men enjoy a spin in an automobile."[12] There is no established proof that this description of Butler's lifestyle is totally or even partially accurate.

* * *

Butler launched the *Sunday News* with repeated assurances to its readers that the newspaper would not be a political organ, stressing that it would be an independent newspaper not under the domination of any party. When he started the *Buffalo Evening News*, he reiterated that pledge of political neutrality.[13]

Politically, the *News* history was one of extremes, particularly where Grover Cleveland was concerned. It was way out front in 1882 leading a campaign to secure the gubernatorial nomination for the then Buffalo mayor, publishing reams of laudatory material, including numerous testimonials the paper solicited from prominent citizens. Although it had not supported Cleveland's election for mayor in 1881, the *News* kicked off a major effort for his gubernatorial quest. Front-page stories extolling Cleveland were displayed under the heading, "The Cleveland Boom."[14] The *News*'s campaign for Cleveland even included displaying a large portrait of him over the front of its office building on Main Street topped by an electric arc light. Thousands of western New Yorkers came to see it. Cleveland won the democratic nomination and then the race for the governor's seat.[15]

Cleveland acknowledged the role the *News* played in his election in a letter to Butler in 1884, stating, "That you have been my warm current and disinterested friend from first to last I desire now to acknowledge and to thank you for all that you have done for me. You have demonstrated again that you don't take on things to lose. I hope you will take the liberty of suggesting anything that appears to you to be helpful in the campaign and I shall presume upon your friendship enough to ask you to do any reasonable thing that occurs to me to be of use. I shall be glad to hear from or see you at any time."[16]

In the spring of 1884 the *News* gave its complete and wholehearted support to Cleveland's campaign for the presidency. Republican James G. Blaine opposed Cleveland in a bitter campaign that may have been the low point in American politics. Each side was guilty of spreading wild rumors.[17] In July 1884 the *Buffalo Telegraph*, a Scripps paper, published "a terrible tale, a dark chapter in a public man's history, the pitiful story of an illegitimate baby of a clerk at a Buffalo department store."[18] Cleveland never admitted paternity although he apparently contributed to the support of the child later on.[19] Three Scripps papers published the story. In the *Cleveland Penny Press* the story read: "Grover Cleveland—a reveler in the domain of lust. . . . A record of drunkenness and brutality. . . ." The *Detroit News*, the parent paper of the Scripps chain, took a different stance: "The mere infirmities of nature in men and women, whether they occupy a public or private position, should be as sacred from newspaper interviews as the physical diseases of which they may be so unfortunate as to be the victims. We protest any discussion whatsoever of purely private sins of candidate for public office."[20] On August 10, 1884, the *News* gave the other side of the Cleveland scandal, protesting his innocence but never ran the original scandal story.[21]

A sharp difference with President Cleveland over United States tariff policy ended the honeymoon between Butler and Cleveland. The president's tariff message in 1887 calling for the abolition of high tariffs infuriated Butler who felt very strongly that tariffs were necessary for the protection of American industries and jobs. He felt government should always do all it can to provide employment. He disliked England and he saw high tariffs as detrimental to that island nation. Without them he felt England could flood the country with low-cost goods and set the prices it wanted. Butler felt betrayed by Cleveland.[22]

When Cleveland ran for reelection in 1888, he did so without the support of the *News*. In fact, the paper that had been such a strong supporter four years earlier now vehemently called for his defeat.[23] The *News* supported Chauncey Mitchell Depew as the Republican nominee, but he did not get his party's support. It went to Benjamin Harrison, who won the support of the *News* while the paper carried on a crusade of attack, criticism, and ridicule of Cleveland. Harrison was elected with more Electoral College votes, although Cleveland had ninety thousand more popular votes.[24] In the aftermath of his defeat Cleveland asserted that Buffalo was "the place I hate above all others" and despite the fact that he was married to a Buffalo woman, he never returned to the city.[25]

When Butler broke with Cleveland, the publisher abandoned any pretense of political neutrality and became a staunchly dedicated Republican.[26] His partisanship was ardent. For example, in a July 29, 1900, memo to his managing editor, William McIntosh, Butler wrote, "Above all things be in with President Taft whatever he does."

The *News* under the stewardship of Butler; his son, Edward H. Butler Jr.; James H. Righter; Mrs. Edward H. Butler Jr.; and finally that of Henry Z. Urban never again endorsed a Democrat for the presidency. The paper did from time to time endorse Democrats for local offices and, although rarely, for state offices. It was not until 1977, when Warren E. Buffett purchased the *News*, that the ban on endorsing Democrats for the presidency finally ended. In my first meeting with Buffett, shortly before he finalized his purchase of the *News*, he informed me that the *News* should endorse candidates for all offices, local and national, based on the principle of supporting whomever the *News* editorial board decided could best serve the interests of the electorate, regardless of their party designation.

* * *

A major change in Butler's labor philosophy occurred in 1892. His response to a rail strike that year differed significantly from his position on another rail strike fifteen years earlier. During the railroad strike of 1877, the then-twenty-seven-year-old publisher of the *Sunday Morning News* defended laborers and encouraged them to exercise their political will against capitalists and the state.[27] Fifteen years later, Butler was an affluent publisher with great influence in the community, who took a different tack when another outbreak of fierce rail strikes brought violence to Buffalo. The *News* sided with the rail companies, replacement workers, and displaced passengers. It condemned the lawless strikers. An editorial called the strike bad business and said the strikers should be punished. The editorial counseled union officials to prevent damage at the railroads and warned, "There is sufficient force in Buffalo to deal with it effectively."[28]

Then, on August 16, 1892, a strident *News* editorial said that the state militia should be sent to Buffalo to control the activity of strikers. Another editorial condemned sympathy strikes and still another said, "Here is their lesson of the strike. The militia is the one and sole dependence of our citizens for protection from riot and destruction to property."[29]

Observers of the labor movement have stated that the impact of the 1877 strike was more far-reaching in Buffalo than the one in 1892, although Butler and the *News* reacted much more negatively toward labor in 1892 than fifteen years earlier. Labor observers claim that the difference was due to the position in life that Butler had attained in the intervening fifteen-year period and with that change the dramatic shift in his relationship with the workingman. However, despite Butler's long-held concern for the plight of the workingman, he had always shown distaste for labor violence that had the potential to overturn the existing social structure.[30]

Countless stories are recorded about his concern for *News* employees and his acts of kindness toward them that he did not make public. A *News* editorial during the 1892 strike said that the bond between worker and the boss should be stronger than between worker and a colleague.[31]

It is significant that throughout this period, the *News* had no labor strife despite the ever-improving financial condition of the newspaper. In a "History of the *News*" prepared by the business department around 1901, Butler said, "The *News* is making more money today than it ever made. But if the *News* were not making money, if it were running a loss, I could run this paper all the rest of my life and pay the bills out of the money it has already made without feeling the strain in the slightest degree."[32]

The loyalty of its employees to the publisher remained constant and Butler's confidence in himself and his actions remained as strong as they were when he was a young man preparing to launch the *Sunday Morning News*.

In an interesting letter to the chairman of the American Newspaper Publishers Association on May 17, 1912, Butler, a supporter of unions in his early days as publisher, wrote: "The members of my pressroom are members of the union but I do not recognize the union's rules nor shall I. I pay the best wages going but I do not propose having men run my office under rules, rules, rules. . . . The publishers in this country can tell everyone how to run their business and cannot run their own. A new stand will have to be taken."[33]

An insight to Butler's feelings about *News* employees is made clear in a letter he wrote August 16, 1912, in response to an inquiry from a federal commissioner.

> In regard to [inquiry] No. 2, the policy of the company towards its employees, I would say it is not a company. I am sole owner and organizer of The *News*. In regard to question four, pension and retirement plans. I take care of my people when they get old if they are worthy of it. I retire them when they are no longer able to work. I have no set rules for that.
>
> Section 6, safety appliances, hygiene and sanitation: I would say that I have studied these points. All my employees work by daylight and not artificial light. . . . According to the *Typographical Journal* I have the best composing room and the best light in the United States.
>
> As to sanitation I have a system that I have not found equaled anywhere. I have an ice-manufacturing machine in my building. Through this I pass all the water used in the building. It is first filtered, then boiled, and then distilled. This, through a circulating process goes to every compositor or printer in my employ. There is a cup for each one eight feet from the machine and they have pure distilled ice water, the best in the world. It is so pure that the surgeons of our city say that they would use it in operations.[34]

With the development of the automotive age, Butler became an ardent exponent of this mode of transportation, again for his personal pleasure and for business purposes. At one time he had as many as eighteen cars for his personal use. By 1911 his cars included three E.

R. Thomas vehicles, a Packard, two Pierce Arrows, a Mercedes, two Renaults, an Overland, a Chalmers-Detroit, a Detroit Electric, and some lesser-known brands.[35]

Butler helped form the local Automobile Club and the *News* frequently published road maps of short tours it recommended for family Sunday auto outings. *News* reporters were envied by those from the other Buffalo newspapers, arriving at the scene of news events first in their *News* cars while competitors had to rely on taxis or streetcars. The *News* conducted a continuing campaign for better roads for many years.[36]

Horses and autos were important to Butler, but his true sense of showmanship was manifested through the years in the buildings the *News* occupied and his personal residences. The *News* itself has always occupied buildings in the downtown sector near the waterfront. In addition to the founder's determination that the paper be housed in a significant structure, Butler also felt that as owner of the newspaper, his residence had to be significantly above others in the community in grace and grandeur. He felt that he accomplished this goal when he purchased a mansion at Delaware Avenue and North Street in 1908 that he believed was the most beautiful in the country.[37]

The mansion, six years old and one of the last works of architect Stanford White, was the largest residential sale in Buffalo at that time.[38] Built over a three-year period from 1895 to 1898 for a cost of nearly $175,000, it was considered to be a palatial residence.[39] More than a century later and several changes in ownership, the residence is still generally referred to as "the Butler mansion" although the family no longer owns it.[40]

Butler's attitude about structures for his business and residence is exemplified in a memo he wrote to his managing editor in 1907. "The people abroad trust much to appearances," he wrote to William McIntosh. "The man who lives in a small house is generally regarded about the size of the house."[41]

Despite ever-increasing ego-building endeavors, Butler never diminished his efforts to strengthen his newspaper. As he did with the *Sunday Morning News*, he continued to promote scores of community reforms, in line with his aim to have the paper be "the voice of the people." The *News* protested the long working hours of children;

The Butler mansion at the corner of Delaware and North in Buffalo. Now the home of the University of Buffalo School of Management. (Butler Family Papers, courtesy E. H. Butler Library Archives, Buffalo State College)

warred against "odious undertakers"; enhanced its letters to the editor column to make it a strong outlet for reader opinions and complaints; campaigned vigorously for elimination of dangerous railroad grade crossings; and supported development of more and larger parks, riding paths, bike trails, libraries, and harbor improvements. No community concern or problem was too small or too large for the *News* to comment upon and often campaign for over extended periods of time.

The early 1900s were exciting times for newspapers. They were the people's only news source. Late-breaking news called for "Extra Editions" and on election nights newspaper boys ran through the street yelling "Extra paper!" They would receive five to ten times the price of a one-cent paper from anxious buyers. Newspaper competition was changing in Buffalo. The staid *Commercial* no longer dominated the evening field. Readers preferred the lively, feature-filled *News*, *Times*, and *Enquirer*. The *Commercial* was sold in 1924 and two years later it disappeared. In 1926 the Democratic *Courier* and the Republican *Express*, both under the control of W. J. Connors, were merged into the

Courier-Express, a morning paper. The two papers separately had been sharing 100,000 readers while the *News* and the *Times* were circulating over 100,000 each. The *Enquirer*, which had been renamed the *Star* and converted to a tabloid paper like the *New York News*, was discontinued. The evening field was left to the *Buffalo Evening News* and the *Times*.[42]

Notes

1. "Producing the News: A Lesson in Progress," *Buffalo News* centennial publication, October 12, 1980, p. H-16.
2. Alfred Kirchhofer files, Butler Family Papers, E. H. Butler Library Archives, State University College at Buffalo, box 2, Kirchhofer, "History," chap. EHB Sr., p. 6F.
3. When I started at the *Buffalo Evening News* as a reporter in 1949, I worked at this location. One thing I remember vividly is that there were fresh flowers at the front counter in the lobby of the *News* Building every morning. The practice had originated with the founder of the paper, and was continued by his son and his son's son-in-law and by his son's wife.
4. Kirchhofer, "History," chap. EHB Sr., p. 2D.
5. Ibid., p. 3D; Jerry Goldberg, "Edward H. Butler and the Founding of the *Buffalo Evening News*: The Life and Times of One of the Last Publisher-editors" (master's thesis, State University of New York at Buffalo, 1997), p. 86.
6. Kirchhofer files, Butler Family Papers, box 1.
7. Ibid.
8. Marjorie Van Antwerp, interview by Sister Martin Joseph Jones, October 13, 1981, Butler Family Papers, p. 3.
9. Goldberg, "Edward H. Butler," p. 20.
10. Kirchhofer files, Butler Family Papers, box 3.
11. Ibid.
12. Ibid., box 11.
13. Michael Dillon, "From Populist to Patrician: Edward H. Butler's *Buffalo News* and the Crisis of Labor, 1877–1892," *American Journalism* 16, no. 1 (1999): 43; Goldberg, "Edward H. Butler," p. 58.
14. Goldberg, "Edward H. Butler," p. 77.
15. *Buffalo News*, October 12, 1980, p. H-7.
16. Goldberg, "Edward H. Butler," p. 80.
17. Ibid.
18. Kirchhofer files, Butler Family Papers, box 3.

19. *Buffalo News*, October 12, 1980, p. H-7.
20. Kirchhofer files, Butler Family Papers, box 3.
21. *Buffalo News*, October 12, 1980, p. H-7.
22. Goldberg, "Edward H. Butler," p. 82.
23. Ibid., p. 81.
24. Kirchhofer files, Butler Family Papers, box 3.
25. Ibid.
26. Goldberg, "Edward H. Butler," p. 83.
27. Dillon, "From Populist to Patrician," p. 48.
28. Ibid., p. 52.
29. Ibid.; Goldberg, "Edward H. Butler," p. 91.
30. Dillon, "From Populist to Patrician," p. 51.
31. Goldberg, "Edward H. Butler," p. 93.
32. Ibid., pp. 88, 89.
33. E. H. Butler Sr., 1870–1913, Butler Family Papers, box. 2
34. Goldberg, "Edward H. Butler," p. 93.
35. Ibid., p. 86.
36. Kirchhofer, "History," chap. EHB, pp. 3D, 4D; Goldberg, "Edward H. Butler," pp. 86, 87.
37. Kirchhofer files, Butler Family Papers, box 1; Goldberg, "Edward H. Butler," p. 88.
38. Kirchhofer files, Butler Family Papers, box 11.
39. *Buffalo Architecture: A Guide* (Cambridge, MA: MIT Press, 1996), p. 141.
40. The mansion designed by Stanford White was built in 1896 for a Buffalo banker. He sold it to Edward H. Butler and the family owned it until it was donated to Roswell Park after the death of Mrs. Kate Butler in 1974. The hospital was unable to keep the mansion and it fell into disrepair until the Delaware North Companies, Inc. purchased it in 1979. They launched a $6 million restoration project to make major repairs to the exterior. Much of the interior also had to be restored because of the rather questionable decorating taste of Kate Butler. Varity Corp. bought the property in 1990, and in 1999 multimillionaire Jeremy M. Jacobs acquired the architectural treasure. He gave use of the mansion and the carriage house to the University of Buffalo School of Management in December 1999, and seventeen months later donated both structures to the university for school functions and the School of Management.
41. Goldberg, "Edward H. Butler," p. 89.
42. A. Gordon Bennett, *Buffalo Newspapers since 1870*, Adventures in Western New York History (Buffalo, NY: Buffalo News and Erie County Historical Society, 1974), pp. 4, 5, 7, 8.

6 Heights of Power

Two major *Buffalo Evening News* campaigns at the start of the twentieth century brought great satisfaction to publisher Edward H. Butler Sr. One he considered to be the major story of his career because of the world focus it put on Buffalo. He was enormously proud, too, of the other campaign because the *News* overcame so many obstacles to achieve its aims that were so important for the progress of his city.

In 1898 the *News* started beating the drum for what was to become the Pan-American Exposition of 1901. Most observers at the time, including many competing papers, credited Butler's *News* with creating the environment that resulted in the exposition taking place. It was known throughout the world as Buffalo's crowning glory. It was a typical Butler campaign, pulling out all the stops to create a positive environment and impetus for the endeavor.[1]

Although the exposition brought approximately fifty million dollars into the city, success could be measured not only in monetary terms, but also in the many benefits accruing to the city. These included increased industries, a greater volume of products, increased value of real estate, and the favorable impression hundreds of thou-

President McKinley in a horse-drawn coach shortly before he was assassinated at the Pan-American Exposition in 1901. (Courtesy *Buffalo News*)

sands of people gained from seeing Buffalo.[2] Numerous inquiries came from businesses all over the country about the availability of factory sites in the city as well as a labor supply and shipping facilities. In the following years factories seemed to spring up overnight. Buffalo changed from an underdeveloped community to the eighth-largest city in the United States[3] with a population of almost four hundred twenty-four thousand. The population grew by 47 percent from 1890 to 1910.[4]

The success of the world's first hydroelectric plant was demonstrated at the 1901 exposition, when it was lighted by electricity generated from Niagara Falls. A story on the front page of the May 17, 1893, *Buffalo Evening News* stated that city residents were very slow to embrace the use of electricity in their homes. This reluctance was attributed to a dislike of the wires and poles required and the initial cost of wiring that was about three dollars and fifty cents a light. They also feared that the cost of the electric service would be far higher than the cost of the gas they were accustomed to using. There was only a limited amount of power available until a transmission line to Buffalo, from what later became known as the Adams Station, was completely powered in 1896 making more power available for industry, streetcars, and lighting.[5] By 1887 the city had sixty-seven hundred gas street lamps and 546 electric street lamps.[6]

The exposition got off to a glorious start, but on September 6, 1901, assassin Leon Czolgosz shot Pres. William McKinley as the president greeted visitors at the Temple of Music. McKinley died eight days later and Czolgosz was tried and executed in the electric chair by the end of the following month. The *Buffalo Evening News* of October 29, 1901, quoted Czolgosz as saying, "I killed the President because he was the enemy of the good people—of the working people. I am not sorry for my crime."[7]

The day of the shooting the *News* published three extras and in the period following, as the president fought for life, the *News* had in-depth coverage each day. Publisher Butler cited the shooting and its aftermath as the major story of his career.[8]

Following McKinley's death, Butler felt strongly that the city, the site of this national tragedy, had to do something to commemorate the occasion. He felt confident that this effort would be well met, but he had to experience a long period of frustration before a satisfactory conclusion was reached. Editorials in the *News* called for the erection of a Buffalo monument to the late president. A commission was established to carry out such a project and Butler, who had initiated the idea, was named chairman.[9] Although the state senate and assembly had Republican majorities, and Gov. Benjamin B. Odell Jr. was a Republican, the measure to set up the commission and appropriate $100,000 for a suitable monument was met with apathy and remained in committee.[10]

Tiring of the inaction, Butler instructed his Albany correspondent, Ed Scanlon, to personally intervene with the governor and get a clear indication of his intent on the bottled-up legislation. When Scanlon reported that he was unable to get a commitment from the governor, Butler instructed him to ask the governor the same question every single day from then on. Back then, the governor held a press briefing daily. Thus started a daily ritual, with Scanlon asking the governor about his intentions and the governor each day replying that he would not move the measure. Finally, the *News* reporter and the governor tired of the routine and agreed to set up a system that would save everyone from hearing the same thing at each press briefing. Scanlon would lift one finger, an indication to the governor that he was going to ask about the McKinley monument. The governor, in response, would raise two fingers, indicating that he had not changed his mind on the matter.[11]

The finger-waving routine went on for some time while the *News* publisher continued to fume. Finally, he instructed Scanlon to again see the governor in his office and inform him that unless he directed the legislative committee to act positively on the monument bill, the *News* would not support his reelection and would instead support a Democrat.[12]

Butler's threat ended the impasse. The governor publicly proclaimed support for a monument and the projected $100,000 appropriation. He used his influence with the legislative leadership and the measure quickly passed both houses. The obelisk known as the McKinley Monument was unveiled on September 5, 1907, in Niagara Square in front of Buffalo City Hall.[13] Butler's perseverance and his willingness to use the power and prestige of the *News* to accomplish what he felt was right once again achieved the result he desired on behalf of the community.

During the late 1800s the number of newspapers continued to increase across the Midwest and to the West Coast. The *San Francisco Chronicle* was that city's leading paper until William Randolph Hearst's father gave him the *Examiner* to run. In 1893 the *Examiner* overtook the *Chronicle*, and by 1908 the circulation of the *Examiner* reached one hundred thousand. Hearst moved on to New York and in 1895 purchased the *Morning Journal*, resulting in frenzied competition between the *Journal* and Pulitzer's *World*. The circulation contest between the two papers led to powerful jingo (an aggressive, warlike foreign policy) propaganda by both publications. The Spanish-American War was a result of the popular war fever the papers created. The *New York Herald* and the *Sun* joined them in creating war passions with editorials, news stories, and pictures.[14]

Edwin L. Godkin, an independent commentator on political and social affairs, wrote in the *New York Evening Post* on February 19, 1898:

> Nothing so disgraceful as the behavior of two of these newspapers [the *Journal* and the *World*] this week has been known in the history of American journalism. . . . It is a crying shame that men should work such mischief simply in order to sell more papers.[15]

After the war, Hearst and other publishers, in order to hold on to circulation gains created by the war, entered into a period of "yellow journalism." This meant large, bold, scare headlines; lavish use of pictures; and faked interviews and stories. Many papers in large metropolitan centers practiced "yellow journalism." President McKinley had been a frequent target of Hearst because of the president's antiwar stance. The death of McKinley marked the beginning of the decline of "yellow journalism," and by 1910 there were not many yellow papers left. The *Buffalo Evening News* never practiced "yellow journalism" nor did many other papers in the country including in New York, the *New York Times*, the *Tribune*, the *Sun*, and the *Evening Post*.[16]

During a period of national economic decline in the 1870s, Buffalo was somewhat better off than other parts of the country because of the commercial traffic on the Erie Canal. Nearly a half century earlier on August 9, 1823, the work of canal digging in Erie County was formally started and was completed in September 1825. At that time the canal was the longest artificial waterway in the world, except for one in China. As then constructed, the canal was 363 miles long, forty feet wide at the surface and twenty-eight feet at the bottom, and was only four feet deep. The largest boats used on the canal carried an average of seventy tons of cargo. Buffalo, the transfer point from the lake to the canal, was a major beneficiary and as a result its population and wealth increased more rapidly than any other community in the country at that time.[17]

During this period of general economic malaise that infected most of the nation, Buffalo suffered from a dramatic reduction in lake and canal traffic as a result of stiff competition from the railroads, which by this time were carrying freight for less cost than boats. Canal barges were coming into Buffalo underloaded and returning empty.[18]

Seeking a solution to the problem, in 1902 Butler started a sixteen-month campaign in which the *News* hammered away on the need to widen and deepen the Erie Canal. The effort came to a successful conclusion in the fall of 1903. Butler made the canal project the keystone of *News* editorial policy and refused to let up despite early frustrations that led most in the state to believe that the costly project would never get voter approval. No other newspaper in the state supported it. He was convinced that the city would suffer negative economic consequences if the canal was not improved to make it competitive with the railroads, which had expanded greatly since the canal first opened in 1825.[19]

The *News* publisher considered the canal project so important that he came close to splitting with the Republican Party over it when the Republican state convention of 1902 defeated a resolution calling for enlargement of the canal. Butler was enraged and warned that if it refused to endorse the canal plan at its next state convention "the party need not look for many votes in Erie County." The GOP reacted positively, approving a canal improvement resolution in 1903 to spend not more than $101 million to enlarge the Erie Canal, the Champlain Canal, and the Oswego Canal to a depth of twelve feet.[20]

The history of the canal goes back to 1812 when the state legislature authorized a $5 million borrowing to start construction on a canal. This law was repealed two years later as the War of 1812 broke out and stymied any further talk of a canal project. In 1816 the legislature revived the project with appointment of a canal commission and in 1817 again passed a law authorizing canal construction. In July 1820 the first section of the canal, from Utica to Montezuma, was completed. In 1823 ground was broken in Erie County near Commercial Street in Buffalo, the first canal construction in our area. That phase was finished in 1825.[21]

With the passage of time, the canal lost its competitive edge as rail facilities expanded and rail-carrying rates were reduced. In order to remain viable, proponents said, the canal had to be widened and deepened so that it could permit passage of boats capable of carrying at least 1,000 tons of freight.[22] However, in April 1902 the legislature voted down a proposal to spend $31.8 million to improve the canal.

The project was dealt what many thought to be a deathblow. But in July of that year, at the instigation of publisher Edward H. Butler Sr., the *Buffalo Evening News* entered the picture actively and kicked off its intensive campaign, employing all the resources of its news pages and editorials, to bring new life to plans for canal improvement. Butler felt strongly that the early growth of Buffalo was due to its location on the western terminus of the canal. He made the campaign for upgrading the facility the keystone of *News* policy and his paper became the chief proponent for canal enhancement while most of the print media in the state took the opposing position. They were opposed because of the project's cost and their belief that it would not have positive economic impact.[23]

Butler also exercised his own political muscle, and as a result, when the state Republican convention was held it accepted the *News* position on the canal. The week following, when the Democrats met in convention, they, too, supported canal expansion. When the legislature convened in 1903, the message of Gov. Benjamin Odell was less than friendly to the canal project, kicking off three months of vigorous legislative debate. Finally, a measure appropriating $101 million for the canal project won passage conditioned upon approval of the voters in the November election. The *News* campaign for the canal continued unabated and finally the voters approved the $101 million expenditures by a majority of some 250,000 of the popular vote. The *News* was credited by virtually all the media and political and civic organizations in the state with turning negative feeling about what was then a huge expenditure of dollars into a resounding victory endorsed by the people.[24]

During the sixteen-month period of the canal initiative, the *News* gained twenty thousand new subscribers. Nobody is certain if it was due to the public's approval of the campaign or just fortuitous circumstance. Nonetheless, it was, without doubt, a strident campaign of news stories and accompanying editorials pointing out the pluses of canal improvement for the Buffalo area.[25]

One of the city's problems was that it lacked a railroad connection from the west. The New York Central Railroad repeatedly had attempted to make Buffalo a city on its main line that would connect with lines to the west. The city aldermen, however, resisted all of these efforts that would have enhanced Buffalo's economy. The legislators defended their actions saying it showed their "incorruptibility." Their critics, however, said it was a manifestation of their stupidity. As a result, Buffalo remained on a siding, paying the price in commerce and passenger traffic for rejecting the overtures of New York Central to run trains through the city.[26]

Publishing authorities recognized the *Buffalo Evening News* as one of the great disseminators of news in the country. As a result of a campaign to correct mismanagement in a reformatory, the *News* reputation grew in Europe as a paper that dared to fight for the better treatment of unfortunate youths and men who were committed to the reformatory. This led to better treatment in all penal institutions.[27]

In addition to these major campaigns, Butler took up the cudgel for other community endeavors. As early as 1898 he became a strong advocate for a cancer research center at the University of Buffalo medical school. A year earlier, the state legislature had passed a bill to appropriate $7,500 for a startup effort at UB to investigate the causes and possible cures for cancer. The idea for this effort originated with Dr. Roswell Park.[28] When Governor Black vetoed the cancer research measure, Butler started to make plans to ensure passage of a similar or more liberal measure in the next legislative session. His thoughts, reflected in *News* stories and editorials, paid off and $10,000 was appropriated for a state laboratory in Buffalo to investigate the causes and cure of cancer. This miniscule appropriation was the nucleus of what was to become Roswell Park Memorial Institute in 1946. The battle to give the state's financial support to this effort continued for years as each succeeding legislature balked at approving appropriations for the effort.[29]

Still another local institution enjoyed major support from the Butler family. The founder of the *News* was very supportive of the State Normal School and its role in the community. In 1895 Butler became a member of its board of managers. In 1902 he became president of the school's board. After Butler's death in 1914, his namesake, then the publisher of the *News*, succeeded him in the presidency of the board and continued in this leadership role for the institution when it became Buffalo State Teachers College in 1927.[30]

Edward H. Butler Jr. joined with then Buffalo mayor Frank Schwab in 1927 to get state legislation ceding state hospital property adjoining the school to the college, providing ninety acres to what is now the campus of Buffalo State. Butler was president of the local board of Buffalo State for eighteen years and with his passing he was succeeded by his daughter Kate Butler. The library at the college today carries the Butler family name and many of the archives of the *News* reside in that library.[31]

Butler, long concerned about railroad grade crossings, was an original member of the state's Grade Crossing Commission and served on the commission for twenty-six years. He was a director of the Grosvenor Library for twenty-six years and president of its board for seven years. He was chairman of the State's Board of Electors in 1908. He served as president of the Buffalo Publishers Association and the State Editorial Association, the Republican State Editorial Association, and was vice president of the United Press.[32]

Notes

1. Alfred Kirchhofer files, Butler Family Papers, E. H. Butler Library Archives, State University College at Buffalo, box 4.

2. *A History of the City of Buffalo, Its Men and Institutions* (Buffalo, NY: Buffalo Evening News, 1908), p. 44.

3. Ibid., p. 52.

4. Buffalo and Erie County Public Library, main branch, local history card files.

5. Ralph Greenhill and Thomas D. Mahoney, *Niagara* (Canada: University of Toronto Press, 1969), pp. 158–59; "Dawn of Greatness," *Buffalo Evening News*, November 14, 1896, p. 1.

6. Kirchhofer files, Butler Family Papers, box 4.

7. "Covering Presidents," *Buffalo News* centennial publication, October 12, 1980, pp. H-8, I-8.

8. Ibid.

9. Kirchhofer files, Butler Family Papers, box 4, Charles Armitage, "History of the *Buffalo Evening News*"; Murray B. Light, "A Little Pressure Still Can Get a Lot of Action," *Buffalo News*, April 30, 2000, p. H-5.

10. Kirchhofer files, Butler Family Papers, boxes 1, 11.

11. Ibid.
12. Ibid.
13. Ibid., Light, "A Little Pressure," p. H-5.
14. Frank Luther Mott, *American Journalism, 1690–1940* (New York: Macmillan, 1941), pp. 520–27.
15. Ibid., p. 532.
16. Ibid., p. 540.
17. *A History of the City of Buffalo*, p. 36.
18. William H. Dolan, comp., *Our Police and Our City: The Official History of the Buffalo Police Department and a History of the City of Buffalo*, ed. Mark S. Hubbell (Buffalo, NY: Bensler & Wesley, 1893), p. 191.
19. Kirchhofer files, Butler Family Papers, box 4.
20. Kirchhofer files, Butler Family Papers, boxes 1, 4; *A History of the City of Buffalo*, p. 37.
21. *A History of the City of Buffalo*, pp. 35, 36.
22. Ibid.
23. Ibid., p. 35–37.
24. Ibid.
25. Murray B. Light, "The Erie Canal Has Long Been Controversial," *Buffalo News*, June 4, 2000, p. H-5.
26. Dolan, *Our Police and Our City*, p. 195.
27. *Buffalo Evening News*, March 10, 1914, p. 1.
28. Kirchhofer files, Butler Family Papers, box 3.
29. The *News*, however, never let up on its effort to increase the hospital's funding and furthering its efforts against cancer. This effort continued through the years of *News* guidance under Edward H. Butler Jr. and even beyond that when editor Alfred H. Kirchhofer played a significant role in support for Roswell Park. Roswell Park, under new governance and leadership, has acknowledged the decades-long role of the *Buffalo News* in establishing its national recognition as one of the nation's major research and clinical facilities against cancer.
30. Kirchhofer files, Butler Family Papers, boxes 1, 4.
31. Ibid.
32. Lance Zavits, "The Edward H. Butlers—Father and Son," an address presented at a meeting of the Le Roy Historical Society, August 16, 1958. It was reprinted in full in the *Le Roy Gazette-News* on August 21, 1958.

7 Politics and Death

Butler, highly successful as the editor and publisher of Buffalo's largest circulation Sunday and daily newspapers, had been an ardent Republican since 1887. Even so, he had never given any indication that he was interested in running for elected public office. He had served the Republican Party as a presidential elector at its national convention in 1896 and then again in 1900, and the editorials of his newspapers reflected his dedication to the GOP.[1] Butler had been involved in behind-the-scenes Republican Party politics, lending his support publicly and privately to certain candidates and was not averse to using his newspapers to advance these candidacies through the positioning of stories, extensive news coverage, and supportive editorials.

On June 4, 1901, the *Buffalo Times*, a Democratic Party paper, gave the first public notice that Butler was under consideration by the Erie County Republican Party as its candidate for mayor of Buffalo. The *Times* story almost instantly set off a "Butler for mayor" movement. It followed up the next day indicating support for Butler by key party leaders and an editorial stating that Butler's candidacy "would be received with pleasure by thousands of Republicans in this city, and no doubt, outside of partisan considerations, by many other citizens."[2]

On June 7, Senator Chauncey M. Depew was quoted as saying, "If the local organization wants my advice, I say nominate Mr. Butler."[3] The Democratic *Courier* immediately joined the positive comments, saying that if Butler became the Republican candidate, the Democrats "would need to place a notably strong candidate against him." The *Courier* published a picture of Butler with a caption describing him as a "Man of action, with clean record, who would catch the Independent vote."[4] All the Republican papers in the city immediately lined up in support of a Butler nomination and newspapers throughout the state and in major cities of the East gave the drive for the Buffalo publisher considerable favorable publicity.[5]

The *Brooklyn Times*'s comment was typically laudatory of Butler. One of its editorials stated, "The fact that all the newspapers of Buffalo have come out for an editor emphasized two things. That editor is a remarkable man and has undoubtedly won the respect and the friendship of his rivals in the business. He has, by a life of energy, enterprise and ability, won for himself a leading place in his city and state. . . ."[6]

Members of the GOP executive committee formally offered the mayoral nomination to Butler on July 12, 1901. Not surprisingly, this man of significant wealth and great passion for the newspaper business that brought him that wealth, immediately declined, expressing gratitude for the offer and noting that "my newspaper business and other interests will not permit such exclusive attention to official matters for a term of four years."[7]

Declining the nomination for a mayoral race that Democrats as well as Republicans were certain he would have won deprived Butler of the stepping-stone he needed for future political aspirations. While the mayoral movement made him a bigger figure than ever in New York State politics and brought predictions that he would be a candidate for the U.S. Senate down the line, it was not to be. Had he been mayor of Buffalo, the political events that thwarted any aspirations he might possibly have had for a Senate seat might have turned out differently.[8]

William J. Conners of the *Courier* commented on July 14, 1901, that Butler's decision not to run for mayor would "please those friends and admirers who are confident that he will be chosen United States senator for New York, to succeed [the retiring] Mr. Platt, an exalted office which he would not fail to grace." Out-of-state newspapers echoed those sentiments. The *Boston Herald* ran a story saying that Butler was "slated to be the successor to Senator Thomas C. Platt of New York." The same analyses were made in many New York state newspapers. But it was not to be.[9]

The convoluted maneuvers of New York State politics ended up with Butler opposing Theodore Roosevelt's run for governor of the state. When Roosevelt became president upon the assassination of McKinley, any hope Butler may have had for a Senate seat was gone. When Senator Platt decided to retire in 1909, Roosevelt supported Elihu Root for the Senate seat. It was Root who in 1898 had persuaded the Republican state convention to nominate Roosevelt for the governor's post. Butler's final chance for a major political post was gone.[10]

There is, however, no definitive proof that Butler really had any burning desire for a seat in the U.S. Senate. Without question he thoroughly enjoyed the political infighting within the Republican Party, but there's no record that he truly had targeted a Senate seat as the next step in his career. If offered the opportunity, he may have declined, as he did earlier for the mayoral race.

In the last decade of his life, Butler purchased his mansion on Delaware Avenue and spent more time enjoying the fruits of his successful career, marred only by his increasing physical ailments. He spent more and more of his time traveling in Europe and at his winter home in South Carolina. And he was giving increasing thought to what the future might hold for the *News* after his death. His son, Edward H. Butler Jr., was graduated from Yale University in 1907 and his father undertook the process of grooming him to run the newspapers. Father and son exchanged letters almost daily when the senior Butler was absent from Buffalo. These letters revealed a very strong tie of devotion between the two.[11]

The enormous volume of letters and cables the two exchanged was very telling in one respect; little reference was ever made to editorial matters. Young Butler's training started on the business side of the newspaper and his correspondence with his father rarely involved editorial issues.

The senior Edward Butler had become increasingly aware that his son did not show any real interest in the news side of the business and his correspondence with friends and publishers reflected his concern about this. In one 1910 letter to a New York friend, Butler noted that his son had not fulfilled his hopes that he would develop strong feelings for journalism. He somewhat lamely attributed it to his son's marriage in 1909 to Kate Maddox Robinson.[12] He knew his son was constantly upset by the behavior of his wife, and particularly by her frequent absences from home.

In 1912 Edward H. Butler Sr. yielded the title of *News* publisher to his son but retained for himself the title of editor and proprietor. In effect, the father removed from his son the options publishers generally have of strongly influencing editorial policy if they so desire or in some instances of actually calling the editorial shots. Given his disappointment in his son's lack of real interest and enthusiasm for editorial concerns, the elder Butler made sure that he would retain that role while giving young Butler the publisher's title and duties on the business side.[13]

During the two-year period prior to Butler Sr.'s death, the close relationship between father and son continued. In fact, the newly anointed publisher rarely made a move of any consequence without first writing or calling his father. In one instance, for example, the son queried his father about a problem with the *News* building and added, "I'm waiting your orders for as you know, you are the Supreme Court." Years later, even after his father's death, Edward Jr. would base his reasoning for many decisions on what he thought his father would have done.[14]

Butler Sr., having suffered from diabetes since 1904, found his physical strength greatly weakened. In late January 1914 he came down with a cold followed by mastoiditis. His physicians consulted and determined that due to his general health an operation would be very dangerous. Mr. Butler accepted their decision and with characteristic determination he continued to perform all tasks relating to the newspaper and his family. He was not bedridden and apparently showed some improvement as he went about tending to important business matters.[15]

Sunday, March 7, he spent with his family greatly enjoying an afternoon recalling old times and old friends in an entertaining manner. He sang several old songs that were favorites of his with great personal enjoyment. He collapsed on the morning of March 8, 1914, and his doctors immediately operated. The ear infection had spread to his brain and the disease had progressed too far to be overcome. He died on March 9, 1914, in his Delaware Avenue mansion at the age of sixty-three.[16]

The funeral service was held in Westminster Presbyterian Church with every sector of Buffalo's civic life represented. The chancel was banked with flowers including a floral pillow sent by the International Typographers' Union of the *Buffalo Evening News*. This tribute was from the printers, the men who set the type and "got out the paper." It consisted of a mass of roses and white flowers with an old-time compositor's stick worked in violets and the number thirty in red, signifying the end—that work is finished. He was buried next to his wife in Wilkes-Barre, Pennsylvania, the following day.[17]

Jerry Goldberg, present editorial page editor of the *News*, summed up the elder Butler's life:

> Butler was remembered in death just as he wanted to be understood in life—man who lived with one leg in the mansions of the rich and powerful and the other in the neighborhoods of the poor and dispossessed. . . . The millionaire who owned a fleet of cars and three homes, who helped elect a president . . . died as the wealthy businessman, pioneering journalist and civic leader he was, and the populist he considered himself to be.[18]

Notes

1. Lance Zavits, "The Edward H. Butlers—Father and Son," an address presented at a meeting of the Le Roy Historical Society, August 16, 1958. It was reprinted in full in the *Le Roy Gazette-News* on August 21, 1958. Jerry Goldberg, "Edward H. Butler and the Founding of the *Buffalo Evening News*: The Life and Times of One of the Last Publisher-editors" (master's thesis, State University of New York at Buffalo, 1997), p. 98.

2. Goldberg, "Edward H. Butler," p. 98.

3. Alfred Kirchhofer files, Butler Family Papers, E. H. Butler Library Archives, State University College at Buffalo, box 1, "History," EHB Sr., p. 11-F.

4. Goldberg, "Edward H. Butler," pp. 98–99.
5. Ibid., p. 99.
6. Kirchhofer files, Butler Family Papers, box 11.
7. Ibid., Goldberg, "Edward H. Butler," p. 99; Kirchhofer, "History," EHB Sr., p. 11-F.
8. Ibid.
9. Goldberg, "Edward H. Butler," p. 99.
10. Ibid.; Kirchhofer files, Butler Family Papers, box 11.
11. Goldberg, "Edward H. Butler," p. 111.
12. Ibid., p. 112.
13. Ibid.
14. Ibid., p. 113.
15. Ibid.
16. "Edward H. Butler Dies Following Operation," *Buffalo Evening News*, March 11, 1914, p. 1.
17. Ibid.
18. Goldberg, "Edward H. Butler," p. 105.

8 Following in His Footsteps

The year 1914 was momentous. Worldwide it marked the beginning of World War I, on June 28 in Austria. In the United States, the population had increased by 46 percent over 1890 to over ninety-two million,[1] and the number of daily newspapers published reached the highest point thus far, 2,250.[2] Locally, the death on March 9, 1914, of the *News* founder marked the end of an era in the history of Buffalo newspapers that had been dominated since 1873 by the dynamic and highly respected native of Le Roy, New York. His success had earned him recognition in the Buffalo area for his numerous campaigns to champion the causes of the underprivileged and respect from all facets of the political community for his political acumen. Newspaper publishers throughout the nation had very high regard for Edward H. Butler Sr. for his dedication to reporting news and feature content of the *News*, his constant concern for all of his employees, his work ethic, and a wide range of other considerations that enabled him to achieve great success in his endeavors.

Two years prior to his death he had given his devoted son and namesake the title of publisher and now, with his passing, the younger Butler became the editor and publisher of the *News*. Additionally, under terms of his father's will, Ed Butler Jr. was now owner of 60 percent of the paper and was trustee for the 40 percent left in trust for his sister, Ada.[3] Butler Jr. maintained full control of the paper.

The Butlers always controlled ownership of the paper whether through direct beneficiaries or through trusts. The control of the paper was never splintered and no outsiders were allowed in. This tight ownership of the paper kept the Butler family in total control and not subject to takeovers by hostile groups. One offer came in 1895 from William Conners, owner of the *Courier*, but was summarily rejected by Butler Sr. In 1982 the embattled *Courier-Express* inquired about the *News*'s interest in a joint operating agreement but that was quickly rejected by the Buffett ownership. The single-family ownership or control through trusts by the Butler family, and after 1977 by Warren Buffett, eliminated possible threats of a hostile takeover of the *News* by outside interests.

Almost immediately after he assumed control, Butler Jr. issued a statement to reassure *News* readers and particularly its employees. He stated that "All the various departments that tend to make up a good high-toned moral paper will be filled with the best that means and ability will enable us to command."[4]

Butler Jr. had a better educational background than his father but less practical experience in the newspaper business. He had attended prep school in Pottstown, Pennsylvania, then came home to Buffalo to attend the Nichols School. He later went on to earn his bachelor's degree from Yale University. Born June 19, 1883, he assumed full control of the *News* at the age of thirty-one.[5]

Early in his tenure, young Butler made a move that his father just couldn't bring himself to do although he was aware that the economic viability of the *Sunday News* was in trouble. In 1884 the Sunday paper had a profit of a little over five thousand dollars, down two thousand from the previous year. By 1911 the paper was losing money. The new publisher suspended publication of the *Sunday News* early in 1915, unwilling to continue sustaining losses.[6] This decision made good sense in 1915 since advertising and circulation revenues were flowing more and more toward the daily publication while the Sunday operations at that time were experiencing severe economic difficulties.[7]

Edward H. Butler Jr., president (1914–1956) and publisher of the *Buffalo Evening News* (1912–1956). (Courtesy *Buffalo News*)

This was not what papers, with Sunday editions, were experiencing in larger cities like New York, Chicago, and San Francisco. Their Sunday papers were supported by a new volume of department store and classified advertising, and usually ran sixty or more pages. These papers ran colored comics, a color magazine, and many sections devoted to news and special interests.[8] It seems that once Butler Sr. started the daily paper, he did not keep pace with the trends for Sunday papers in the national market.

Young Butler was familiar with all the departments at the *News*, having undergone a training program instituted by his father some years before. The bulk of this orientation concentrated on the business side of the enterprise and on familiarization with the various production processes, the complexities of circulation, and the problems and policies of the *News* advertising department. Young Butler also had been introduced to newsroom activities and philosophy, but his exposure there was minimal and his interest definitely was more oriented toward business. Butler Jr. realized that he could best serve his newspaper by concentrating on the business aspects while leaving newsroom operations to experienced professionals.

When young Edward succeeded his father, John Joslyn was managing editor and had been in that role since 1910. Butler perceived that Joslyn was having problems with staff and was not too effective in his role. Early in 1915 he appointed John Wells as his managing editor. Wells had been Sunday editor and also wrote a column from time to time. Wells continued as managing editor until 1919 when he resigned to take a job as advertising manager for a department store.[9]

In 1917 William R. Meldrum joined the *News* staff as a reporter after having served as managing editor of the *Niagara Falls Journal* from 1911 to 1916. Meldrum, following his reportorial stint, became an editorial writer and then was designated as the chief editorial writer. He was known for his remarkable memory and his constant admonishments to staffers about his concern for accuracy and attribution. Upon his death in 1953, a *News* editorial described Meldrum as "A man who hewed to the line of his conviction without thought of compromise with expediency. His was the capacity to blend an almost nostalgic feeling for the older virtues with openness to new ideas. That kept him always in the company of true liberals."[10]

Butler in 1920 recruited the gifted and highly respected Mark Rose of the *New York Sun* to become managing editor of the *News*. Rose, a soft-spoken, urbane man who made friends easily, remained with the paper until 1927 when he left to accept a major editorial role with the William Randolph Hearst newspaper empire. Rose is credited with changing the personality of the *News* and making it a truly metropolitan newspaper. He expanded the financial department by increasing staff and allocating it more space. He increased foreign news coverage and earned the respect of his staff, executives of the *News*, and community leaders. Following his stint with Hearst, Rose became a senior editor of *Reader's Digest*.[11]

The *News* established a full-time Washington presence in 1921 when publisher Edward H. Butler Jr. decided that a staffed *News* bureau in the nation's capital would add to the paper's prestige and concentrate on matters relevant to the Buffalo area. He also wanted a

News staffer in Washington who could give him better insight into the national political scene. He appointed Alfred H. Kirchhofer to head up the first *News* Washington bureau in 1921.[12]

Kirchhofer, head of the bureau and at the time the only member of the new Washington bureau, turned out as much copy weekly as most of the larger bureaus of regional papers. In addition, his work capacity and skills as a reporter called him to the attention of his fellow newsmen in the capital and he was elected president of the National Press Club after earlier serving on its board of governors and then as vice president. His stay in Washington was highly productive. He provided the *News* with excellent coverage of the area's legislators and established good relationships with top government officials. He became part of a small group of Washington correspondents regularly invited to background sessions by then commerce secretary Herbert Hoover and was able to provide Butler with Washington insights not available to many. Additionally, he became one of the leaders in the $10 million campaign to construct the National Press Building. The *News* Washington bureau has been housed in the National Press Building since it opened.[13]

Kirchhofer, during his Washington stint, also was elected to the very prestigious Gridiron Club, an organization whose membership at that time was limited to fifty Washington correspondents. Correspondents were rated more highly by newspapers if they belonged, and it was not unusual for a paper to hire away from another paper a reporter just because he held a membership in the Gridiron Club. Kirchhofer set the stage for his successors in the *News* Washington bureau to be accepted as Gridiron members, an honor that all Washington correspondents aspired to but few achieved because of its self-imposed limits on membership.[14]

Butler's decision to hire Kirchhofer proved to be the right one. His performance in Washington so impressed the publisher that on January 19, 1927, Butler invited him, at the age of thirty-five, to return to Buffalo to become managing editor of the *News* to replace Mark Rose, who was resigning. Kirchhofer accepted and on June 21, 1927, he started his long and illustrious career in *News* management. The recruitment of Rose indicated Butler's ability to recognize people with potential and bring them to his newspaper. The appointment of Kirchhofer as managing editor confirmed Butler's ability to identify top talent.[15]

The choice of Kirchhofer was somewhat of a surprise to many at the *News*. They were amazed that he was appointed at such a young age, with his relatively brief experience, and lacking a college degree. He had started his career at the *News* in 1915 as a religion reporter and became a general assignment reporter before being given the city hall and county hall beats. Performing well in those assignments, he was promoted to assistant city editor and in 1916 was assigned to cover Albany's legislative sessions. His Washington bureau experiences had convinced Butler that Kirchhofer was ready to take on the top newsroom job.[16]

With Kirchhofer's promotion to managing editor, the *News* turned to James L. Wright to head up its Washington bureau. Prior to joining the *News* in 1927, Wright had been with the Washington bureau of the *Cleveland Plain Dealer* since 1915 and was an experienced capital reporter. He first came to Washington in 1911 on the staff of the *Washington Times* and later became assistant Washington correspondent of the *Detroit News*.[17]

Wright, like his predecessor as chief of the *News* Washington bureau, was a very active member of the press corps in the nation's capital. He was a member of the National Press Club and president of the National Press Club Building Corporation. He had been admitted to Gridiron Club membership in 1924 and was elected its president in 1934, when he was with the *News*. The presidency of the Gridiron Club carried great prestige and gave the man who held it entrée to many events and off-the-record sessions that other correspondents did not enjoy. Wright also served as chairman of the standing committee of correspondents, which governs the press galleries of Congress. The press galleries are a section reserved for correspondents approved by a congressional committee. Wright served in the *News* bureau for twenty-five years, until his death on December 7, 1952. He had a reputation as one of the better-known political writers in the nation and having been a Washington press figure for more than forty years, he covered many major national stories. He was a very familiar figure at White House news conferences and in the congressional press galleries. He had established relationships with congressional leaders of the Republican and Democratic parties. Wright greatly enhanced the reputation of the *News*.[18]

Jim Wright was respected among journalists for his objective reporting and he also played the behind-the-scenes role of providing publisher Butler and editor Kirchhofer with the machinations of party leaders and insights into the possibilities of pending legislation. Butler and Kirchhofer enjoyed the inside information he provided them. This relationship enabled him to set much of his own agenda on what he would cover on a regular basis. For example, although the wire services provided thorough coverage of presidential press conferences, Wright was permitted by Kirchhofer to cover them because he enjoyed doing it and he successfully made the case that it enhanced his reputation and that of the *News*.[19]

Like his predecessor in the *News* bureau, Wright was a tall man, distinguished in appearance and courtly in manner. He could almost have been considered a clone of Kirchhofer. And there's little doubt, although there are no written records to verify it, that Kirchhofer selected Wright as his bureau successor and was able to get Butler to approve the move. [20]

The passing of Jim Wright in 1952 posed a major problem for Butler and Kirchhofer. Both were convinced that the *News* needed someone to fill that post who had established credentials as a reporter, knew the Washington scene, and would do an outstanding job as an objective reporter while fulfilling their needs for inside information about the capital scene.

They ultimately decided upon Nat S. Finney, who had the credentials they coveted. Finney was awarded a Pulitzer Prize in 1948 for outstanding national affairs reporting for stories describing a Truman administration plan to impose censorship on activities of federal civilian agencies in peacetime. In addition to the Pulitzer, Finney in 1948 received the Raymond Clapper Award for outstanding Washington reporting. Finney joined the *News* in 1953 as Washington bureau chief but retired from the post after just six years in 1969 because of illness. Early in his career he had been a reporter for the

Minneapolis Star and later served in the Washington bureau of that paper and the *Des Moines Register and Tribune*.[21]

He was editorial page editor of the *Minneapolis Star* from 1950 until he was recruited by the *News* to take over as its Washington bureau chief. Finney supplemented his Washington duties with assignments throughout the world. He accompanied President Eisenhower on a trip to France, President Johnson on a mission to Vietnam, and then Vice President Nixon on a trip to the Soviet Union, reporting in depth on these overseas missions for the *News*.[22]

Many journalists felt that Finney should have been awarded another Pulitzer for his *News* reporting on August 26, 1962, that the Soviet Union was installing missiles in Cuba. He was the first reporter in the nation to disclose that information, which was to lead to the historic confrontation between the United States and Russia. An American blockade of Cuba was imposed and the Soviets withdrew the missiles. In 1967 Finney was elected to the presidency of the Gridiron Club, the second *News* Washington correspondent to achieve that high honor.[23]

Following his early retirement due to poor health, Finney continued to contribute articles to the *News*. Many at the paper thought that Finney's career in its latter stages was tainted by definite partisanship in favor of Republican policies and politicians, but most admired the totality of his journalistic achievements throughout his career.[24]

The return of Kirchhofer to the newsroom in Buffalo in 1927 was the beginning of a great partnership between himself and Butler, each highly successful in his field of endeavor. They developed enormous respect and admiration for each other over the years and were able to take the *News* in many new and diverse directions, expanding into radio, television, and even a pioneering effort in the facsimile broadcast of a newspaper.[25]

Butler, a quiet and reserved man, had the same fighting spirit and business acumen as his late father. They were, however, miles apart in personality. His father had an explosive temperament and was definitely a showman. The younger Butler proved through his years as publisher that he was willing to take risks with new ventures and to delegate responsibilities to executives such as Kirchhofer.[26]

Consistent with his laid-back demeanor, Butler made few public remarks about the philosophic approach of the *News*, unlike his father who constantly addressed editorials about such matters. Relatively few public utterances of Butler have been recorded. In one instance, he stated, "Reader confidence is a newspaper's priceless asset. It is something that must be consistently merited to be sustained." He reiterated his belief that independence and integrity were the two key factors needed to retain reader confidence.[27]

From a historian's perspective, much of the younger Butler's role in operating the *News* was not recorded because of Kirchhofer's dominance in community and political affairs and his control of the editorial content and editorial policies of the newspaper. To much of the community at large, the newspaper had become Kirchhofer's instrument. They were not aware of the fact that Kirchhofer was constantly in communication with Butler about the direction he was taking the *News*.

It was through the newspaper that Butler expressed his personal sense of responsibility for public welfare. One of the paper's best-known philanthropies was the Fifty Neediest Families Fund established in 1921. Fifty families in Buffalo who were determined to be most in need of help were given food and money. It was discontinued during the Second World War because new methods of public relief made it unnecessary and increased employment reduced the need for family aid. During his tenure the paper sponsored the Smokes for Soldiers Fund, the summer camp for physically handicapped children with the Buffalo Rotary Club, and an annual Christmas appeal for crippled children.[28]

Butler supported many city and local projects such as the municipal airport that opened in September 1926, the Peace Bridge in 1927, and the New York Central terminal in 1929. Working with Mayor Frank Schwab, Butler in 1927 was successful in getting state legislation passed to cede state hospital property to provide ninety acres for Buffalo State Teachers College on Elmwood Avenue.[29] Also that year he supported the adoption of a new city charter, which provided for a strong mayor to govern the city. The paper fought for traffic improvement, playgrounds, preservation of the city's beautiful trees, and changing the method of paying for repaving streets to a general charge instead of a property tax assessment.[30]

He sponsored an airplane endurance flight that aroused wide interest in 1929. Held at the Buffalo Municipal Airport, it stopped just short of a world record, a record exceeded only twice before. The plane called "The BEN," for the *Buffalo Evening News*, remained aloft for 197 hours. The *News* carried daily stories by the pilot of the plane and the technicians involved in the flight.[31]

While Butler basically maintained a hands-off policy in operating the newsroom, he was very involved in plans to expand the communications outlets of the *News*. He worked closely with Kirchhofer who acted as public spokesperson for the company and the direct contact with the Federal Communications Commission (FCC). Butler's efforts and successes in this arena eventually led to his becoming known among publishers as a leader in the field of communications.

The first *Buffalo Evening News* endeavor outside of the printed word came in 1929. The *News* had been making available some of its news reports to the Buffalo Broadcasting Corporation stations of Dr. Clinton Churchill, a local man, as a means of promoting the *News*. When the Churchill stations started using material from the other Buffalo newspapers as well, Kirchhofer looked upon that as a breach of their agreement and he urged Butler to make application for a *News* radio station. Butler agreed. Businessmen, organizations, and others rallied to support the *News* in its effort to change the situation.[32]

The paper's application set off a bitter fight with the Churchill interests. The *News* made the case before the FCC that it was seeking to break up the monopoly of Buffalo Broadcasting, which controlled four radio stations in the community. Churchill also was president of Churchill Evangelistic Association at the time. Charges and countercharges were exchanged between Kirchhofer and Churchill with each party claiming that its obligations for use of material and time on the stations had been violated.[33]

On September 3, 1929, Churchill notified the *News* that Buffalo Broadcasting was terminating its agreement with the paper. Finally, the battle culminated with radio station WBEN going on the air September 8, 1930. A separate corporation, WBEN Inc., was formed

A view of the newsroom in 1929 showing the horseshoe-shaped copydesk in the center and the bank of telephone booths along the wall to the right. (Butler Family Papers, courtesy E. H. Butler Library Archives, Buffalo State College)

with Butler as president. The FCC had ruled that operation of this new station was in the public interest. Its initial studio was on the eighteenth floor of the Statler Hotel, where it remained for many years until construction of its own facilities on Elmwood Avenue in Buffalo.[34] The station joined what was commonly known as the Red Network of NBC in November 1930.[35]

Butler's problems with radio did not end with the granting of the license to operate. The press associations, concerned about competition, refused to permit use of their material on radio. Butler reacted quickly, setting up an independent newsgathering organization for his radio station. Several years later the news organizations lifted their ban and Butler dismantled the operation he had launched.[36]

The *News* was obviously not adversely affected by the national depression of 1929. Circulation grew by 15 percent between 1930 and 1940, the first year it went over 200,000. Net income from the newspaper increased 70 percent from 1929 to 1940. Six years after the startup of WBEN, Butler formed a separate corporation to purchase radio station WEBR from Howell Broadcasting in 1936. He sold it in July 1942 to Paul Fitzpatrick, former Erie County Democratic chairman who later became the state chairman of the party. Butler, the Republican stalwart, declared publicly that the sale showed his interest in giving the listening public diverse views.[37]

The *Courier-Express* some time later acquired a 75 percent interest in WEBR, which ultimately became a public broadcasting station. The *News*, following the conclusion of World War II, launched an FM sister station for WBEN.[38]

Butler, on December 28, 1938, displayed his willingness to pioneer in another area of communications. He started a facsimile operation that transmitted parts of the *News* each day to fifty area residences. It was hailed as the newspaper of the future, but the bold experiment came to an end on December 21, 1940. The WBEN fax was in effect the same as a small printing press that operated by remote control to reproduce newspaper pages by electrical impulses on receivers. When in operation it published a nine-page edition, taking twenty minutes to transmit each page. The project was launched as an FCC-authorized experiment that worked but was handicapped by its limited exposure, its expense, and an inability to speed up transmission. This early facsimile transmitter is now housed in the Smithsonian.[39]

The next step in the Butler-Kirchhofer communications expansion was much more successful. This was the launch of WBEN-TV known later as WIVB-TV. The original application for a television station, filed in 1939, was rejected but was resubmitted after the end of World War II and won approval of the FCC. WBEN-TV was the city's first commercial television station. Experimental broadcasts started in February 1947 and regular daily telecasting began on May 14, 1948.[40] It was a highly innovative and successful operation from the beginning.[41]

In retrospect, it is of interest to note that the Butler-Kirchhofer moves into radio and television, while farsighted, ultimately undermined the newspaper operations, providing significant outlets for news other than the newspaper. In the latter part of the twentieth century, the explosion of Internet sites added to the competition for the reporting of news events, further undermining the impact of newspapers.

While extending his communications empire to include radio and television, Butler in July 1939 declined an opportunity to buy the *Buffalo Times*, the last Democratic print voice in Buffalo, under the able direction of Norman Mack. Failing to find a buyer, the *Times* went out of business with its final editions on July 30, 1939.[42]

Butler from time to time did let his editors know how he felt on issues that he considered to be important. For example, on March 12, 1941, he addressed a memo to Kirchhofer and to the then editor of the editorial page, William Meldrum. In it he didn't pull any punches: "Please let us always keep in mind that we are opposed to sending an American army to fight in foreign lands and that we are opposed to using the U.S. Navy or Air Force to convoy ships into the belligerent areas."[43]

Although there are no written records to verify it, one has to conclude that Butler did communicate regularly with Kirchhofer and Meldrum on important *News* editorial policy directions. While the 1941 memo to his editors would indicate Butler's strong negative feelings about the United States' involvement in the war in Europe, nothing in the news pages of the paper during the period prior to and after the U.S. entry into the war would indicate any bias in straight news coverage against such involvement.

The Butler home on Delaware Avenue became the focal point for entertaining. Mrs. Butler was considered Buffalo's outstanding hostess and invitations for dinner parties were prized. Mr. and Mrs. Butler, renowned for their hospitality, entertained kings and queens as well as well-known people in national, state, and local politics and the arts. Among those who were entertained were King Albert and Queen Elizabeth of Belgium, Prince Gustav Adolph and Prince Sigvard of Sweden, Herbert Hoover, Alf Landon, Percy Grainger, Paul Whiteman, Bob Hope, and Olsen and Johnson of "Hellsapoppin."[44] The Butlers were frequent overnight guests at the White House during the presidential term of Herbert Hoover. They once traveled to Florida on former president Franklin D. Roosevelt's private railroad car for a fishing trip aboard the yacht *Windswept* that had served several presidents.[45]

During World War II, furniture and works of art from their Paris apartment were taken by the Nazi general Hermann Goering and made a part of his famed salt mine collection. After the war Andrew Ritchie, former curator of the Albright-Knox Art Gallery, served on the United States Commission to review the Goering collection. He was responsible for finding the Butler possessions and returning them to their homes in Paris and in Buffalo.[46]

In 1953 Butler was the recipient of the University of Buffalo's Chancellor's Medal for his "powerful, staunch and courageous leadership in the civic, cultural and educational life of our community, his integrity and the nobility of his character." Among other endeavors for the university, he had chaired its development program in 1952.[47]

Butler was decorated by the Polish and Italian governments for services to their people in America. And he was honored by the National Conference of Christians and Jews for a "lifetime of service in promoting brotherhood."[48]

Butler was also very active through the years in professional organizations. He was president from 1928 to 1930 of the American Newspaper Publishers Association and served for twenty years on the Associated Press board of directors.[49] The training of youthful journalists was a major interest of the publisher. Speaking before the American Society of Newspaper Editors in 1930, he said,

> I sometimes feel that the schools of journalism do not measure up to their responsibilities, thereby unfortunately leaving in the minds of some of their students, who after all are only novices, the idea that they should begin at the top rather than somewhere near the bottom of the ladder.
>
> After a period of training in a school of journalism, when a man has been schooled in work that borders on executive direction, he is loath to go back to the more humble reportorial field, although I am sure you will agree with me that the reporter still is the backbone of the newspaper editorial room. For one thing, therefore, the average graduate of a school of journalism doesn't have the proper sense of values.[50]

This statement showed his attitude toward newspaper work and that accurate reporting was vital. The *News* contributed generously to the creation of the American Press Institute at Columbia University, which was established to enhance the training of newspaper workers already in the field.[51]

The death of Edward H. Butler Jr. on February 18, 1956, resulted in significant changes in the management ranks of the *News*.[52] He held the titles of editor and publisher, and upon his passing, his wife, Kate Butler, assumed the responsibilities of president. She designated her son-in-law James H. Righter as publisher and vice president of the paper. She also promoted Alfred H. Kirchhofer, whom her husband had named managing editor in 1927 and who had become his most trusted and valuable ally at the paper and its affiliated broadcast facilities, to the posts of editor and executive vice president of the *News* and president of WBEN Inc.[53]

Kirchhofer had enormous respect and admiration for Butler. For years after Butler's death, he constantly recalled his close association with him, never once uttering a negative remark about his former publisher. The two appeared to be totally in sync in their philosophy about newspapers and in fact, about the world at large. In labor negotiations with the Newspaper Guild, a negative remark was made by a guild member about the publisher. Kirchhofer was infuriated: "You cannot speak of Mr. Butler that way in Mr. Butler's house."

A close relationship between the individual in charge of newsroom operations and the publisher of the paper is always vital and the Butler-Kirchhofer symbiosis was deep and truly dedicated. It would be hard to replicate. The old cliché about opposites attracting did not come into play here. Both had laid-back personalities but each had the ability to make important decisions without undue equivocation.

Butler Jr. had the wisdom to rely greatly on the counsel of Kirchhofer in areas in which he did not feel comfortable. Kirchhofer, in his wisdom, never acted on important matters outside of the newsroom without conferring with Butler.

Butler's will deeded 50 percent of his interest in the *News* to his wife, Kate, with the remainder in trust for life income for his daughter, Kate Righter. His gross estate was valued at $9,240,384. Of this, $8,681,000 was the value of his interest in the *News*.[54]

Notes

1. John W. Wright, ed. *The New York Times 1998 Almanac* (Middlesex, England: Penguin Reference Books, 1997), pp. 264–65.

2. Frank Luther Mott, *American Journalism, 1690–1940* (New York: Macmillan, 1941), p. 549.

3. Alfred Kirchhofer files, Butler Family Papers, E. H. Butler Library Archives, State University College at Buffalo, box 1.

4. Lance Zavits, "The Edward H. Butlers—Father and Son," an address presented at a meeting of the Le Roy Historical Society, August 16, 1958. It was reprinted in full in the *Le Roy Gazette-News* on August 21, 1958.

5. Ibid.

6. It was not until November 13, 1977, under the new ownership of Warren E. Buffett that the *News* once again had a Sunday newspaper outlet.

7. The situation changed dramatically as the twentieth century neared its close and Sunday operations became vital to the economic viability of newspapers. Buffett, aware of this trend, reversed the long-standing *News* resistance to buck the *Courier-Express* monopoly on Sunday to get the *News* back into that operation, without which the *News* could not have survived.

8. Mott, *American Journalism*, pp. 584–85.

9. Ralph Dibble, "The *Buffalo Evening News* Is Born," *Buffalo News* centennial publication, October 12, 1980, p. H-6.

10. Ibid., *Buffalo News* library files, obituary and editorial, April 14, 1953.

11. Dibble, "The *Buffalo Evening News* Is Born."

12. Kirchhofer files, Butler Family Papers, box 4.

13. Alfred H. Kirchhofer Papers, Buffalo and Erie County Historical Society Archives, C67-6, box 7.

14. Ibid., box 11.

15. Ibid.

16. Ibid.

17. E. H. Butler Jr. files, Butler Family Papers, box 1, file 19.

18. Kirchhofer Papers, Historical Society, box 34, *Washington Post*, obituary, December 8, 1982.

19. Ibid.

20. Ibid.

21. Ibid., box 35.

22. *Buffalo News* personnel files.

23. Ibid.

24. *Buffalo Evening News*, obituary, December 21, 1982.

25. Kirchhofer Papers, Historical Society, box 10; Lewis G. Harriman, *Buffalo Evening News and Its Courageous Leader Edward H. Butler* (Buffalo, NY: Newcomen Society in North America, 1955), p. 10.

26. Zavits, "The Edward H. Butlers."

27. Harriman, *Buffalo Evening News and Its Courageous Leader*, p. 16.

28. Ibid.

29. He succeeded his father as president of the State Normal School Board of Managers in 1914. The school became Buffalo State Teachers College in 1927.

30. Harriman, *Buffalo Evening News and Its Courageous Leader*, p. 14.

31. Kirchhofer files, Butler Family Papers, box 4.

32. Ibid., boxes 8, 10.

33. Ibid.

34. Ibid.

35. Ibid., box 10.

36. Ibid.

37. Ibid.

38. Ibid.

39. Ibid.

40. Ibid.

41. With the 1977 sale of the *News*, the Butler estate retained ownership of the radio and television stations that were then sold off individually.

42. Kirchhofer files, Butler Family Papers, box 4.

43. Ibid., box 1.

44. *Buffalo News* obituary of Mrs. Butler, August 5, 1974.

45. Ibid.

46. Ibid.

47. Kirchhofer files, Butler Family Papers, box 1.

48. Ibid.

49. Ibid.

50. Harriman, *Buffalo Evening News and Its Courageous Leader*, pp. 20, 21.

51. Ibid.

52. *Buffalo Evening News*, obituary, February 20, 1956.

53. Dibble, "The *Buffalo Evening News* Is Born," p. H-6.

54. Edward H. Butler Jr. file in the *Buffalo News* library; Kirchhofer files, Butler Family Papers, box 1.

9 AHK
The Beginning of a Legend

When Butler invited Alfred H. Kirchhofer to return to Buffalo to become his managing editor,[1] he made a move that proved to be unbelievably successful for the *News*, and one that influenced the paper's operations for the next forty years. AHK, as he was called by most, had risen to top management in a relatively short time. Prior to joining the *News* in 1915, he had limited experience, starting at age eighteen as a copy boy and then as a reporter for the *Buffalo Commercial*, followed by stints at the *Buffalo Times* and the *Buffalo Courier*. These jobs covered a five-year period prior to his joining the *News* staff. In 1914 he and his friend Samuel Mayer started the *Western New York Post* in Lancaster. Emma Shurgardt, who became Kirchhofer's bride on January 27 of that year, served as secretary. They had one son, Robert, in their long and happy marriage. Unfortunately the fledgling paper did not fare as well and closed after just one year.[2]

When Butler appointed Kirchhofer managing editor in 1927, he launched a management career that lasted until Kirchhofer's retirement from the paper in April 1966.[3] The thirty-nine years of the Kirchhofer era (1927–1966) saw significant changes in Buffalo and at

Alfred H. Kirchhofer (AHK), editor of the *Buffalo Evening News* from 1927 to 1966. (Courtesy *Buffalo News*)

the *News*. When he returned to Buffalo from Washington, the city population was on the rise with a 1930 census figure of 573,076 increasing to 575,901 by 1940 and 580,131 by 1950.[4]

The *News* in 1951 was able to report that Buffalo was the fifteenth-largest city in the United States and the eleventh-largest industrial center in the country. It was the nation's largest inland water port and the second-largest railroad center with twelve rail terminals serving some forty-five thousand trains a year and five rail passenger terminals serving fifty thousand trains each year. The booming metropolis of Buffalo was the third-largest producer of steel in the United States with five iron and steel plants employing thirty thousand workers. It was the leading flour milling center in the world. As the city continued to grow in population and in economic activity, so did the *News* under Butler and Kirchhofer.[5]

News coverage of local, state, and national politics was very thorough during the Kirchhofer era. Involved were the local political writers, the Washington bureau, the Albany bureau, and the editorial writers. One of the most celebrated political writers was Jack Medoff, who was hired by Kirchhofer in 1927 and was the principal political reporter for decades before he retired thirty-nine years later in 1966. Medoff's newspaper career started in 1921 with International News Service. He then worked on several smaller papers prior to joining the *News* staff.[6]

I was a young copyeditor who had been assigned to the desk only a few weeks earlier when the copydesk chief, Ned Prentiss, gave me a Medoff story for editing. Medoff had written the first two paragraphs and the rest of the story was a pasteup of a Republican Party handout. I pointed that out to Prentiss who shrugged his shoulders and said that it was not unusual. I told him that I was going to take up the matter with Kirchhofer. He smiled and said I would be wasting my time. He was right. Kirchhofer said that Medoff knew what he was doing and that "a neophyte had a lot of nerve challenging the work of a long-time professional." He then added that I must not change any of Medoff's stories because "he knows what he's doing and has been doing it for years and he knows what I want in political stories." Chagrined, I returned and was greeted by the laughter of the copydesk rim. I nevertheless informed Prentiss that given this order, I did not want to handle any more Medoff stories and he agreed that would be a good idea. My colleagues on the desk told me that numerous Medoff stories consisted of a few paragraphs he himself wrote and a pasteup of a handout from the Erie County Republican Party headquarters. Kirchhofer, they said, was aware of this and would not countenance any criticism of the practice.

Medoff made no realistic attempt to be impartial in his political stories and he was rewarded when he finally retired. Upon his retirement he was named public relations director for the county Republican Party and this was followed by his appointment as economic coordinator for the Republican county executive, Edward Rath. In 1970 he was named western New York public relations director for Gov. Nelson A. Rockefeller's reelection campaign.[7]

Only a year after he was appointed managing editor, Kirchhofer accepted the role as associate director of publicity for the Republican National Committee, handling the publicity for Herbert Hoover's 1928 run for the presidency. He had gotten to know Hoover when he headed up the *News* Washington bureau. Hoover was elected but then lost his reelection bid in 1932 to Franklin D. Roosevelt.[8]

In a letter to Hoover written September 1, 1931, Kirchhofer commented on Hoover's problems with the press and advised him to

> Never let a newspaperman know that he has hit or hurt you. When he becomes aware of that, an unholy zeal possesses him to go ahead and repeat it. . . . Keep using the friendly press to carry all the news you can create and to create enough news . . . that the opposition

> press simply has got to carry your news statements and your viewpoint. In other words, flood the opposition with material they must use, which also will overshadow their attacks. . . ."[9]

AHK continued his correspondence with Hoover for years, generally alluding to him as "chief" in his salutation. His feeling for Hoover is indicated in a letter to him in 1938 that ends with "renewed considerations of my devotion [to you]." In a July 5, 1930, letter to President Hoover, Kirchhofer wrote fifteen single-spaced typewritten pages of advice on a wide range of topics. Hoover's response was only one sentence of fifteen words, acknowledging receipt of Kirchhofer's long letter. But their relationship continued to be very close and cordial.[10]

The Republican candidate for president in 1936 was Alfred Landon and the party asked AHK to serve as the director of publicity for the GOP National Committee. "You can name your own salary," the party chief wrote AHK on January 11, 1935. Kirchhofer responded that he would have loved to have been able to accept the job but couldn't because Butler was unwilling to give him a leave of absence. Butler was ailing at the time and wanted AHK to remain in Buffalo and tend to affairs at the *News*.[11]

Although Kirchhofer remained at the paper during the 1936 campaign, he did give advice and counsel to Landon. In fact, following his defeat Landon wrote him: "Looking back on the campaign, I wish now that I had kept in closer touch with you in shaping some of my speeches." Landon and Kirchhofer maintained a steady and extensive exchange of letters for more than two decades.[12]

In 1942 AHK turned down Thomas E. Dewey's request that he handle public relations for his 1944 presidential bid but he did maintain an extensive correspondence with the Republican candidate, making many suggestions on how his campaign for the presidency should be run and what positions he should take on important issues. Dewey, the New York governor, was the Republican candidate for the presidency. Roosevelt defeated him. Dewey headed up the GOP ticket again in 1948 and was defeated by Harry S. Truman. On December 16, 1948, following his defeat by Truman, Dewey wrote to AHK, inviting him to "Come on down so we can have a postmortem. You are the only man in the U.S. to whom I have issued such an invitation."[13]

Kirchhofer's deep involvement with politics and politicians was more extensive than that of most editors of his time but the hands-off attitude of virtually all editors in today's newspaper world was not the abiding passion during the years he was the chief of news operations for the *News*. His advice and counsel to presidential candidates now would be considered a definite conflict of interest for an editor.

Their contemporaries and history designate individuals as legends as the result of their deeds as well as their idiosyncrasies over a period of time. AHK filled that bill well. His accomplishments through the years were quite remarkable and he had some personal traits that were most unusual.

Symbolic of the Kirchhofer legend most apparent to all who came in contact with him was the chair next to his desk on the newsroom floor. He utilized that desk in the morning hours before moving to his private office prior to his lunch period. The chair was bolted to the floor, two feet and six inches from his desk, far enough away to be uncomfortable for most who occupied it when meeting with him.[14]

I remember well my first exposure to Kirchhofer in early August of 1949. I had an appointment with him about the possibility of my joining the *News* staff. I tried to move the chair at his desk forward so I could comfortably speak to him. My efforts were to no avail; it just would not move. Montgomery Curtis, city editor during the 1930s and 1940s, later told me that Kirchhofer was a fastidious man who "did not want boozy salesmen or politicians getting too near him." The chair was unbolted the day after Kirchhofer retired with virtually everyone in the newsroom gathered around to watch the event.[15]

I don't completely concur with the explanation by Curtis, who later became director of the American Press Institute. My belief is that the bolted chair was to keep any and all persons from getting too close to him. He was a hypochondriac who was fearful of the germs anybody near him might carry. I remember numerous occasions listening to him placing a luncheon order with one of the copy aides. His instructions to the aide always carried a stern warning to "wash your hands thoroughly before getting my lunch."

Adding to the Kirchhofer legend was the *News* stylebook, which he fashioned and rigidly enforced. It was known throughout the newspaper business for its primness. Use of words such as "rats" and "snakes" were verboten. In the *News* they had to be referred to as "rodents" and "reptiles." The word "rape" was outlawed and substituted for it was "criminal assault" even though the two were not synonymous. "Abortion" was also on the banned list; it had to be referred to as "an illegal operation."[16]

The AHK stylebook also stated: "Avoid these words unless approved by someone in authority—adultery, call girl, ex-con, homosexual, lousy, love nest, orgy, pregnant, prostitute, sexy, socialite, stink, strip tease." When one of these words did appear in the *News*, the editor who authorized it generally was called to account for its use. Motherhood, the stylebook counseled, could not be "treated as a situation comedy" and it ordered, too, that "stories of illegal, immoral or antisocial activities" had to omit "the instructions." One could not refer to a rat in a front-page story "unless it bit Eisenhower or he bit it."[17]

Kirchhofer was a dedicated practitioner of accurate reporting but many staffers felt he carried it too far with his insistence that the middle initial of any person mentioned in a story had to be included. He produced a constant flow of notes to reporters questioning the omission of a middle initial. Many, as a result, resorted to fabricating a person's middle initial to avoid receiving an AHK note. There are those of us who would insert a "J" for John or "F" for Francis if we were doing a story about a Catholic male and had neglected to get his middle initial.

The Kirchhofer legend also included his passion for the color blue. All of his memos were on blue paper. He used only blue lead pencils. He drove a dark blue Cadillac exclusively through all his years in management. His attire at the office always was a dark blue suit, generally accompanied by blue shirts. In a letter to Edgar May, a *Buffalo News* Pulitzer Prize winner, AHK explained his blue passion: "When I left Washington in 1927, Amery Marks, then managing editor of the *Washington Herald*, said he had only one bit of advice. He said 'get yourself a blue pencil and use blue note paper. Then when the staff hears from you nobody will be able to say they didn't recognize it.'" AHK accepted the advice but carried it to the extreme. There is no doubt, though, that it produced the desired results.[18]

Kirchhofer's notes to staffers and his top editors were generally brief but pointed. They reflected his personality. Small talk was somewhat foreign to this basically taciturn man. This resulted in the feeling of many in the community and on staff that he was a severe, humorless individual. Carl Lindstrom, one respected editor of his time, wrote in *Editor & Publisher* in 1937 when Kirchhofer was elected president of the American Society of Newspaper Editors that AHK could "seem downright terrifying, less because of what he says than because of his disconcerting brevity and devastating silences." Lindstrom, however, caught the essence of the man, referring to him as "a born newspaperman of incredible competence and frequent brilliance, absolutely devoted to the highest standards of newspaper work, a perfectionist who is intolerant of everything but the best writing and editing; the possessor of an uncanny instinct for the hidden error or the missed point or angle."[19]

Kirchhofer did indeed terrify many staffers who did not have much opportunity to deal with him except as recipients of his blue notes. They for the most part were unaware of other facets of his personality. When staffers had personal problems that came to his attention, he often took steps to remedy them. He would never admit to having this "soft side" but he certainly was not a man without a certain amount of compassion for embattled members of his staff.[20]

As tough and gruff as AHK appeared to most, he did have a sense of humor, although it did not surface too often. I recall an incident where I, as news editor at the time, had loudly expressed my unhappiness with the work of a member of the city desk. My outburst was obviously heard by many in the newsroom. The following day I received a blue note requesting my presence in the editor's office. When I entered his office, AHK without any preliminary conversation handed me a book and advised me to read it and see if I could learn enough from it to further my ambitions at the *News*. The book was Dale Carnegie's *How to Win Friends and Influence People*. He counseled me that a temperate response often achieved more than outbursts of temper, and without further ado dismissed me. Prior to turning from his desk, I detected a whisper of a smile on the editor's face.

Small samplings of Kirchhofer's general memos to the staff reflect some of his thinking about the newspaper business. In 1939, shortly after the *Buffalo Times* suspended publication, he wrote: "The integrity of newspapers these days is questioned as never before. . . . Let us guard against doing that which will give any just critic cause to say The *News* is arrogant, careless, or not responsive to its public obligations."[21]

Given his enormous workload, it's no wonder that AHK had little or no time at all for leisure activities of any kind or the cultural pursuits of music, drama, or even books. His was the life of a true workaholic. He relished his work and never was heard to complain about the countless hours he devoted to it. He spent many hours at home working for the *News*. Every morning he would come into the newsroom with clippings from the *New York Daily News* of stories that had not appeared in the *Buffalo Evening News*. He would order the wire desk to verify the material in the New York paper and get something in the *News* to cover the situation. What surprised many was that this conservative editor so carefully monitored the New York tabloid that certainly was not a conservatively oriented newspaper. I had the temerity to ask him about this once and his response without hesitation was that the *New York News* often carried interesting material that his desk people tended to overlook in their quest for the most significant and not necessarily the most interesting news items.

Kirchhofer's philosophy on the local scene emphasized totally thorough coverage. He followed the philosophy laid down many years prior to his time by the paper's founder, Edward H. Butler Sr., who insisted that no local news item was too insignificant to be covered by his newspaper. One device Kirchhofer utilized to carry out this precept was a "Daily News Summary." It was run each day in agate type and included all the births, marriages, court judgments, bankruptcies, fires, and a range of other material relevant to Buffalo. The summary also carried the entire Buffalo Police Department blotter for the previous day. The city desk editors never were too happy with the news summary because of the manpower needed to gather the material. On the other hand, *News* readers loved it, perhaps because of the gossip material it provided.

Another practice AHK introduced to ensure that no local news was missing from his paper was his insistence that the *News* carry at least one paragraph, or more if warranted, on any local news item that appeared in the morning *Courier Express* if the *News* had not covered it. Implementation of this started early in the morning when one of the assistant city editors reviewed that day's early edition of the *Courier*. If he found a *Courier* item that the *News* had not covered, he'd clip it and then assign it to a *News* reporter who would shortly be reporting for work.

A strict rule mandated that before the *Courier* item was rewritten, all the information it contained had to be verified. This took a great deal of time because it was not always easy to contact the individuals cited in the *Courier* story. It often led to problems. For example, Ed Hale was assigned to cover an evening meeting of no great consequence. The *Courier-Express* reporter was late arriving at the meeting site so Hale, who was not averse to playing games from time to time, deliberately gave the *Courier* reporter a good deal of incorrect information about what had transpired before his arrival. The *Courier* reporter wrote his story, incorporating all the false material Hale had given him. When Hale came to work at the *News* later that day, he found that his story of the meeting had been altered to contain the nonfacts in the *Courier* story that he had fed the opposition reporter. The verification rule obviously had failed and the *News* reporter checking that *Courier* clipping just picked up the phony information that Hale had fed to the *Courier*. Hale relished telling this story many times through the years. The city desk was not too happy with him when they learned what he had done.[22]

Hale for years mystified his newsroom colleagues with his habit of constantly passing his hand in front of his eyes, appearing to swat nonexistent insects. When questioned by friends about his actions, Hale never would give a definitive response. Finally, however, tiring of the continuing inquiries, he confirmed that he had an optical problem and was plagued by a constant array of spots that appeared to be flying insects approaching him. He acknowledged that he was aware there really were no insects buzzing around him but said he couldn't stop his meaningless swatting habit. Once that became known, the staff finally stopped asking Hale why he was trying to bat away insects that they could not see. Hale eventually left the *News* to take over ownership of the *Adirondack Enterprise*. We never did learn if his problem was cleared up.

Kirchhofer's many decades of stewardship over the editorial product of the *News* resulted in thousands of routine stories, the initiation of numerous investigative stories that led to community reforms, and inevitably some nasty battles with political figures. Over the years, Kirchhofer assembled a staff of highly qualified reporters and editors who could produce a product that would satisfy his highly critical standards. Although he had never attended college, AHK recognized the importance of a college education for his staffers and in the last twenty-five years of his editorship the majority of the people he hired possessed college degrees, many with master's degrees. Even then, however, he was astute enough never to make the college degree a mandatory requirement for hiring. In today's environment a college degree is an accepted "must" in hiring of newsroom people, with the possible exception of copy aides. But back in 1927, Kirchhofer was named managing editor based on his background as a fine reporter on the paper's cityside staff and his outstanding performance as the paper's first full-time Washington correspondent. The fact that he had not attended college did not deter Edward H. Butler Jr. from naming Kirchhofer to the top newsroom job.[23]

It takes people with different educational backgrounds, divergent motivation, differing approaches to their jobs, opposing political orientations, and a whole range of other differences to produce a successful newspaper. The *News*, since its inception as a daily in 1880, has been successful in putting together a workforce dedicated to the success of the enterprise and carrying out their assigned duties. Greatly responsible for this environment was the spirit of Edward H. Butler Sr. He had always stressed that everyone involved in producing the paper each day, from the flyboy (apprentice) in the pressroom to the editors in the newsroom, was important to the operation and each had to contribute to make the paper respected and successful.

The *News* copydesk in the period from the late 1940s and the decade that followed boasted a cadre of very talented veteran editors, some of whom were quite colorful characters. Ned Prentiss was the longtime head of the copydesk operation or in newspaper lingo, the slot man. In those days the *News* had an eight-column format and each edition always carried an eight-column banner headline over the lead story. The slot man almost always wrote the banner head, a task that Prentiss particularly relished. He utilized one technique that made the job easier. When he was having a tough time writing the banner he was not above making some changes in the story so that it would reflect the headline he had come up with. This was not exactly the proper thing to do but he insisted that the changes he made in the text did not alter the principal thrust of the story. The practice was not proper and was in fact reprehensible. When questioned about it, Prentiss would always respond, "I didn't really change too many facts. No harm done and nobody really cares."

Prentiss had a love affair with automobiles. He loved to drive and fortunately he was an exceptionally good driver. Snowstorms never stymied Prentiss. On many occasions, when traffic was snarled during storms, he would drive for miles on the sidewalks of Main Street to get from the *News* to his home in Williamsville. It was a foolhardy thing to do but he got away with it time and time again over the years without mishap to himself or pedestrians.

One of Prentiss's copyeditors was Ralph Spinning, a man who didn't communicate too well with the other deskmen but was a superb wordsmith and a very fine editor. Spinning would start his shift each day by laying out a half dozen pencils in front of him, pull a knife from his pocket, and then slowly, meticulously sharpen each pencil to a very fine point. That task completed, he would begin editing. In all his years on the desk, he never deviated from this routine. Most days, Spinning would go through his entire shift without uttering a word to anybody on the desk.

Another one of the copyeditors at that time was Arthur Buck, a man filled with prejudices of all kinds and who made no attempt to hide them. His nasty remarks infuriated most of his colleagues and on one occasion one of them hurled a glass glue pot at Buck, who had just finished a snide attack on Jews and African Americans.

A newsroom fixture for years was Nelson Griswold, the city editor from January 1948 until January 1961. He had a nasty disposition and was disliked by his own staff and others in the newsroom. He had joined the *News* in 1935 as an assistant city editor. In 1961 he was moved to the radio and television operations, becoming director of news and public events for Channel 4 and WBEN radio. He returned to the *News* as chief librarian in 1964 and retired in June 1970.[24]

Griswold was city editor in the days before ethical considerations ended the practice of journalists accepting gifts from various sources. As city editor, Griswold was showered with dozens of bottles of liquor each Christmas season from individuals and community organizations seeking to curry favor with him. Almost immediately after the holiday season Griswold would compile a list of liquor he was offering for sale to staffers, complete with a pricing structure that made his wares competitive with the liquor stores. The extent of his liquor list was amazing. He was aware of the many snide remarks made by staffers about his sales efforts but these never seemed to bother him. The practice of staffers accepting gifts from sources was finally banned in the early 1970s but it was done over the protests of many of the traditional gift givers who feared that their influence would wane as a result.

Griswold's number-one assistant for many years was Ed Lebherz, who had the exact opposite personality of his boss. Lebherz was a friendly, outgoing man who worked well with the younger reporters and was liked by most of the staff. On the other hand, he was not as good of an editor as Griswold. He had difficulty in making quick decisions so necessary in his city desk role. Lebherz was a paper shuffler, constantly moving material from the top of the pile in front of him to the bottom of the pile and continuing that process for long periods before finally plucking one story out and tackling it.

During the many years Griswold served as city editor, he had a great many assistants on the desk. He was not a pleasant man to work for and as a result a good number of his assistant city editors were unhappy in their roles. One of the exceptions was Clemenceau (Kelly) Simon who served as an assistant city editor for twenty-eight years. A friendly, self-effacing man, he was a stabilizing influence on the city-side staff. He somewhat offset the negative vibes the staff often suffered from dealing with Griswold. Simon, who started at the *News* in 1959, retired in 1981 but continued to do some part-time duty on the desk until 1988. He died in February 2003 at the age of eighty-three.[25]

The *News* through the years has had its share of "characters" and each in his own way, with his particular idiosyncrasies, contributed to the *News* reporting environment. The public perception of newspapers in the thirties and forties was that a lot of newspapermen were heavy drinkers. The plays and movies of that time like *The Front Page* and *His Girl Friday* played this up, and, as it happens, the perception was not entirely wrong. The *News* had its share of heavy drinkers in the newsroom, all unwittingly hired by Kirchhofer.

When I first came to the *News* in 1949, I was assigned a temporary desk near the city desk and the rewrite men. It was the rewrite person's job to assimilate copy from the reporters calling in a breaking story and rewrite the copy for the next edition. I was seated near Nick Carter, a crackerjack rewrite man. I couldn't understand why he kept bending down for a few seconds every half-hour or so. Innocently, I asked Ed Lebherz why Nick was constantly bending down. I was informed that Nick always kept a bottle of liquor in his desk drawer and in it was a very long straw. He would bend down, draw on the straw, and in this way got his alcohol fix on a regular basis. I was told that his habit was tolerated because Nick was such a fine rewrite man and the editors felt that his alcohol intake likely helped him achieve that level of expertise.

Dick Engler was an absolutely superb reporter despite his severe drinking problem. He was a nightside reporter in the early 1950s when the *News* was still an afternoon-only newspaper. I worked with Engler for a couple of years and vividly recall his working habits. We would report for work at 4 PM and then, after getting our assignments for the night, would go out to dinner shortly after five. Night after night, Dick would order a bowl of oyster stew. This, he said, lined his stomach. Next he would imbibe one martini, followed by a second, and then a third. We would go off to our assignments and much to my surprise, Dick was more than able to do so. Hours later, we would be back in the newsroom and Engler invariably would tell me he was going to take a short nap. He asked me to awaken him in half an hour. With that, he would go into the sports department, which then was immediately adjacent to the newsroom, lie down across the top of a few desks, pull his ever-present hat over his eyes, and within seconds be asleep. When I would awaken him, he'd stagger over to his own desk, tip his hat back, and bang out his stories. Dick was a hunt-and-peck typist and very nimble, typing about as fast as any touch typist.

The night city editor, Julius Johnson, who also had a drinking problem, said that Engler's copy always was clean, needing very little work, and always was very thorough. After some time, Engler left the *News* and went to the *New York Daily News*, where he performed well until he retired to Maine some years later. His wife told me that Dick hated to leave Buffalo but his physician had convinced her he needed to get away from his drinking friends in Buffalo or he would surely develop cirrhosis of the liver.

Johnson had his own drinking routine that was repeated nightly. Just about every hour or hour and a half, he would leave his desk and be gone for about half an hour or so. There was a bar directly across from the *News* building and that was his destination on a regular basis. I don't know if his liquor intake played any role, but Johnson was not the sharpest editor.

A staffer who had a serious drinking problem for years was Jerry Allan. Allan joined the *News* in 1956 and was named Albany correspondent in 1967. He was a hard worker who, when the state legislature was in session, often would file as many as seven stories a day. Admired by the other correspondents in the state capital, he was elected president of the correspondent's association and in 1973 won its award as the outstanding correspondent covering state government.[26]

Allan was an alcoholic and one day he didn't turn up at his desk in Albany and was missing the next few days. His Albany colleagues suspected he was off on a binge and they alerted the then governor Nelson Rockefeller about Allan's absence. The governor was fond of Allan, who was the one correspondent who called him Rocky to his face and was able to get away with it. He assigned several state troopers to help in locating the *News* correspondent. They did find him in a fleabag hotel, brought him back, and then hospitalized him for alcoholism treatment. Upon his release from the treatment center, I met with Allan in Albany and informed him that I would have to fire him if he ever again went off on an alcohol binge. Allan pledged that he would reform and, in fact, he did. I never again heard that Allan had resumed drinking. Instead, he substituted enormous amounts of coffee each day and substantially increased his cigarette smoking. Allan continued performing as a very effective reporter until his retirement years later to the Carolinas.

An incident that always brings a smile to my face occurred in the same time period. My wife and I had a small gathering of friends in our home one evening in the 1960s. One person there was Charley Michie, an outstanding editorial writer. At one point somebody pointed out that Michie had gone to the bathroom some time ago and had not reappeared. I knocked on the bathroom door repeatedly and called Charley's name over and over again. There was no response so I opened the door and was shocked to see him lying in the bathtub wrapped in the shower curtain. By this time his wife was standing beside me and she was hysterical, certain her husband had collapsed and died. In fact, as we later figured out, Charley was totally inebriated and had staggered and grabbed the shower curtain to steady himself. The curtain came down and he landed in the bathtub. We let Charley sleep it off in the tub before he and his wife departed. The incident was no surprise to his wife who said his bouts with alcohol were not unusual.

Perhaps one of the most studious reporters of all the years in the newsroom was Ralph Wallenhorst. He was the victim of his knowledge of shorthand, which enabled him to record verbatim virtually all he heard when covering a meeting. He would return to the newsroom with a stenographer's pad filled with his shorthand notes. It would then take him hours to write a story. Unlike other reporters who had learned to take notes on only the most germane material they heard at a meeting, Wallenhorst had to go through page after page of his shorthand notes and then use only the best material for his story. He was thorough to a fault but his inability to produce a story quickly was most annoying to the city desk.

AHK, who rarely consulted with any of his editors before making a hire, had an uncanny ability to recognize good talent. For example, he had put together a superb team of reporters and editors for the financial department that has never been equaled since. The names Hilton Hornaday, Harry Waddell, Jerry Wood, and Jimmy Collins will not be forgotten by readers of the business pages in the Kirchhofer days. One can add to that list the name of Bob Watson, the finest business writer ever employed by the *News*. In addition to his reporting duties, Watson wrote a Saturday column that for years was the popular Saturday feature of the business pages. And this was in the time period that business pages were not the best-read pages in the paper. Watson was a superb reporter and an excellent writer. He commanded attention and he got it.

Kirchhofer was equally adept at recruiting top-notch talent for other sectors of the newsroom. He hired Art Goldberg as a rewrite man and there were few who could match his talents. In addition to his ability to gather and collate information from many reporters, he had a wonderful sense of humor that was manifested in his daily fascinating weather stories. His stories always had a touch of humor as well as being informative. For years they were reader favorites.[27]

Two cityside reporters whom Kirchhofer hired without consulting any of his editors proved his instinctive ability to recognize potentially fine talent. The two, Ed Kelly and Ralph Dibble, had long and illustrious careers with the paper. Kelly came to the *News* in June 1944 immediately after getting his master's degree in journalism from Columbia University. Initially he covered all kinds of news and was assigned from 1950 to 1954 to assist the Albany correspondent while the legislature was in session. But it was as a labor reporter specialist that Kelly really made his mark and won state and national recognition before his retirement in 1983. He had completely and conscientiously covered labor news for thirty-four years on a full-time basis.[28]

Labor and management sources had the greatest respect for Kelly's integrity and his absolute insistence on being fair to all parties in disputes. His coverage in 1949 of the violent Bell Aircraft strike was his most challenging assignment and proved conclusively his enormous value to the *News*. None of his successors on the labor beat have been able to equal his ability.[29]

Kirchhofer hired Ralph Dibble in 1953 from the *Utica Press and Observer Dispatch*, where he served as state editor and city editor. In his long career at the *News* he worked as a reporter, rewrite man, and assistant city editor. He performed all of his duties extremely well and earned the respect of all news editors. No project was too tough for Dibble to tackle. He was unflappable. Anytime a difficult or particularly sensitive story had to be written the word always was "give it to Dibble." It would be done and done well with a balanced approach.

Dibble's longest and most arduous project was producing the bulk of material for the *News* Centennial section, October 12, 1980. He wrote the main story that had some fourteen thousand words and took about eight months to research and write. In addition, he prepared thirteen other articles for the section. A laid-back man, Dibble was a superb craftsman and a great example of the type of talent that Kirchhofer was able to recruit in his years as editor of the paper.[30]

Another longtime feature of the *News* was its picture page. Edited for years by another AHK hire, Fred Kosslow, the page carried the best local and wire pictures available. No advertising ever appeared on the picture page. Kosslow was of some assistance to Kirchhofer in developing a photographic staff for the paper. Kirchhofer was aware of his lack of expertise in this area and in this case deviated from his customary practice of ignoring the input of his subordinates.

When Kirchhofer became managing editor in 1927, not much attention had been given to the photographic staff. Lines of responsibility were not clearly defined, and this would remain the status quo for many years to come. On staff at the time was Cornelius "Ken" Kennedy, who had started his career at the *News* back in 1907. In his early years on staff, he served as an artist and produced sketches for the paper in addition to occasional photos. A wonderful, likable man, Ken was everybody's favorite and a photographer who enjoyed his work. I can recall as late as the early 1950s going out on assignment with Ken. He utilized "flash powder" instead of flashbulbs in taking his photos and he set up his big, boxy camera on a stationary tripod for setup shots. Habits, he said, were not easy to change and he was convinced that "the old-fashioned way still produced the best results."[31]

Walter Bingham was hired as a reporter in 1923 and ten years later, in 1933, Kirchhofer shifted him to the photographic staff. He became a fine photographer who was popular with the staff and the public until he died in 1951 at the early age of forty-nine. Also on the photo staff at that time was George Butler who had joined the *News* in 1929 and continued shooting until his retirement forty-four years later. Ralph Hinkson, the fastidious dresser and man-about-town, became a staff photographer in 1928 and continued in that role for forty-one years.

Barney Kerr had a long and interesting career at the *News*. He started at the paper in August 1937 and became a staff photographer in January 1941. The shift from clerical to professional status resulted in a two-dollar weekly pay raise from eighteen to twenty dollars. Kerr was named chief photographer in March 1953 when Cornelius Kennedy retired. Kerr was the first *News* photographer to use a sequence camera in sports photo coverage and the first to utilize a strobe light. In 1966 he also took the first color photo ever to be published in the *News*. Early in his career he used a red-bellows camera with an air compression shutter shooting pictures with the last of the glass-plate film. Kerr, who retired in June 1983, said his most exciting assignment was the coverage of the 1971 Attica Prison riot. His aerial shot from a helicopter was used in a two-page spread by the famous German magazine *Stern*. Photos of the riot taken by Kerr and other *News* photographers were published in newspapers and magazines throughout the world.[32] When Barney Kerr retired in 1983, Roy Russell, who had been a *News* shooter since June 1969, was elevated to the chief photographer's position.[33]

Merrill D. Mathews was hired as a copyboy in 1941 and was advanced to a photographer's role by Kirchhofer in 1950. Mathews was particularly adept at taking photos of children and animals and had many one-man exhibits of his work. His career ended much too early with his death in 1976.[34]

In the early period of his management career Kirchhofer obviously had no hesitation about moving people into different positions to fill staff needs. In most instances his judgment was vindicated by the performance of those he shifted. On the other hand, he had some strange personal hang-ups that resulted in job switches. For example, he instituted a policy that could not be justified legally or morally in today's environment. Female copy aides who announced an intention to wed were relieved of their job duties. For a reason never enunciated publicly, he would not countenance having any married copygirls.

Some in this category voluntarily left the *News*, a few moved into other *News* departments. Still others were reassigned in the newsroom, strangely enough, to positions as staff artists, although they had no previous experience or special aptitude for those jobs. The result was an art department that basically had some members with no particular skills as artists.

The newsroom art department in Kirchhofer's early years in management had no relationship to the department as it evolved later on. The artists created no graphics. They did not design any layouts. In effect, the artists only did touch-ups on photographs, eliminating some images or enhancing others. They did this with cotton-tipped sticks that they constantly wet with their tongues. Creativity and ability was at an absolute minimum. The artists carried out Kirchhofer's instructions, eliminating any and all cleavage in a woman's dress; obliterating belly buttons; extending a woman's skirt, shorts, or bathing suit to cover more of her body.

Kirchhofer's morality mandates extended also to the printed word. Motion picture ads were carefully scrutinized to remove or blur any words that he found offensive. Countless titles of movies were altered to meet his standards and if the companies releasing the movies objected to the changes he insisted upon, the ad was refused. I recall vividly one incident. He had rejected one ad for a movie whose title he found to be objectionable and a substitute title for the film was used in the ad that finally was accepted. When the movie was reviewed, its real title was used in the review. Kirchhofer was incensed. I, the news editor at that time, said we could not review a movie without its proper title and insisted it had to be done. I finally prevailed in that battle but it was a victory that left a bitter taste.

The art department didn't change or grow until 1959 when John Manion, a copydesk and news desk veteran, took the job as picture editor. This was the beginning of the evolution of the art department into a real art department.[35]

Kirchhofer's very strong feeling about the role of the media in maintaining morality changed somewhat with the passage of time but he remained steadfast in his intense effort to have the *News* be the beacon of strict morality. As the years rolled by, he slowly but steadily came to grips with the need to accommodate to the newer environment and he reluctantly moved in that direction.

Composing room personnel who were employed by the *News* in the 1950s remember the production superintendent at that time who spent the vast majority of his time in his office at his desk reading the Bible. George Lowe didn't provide much direction or supervision to his staff and always acted annoyed when anyone would approach him with an inquiry, interrupting his Bible studies.

Given his tremendous involvement at the *News* and so many other areas, the tributes to Kirchhofer often tend to overlook his dedicated involvement in developing the *News* product for so many decades. He often said in speeches and in conversations with staffers and friends that his greatest pleasure came from working with staff in creating stories, perfecting them, and bringing them to the publication stage. Additionally, he relished his role in establishing editorial policies that guided the newspaper and that he felt gave better service to improve his beloved Buffalo.[36]

The first big local story to occur under the Kirchhofer's stewardship was the opening of the Peace Bridge in August 1927. Shortly thereafter, in June 1929, the New York Central Terminal was opened. Although both were scheduled events, the coverage in the *News* indicated what would occur under Kirchhofer—complete detail, including sidebars and accompanying photographs.[37]

Although the days of investigative reporting did not really flourish until Watergate in 1972, the *News* under AHK's guidance was not reluctant to look into situations that he felt needed exposure in the media and to be augmented by editorials to bring about reforms. For example, on August 26, 1931, the *News* broke its first story exposing what it said was inadequate pay and improper treatment of workmen involved in the construction of Attica State Prison and other state projects. The continuous campaign by the *News* resulted in the paper earning a place on *Nation* magazine's 1931 roll of honor in journalism.[38]

Two years later, the *News* initiated a campaign for legislation to assure privacy of individual income-tax reports that resulted in a series of reforms. And in that same year of 1933, its reporters on the local scene forestalled political manipulation of funds in the construction of a fifteen-million-dollar sewage disposal system. The *News* stories were a major factor in the saving of enormous amounts of taxpayer dollars.

Then in 1938, the *News* launched a two-year investigation of city affairs that disclosed misuse of funds and misconduct by many city officials. It resulted in the appointment of Buffalo attorney Frank Raichle as a special prosecutor who succeeded in getting convictions against thirteen city officials, including Mayor George Zimmerman. The outcome of this bribery probe was a major victory for the *News* in its long and detailed investigation of civic malfeasance.[39]

A Kirchhofer memo to staff in March 1941 is reminiscent of similar ones that Edward H. Butler Sr. might have written in the 1880s. It stressed that "brief, compact writing is a prime essential. Five hundred words still is the standard by which to gauge how long or short a story should be."[40]

Despite these instructions to staff, AHK was willing to cast them aside when a subject dear to his heart was involved. A prime example was his strong concerns about Communism and the threat he perceived it could present to the American way of life. One veteran *News* staffer, Fred Turner, spent most of his time and energy on stories about Communist activity on the Niagara Frontier, real or imagined. Turner was an excellent reporter who wrote very lengthy and at times unwieldy stories about suspected Communists and Communist front organizations. These generally were given front-page display and occupied large amounts of space.

AHK was so absorbed in this thrust against the red menace that it ultimately brought him into direct confrontation with another facet of his life to which he had dedicated a great deal of time and conviction. For years he had been active in the affairs of Buffalo's First Presbyterian Church, a highly respected institution. He was the ruling elder of the church in the 1950s but in 1953 he took issue with the Presbyterian Church on the topic of subversive activity.[41] In a June 1953 letter to the editor of the national church publication *Presbyterian Life*, he wrote, "There is indeed no reason why a congressional committee investigating subversive activities [the McCarthy committee] should overlook any field, the clergy included. . . . The record clearly shows that there have been quite a few clergymen whose names have appeared on Communist front organization's letterheads. . . . Dr. Blake seems singularly uninformed about many aspects of the Communist conspiracy and its ramifications in the country."[42] (Dr. Blake was the stated clerk of the General Assembly of the Presbyterian Church, USA.)

AHK then resigned as the dean of First Presbyterian Church because "I disagree so fundamentally with some of the things that are being done in the home of the Presbyterian Church, USA." In effect, AHK was defending McCarthyism. He publicly stated, "To say that McCarthyism . . . is the greatest threat to freedom in America ignores the threat of the Communist criminal conspiracy that has been operating here. Had it not been for the congressional committees which have exposed these sinister ramifications, our freedom indeed might be in danger."[43]

For Kirchhofer to direct such criticism at the Presbyterian Church and to relinquish his key role in the local church had to be a most difficult and emotional decision. However, it supported his stridency on the Communist issue that the *News* in its news stories and editorials had concentrated on for so long. An ardent patriot, he never deviated in his dedication to eradicating what he felt was a threat to the nation.[44]

Although Kirchhofer always gave priority to careful, detailed coverage of local news, he always kept national and international news in proper perspective and gave these events more coverage than the average regional newspaper in the nation. A review of the *News* from the years 1927 through 1956 would provide any reader with a full appreciation of the historical events that transpired in those years.

The *News* coverage of two nonscheduled news events really indicated what could be expected from it under Kirchhofer. The first was the Lucidol plant explosion in September 1953 that resulted in nine fatalities and injuries to twenty-seven others. And even more dramatic was the March 1954 Cleveland Hill School blast in Cheektowaga that killed eleven and injured nineteen. Both of these tragic events were given extensive *News* coverage for days, with every facet of the events thoroughly explored and explained. The school fire, in particular, captured the attention of the entire area, given the involvement of so many children. The *News* coverage of the event and particularly of its aftermath was unbelievably detailed and was typical of his approach to coverage of major local news events in all the years of his stewardship.[45]

Kirchhofer's city editors and their assistants were fully aware that he was a stickler for detail and that they had to arrange for total coverage of news events to satisfy the boss. His philosophy would excuse overkill in coverage but would never countenance gaps in covering every conceivable aspect of a story. In fact, what constantly amazed his editors was his ability to spot what he felt were gaps in coverage that they thought were competently covered.

Notes

1. Ralph Dibble, "The *Buffalo Evening News*," *Buffalo News* centennial publication, October 12, 1980, p. H-6; Alfred Kirchhofer files, Butler Family Papers, E. H. Butler Library Archives, State University College at Buffalo, boxes 1, 14; Kate Robinson Butler files, Butler Family Papers, E. H. Butler Library Archives, State University College at Buffalo, box 1; Alfred H. Kirchhofer Papers, Buffalo and Erie County Historical Society Archives, C67-6, box 35.

2. Kirchhofer Papers, Historical Society, biographical note.

3. Kirchhofer files, Butler Family Papers, boxes 1, 7.

4. Buffalo and Erie County Public Library, Main Branch, History of Buffalo, card file.

5. Mark Goldman, *City on the Lake: The Challenge of Change in Buffalo, New York* (Amherst, NY: Prometheus Books, 1990), p. 167.

6. *Buffalo News* personnel files.

7. *Buffalo News* clipping file.

8. Kirchhofer Papers, Historical Society, box 8.

9. Ibid., box 12.

10. Ibid.

11. Ibid., box 8.

12. Ibid.

13. Ibid., boxes 10, 11 .

14. Ralph Dibble, "Kirchhofer Dominating Figure," *Buffalo News*, October 12, 1980, p. H-12.

15. Ibid.

16. Ibid.

17. Ibid.

18. Ibid.; Kirchhofer Papers, Historical Society, box 16; Dibble, "The *Buffalo Evening News*."

19. Dibble, "Kirchhofer Dominating Figure."

20. Ibid.

21. Kirchhofer files, Butler Family Papers, box 1.

22. Pat Higgins,"My Mind's Eye" (unpublished memoir).

23. Dibble, "Kirchhofer Dominating Figure."

24. *Buffalo News* personnel files.

25. The *Buffalo News*, February 5, 2003, obituary, Sunrise edition, p. D-7.

26. Ibid.

27. Ibid.

28. Ibid.

29. Murray B. Light, "The News—Your Newspaper," *Buffalo News*, October 9, 1979, second front page.

30. "A Real Pro Pens History of News," *Buffalo News*, October 12, 1980, p. H-5.

31. "The News Photographers: Real Shooting Stars," *Buffalo News*, October 12, 1980, p. H-7.

32. Murray B. Light, "Your Newspaper," *Buffalo News*, June 7, 1983, second front page.

33. *Buffalo News* personnel files.

34. "The News Photographers," p. H-7.

35. Ibid., p. H-10.

36. Ibid.

37. "Bridge Ceremony Hailed as Influence for Peace," *Buffalo Evening News*, August 8, 1927, p. 1; "Buffalo Pauses to Join Railways in Terminal Dedication Ceremony," *Buffalo Evening News*, June 22, 1929, p. 1.

38. Lewis G. Harriman, *Buffalo Evening News and Its Courageous Leader Edward H. Butler* (Buffalo, NY: Newcomen Society in North America, 1955), p. 23.

39. Kirchhofer files, Butler Family Papers, box 4.

40. Ibid., box 1.

41. Kirchhofer Papers, Historical Society, box 24.

42. Ibid.

43. Ibid.

44. Ibid.

45. "9 Killed, 27 Hurt in 'Hydrogen' Blast," *Buffalo Evening News*, September 23, 1953, p. 1, "11 Pupils Killed, 19 Hurt in Explosion," *Buffalo Evening News*, March 31, 1954, p. 1.

10 AHK
The Imprint of the Legend

The death of Edward H. Butler Jr. resulted in significant changes in the management ranks of the *News*. His widow, Kate Butler, assumed the responsibilities of president and she promoted Alfred H. Kirchhofer to editor and executive vice president of the paper as well as president of WBEN Inc.[1]

A legend is a well-known person whose actions or views are frequently talked about during his or her lifetime. If this is the case, Alfred H. Kirchhofer, who presided over the *Buffalo News* editorial operations as managing editor from 1927 to 1956 and as editor from 1956 to 1966, is indeed a legend. In fact, his influence over many other sectors of the *News* as well gave rise to his status in the newspaper world as a legend. So dominant was his status that he overshadowed the publishers under whom he served, particularly Edward H. Butler Jr.

Butler and Kirchhofer made an excellent team. Butler never had shown too much interest in the editorial product and, according to business office executives there at the time, he wisely exempted himself from editorial matters although from time to time he would inform his editor what his feelings were on certain subjects. This involvement was minimal, however. On the other hand, Butler quickly came to value Kirchhofer's suggestions on corporate matters outside of the newsroom purview and did not appear to resent his involvement. Mutual respect was the key to their fine relationship and the result was ideal teamwork between the editor and the publisher, which was beneficial to the entire enterprise for many years.

Butler's involvement with local institutions was enormous and he took these responsibilities seriously, contributing his knowledge and prestige to all with whom he was affiliated. His capacity for work and willingness to dedicate his time and energy to so many causes amazed community leaders.

The key to the success of any newspaper, big or small, is its news product. Everything flows from that base but it can't stand alone to make a newspaper financially viable without meeting the demands of its consumers, meaning the readers. Advertising and circulation that produce the revenue needed for financial success of a newspaper are basically dependent on the news product.

The news content can only be produced by the staffers in the newsroom, making the selection and hiring of the *News* staff the most important function of the top editors in the newsroom operation. It's the first priority without any question, and the editor of a paper who delegates total responsibility for staff recruitment and hiring abrogates his chief responsibility. The finest advertising department and circulation department staffs can perform flawlessly but in the long term their efforts fail if the newsroom fails to deliver a top-grade product.

The editor, of course, needs the resources to get the job done and providing those resources is the responsibility of the publisher. The editors of the *News* through the more than one hundred years of its existence have been fortunate in working for publishers who fully understood their responsibility in this area. Edward H. Butler Sr. had financial hardships in the early days of the *News* but didn't stint in providing the needed dollars to hire the best editorial staff available. And even in the early days of the Buffett ownership of the paper, when the operation was losing millions of dollars annually, the newsroom was basically exempt from staff cutbacks and job freezes.

Bruce Shanks, winner of the 1957 Pulitzer Prize for his political cartoon "The Thinker." (Photo by George J. Butler, courtesy *Buffalo News*)

The editor has the responsibility of allocating the financial resources available to him. Some believe that targeting stories to win Pulitzer Prizes proves his worth and that of his staff. Others feel that concentrating resources to provide continuing daily thorough news coverage is the road to success. The *Philadelphia Inquirer*, for example, has won more than its shares of Pulitzers, many for stories that had little or no impact on its daily readers. Editors of the *Buffalo News* through all of its history have not been too concerned about the kudos that come to a newspaper in winning Pulitzers and other top national awards, although they are gratified when they come to the paper. The concentration has always been on consistent quality coverage, particularly of local news.

The *News*, since its beginning as a daily in 1880, has won three Pulitzers with two of the three the result of an individual's particular talents. Both of these Pulitzers were to *News* editorial cartoonists, Bruce Shanks and Tom Toles.[2]

Shanks won his Pulitzer in 1957 for his cartoon "The Thinker," a portrayal of an American worker pondering newspaper accounts of corruption among union leaders. The long-time editorial cartoonist had produced an exceptionally fine body of work through the years and his cartoons were frequently reprinted in many other newspapers and magazines. Shanks was a well-liked and highly respected figure in the newsroom. He was admired by all for his outgoing personality, his modesty, and his friendliness with the vast majority of staff, from copy aides to the top editors. Whenever a staffer departed for another job or retired, Shanks was never known to reject a request that he do a special cartoon to be presented to the individual who was leaving. Nor did he ever get upset over the frequent jibes he received about his perpetual problem with excess weight.[3]

A second *News* editorial cartoonist, Tom Toles, was the recipient of a Pulitzer Prize in 1990 for his series of cartoons published in 1989 on a constitutional amendment banning flag burning.[4] (For more on Toles, see chapter 21.)

Another *News* Pulitzer Prize was earned by Edgar May in 1960 in the "best local reporting" category. May was only thirty-one when he wrote his 1960 series "Our Costly Dilemma." It resulted from his six-month stint when he went undercover and worked as a caseworker for the Erie County Department of Social Welfare. He uncovered numerous problems in the welfare system. May joined the *News* staff only two years prior to this assignment. Editors told staffers who were puzzled by May's absence from the newsroom during this period that "Ed May has left us." After winning the Pulitzer Prize, May did leave the staff. He moved to New York. He wrote a book, published in 1964, titled *The Wasted Americans.* He later went on to become an assistant to the director of the Peace Corps and still later was appointed an assistant director of the U.S. Office of Economic Opportunity.[5]

A major innovation in the Kirchhofer era occurred on October 4, 1958, with the inauguration of the weekend edition, which featured ten pages of color comics, the nationally syndicated *This Week* magazine, and the tabloid *TV Topics.* When television came on the scene and started to increase its audience and its ability to garner advertising, the *News* didn't ignore it as many other papers did. Instead, the *News* almost immediately added the schedules for TV programming to the paper, ran a daily TV column, and began publication of the weekly *TV Topics.* Kirchhofer decided to meet the electronic competition head-on, and it was a very wise decision. The *News* today provides more comprehensive television and radio information than most papers do. In 1977, before the sale of the paper to Warren Buffett, the *News* owned an AM and an FM radio station as well as the CBS television outlet, and used its daily TV-radio column to shamelessly promote all three. Now the coverage is complete and impartial and a credit to the *News.*

The weekend edition was the *News*'s response to the Sunday *Courier-Express* and while its circulation and advertising volume started slowly, it gradually gained momentum in both areas. It was launched as circulation and advertising in Sunday newspapers was continuing to grow nationwide. The *Buffalo Courier-Express* was enjoying that same success but given the *News* decision not to challenge the *Courier* on Sundays, the weekend edition was its attempt to capture some of the Sunday market advertising and circulation revenues.

Initially, reader and advertiser response to the weekend package was disappointingly slow, but eventually the *Weekend News* continued to garner the interest of readers and advertisers. Some preprint ads, long exclusively in the *Sunday Courier*, had even migrated to the *News* weekend paper.[6]

The conversion of its Saturday paper into a weekender with many features such as color comics and a TV magazine normally found only in Sunday papers was innovative for the *News*. The weekend edition was terminated in 1977 when the *News* launched its own Sunday paper. Much of the weekend material was carried over into the new Sunday publication. Another important milestone occurred on July 26, 1958, with the introduction of the first color used as part of a regular edition of the paper.[7]

In the many years of Kirchhofer's stewardship over the editorial policies of the *News*, his most bitter personal battle occurred during the years that Frank Sedita was mayor of the city. In October 1959 the State Investigation Commission launched an inquiry into Buffalo police and gambling activities in Buffalo. The Republican state legislature and Gov. Averill Harriman, a Democrat, had established the commission the year before. That set off a long, vitriolic verbal exchange between the mayor and the *News*, one that reached its peak when the commission sent a questionnaire to all Buffalo police. The mayor and Police Commissioner Frank Felicetta directed the police officers to refrain from answering it. That directive infuriated Kirchhofer and was the spark that ignited the ensuing battle between the mayor and the *News*.[8]

Crime Commission chairman Goodman Sarachan told the police to ignore the Felicetta directive and asked them to respond to the fifteen questions of the Crime Commission. The *News*, in a strong editorial on April 21, 1960, stated that "If the police record is clean, with nothing to hide, why should there be any hesitation about cooperating fully with the commission to ferret out all the facts?"[9]

The following day, another *News* editorial defended the Crime Commission actions and said, "An effort is being made in some official city quarters to discredit the State Crime Commission investigation of the Buffalo Police Department as a politically-inspired attack on a Democratic city administration." Two days later, Mayor Sedita launched his major attack in a television broadcast, criticizing the commission for its investigation and the editor of the *News* for supporting it. The mayor pulled no punches, accusing Kirchhofer of using the editorial pages of the *News* as a "personal vehicle of hatred and vindictiveness" and adding that this "venom is slowly but surely seeping into its news columns." The mayor added fuel to the fire as he went on to say:

> I say to you, Mr. Kirchhofer, that the unprincipled, vicious, inexcusable campaign of untruths and half-truths that you have consistently maintained against me and my administration is the kind of thing if practiced wholesale by the press everywhere would invite legislative intervention. You have made the editorial pages of a great newspaper your own, personal vehicle of hatred and vindictiveness. You have made it your dedicated policy to criticize, ridicule and demean anything connected with me or my administration and to hold up our city to ridicule and contempt throughout the country.[10]

On October 27, 1961, the *News* published a front-page editorial calling for election of Chet Kowal, then city comptroller, to defeat Sedita in the mayoral election. It was a vitriolic editorial, citing Sedita's position on the Crime Commission. Sedita was defeated in the Democratic primary by North District councilman Victor Manz and ran as an independent in the election. Manz and Sedita split the Democratic vote and Republican Chet Kowal won the election. Sedita, however, regained the office of mayor in the election of 1965 and again in 1969.[11]

Kirchhofer's background as the *News* correspondent in Albany and later as its first Washington bureau chief whetted his appetite for politics and it remained a consuming passion of his throughout his career as the head of the paper's news operations. Even after his retirement in 1966, his intense interest in politics never waned. As I noted in the introduction, he was engaged in writing a history of the *News* and spent thirteen years in the endeavor. Unfortunately, he never completed it because he became bogged down in research and in recounting the details of every elected contest for offices in Erie County as well as internal party battles for committeemen and ward chairman. Politics had become an obsession that he could not shed.

The efforts of *Buffalo News* staffers have been rewarded countless times over the years with commendations from the State Society of Editors and the State Publishers Association. These awards have gone to reporters, editors, photographers, and staff artists in competition with other major newspapers in New York State. Various foundations and professional organizations in many different fields also have frequently cited staffers. It should be noted, however, that the *News* has never endorsed staff entries in competitions sponsored by commercial enterprises that tend to be self-serving, seeking only to enhance their image.

A prestigious organization, the National Conference of Editorial Writers, has consistently recognized the excellent work of *News* editorial writers. The *News* always has taken special pride in its editorial page and the work of its editorial board and its editorial page cartoonists.

News editorial writers are separated physically from the newsroom staff but communication between editorial writers and reporters and editors is constant. Reporters and editors are useful sources of information for editorial writers although they are not asked to express their own likes and dislikes in contributing facts about their beats to the editorial writers.

The number of editorial writers has varied through the years from one to four but in recent times three editorial writers and the editorial page editor comprise the editorial board writing team. Millard C. Browne served as chief editorial writer until 1969 when his title was changed to editorial page editor. He reported directly to Mr. Butler and later to Kirchhofer. A brilliant but highly sensitive man, Browne was a liberal with very strong feelings about the protection of civil liberties, desegregation, strict interpretation of constitutional guarantees, and the need for government to assist the needy.[12] Browne did not shy away from battling fiercely for positions about which he felt strongly. He and publisher Henry Urban had many a battle about the position the *News* would take on Watergate and Browne came close to resigning over the issue. When Browne became particularly agitated, his aquiline nose would quiver. When that occurred, you knew that the normally reserved intellectual was very upset and would marshal all of his arguments to reinforce his position. Browne retired in January 1980 and moved to a home near his alma mater Stanford University.[13]

In addition to the close scrutiny he maintained over the *News* product, AHK worked closely with Butler in planning the expansion of the physical plant as the paper's circulation continued to increase

In April 1973 the new home of the *News* office building opened at Scott and Washington streets immediately adjacent to the printing and distribution center that opened in 1958. (Photo by Dick Mueckl, courtesy *Buffalo News*)

and the growth in advertising resulted in ever-larger papers. In 1958 a new mechanical building at Scott and Washington streets was opened. It comprised 180,000 square feet of space and contained the pressroom, stereotype department, mailroom, loading docks, and provision for newsprint storage. Five new Wood presses were also introduced and included four-color units.[14]

In December 1969 ground was broken for a new office building at the intersection of Scott and Washington streets and it was put into use in April 1973, ending the split operation that had been utilized for years with the pressroom at that site and the office building at Main and Seneca streets. Designed by Edward Durell Stone, the office building is a five-story structure featuring recessed first and fifth floors. It also has a magnificent tropical garden in a thirty-six-foot well from the fourth-floor level to the skylights atop the fifth floor.[15]

Kirchhofer's enormous capacity for work was well known by political and business leaders in the community. It also amazed editors and publishers in the newspaper industry. In addition to the numerous full-time duties he had at the *News* and its related broadcast enterprises, he deeply involved himself in many professional organizations and community endeavors. His role in most was more than superficial, taking on responsible policy-setting functions. Kirchhofer served as a director of the New York State Society of Newspaper Editors from 1961 through 1963, chairman of the St. Bonaventure University Advisory Council for Journalism, and a key member of the Syracuse University School of Journalism Advisory Council.[16] He was a member and former president of the National Press Club during his time at the *News* Washington bureau, and was elected to membership in the prestigious Gridiron Club during that period.[17]

On the local scene Kirchhofer served on numerous boards and committees, including the Buffalo Philharmonic Orchestra Society, the Buffalo Fine Arts Academy, the Buffalo Chapter of the American Red Cross, the Roswell Park Memorial Institute Board of Visitors, the Children's Hospital Advisory Board, the Erie County Civil Defense Council, University of Buffalo Foundation, University of Buffalo Council, the Board of Millard Fillmore Hospital, and a host of others.[18]

He was a major benefactor of Roswell Park, dedicating hundreds of hours each year fighting for more state funding for the hospital's physical plant and for its research activities. He was very involved with the Roswell Park Division of Health Research, Inc. and served for years on its board of directors.[19]

Kirchhofer was honored by numerous universities and journalism organizations for his contributions to journalism and the communities served by the *News*. Buffalo born and bred, AHK had a life replete with remarkable achievements. He never attended college but later was awarded several honorary degrees. His education was at Buffalo's School 31, the old Central High School in Buffalo, and then night classes at the city's YMCA Institute.[20]

In a 1980 special section of the *News*, I, who had been hired by AHK in 1949, wrote the following,

> AHK is without doubt the most dominant figure in Buffalo area media in the twentieth century. His foresight was remarkable. As an editor, his demand-levels were so great they produced fine journalism and spawned hundreds of fine journalists over the years.
>
> He always had the respect of his staff because the demands he

made on himself were always greater than those he made on them. His respect for detail and accuracy was infinite as was his capacity for work.[21]

NOTES

1. Kate Robinson Butler files, Butler Family Papers, E. H. Butler Library Archives, State University College at Buffalo; 1955–1975 files, E. H. Butler Collection, box 1.
2. *Buffalo News* Library, *Buffalo News* personnel files.
3. "Array of Honors for the *News*," *Buffalo News* centennial publication, October 12, 1980, p. H-9.
4. Murray B. Light, "The News—Your Newspaper," *Buffalo News*, March 27, 1990, second front page.
5. "Array of Honors for the *News*."
6. Alfred H. Kirchhofer Papers, Buffalo and Erie County Historical Society Archives, C67-6, box 1; Alfred Kirchhofer files, Butler Family Papers, box 5.
7. Ibid.
8. Kirchhofer Papers, Historical Society, box 28, files 9, 10.
9. Ibid.
10. Ibid.
11. Ibid.
12. *Buffalo News* personnel files.
13. Light, "The News Your—Newspaper," *Buffalo News*, January 7, 1980, second front page.
14. "Producing the News," *Buffalo News*, October 12, 1980, p. H-16.
15. Ibid.; *Buffalo News* files.
16. Kirchhofer Papers, Historical Society, box 11.
17. Ibid.
18. Ibid.
19. Ibid., box 12.
20. Ibid., biographical note.
21. Ibid.

11 Paul Neville
The Stadium Is the Issue

Alfred H. Kirchhofer brought Paul Neville to the *News* in June 1957 as his assistant and later promoted him to managing editor on January 2, 1959. He recruited Neville from Indiana's *South Bend Tribune*, where he was managing editor. Prior to that Neville had been a reporter, political writer, and sports editor of the *Tribune*. A native of Massachusetts, he started his newspaper career at two newspapers in that state, the *Worcester Post* and the *Boston Herald*.[1]

Neville is credited, and rightfully so, with persuading Ralph Wilson to make the Buffalo Bills the seventh franchise in the newly formed American Football League. Wilson met with Neville in 1959 in the *News* offices and that meeting led to Wilson's decision to join with the AFL. He had asked and received Neville's pledge that the *News* would be a strong supporter of a football team in Buffalo, but to his credit Neville, who was managing editor at the time, did point out that he would not rule out legitimate criticism of the team's performance when warranted.[2] I was present at that meeting and reinforced what Neville said because I felt it was important for the record.

The shift from Kirchhofer to Neville in the top editorial position at the *News* in 1966 was quite dramatic. Most staffers at the paper and many editors around the country were surprised by the appointment of Neville as executive editor. They never thought that Kirchhofer would pick as his successor one who was so totally different in personality and interests than he. Neville had an outgoing personality with an abiding love of football and enjoyed long lunches with friends almost daily. AHK had rarely accepted luncheon engagements and never manifested much interest in any sport. Neville was an expansive extrovert; AHK was by nature austere.[3]

Neville was a good newspaperman who became too emotionally involved in the county legislature's debate over an open stadium downtown or a domed stadium in Lancaster. Neville set aside the very basic principles of journalism he enunciated in a memo to the staff upon his promotion from managing editor to editor in 1966. In it he wrote, "I believe a newspaper should be respected and not necessarily be universally popular. They [readers] may not like it but they will respect the paper if it is honest, fair, and objective."[4]

Contrary to a long-standing practice at the *News* and at other first-rate newspapers, Neville ordered editorials run on the front page of the paper on behalf of a domed stadium. As one of his key assistants, I constantly counseled against this practice. Neville himself wrote these strident editorials and he frequently summoned me to his Snyder home at night to assist him in the endeavor. He had become absolutely obsessed with the stadium matter and spent the majority of his time for a lengthy period on the issue, meeting with legislators and community leaders in his endeavor to convince them that a domed stadium was needed in Erie County given the sometimes severe weather during the football season.

During this period Neville almost daily ordered changes in stories about the stadium battle in the county legislature, often doing the rewrites himself and injecting editorial comments into news stories to the chagrin of the County Hall reporters and the staff in general. It was a trying period for many. The *Courier-Express*, taking an opposite stand on the stadium, responded with its front-page editorials and slanted stories. I have often felt this was the saddest period in Buffalo newspaper history. Honest and objective journalistic practices were set aside in the heat of this bitter battle.

Paul E. Neville, managing editor, 1959–1966. (Courtesy *Buffalo News*)

Neville's role as the top editor of the *News* came to an untimely end after only three years. He suffered a cerebral hemorrhage at his desk on June 20, 1969, and died two days later. His death came just two days after the Erie County Legislature had approved a plan for a domed stadium in Lancaster, south of the city. It was the successful conclusion to a campaign that the *News*, under the leadership of Neville, had fought for so long and vigorously. [5]

The county legislature never built the domed stadium despite the vote of approval since all the bids came in way over original estimates. Additionally, charges of bribery led to an ugly period of indictments, trials, and prison terms. Legislators Frederick Pordum and Frank Ludera were convicted of conspiracy to accept bribes on June 16, 1970, and sentenced to three years imprisonment. Later, five architects involved in the project were indicted on charges of conspiracy and bribery.[6] Ultimately, an open-air stadium was built in Orchard Park, and is now the home of the Buffalo Bills.[7]

I have long been saddened and surprised by the accusation of Lillian Neville that I was responsible in part for bringing on her husband's fatal stroke. She had witnessed countless sessions in the Neville home where her husband and I vigorously argued the direction he was taking in the stadium battle, particularly about his insistence on front-page editorials and what I considered to be his distortion of news stories on the issue. She was unaware that Neville and I, despite our differences on this particular issue, had remained good friends and that our differences never endangered that friendship.

When Neville collapsed at his desk, I followed the ambulance to the Buffalo General Hospital and then called Lillian to tell her that Paul had been hospitalized. When she arrived at the hospital we spent the next ten hours awaiting word on Paul's condition. Meanwhile, she smoked continually. I had been off cigarettes for more than five years but finally, about 11 PM I weakened and asked her for a cigarette. That was a move I never should have made. It got me back in the habit that has remained with me ever since.

While Neville distorted news reporting on the domed stadium, he reformed the political reporting of the paper that for too long had reflected Jack Medoff's bias in favor of the Republican Party. Coverage of the local political scene always has played a major role in the *Buffalo News*, more so than in many other newspapers in the nation. The paper's fascination with politics and politicians has never ebbed since Edward H. Butler Sr. launched the *Sunday News* in 1873. Media consultants today say that readers and viewers aren't too interested in politics and that this coverage should be limited. That may be a valid observation in many areas of the country, but the residents of western New York appear to be the exception to that finding. Perhaps it is because their fathers, grandfathers, and great-grandfathers were nurtured on the *News* that always placed strong emphasis on its coverage of politics and utilized many of its most talented staffers for that purpose.

When Jack Medoff retired from the paper in September 1966, George Borrelli filled the chief political reporter's role. He had covered government and politics for eight years at the *Courier-Express* before joining the *News* in 1963. A Syracuse University graduate, he also reported for the *Syracuse Post-Standard* for two years. In his first three years at the *News* he served an apprenticeship of sorts with Medoff, doing occasional political stories when Medoff was away.[8] With Medoff's retirement, Neville assigned Borrelli to the political beat on a full-time basis. And with that change a different approach to our political reporting occurred. Borrelli was an objective reporter who did not follow a Republican or Democratic line in his approach, which was strictly factual reporting without the apparent bias that had pervaded much of the work of Medoff. Neville approved of Borrelli's approach. The GOP bias in the *News* remained where it should have been in the first place, in editorials. These continued to favor Republican candidates in the major races until the sale of the paper in 1977.[9]

Borrelli retired in June 1992 after twenty-nine years at the *News* and a total of thirty-eight years in the newspaper business. His was a distinguished career as a fine, objective reporter and he earned his reputation for integrity. He had good sources in both major parties. They respected his impartiality and willingness to listen and to report on all sides of any issue.[10]

It is in the area of critical analysis that sharing a critic's feelings creates vital links with the readers. Paul Neville in his brief tenure as editor brought two fine columnists to the *News* who had this capacity.

Janice Okun joined the paper in 1968 to take over the long popular "Kitchen Counsel" column. A Cornell University graduate with a degree in nutrition, Okun early on in her *News* career established her credentials by providing readers with good cooking advice for the average housewife, stressing recipes that were not expensive to create. The Taste Test panels she instituted quickly became reader favorites and her columns rating new packaged products also hit the mark with readers.[11]

Okun really became well known in 1974 when she started doing weekly restaurant reviews. She enjoyed doing them and readers became dedicated to the reviews. It quickly became common knowledge that when Okun wrote a favorable review of a restaurant it would become difficult to get a reservation in that place for weeks following the review. When she did a negative review, the restaurant didn't fare too well and Okun had to put up with complaints from the owners. She often would return to a restaurant for a second review to satisfy herself that her initial review was fair to the owner and to the patrons.[12]

Okun reviewed the high-priced restaurants in western New York and southern Ontario, but aware of the diversity of her readership she also reviewed those whose price range was significantly lower. Always aware of her impact on the patrons of a restaurant as well as on the ownership, she never used the sledgehammer approach in a review even she when gave a negative review of a restaurant.[13]

Well respected by her peers throughout the nation, Okun has served as president of the Society of Food Journalists and is one of the best-known newspaper food critics in the country. She has traveled extensively throughout the world, studying foods of various countries and bringing fresh ideas to her host of readers. As her editor, I always found her to be balanced in her approach. The only problem I ever had with her was her use in reviews of the word "veggies" when referring to vegetables. When I could tolerate it no longer, I ordered a ban on that juvenile word.[14]

One of the most popular features in the *News* for more than thirty-two years was the column written by Bob Curran, who was recruited by his close friend Paul Neville in June 1967. Curran was our in-house conservative who often would write that "I'm a flag waver and proud of it."[15]

An unabashed patriot, Curran had served as an Army Ranger in World War II, with service in France, Belgium, Luxembourg, Holland, and Germany. He was awarded the Silver Star, the Bronze Star, and two Purple Hearts. Through the years he dedicated hundreds of his columns to those serving in the armed forces and many were in the form of letters to GIs, keeping them informed about events on the home front.[16]

Curran, who wrote five columns a week for many years, was a great favorite of area veterans organizations, always ready to publicize their events. He was guest speaker at hundreds of functions sponsored by posts of the many veterans organizations. Invariably he would wind up his talks, as he did so many of his columns, urging his listeners and readers to "hang tough." A tireless champion of veterans' causes, he constantly urged his readers to "say a prayer for our guys over there."[17]

Curran came to the *News* with an interesting background. He had been the television editor of Fawcett Publications, editor of *Cavalier* magazine, the creator of radio and television ads for a New York advertising agency, sports publicity director for NBC, and sports columnist for the national publication known as *Family Weekly.* Curran authored seven books before joining the *News* staff. The first was *The Kennedy Women* published in 1963. In 1965 came publication of *The $400,000 Quarterback* [Joe Namath] *or the League that Came in from the Cold* about the American Football League. It made several bestseller lists.[18]

The very popular *News* columnist Bob Curran (*right*), author of "Curran's Corner." (Courtesy *Buffalo News*)

Curran had several favorite topics and wrote about them repeatedly year after year. In addition to his dedication to veterans and their organizations, he was a big Buffalo booster. He rarely had a good word to say about any member of the Kennedy family despite the fact that he was a native of Massachusetts. He consistently denied he had any animosity toward the Kennedys but a perusal of his columns over the years proves the opposite. On the lighter side, he enjoyed writing columns bashing outdoor picnics, a favorite activity of Buffalonians when the weather was good. These anti-picnic columns were written in a lighter vein and while many readers disagreed with his point of view, they obviously enjoyed his expression of distaste for the pastime.[19]

Curran was not a favorite of many *News* copyeditors who had to edit his material. He didn't believe in cleaning up his copy before turning it over to an editor. Correcting his spelling and grammatical errors was the bane of the existence of many copyeditors. His was a loose, breezy writing style that was quite readable when the finished, edited version appeared in the paper. Many of Curran's columns were written when he was "under the weather" after imbibing too many alcoholic beverages. The good work of editors frequently salvaged his final product.[20]

"Curran's Corner" was a very popular feature for more than three decades of his stay at the *News* prior to Bob's retirement. He was an outgoing, friendly person whose every spoken word was delivered through clenched teeth, a mannerism for which he became well known. Curran was a familiar figure on the lecture circuit, finding it difficult to turn down a request that he address groups. He always did so without any text or even notes but generally left behind a satisfied audience who enjoyed his many anecdotes and his patriotic themes. If you had to select a *News* staffer who most typically personified the old-time movie representation of a newspaperman, it would have to be Bob Curran. He was the recipient of countless national and local awards for his columns, particularly those dealing with veterans.[21] Curran retired in March 1999 and died on March 13, 2003, in a veterans home where he moved in 2001 to be closer to his sons.[22]

Another staffer who joined the *News* in 1967, the same year as Curran, followed a totally different career path. Unlike Curran, who had vast experience in the world of communications prior to being hired by the *News*, Lee Coppola only had limited summer experience with the Associated Press from 1962 to 1965 while still a student in St. Bonaventure's journalism program. He then served as an army information officer from 1965 to 1967. He joined the *News* in 1967 and from that time until 1983 was on general assignment and finally filled the role of an investigative reporter.[23]

With the contacts he developed in law-enforcement circles as well as in the underworld, Coppola made a name for himself writing on organized crime. In 1974 he produced a significant series on Stefano Magaddino. Titled "The Don Nobody Knew," the series about the underworld boss for some fifty years provided more facts and insight about the Mafia chieftain than had previously been disclosed.[24]

A year later, in 1975, Coppola produced a series of stories on Tom Leonhard's search for his children who were living with their mother and government informant Pascal Calabrese while Calabrese was hiding from the Mafia. A gripping story, Coppola's series prompted the movie *Hide in Plain Sight*.[25]

In January 1979 the *News* broke the first of a continuing series of Coppola stories on the Onyx Corporation, a so-called minority company, and its ties to Laborers Local 210, long an object of FBI scrutiny. Onyx had been awarded a significant contract for construction of Buffalo's Light Rail Rapid Transit system. Coppola's many months of research unearthed the facts that led to the downfall of Onyx.[26]

Coppola's standing in the community reached a high level following the excellent work he had been producing for the *News* and the local television stations were anxious to secure his services. In 1983 he signed with WKBW-TV as an investigative reporter and stayed there until 1987 when he shifted to WIVB-TV as its investigative reporter. He was with the station until 1992 when he was named assistant U.S. attorney for the western district of New York. He earned his law degree from the University of Buffalo in 1983 going to school nights while he was at the *News*. In 1996 he was invited to become the dean of journalism at St. Bonaventure University and has served in that role with distinction to the present time.[27]

Notes

1. Alfred Kirchhofer files, Butler Family Papers, E. H. Butler Library Archives, State University College at Buffalo, boxes 1, 5, 11; Alfred H. Kirchhofer Papers, Buffalo and Erie County Historical Society Archives, C67-6, box 20; Ralph Dibble, "The Buffalo Evening News Is Born," *Buffalo News* centennial publication, October 12, 1980, p. H-6.
2. *Buffalo News*, October 12, 1980, p. H-6.
3. Ibid.
4. Kirchhofer Papers, Historical Society, box 20.
5. *Buffalo Evening News*, June 23, 1969, and June 25, 1969; *Buffalo News*, October 12, 1980, p. H-6.
6. "Appeals Court Unanimous in Dome Ruling," *Buffalo Evening News*, November 19, 1971, p. 1.
7. *Buffalo News*, October 12, 1980, p. H-6.
8. Murray B. Light, "The News—Your Newspaper," *Buffalo Evening News*, June 19, 1979, second front page.
9. *Buffalo News* personnel files; Murray B. Light, "Your Newspaper," *Buffalo Evening News*, June 23, 1992, second front page.
10. Ibid.
11. *Buffalo News* personnel files; Murray B. Light, "Your Newspaper," *Buffalo Evening News*, February 19, 1980, second front page.
12. Ibid.
13. Ibid.
14. Ibid.
15. *Buffalo News* personnel files; Light, "The News—Your Newspaper," *Buffalo Evening News*, August 14, 1979 and November 13, 1979, second front page.
16. Ibid.
17. Ibid.
18. Ibid.
19. Ibid.
20. Ibid.
21. Ibid.
22. *Buffalo News* obituary, March 14, 2003, p. C1.
23. *Buffalo News* personnel files,
24. Ibid.
25. Ibid.
26. Ibid.
27. Ibid.

12 Dissension in the Family

Following the death of Edward H. Butler Jr. on February 18, 1956,[1] his wife, Kate Butler, designated her son-in-law, James H. Righter, as publisher and vice president of the *News*. He was the third publisher in the newspaper's history.[2] The new publisher had married the Butlers' daughter, Kate, in 1943. A native of Philadelphia, he attended the Drexel Institute of Technology and the U.S. Naval Academy. He achieved the rank of a lieutenant commander in the navy when he was discharged in February 1946. Following his navy service, Righter joined the business staff of the *News* in April 1946 and was named assistant business manager in April 1949.[3]

Righter was an effective publisher, concentrating his efforts on advertising, circulation, and production and wisely leaving editorial matters in the hands of Kirchhofer. The relationship of Righter and Kirchhofer never approached the level of trust and cooperation that previously had existed between Butler and Kirchhofer but it was a satisfactory one nevertheless. They respected each other and Righter, aware of the high regard Mrs. Butler had for AHK and his long history and knowledge of the *News* people and practices, would counsel him from time to time on matters that normally would not be in the editor's domain.[4]

Kirchhofer became involved in an internal dispute that was not of his making but which resulted in his having to take a stand against a member of the *News* ownership, which he revered so greatly. It started with a March 7, 1960, article in *Time* magazine headlined "The Voice of Buffalo."* The *Time* piece, illustrated with a picture of AHK, stated, "*The Buffalo News* is a big circulation, powerful and prosperous example of the U.S. provincial daily, whose voice rings commandingly at home but is rarely heard outside. The city's brawling political affairs are covered . . . with the thoroughness of a paper whose editor believes that politics and government turns out to be our job."[5]

"The *News* Republicanism," the *Time* article continued, "usually confined to the editorial page, gives local Democrats the conniptions. The *News* remained in the hands of Butler's heirs but Alfred H. Kirchhofer runs it. . . . On the *News* masthead his name stands above that of the publisher, James H. Righter, a Butler son-in-law."[6]

"The *News* stylebook, largely drafted by Kirchhofer and cast in his own stern image, warns that 'motherhood is treated as an institution, not as a situation comedy.' The *News* has become an ingrained Buffalo habit that grew with the city, and faithfully reflects its image: solid, conservative, industrious, and at first glance, colorless."[7]

The *Time* article, basically a positive piece of national publicity for the *News*, infuriated Kent McKinley, husband of Marge McKinley, granddaughter of Edward H. Butler Sr. and a vice president of the paper. On March 8 he fired off a letter to Mrs. Butler, *News* president, as proxy for his wife. He wrote,

> We were amazed and annoyed at the article that appeared in *Time Magazine* giving Alf Kirchhofer the big buildup at the expense of the Butler family. . . . It would be my suggestion that the first order of business is to change the masthead of the *Buffalo Evening News* and it would appear appropriate that Mr. Kirchhofer's retirement be considered for the good of the morale of the newspaper. His story did the owners little good and was ill advised. There are younger men available that can't be kept on indefinitely if the iron rule carries on of a past decade. It's time for a change.[8]

---

*©1960 TIME Inc., reprinted by permission.

The McKinley letter was a bombshell in the executive offices of the *News*. Legendary AHK was being challenged as never before. Publisher James Righter on March 22 sent Kirchhofer a memo stating that Mrs. Butler "has directed that the masthead be modified so that my name as publisher appears directly below the name of Mrs. Butler as president and above yours as editor. *Time* gave the appearance of a break in the continuity of the Butler family."[9]

James H. Righter, publisher, 1956–1971. (Courtesy *Buffalo News*)

Two days later, on March 24, Kirchhofer responded to Righter with a memo to Mrs. Butler in which he stated, "The sequence in which the names have appeared in the masthead since you became president specifically was directed by you. It was done at a time when, you will recall, I urged and pleaded that Mr. Righter be appointed publisher. . . . I did not see the article nor did I have any inkling as to what might be printed."[10]

The AHK note to Mrs. Butler added that he refused to pose for a picture for *Time* and that he told the writer nothing about himself. "I have worked at my job day and night," the obviously upset editor said. He then went on to relate his accomplishments at the paper and the radio and TV stations, and ends his uncharacteristically long memo with the statement that "I have great respect for family pride. I submit that much of what I did over the years has enhanced the prestige of the Butler family. Family pride also entails noblesse oblige which I think has been afforded to me in the present circumstance because I have been blamed for something for which I have no responsibility whatever."[11]

On March 25 Righter ordered the change in the *News* masthead, placing his name above Kirchhofer's. The ugly episode, the only

(*From left*) Mrs. Edward H. Butler; James H. Righter; his wife, Kate Butler Righter; and their children, Edward and Kate. (Courtesy *Buffalo News*)

known one in AHK's long, illustrious career with the *News*, was finally over.[12]

In 1960 William M. Fallis came to the *News* as a temporary consultant to Righter to work on circulation problems relating to the startup of the then new north edition. To boost circulation, the *News* wanted to start special sections in the paper for a particular geographic area. The north edition would carry stories of special interest to readers living in the suburbs located north of the city. At that time a Pittsburgh consulting firm employed Fallis. Righter was impressed by Fallis and hired him as assistant to the publisher in September 1960. He reported directly to Righter and had many responsibilities assigned to him by the publisher. In April 1968 Righter asked Fallis to chair a committee planning the future home of the *News* at Scott and Washington streets.[13]

Two days after Executive Editor Paul Neville's untimely death on June 22, 1969, I was summoned to Jim Righter's office. He informed me that he was going to announce the next day my appointment as managing editor for news and Elwood M. Wardlow, then an assistant managing editor, as managing editor for administration. The arrangement was unusual and somewhat unique at that time in the newspaper business. Righter was aware of that but said he decided on this path to take advantage of what he felt were the strengths of both of us. He also acknowledged that it might create some internal conflicts but he felt that given our close friendly relations over the years, problems of jurisdiction could easily be overcome.[14]

Righter made it plain that as managing editor for news I would be in total control of all nonpaid matter in the *News*, with the exception of the editorial page, which would be the responsibility of Millard Browne, editorial page editor. I would, however, be a member of the editorial board and Righter said he anticipated that I would have significant input on the *News* editorial page policies.[15]

Wardlow, Righter said, would in effect continue the work he had assumed under Neville as an assistant managing editor. He would handle the numerous administrative duties involved in an organization of some two hundred newsroom employees. He also would be primarily responsible for dealing with the Newspaper Guild, the union that represented newsroom personnel, and he would continue his role in working with editorial department heads on scheduling vacations and days off to minimize overtime. Interviewing and hiring newsroom interns and maintaining the very important role of representing the *News* in dialogue with community leadership and organizations were his responsibilities.[16]

Righter respected the judgment and authority of the editor and basically kept his hands off editorial matters. He did hold weekly luncheon meetings with Wardlow and Millard Browne and myself. The focus of these Buffalo Club sessions generally was on state and local political matters. He rarely was peremptory in ordering a specific editorial stance but was successful in planting seeds of what positions he would be happiest to see the paper espouse.

Wardlow and I and our spouses experienced several highly enjoyable visits to Washington, DC, as guests of Righter and his wife, Kate, at the annual Gridiron dinner weekends. Washington bureau chief Lucian Warren was the *News* Gridiron Club member during that period and he and his wife, Katherine, were extremely gracious in entertaining the Buffalo contingent from the *News*. During these years only men were allowed to attend the Gridiron dinner but Jim and Kate always planned a weekend that was enjoyable for all. A highlight of the trip for several years was the invitation to attend Sunday morning services and breakfast at the White House. Richard Nixon was president and he and his wife and their two daughters were always in attendance. The Reverend Dr. Billy Graham conducted the service each year. At the breakfast following the service, President Nixon, who always was gracious during these affairs, generally engaged me in conversation about the Buffalo Bills.

Lucian C. Warren succeeded Finney in 1968 as *News* Washington bureau chief. The Jamestown native, who retired from full-time *News* duties in 1978 after ten years as bureau chief, followed in the path of his predecessors, achieving top positions in the Washington journalism community.[17] Prior to his retirement, Warren at various stages in his career was president of the National Press Club, president of the Gridiron Club, and chairman of the Standing Committee of Correspondents. Veteran Washington correspondents could not recall any other correspondent of a regional newspaper who had held all three of these important posts.[18]

Warren was the second *Buffalo News* reporter to be elected president of the Press Club, following in the footsteps of its first Washington correspondent, Kirchhofer, who held that position in 1927. Old-time club members credit Warren with leading the fight to break the color line at the club when he was president in 1955. Warren for years was the most popular and respected member of the Gridiron Club. After his term as president was completed, Warren served for many years as secretary of the Gridiron Club and in that post was the most influential member in allocation of tickets to its dinners, a commodity that was scarce and treasured by the nation's leading politicians and journalists. Warren also was a participant for many years in the cast of journalists who annually staged the famed Gridiron Club shows at the dinner.[19] The cast of the show was always made up of members of the Gridiron Club although professional actors and actresses in a few vital roles supplemented it. The late Carl Rowan, a former Buffalonian and a well-known columnist and author, was always in the show because he had an excellent singing voice. Members of the club write the script and the songs of the show, which is a good-natured roast of political events and people in the news.

Warren's newspaper career started with the *Jamestown Evening Journal* when he was still in high school. He then worked as a reporter for the *Buffalo Courier-Express* from 1937 to 1943 and became its Washington correspondent in 1945. In 1968 he was recruited by the *News* to head up its Washington bureau, following the passing of Nat Finney.[20]

Like Finney, Warren did not confine his reporting to the activities of Buffalo-area congressmen. He enjoyed covering the White House and was a familiar figure at the *News* desk in the White House pressroom. In 1970 he wrote a comprehensive series featuring exclusive interviews with the Nixon cabinet and top members of the White House staff. His bylines for the *News* covered stories from Vietnam, Eastern Europe, and Scandinavia as he accompanied President Nixon on many of his overseas trips.[21]

Among the many honors accorded Warren was an Ernie Pyle Award for the stories he wrote from Vietnam. In 1986 he was inducted into the Journalism Hall of Fame of the Washington Chapter of the Society of Professional Journalists. A man of enormous energy and enthusiasm with a winning, infectious laugh, Warren had many friends among the nation's political leaders as well as the Washington press corps. He loved his work and his capacity for it was amazing. In addition to his regular job, he was published from time to time in *Esquire*, *Parade*, and the *New York Times Magazine*, *Family Weekly*, and other periodicals.[22]

After his retirement, he and his wife, Katherine, traveled around the world and Warren filed numerous dispatches for the *News* during that journey. A Phi Beta Kappa graduate of Denison University, Warren never lost his thirst for learning. He died at the age of seventy-five on December 12, 1988.[23]

Jim Righter's alcoholic intake at our Buffalo Club weekly luncheon meetings increased by early 1970 to a disturbing level. It was difficult to believe how he could function properly after consumption of two and often three of the very potent club martinis. Righter did return to his office after these luncheons but his ability to perform his duties those afternoons had to be impaired by his luncheon libations.

Righter was active in community affairs during the period that he was *News* publisher. He was a director and later board chairman of the Buffalo Philharmonic Orchestra, a director of the Buffalo Fine Arts Academy, and chairman of the board of trustees of Villa Maria College. He attended numerous luncheons and dinners.[24]

A well-spoken and articulate man, he always was well groomed and affable. Righter was on good terms with many of Buffalo's top business and community leaders and was a well-liked and respected spokesman for the *News*. Politically he was fully aligned with the Republican loyalties of Mrs. Butler and Kirchhofer, although he basically was not an active political participant.[25]

Mrs. Butler was spending a good deal of time during the years of her presidency in her favorite country, France. When she was in residence at her Delaware Avenue mansion, she would hold weekly luncheons there with the top executives of all the *News* departments and was briefed on what was taking place in her company. As time went on, it became apparent that she and her son-in-law did not get along too well. There was no open break, however, until the fall of 1971.

There had been recurring reports from various sources that Righter was having an affair with his secretary. At one point earlier in the summer of 1971 I broached the subject with Righter and cautioned him that his mother-in-law was bound to pick up on these rumors from her Buffalo friends. Righter's response was that it didn't matter because, he said, she could not operate the paper without him at the helm. Unfortunately for him, Righter had underestimated the wrath of Mrs. Butler when she learned about his affair and his career at the *News* ended quickly. I was at my desk in the newsroom one day early in September 1971 when my phone rang at about eleven in the morning. It was Mrs. Butler who, without any preliminaries, summarily ordered me to announce that Mr. Righter no longer was the *News* publisher, and was no longer an employee. Mrs. Butler would assume the role of publisher. She did not cite any specifics but I knew what had brought it on.

After a momentary pause, I regained my composure and told her that we should not be making an announcement of that import in the midst of a publishing cycle, especially since the first edition of that day already was running. I suggested that she and I meet and determine how we would couch the announcement and how it would be played in the paper. Initially, she insisted that she wanted no delay in informing the public but then reluctantly agreed to wait until the next day.

Mrs. Butler and I did meet later that afternoon and the announcement about Righter appeared on the main local page of the *News* the next day with the customary phrase that he would be pursuing other interests. Righter was fifty-four at the time. He and his wife divorced and he later remarried and took up residence in Amherst while continuing with some of his earlier community associations. He died on June 9, 1984, at the age of sixty-seven.

I was saddened by Righter's fate at the *News*. He had been a good publisher and we had established a good relationship. I would never forget that he was responsible for my status at the paper, promoting me to managing editor upon the death of Paul Neville. At the same time, he had also named Elwood M. Wardlow managing editor for administration and the two of us worked together for eight years after Righter left the paper. What I described in a column addressed to readers as a "shotgun wedding" for Wardlow and myself continued for ten years, finally terminating on November 1, 1979, with Woody's resignation from the *News*.[26] The arrangement of dual managing editors worked well for some years but frankly deteriorated with the passage of time as conflicts between the managing editors began to surface and fester. When Warren Buffett assumed control of the paper he expressed his disenchantment with the arrangement and in various subtle ways let his unhappiness become known. Many felt that Wardlow became increasingly aware of the owner's feelings and that he wisely decided after twenty-seven years at the paper that it was time for him to explore other options. After leaving the *News*, he became an associate director of the American Press Institute, a role that he enjoyed and in which he performed exceptionally well.

After Jim Righter's departure, William Fallis stayed with the paper. When Henry Urban became publisher in 1974, he named Fallis a senior vice president and treasurer, with all department heads reporting to him except editorial and accounting. He represented Urban on the Blue Chip Committee planning the start of thc *Sunday News*. He was respected for his ability to resolve complex problems and for getting people to work together to resolve problems. He left the *News* after its sale to Warren Buffett and took up residence in Florida.[27] About the same time, George T. Mosely also departed. Mosely had been the chief labor negotiator for the paper for many years with the thirteen unions that represented employees.[28]

Notes

1. *Buffalo Evening News*, obituary, February 20, 1956.

2. "Kirchhofer Era Begins," *Buffalo News* centennial publication, October 12, 1980, p. H-6.

3. Ibid.

4. Ibid.

5. "The Voice of Buffalo," *Time*, March 7, 1960, pp. 66, 69; Alfred H. Kirchhofer Papers, Buffalo and Erie County Historical Society Archives, C67-6, box 17.

6. Ibid.

7. Ibid.

8. Kate Robinson Butler files, Butler Family Papers, E. H. Butler Library Archives, State University College at Buffalo, box 1.

9. Ibid.

10. Ibid.

11. Ibid.

12. Ibid.

13. Ibid., "Corporate Suite Key to News Family," *Buffalo News*, October 12, 1980, p. H-14.

14. "The *News* Appoints Two as Managing Editors," *Buffalo Evening News*, June 30, 1969.

15. "Kirchhofer Era Begins at the *News*," *Buffalo News*, October 12, 1980, p. H-6.

16. Ibid.

17. *Buffalo Evening News*, obituary, October 12, 1980.

18. Ibid.

19. Ibid.

20. Ibid.

21. Ibid.

22. Ibid.

23. Ibid.

24. *Buffalo News* personnel files.

25. "Kirchhofer Era Begins."

26. Murray B. Light, "The News—Your Newspaper," *Buffalo Evening News*, October 27, 1979, second front page.

27. "Corporate Suite Key to News Family," *Buffalo News*, October 12, 1980, p. H-14.

28. *Buffalo News* personnel files.

13 The Support Team

When publisher James Righter named two managing editors, Elwood M. Wardlow and myself, to run newsroom operations, he created a situation that had never before existed at the *News*.

I felt comfortable in my ability to carry out my responsibilities and to allay concerns of staffers. I made a determination that my initial moves would be glacial rather than draconian. I had no desire to see *Editor & Publisher* headlines about major changes in the *Buffalo Evening News*. Moves I felt had to be made would be done a step at a time over an extended period.

Wardlow and I were well known to the staff but there was considerable newsroom speculation on how the unique split of responsibilities could be carried out without friction. Wardlow and I were aware of possible problems but were convinced that our long-term friendship would carry us smoothly over the bumps in the road that inevitably would arise.

Longtime staffers were fully aware that Wardlow enjoyed involvement in administrative details that I looked upon as minor irritations and really preferred not to be bothered with. For the most part they also respected my news judgment, my abhorrence for those who

Elwood M. Wardlow (Woody), managing editor for administration, 1969–1979. (Courtesy *Buffalo News*)

would even attempt to influence news stories and news play, and my willingness to challenge any *News* executive or outsider who attempted to influence newsroom judgment.

Almost from day one of my appointment, I had made a determination to call a halt to a practice of Kirchhofer's that I had long felt was reprehensible and out of step with the journalism of the day, although it was not considered in that light during his days as editor—namely, his deep involvement in Republican Party politics.

The matter, in fact, came to a head rather quickly. Shortly after my promotion, Erie County Republican bigwigs and the party's chief financial supporters asked for a meeting to discuss *News* support for candidates they were considering for endorsement. I categorically rejected their overtures, saying the *News* would not participate in prejudgment of any candidate. That, I told them quite emphatically, was the role of the party and not of the *News*. I informed them that the paper would pass judgment on candidates for public office only after they were officially candidates of their party.

It took about three years before the GOP leadership finally gave up badgering me to participate in selection of their candidates, a role they insisted Kirchhofer had always played. They were quite upset with my stance, which I emphasized would not change. The GOP chieftains never made reference to Neville having followed Kirchhofer's practice of party involvement.

Prior to Neville's death and my promotion, I had been news editor, a very important role in the *News* newsroom establishment. All local and wire copy flows from various desks of origin to the news desk, where a determination is made of how stories will be positioned in the paper and how much space will be allocated to each one. The news editor, who has several assistants, has to have a good relationship with the managing editor. He confers with him frequently during each publication cycle. A key operative in the newsroom operation, the news editor has to have the confidence of the chief newsroom operative; has to have a commanding personality to deal with the city editor, wire editor, and copydesk chief; has to be able to make decisions quickly and competently; has to have the patience to deal with those who challenge decisions or are not able to provide the immediate answers he needs to make the vital editorial decisions. The news editor has to be strong, confident, and intelligent. He has to pass judgment on countless stories each day and although he confers regularly with the supervising editor of the newsroom, he has to review and make judgments on dozens of stories without any assistance from his superior.

I had no difficulty deciding on who to name as my successor in the news editor's role. Foster Spencer had been my first assistant on the news desk since 1967 and had proven he could effectively assume the role as leader of the news desk. Spencer joined the *News* in January 1966 as a copyeditor. He had been employed previously as the Sunday editor and a feature editor for the *Springfield Republican* in Massachusetts.[1]

Spencer could best be characterized as a "newspaperman's newsman" who loved his work, had excellent news judgment, and was always aware of the sensitivities of readers. He was totally candid and pulled no punches in expressing his feelings and in saying what he believed. He was well liked and respected by the staff, all of whom were aware that Spencer's prime motivation at all times was to produce a paper that would meet the needs of his mythical reader, "Sweeney."

In his role as news editor, Spencer invariably made the news judgment calls that I rarely felt the need to challenge. When I was away from the newsroom, I always felt comfortable knowing that he was calling the shots and would do nothing that would come back to haunt me later.

Spencer's prime interests were sports, crossword puzzles, golf, and wine making. He was respected by members of other *News* departments and frequently was called upon to emcee their retirement parties. The vast storehouse of jokes that he delivered so well made him ideal for these affairs.

Spencer participated in many professional organizations, serving as president of the State Society of Newspaper Editors in 1983–1984 and as president of the State Associated Press Managing Editors Association in 1976–1977. He frequently served as a judge in many secondary school and college newspaper competitions. He lost his battle with lung cancer on March 27, 1997, at the age of sixty-four. He had been a respected and valuable member of the *News* staff.[2]

At the time I appointed Spencer news editor, I advanced Bill Malley to the position of assistant news editor, starting him on his successful path to newsroom management positions that he held until his untimely death at an early age in 1989. Malley had served from time to time on the news desk and loved the assignment. He had proven that he had all the attributes needed for full-time employment on that desk. In fact, some years later, in October 1977, Malley was very upset when I informed him that the *News* was going to start publication of a weekly Sunday magazine in its new Sunday paper and that I wanted him to serve as the magazine's editor. Malley, who was never reticent about venting his opinions, vigorously protested his assignment to this important position.[3]

Certain that he had the organizational skills, judgment, and flair necessary to launch a Sunday magazine, I resisted Malley's pleas that he be permitted to remain on the news desk. He reluctantly started work on putting together the magazine. As I had anticipated, he did a splendid job of formulating a publication in a very short period of time.

In 1982, following the close of the *Courier-Express*, I utilized Malley's talents in the formulation of our new sunrise edition, and for the next five years he supervised its publication. In 1987 I handed him another challenging assignment, the redesign of the entire newspaper. Working with our outside consultant, Malley met with all newsroom department heads and numerous reporters and editors, lessening their concerns about changes to be made.

(*From left*) Murray B. Light, editor, and his top newsroom managers, Foster Spencer, Bill Malley, and Ed Cuddihy, in a 1980 photo. (Photo by Robert Stoddard, courtesy *Buffalo News*)

Unfortunately, this fine newspaperman's life came to a premature end at the age of forty-nine when he was killed in an automobile accident in May 1989. He was, as I said in a farewell tribute to him, "a hard-driving perfectionist, a man of conscience, a man for whom no detail was too small, a man with a probing mind who never was afraid to challenge the accepted. And an editor who had an abiding concern for fairness and for the reputation of the person about whom we wrote."[4]

I had great respect and admiration for Malley, whom I had dubbed my "madman." I could always depend on him to challenge any decision I made that bothered him for any reason and the ensuing dialogue with him was invariably productive. To his credit, when final decisions were made, Malley carried them out faithfully. Malley was a deputy managing editor at the time of his fatal accident.[5]

In putting together my management team, I had no problem in deciding the name of the person I needed to run the all-important city desk in the role of city editor. Ed Cuddihy had started his career at the *News* as a summer intern and became a staffer in June 1961. In his reporting years he earned the plaudits of his editors for his maturity, intelligence, and dedication and in April 1967 he was named an assistant city editor. I, as news editor, had observed Cuddihy's editing skills and his ability to relate well to the reporting staff. When Bud Wacker decided to take early retirement in April 1977, my choice to succeed him was easy. Cuddihy became the *News* city editor that month and, as I had anticipated, he became a steady, reliable, unflappable editor in a most difficult and sensitive job. In recognition of his fine work, I named him an assistant managing editor in November 1979.[6]

After Cuddihy had proven without any doubt his management abilities, ten years later I again promoted Cuddihy, naming him a deputy managing editor. This was in recognition of his fine city desk oversight plus the added responsibilities he had taken on as the key newsroom overseer of the ever-growing electronic systems and some personnel responsibilities beyond the normal scope of the city editor. Cuddihy had become a very important newsroom management personality and had fully earned his promotions and the respect of the entire staff.

The *News* was one of the last major metropolitan newspapers in the country to convert newsroom production from paper to computer. The metamorphosis took place in 1985 under Cuddihy's direction. Offering him the leadership role in the conversion was an easy decision, given his previously acquired knowledge in the field. Typewriters were phased out, and all staffers produced their stories on computers. All editors did their jobs on computers as well, with output going directly to the composing room for typesetting. Cuddihy was relieved of his city desk responsibilities so that he could direct all his efforts to set up a computer front-end operation for the newsroom. He set up a systematic program of training for staffers, to implement the transition to an SII front-end system department by department. In the four-month period from June through September, Cuddihy's targets were implemented with only occasional delays. Working with Cuddihy on some of the technical problems was the very capable Barry Breig, at that time *News* director of systems.

About a year later, in the fall of 1986, the Apple-MacIntosh graphics system was introduced in the graphics department, again under Cuddihy's direction with the assistance of Breig and staff artist John Davis.

Thanks to Cuddihy's efforts and the fine cooperation of various department heads, the transition to electronic systems suffered few of the problems encountered in many newspapers. The first-generation systems have long been replaced by upgraded, more sophisticated ones serving the newsroom and the production departments.[7]

Cuddihy's great work ethic, outstanding relationship with staffers, and loyalty to the *News* and its top executives was capped in 1999 with his promotion to one of two managing editor positions by my successor as editor, Margaret Sullivan. It was a choice that was well received by newsroom staffers as well as members of other *News* departments.

One of the most emotionally upsetting events during my stint as managing editor involved Louis (Bud) Wacker, a longtime colleague who had joined the *News* the same year that I did. Wacker's involvement with the paper actually preceded mine since he served as its University of Buffalo campus correspondent while still a student. His fine work in that role led to his being hired as a reporter.

In his eight years as a reporter Wacker proved his versatility, his toughness, and his ability to function in various capacities. He reported on local men serving in the Korean War, did fine reporting on a trip to Antarctica, and on an entirely different level proved his worth in covering the state legislature in Albany. In 1957 he joined the city desk as an assistant city editor and quickly proved worthy of the assignment. In 1960 he was promoted to city editor.[8]

As city editor Wacker was tough, demanding excellence at all times, and concerned only with results from his staff. He never wanted to hear excuses for less than the best performance. In recognition of his fine work he was promoted to assistant managing editor and in 1973 to deputy managing editor.[9]

As managing editor, I met with Wacker each morning to discuss the day's local news agenda and a myriad of staff matters. Additionally, he and I conferred countless times each day. With the passage of time, staff complaints about Wacker began to mount. The people reporting to him felt he was too tough, too demanding, and often rude in dealing with them. Most respected his ability but said he was abrasive and that they could not establish a relationship with him that would be conducive to improved performance on their part.

I talked to him repeatedly about the changing times and changing newsroom environment that mandated he ease up in his relations with staffers, explaining that his demeanor was counterproductive. Finally, I suggested that it might be time for him to change jobs after he informed me that he didn't feel that at this stage of his career he could change his approach.

In 1977 Wacker resigned and joined the Buffalo State Teachers College journalism faculty.[10] I hated to lose a good friend and fine city editor, but he and I agreed it was best for all concerned. He was on the college faculty for ten years and was instrumental in turning a mediocre program into a good one. Upon retirement, he went to Florida and later returned to Buffalo in 1999. He died on February 8, 2001, at the age of eighty- two.[11]

Notes

1. *Buffalo News*, obituary, March 28, 1997.
2. Ibid.
3. Murray B. Light, "Your Newspaper," *Buffalo News*, December 8, 1987, second front page.
4. *Buffalo News*, obituary, May 1, 1989.
5. Ibid.; Murray B. Light, "Your Newspaper," *Buffalo News*, May 2, 1989, second front page.
6. Light, "Your Newspaper," December 8, 1987.
7. *Buffalo News* executive committee meeting, October 4, 1986.
8. *Buffalo News*, October 12, 1980, p. H-8.
9. Ibid.
10. Ibid.
11. *Buffalo News* personnel files.

14 Another Butler Publisher

Born in Atlanta, Kate Maddox Robinson attended Wesleyan Female College and married Edward H. Butler Jr. on February 2, 1909. They had a child who was born in 1915 but died a few years later in 1919. A second child, Kate, later became the wife of James Righter in 1943.[1]

In 1962 Kate Butler gained full control of the *News* and its radio and television stations by buying the minority interest held by Mrs. Kent McKinley of Sarasota. Mrs. McKinley was a granddaughter of Edward H. Butler Sr. Her mother, Ada, had inherited 40 percent of the *News* from her father and she in turn left it to her daughter, Mrs. McKinley, upon her death in 1934. As part of the sale agreement, Mrs. McKinley resigned as vice president from the *News* board in return for forty-eight thousand shares of stock and $1.4 million for *News* bonds.[2]

Following her dismissal of Righter, Mrs. Butler assumed the duties of the *News* publisher in addition to her role as president.[3] A strong-willed woman, Mrs. Butler, who previously had spent much of her time in Paris, took her responsibilities very seriously and was generally in her office six days a week once she became publisher.[4]

Kate Robinson Butler, *News* president (1956–1974) and publisher (1971–1974), and WBEN president (1967–1974). (Butler Family Papers, courtesy E. H. Butler Library Archives, Buffalo State College)

I met with Kate Butler some months after Righter had named me managing editor in 1969. She was back in Buffalo after another stay in Paris and she summoned me to her office. She wanted me to know that she had not been aware that Righter had named me managing editor and although she had nothing personal against me she felt I was too young for such an important role at the *News*. I was forty-three at the time. I suggested that many of the editors and even publishers in the Gannett newspaper chain were younger than I. She dismissed that as irrelevant and said that she thought Righter had made a mistake in his appointment. It was the first and last time she ever brought that subject up.

It was after she assumed the role of publisher in 1971 that I got to know Mrs. Butler well. The phone at my desk would invariably ring every Saturday morning at almost exactly the same time—10:45—and it was always Mrs. Butler's secretary informing me that "Mrs. B" would like to meet with me if I could spare a few minutes. My response, naturally, was that it would be fine. The "few minutes" generally lasted at least thirty and often sixty or more minutes. We became good friends and I looked forward to these sessions. The subject matter of our conversations ranged widely with Mrs. B letting me know her thoughts on many subjects, particularly on people she liked or disliked, but never giving me any specific orders.

These weekly sessions in Mrs. Butler's office gave me an opportunity that not too many at the *News* had to learn a good deal about her. Seated behind her beautiful, leather-topped semicircular desk that she had imported from France, when upset Kate Butler would rise from her chair, pull herself up to her full stature of slightly more than five feet, and pound her desk. She could be stubborn and not easily swayed from her strongly held opinions.

For the first seven months or so of those weekly sessions, I never failed to bring up the matter of the *News*'s refusal of engagement or wedding photos of African American women. None had ever appeared in our Saturday "Society Pages." I said that the policy had to be changed, that it was discriminatory, and that it ignored an ever-increasing segment of the city's population.

Week after week, Mrs. Butler rebuffed my overtures on the subject. A southerner by birth and upbringing, she retained the prejudices of her youth. But the breakthrough came when I informed her that the state Human Rights Commission had made an inquiry about our practices in this area. Her immediate reaction was that the *News* was her property and she could do as she pleased but almost in the same breath she told me to go ahead and start using photos of African American engagement and wedding pictures. She did so with great reluctance and with the warning that it wouldn't take long before black women would dominate the society pages. I assured her that this would not happen, and that our major problem would be to encourage them to submit their photos, given the past practice of the *News*. In fact, even now, so many decades after the shift in policy, the *News* still does not receive sufficient submissions from African Americans despite efforts to encourage them.

My good relationship with Mrs. Butler suffered a severe setback at one point. I had purchased the serial publication rights to *My Life with Jacqueline Kennedy* by Mary Gallagher, personal secretary to Mrs.

Kennedy before, during, and after John F. Kennedy became president. The book detailed Gallagher's experiences in the White House and matters that previously had not been made public. We preceded publication of the first installment with radio and television spots and many house ads in the paper informing our readers of the coming event.

The *News* at the time was a six-day afternoon publication and the first chapter of the book was scheduled for Saturday publication. On the scheduled launch day, I received a call that Mrs. Butler wanted to see me immediately. That was surprising since it was not the customary 10:45 call to summon me for our weekly meeting. When I entered her office, I could immediately see that the publisher was very upset. I quickly found out why.

She informed me that she had heard on television the previous night that the *News* would be publishing the memoirs of Mrs. Kennedy's White House secretary. In no uncertain words, Mrs. Butler let me know that she would never want any of her hired help to write about her private affairs and that it was reprehensible to publish such a book.

I informed her that we had been advertising publication of the book for several weeks and that I was surprised that she was not aware of it until this time. The first edition of that day's paper was about to go to press with the initial chapter of the book serialization on the front page. Mrs. Butler pounded on her desk and vigorously restated that she was totally opposed to its publication and wanted me to immediately pull it from the paper.

My rejoinder was surprise and I said that we had to go forward with the book serialization given all the advance publicity. I'll never forget her exact words to me, "Mr. Light, you know how I feel about this. Go back to your desk and think about it and get back to me in half an hour with your decision on what you are going to do. I feel strongly about this."

I returned to her office about twenty minutes later and informed her that I was sorry to have to go against her specific order but given the circumstances, I was committed to going forward with publication of the book serialization, starting that day. It was then that she dropped the bombshell, saying that given that she had no alternative but to inform me there was no need for me to report to work Monday. I had been fired.

Returning home after the first edition press run ended, I informed my wife of the day's events. I had not anticipated that I would be fired but I was confident I could find new employment rather quickly although I was very saddened about ending my *News* career on such a sour note. She agreed that I could not go back on my word to *News* readers.

Later that day, my wife and I and our three children were at the dinner table when the phone rang. My eldest daughter answered and informed me that Mrs. Butler was on the line. Mrs. Butler wasted no words. I can recall almost verbatim her conversation.

"Mr. Light, I've been upset all afternoon at the action I took this morning over our disagreement. Frankly, I was surprised that you would not follow my dictates. I am not used to any of my executives going against my orders.

"But, angry as I was with you, I do realize that your courage in standing up to me was an indication of your integrity, a trait that is good in an editor. I want you to continue to be my editor and I'll see you in the office Monday. Good evening, Mr. Light."

I took the initiative that Monday of requesting a meeting with Mrs. Butler. After thanking her for reconsidering her action, I informed her that out of consideration for her feelings, I would give orders that the book serialization be carried on inside pages of the *News* rather than on the front page. I also told her that I had read all of the segments again and removed several passages that I thought would offend her. She thanked me and from that point on our good relationship was reestablished, with the incident never again mentioned.

One of the major decisions Kate Butler had to make after the death of her husband related to a new office building for the *News* at Scott and Washington streets. Mr. Butler pursued the idea for some time, realizing the need to unify the editorial and business operations with the press building facility already in place there. No final decision had been made at the time of his death.[5]

Mrs. Butler's preference was to remain at 218 Main Street, an address with which the *News* had been identified for so many years. But she had come to the realization that the city was determined to move ahead with its redevelopment project and needed the Main

Street site. She reluctantly told the board of directors to move ahead with plans for an office building at Scott and Washington.[6]

Having made this decision, Mrs. Butler then involved herself deeply in the project. She selected the architectural firm of Edward Durell Stone after visiting several of the projects he had designed. She was determined that the new *News* building would be a tribute to her late husband and in fact shocked other executives of the paper when she informed Stone's people that cost was not a factor. She wanted a beautiful building, one that would win the plaudits of the newspaper industry, as did the one built under the senior Edward H. Butler's stewardship at 218 Main Street in 1896.[7]

Unfortunately, Mrs. Butler never did see the interior of the *News* building at One News Plaza. By the time construction had reached a point of near completion, her health had deteriorated to a point that she could not enter the building. She was driven around the perimeter of the structure one day and she was satisfied by the assurance of others that it would have made her proud. The *News* occupied its new office building in April of 1973.[8]

My weekly Saturday meetings with Mrs. Butler took a strange twist in 1974, the last year of her life. She had become obsessed with death and week after week she brought up the subject, initially ordering that when she passed away her age was not to be mentioned in the obituary. Her grandson, Edward Butler Righter, told me later that she was so vain about her age that even the family was unsure how old she was when she died.

When she did pass away on Saturday, August 3, 1974,[9] I was out of town and received a call at the hotel where I was staying from the Associated Press in New York City. The editor in charge said that AP wanted to put an obituary of Mrs. Butler on the national wire but had a problem because nobody at the *News* knew her age and the AP rule mandated that an age had to be included in obituaries. I informed the AP editor that I had promised Mrs. Butler that her age would be kept confidential upon her death and that I would not divulge the information. But because I felt it was important that the obituary go out on the AP wire, I convinced him to just say that she was in her nineties. He agreed and that's the way it appeared in newspapers around the country.

Her concern about age can be attributed to vanity and was not that unusual a request but her other statements and requests of me can, I believe, only be attributed to a deterioration of her mental processes, not unusual in a person of her age. She was convinced that "they will bury me when I am still alive" and wanted me to stick a dagger in her heart to make sure she was dead before she was buried.

I heard that statement repeated frequently in her last year. She never identified whom she meant by "they." She also insisted that I promise to be at her wake to affirm that she was indeed dead and to check on her body from time to time to be sure that "they" were not burying her alive.

I did not succeed in convincing her that her fears were unfounded, but to keep her calm I did pledge that my wife and I would be at the wake daily until her burial. We kept that promise. The wake was held in the Butler mansion on Delaware Avenue and my wife and I were the only two nonfamily members in attendance throughout the two days and evenings.

Mrs. Butler's will, dated October 5, 1971, left her estate to her daughter, Kate Butler Righter Wallis, and to her two grandchildren, Edward and Katie, the children of her daughter and Jim Righter. Each also received $100,000. Henry Z. Urban and Edward Righter were named executors of the estate.[10]

Mrs. Butler's two prime interests outside of the *News* were the University of Buffalo and the Buffalo Philharmonic Orchestra. Both of these institutions were beneficiaries of her financial assistance through the years. She was elected to the University Council of UB in 1920 and served on it until she resigned in 1960. In 1958 she was named Woman of the Year by the Buffalo Philharmonic Society and for years reportedly contributed to the salary of the orchestra's musical director.[11]

Mrs. Butler's relationship with her daughter, now Kate Butler Righter Wallis Wickham, had deteriorated years earlier. In an extensive interview with Sister Martin Joseph Jones, who was the archivist of Buffalo State College, Mrs. Wickham made no attempt to hide her animosity toward her mother. The daughter had been married to James Righter, who served as publisher of the *News* from 1956 to 1971 before being fired by Mrs. Butler. After their divorce she married Bruce Wallis, a newsprint company executive, and following his death she wed Dr. Robert Wickham. In the interview, Mrs. Wickham said her mother "was very independent. She would take nobody's advice, which was very difficult for the family. . . . She was definitely an egotistical lady." She also added that Mrs. Butler "was very difficult and gave him [Mr. Butler] many heartaches. . . . She had a dual personality. She found it very difficult to express her feelings and so consequently she did things that were in some cases unforgivable. . . . She made life very difficult for the rest of the family. She was very difficult in the business as far as my husband [James Righter] was concerned."[12]

In an interview in 2002, Mrs. Wickham said that her negative remarks in her interview with Sister Martin so many years earlier were prompted by her mother's firing of her husband and her mother's jealousy of him. She said her mother wanted more of her attention and felt she didn't get it because of Jim Righter. She also stressed that she felt sorry for her mother more than she felt anger toward her. Kate added that she and her father had enjoyed an excellent relationship throughout his lifetime.[13]

In her younger days Mrs. Butler was involved in riding, skeet shooting, skiing, and fishing. She was especially proud of a forty-eight-pound wahoo she caught and for a time held the record for bonefish caught off the coast of Marathon, Florida. She skied in the Adirondacks, where the family maintained a lodge, and in Europe on her frequent trips.[14]

Notes

1. Alfred Kirchhofer files, Butler Family Papers, E. H. Butler Library Archives, State University College at Buffalo, box 1.

2. Kate Robinson Butler files, Butler Family Papers, 1955–1975, *Buffalo News* files, pt. 1, box 5.

3. Ibid., box 1; *Buffalo News* centennial publication, October 12, 1980, p. H-6.

4. Marsha Ackermann, "100 Years of Pride," *Courier Express*, October 1980.

5. Kirchhofer files, Butler Family Papers, boxes 3, 5; "Producing the News," *Buffalo News*, October 12, 1980, p. H-16.

6. *Buffalo News* files; *Buffalo News*, October 12, 1980, pp. H-3, H-6; *Buffalo News*, obituary, August 5, 1974.

7. Ibid.

8. *Buffalo News*, October 12, 1980, p. H-6.

9. *Buffalo News*, obituary, August 5, 1974.

10. Kate Robinson Butler correspondence files, Butler Family Papers, pt. I-V, box 9.

11. *Buffalo News*, obituary, August 5, 1974.

12. Kate Wallis, interview by Sister Martin Joseph Jones, Butler Family Papers, pp. 9, 10.

13. Kate Wickham, interview by Murray B. Light, September 25, 2002.

14. *Buffalo News*, obituary, August 5, 1974.

15 The Right Man for the Time

Two weeks after the death of Kate Robinson Butler on August 3, 1974, the *News* board of directors named Henry Z. Urban president and publisher, the first nonfamily member to head up the enterprise.[1] The fifth publisher of the *Buffalo Evening News* was elevated to that position one hundred and one years after Edward H. Butler started the *Buffalo Sunday News* in 1873. Urban had started his career with the paper in the business department in 1953 with no previous newspaper experience. He was different in most respects from the founder and first publisher of the paper, but like Butler he fired off numerous memos to his department heads, primarily to express his unhappiness with things he didn't like. Unlike the hard-driving, ambitious, adventuresome Butler who never shied away from new ventures, Urban was reserved and fastidious in dress and manner, conservative in every respect. Normally even-tempered, he became irascible on occasions when he felt readers were not being well served.[2]

Urban was the third generation of an old Buffalo family that came to the city in 1832 and established a successful flour-milling business, which had the country's first flour mill to be run by electricity. Urban joined the family business after his graduation from

Henry Z. Urban, president and publisher, 1974–1983. (Courtesy *Buffalo News*)

Yale University in 1943. He saw action in the Pacific during World War II as a navy gunnery lieutenant on a cruiser that was damaged in fighting off the Philippines. Following the war's end he joined the family company, the George Urban Milling Company, and became treasurer and director until leaving to join the *News* in 1953.[3]

Urban had been a childhood friend of Kate Butler, granddaughter of Edward H. Butler Sr. He and his family were well known to the Butlers. He says Edward H. Butler Jr., the publisher of the *News*, hired him for the business office to work under the supervision of Edgar Steeb, the longtime general manager.[4]

Newsroom and community speculation was that Urban had lost out in a family struggle for the control of its flour-milling business and that he was hired by the *News* as a favor, despite his lack of any experience in the newspaper business. By his own admission Urban for years had no meaningful duties to perform. He sat at a desk in a small office off the main lobby and checked each edition of the paper for typographical errors. Like a good soldier, he did this and other menial tasks without complaint.

Finally, in 1957 he was promoted to assistant business manager and served in that capacity until 1962 when he was named business manager and assistant treasurer. In 1971 he was named treasurer and elected to the *News* board of directors. Throughout this period he had earned the respect of everyone at the paper with whom he came in contact. He was particularly known for his friendliness, his politeness, and his total dedication to the *News* and to the Butler family.[5]

Even after he became publisher, Urban continued to express concern to his department heads over typographical errors, late press runs, wrinkled papers, and inking problems. Known throughout the building and the industry as the man who deeply cared about *News* readers and advertisers, he was commonly described as a "reader's publisher." The things that annoyed many readers annoyed him as well, and he constantly strove to minimize these annoyances. He was a very familiar figure around the *News*, constantly checking on conditions in the various departments and never failing to exchange greetings with employees.[6]

In a day and age when many of the common courtesies of the past had gone out of style, Urban continued to observe them. For example, he never failed to tip his hat when he passed a woman on the street that he knew. Even his eating habits were somewhat unusual. He never picked up a sandwich, but instead he utilized a knife and fork at all times.

When the *News* started Sunday publication in 1977, Urban visited the production department about 11:30 every Saturday night. His feeling was that these employees had to work Saturday nights and he wanted them to know that the publisher was aware of this and appreciated their working when other people did not have to. Urban continued this practice until his retirement on July 1, 1983. On these nocturnal visits, he shed the customary gray suit, button-down-collar shirt, and narrow tie that he wore each day at the office and donned an old sweater, casual pants, and a somewhat rumpled coat.[7]

There was one area where he became much more aggressive and involved than his two immediate predecessors, Kate Butler and Jim Righter. A deeply committed political and social conservative, he was quick to fire off memos to me when I was the managing editor for news and later the editor of the *News*, challenging the positioning of news stories and commentaries on political issues and of editorial stands taken by the paper.

Although totally different in personality than the founder of the *News*, Urban did emulate Edward H. Butler Sr. in one respect. Like the founder, he was not bashful about sending memos to his editor about his personal views and his desires to see these reflected in the news and editorial pages. Publishers Edward H. Butler Jr., Jim Righter, and Mrs. Edward H. Butler Jr. had been very sparing in their requests to the editor. Henry Urban repeatedly sent memos.

Under other circumstances, a publisher's incursion into the editor's area of influence could have caused serious internal problems. Fortunately, Urban and I enjoyed a good personal relationship and what could have developed into a major problem never reached that stage. We respected each other and compromises were reached in some minor areas of difference, while others were conveniently set aside without the editor responding to the publisher or compromising an editorial position.

I was frank in responding to most of Urban's memos stating his position and why he felt it was best for the newspaper. Because we liked and respected each other, the exchange of memos never became acrimonious. I learned through the years how to finesse those areas that had the potential to cause a major problem between the publisher and the editor, a situation that is never healthy for a newspaper.

Urban did have one habit in dealing with me as an editor that was most annoying and that I felt was unworthy of him. When I disagreed with him over an editorial matter, he would always try to trump my argument by saying that he was just following what he felt Mrs. Butler would have wanted.

I was aware of Urban's very conservative views on politics and social issues and while I personally differed with many of these, I also respected him. I was acutely aware that Urban's orientation at the *News* since his hiring in 1953 had been on the business side of the enterprise and that he could not be expected to be sensitive to the concerns, philosophic and otherwise, of the newsroom.

My files contain numerous memos from Urban. A great number deal with Watergate and other political matters; as well as concerns about what he considered to be antibusiness stories; commentary on TV programming; criticism of individuals, particularly sports personalities; and reflections on social matters such as marriage and what he considered to be unfair attacks on area institutions.

Some typical Urban memos dealing with Watergate were unceasing and caused great discomfort both to me and to Millard Browne, the editorial page editor. We both felt we could not justify following the path the publisher preferred. For example, he wrote, "As I said before several times, I think the public is getting fed up with nothing but headlines on Watergate. Please whenever possible use our eight column head for something else."[8] On another occasion he wrote, "Unless in your judgment it is very essential, I do not want the Watergate trial dominating our front page. It is my definite feeling that the readers are tired of being bombarded with this thing. I know I am."[9]

Analytical pieces on the Nixon role in Watergate and opinion poll stories on public reaction to the affair generally brought a phone call from the publisher's office or a memo with a negative reaction from him. Millard Browne was in an extraordinarily difficult situation in dealing with Urban on Watergate editorials, given that a publisher's role on a paper's editorial position is definitely within his prerogative. Browne at one point informed me that he was going to resign because of his frustration with Urban over Watergate. I urged him to continue his role at the *News* and do all he could to keep a proper and needed perspective on the Watergate affair. Browne finally agreed to stay on and pulled some of his punches and steered a careful course for many months. A skilled and highly intelligent editor, he did manage to keep the *News* in a respectable position with his editorials.

On other political matters Urban was just as outspoken in his demands. For example, in an October 6, 1976, memo to me, he wrote, "I was disappointed with the picture of President Ford, especially in comparison with the good one of Mr. Carter next to it. . . . I expect to see a picture of President Ford just about daily until November."[10]

On January 5, 1976, he wrote, "I was surprised to see Lu Warren [*News* Washington bureau chief at that time] predicting Humphrey winning over Ford and also very sorry that you allowed him to do so. . . . I do not want members of our staff going on record with a Ford defeat. The publisher of this paper thinks Ford will win and certainly will see to it that the paper will do all it can to insure a victory."[11]

His concern about political content is illustrated by other situations. Fortunately, I was able to ignore or finesse most of his requests.

On August 4, 1977, Urban sent me a memo that expressed his frustration. It stated, "In the future before any story, feature, or editorial in which I have expressed a special interest is released . . . a final corrected proof must be submitted to me for approval." Except in the case of editorials, where a publisher's approval is not unusual in any newspaper, the order in this memorandum was never put into effect. Nor was it ever mentioned in the future.[12]

Urban's conservatism extended beyond politics. It was even manifested in the area of sports. When Jim Ringo was relieved of his Bills coaching duties in 1977, Urban was upset with the headline that said Ringo was fired. "In my opinion, it (fire) is a very degrading word and I do not even like to see it used in the body of a story." He also expressed his unhappiness with sports commentaries about the Bills at that time. "Please see what you can do to get somewhat of an upbeat feeling about the team's situation," he wrote in a memo to me. "I am anxious to have a positive viewpoint towards the Bills from now on as they seek to get out of their doldrums."[13]

Another of Urban's pet peeves involved the paper's local television columnists. According to him, "every decent family show that gets away from filth and bedroom humor ends up with a load of sarcasm and cynicism." And he added in an April 8, 1974, memo to me, "If there is not a definite about face on this type of writing, I will ask you to make personnel changes." A Jeff Simon column prompted this memo but others were aimed at TV critics Hal Crowther and Gary Deeb. Through the years Urban's tastes in TV programming were usually out of sync with those of *News* writers. Urban approved of only family-oriented shows and was upset when any of these were criticized.[14]

The bulk of Urban's memos expressed his concern for what he saw as an "anti-business" attitude in many stories. He flooded my desk with a continuous stream of memos on this subject, most of which I felt were unwarranted. For example, on January 14, 1974, Urban objected to a national labor story that reported one hundred thousand people had been laid off because of the energy crisis. The story had been displayed as the top story on the front page. Urban did not dispute the validity of using the story but in a memo to me he said, "We have to report these stories but not feature them. The 100,000 laid off in our headline were a very small percentage in our labor force nationally. . . . We should inform but not scare."[15]

A column by the financial editor citing criticism of two Buffalo banks for the paucity of women on their boards brought an April 24,

1978, memo from Urban, saying, "This is not the time to have an anti-business feeling in the community." A July 5, 1978, memo asked the editor to inform the staff "to stay away from anti-business columns." What prompted that memo was a column discussing limitations some companies were putting on personal calls by employees on company time.

When three major Buffalo companies applied to the city for property tax refunds on July 10, 1978, the story was given the page-one lead because of its potential impact on the city's revenue stream. The then city comptroller Robert Whalen criticized the companies for "monumental insensitivity." A memo from Urban's office commented, "I am worried about giving Whalen front page headlines to lambaste three leading Buffalo firms about a business decision they made. We must be extra careful not to give people the impression we are anti-business. Please ask your people to watch this closely. It is very important."[16]

Despite bombarding his executive team with memos, Urban was well liked by all of them. They respected the publisher's prerogatives as an overall watchdog of operations and some thought his criticisms were right on the mark. In the case of news operations, his memos all came directly to the editor and I was gratified that the publisher did not undermine my position by expressing his opinions to staff members. While I finessed most of Urban's requests without compromising my position and that of the paper, we still maintained a good working relationship.

If one were to fault Urban for the period of his *News* stewardship, it would relate to his conservative approach in some business matters. For example, the *News*, unlike most large metropolitan newspapers, paid top dollar for its basic raw ingredient, newsprint. The newsprint mills did negotiate discount prices based on volume of product ordered from them. The *News* bought its newsprint from as many as six or seven mills and as a result paid top dollar for all of its tonnage. Urban defended this practice as a hedge against any mill strikes, not an unusual event at the time. With a multiplicity of suppliers, the *News*, he said, would not be faced with a problem if one or even several were struck.

But above all else, Urban had a moral compunction against seeking to buy newsprint at a negotiated discount. He said the paper was steadfast in charging all its advertisers fixed rates for their ads, a practice instituted by the founder, and given that, it would not be fair to ask *News* suppliers to sell product to us at a discounted price.

Following Warren E. Buffett's purchase of the paper in 1977, the *News* cut back on the number of mills it dealt with and negotiated an improved price structure based on volume. To protect against mill strikes, we also increased our storage capacity for newsprint.

It would have been difficult to find any rank-and-file *News* employee who had anything but good things to say about Henry Urban. He was well regarded by all. Among other things, they were aware of his Saturday night visitations to the production departments and respected him greatly for this.

A story that will be forever engraved in the minds of *News* employees resulted from Urban's actions during the infamous Blizzard of '77. Urban, like a great many of the employees, was stranded at the *News* offices the Friday night that the storm raged and didn't leave for his Tudor Place home until late Saturday. When he left the paper he took with him a supply of Friday and Saturday papers that he personally delivered to houses in his neighborhood despite the still horrendous conditions.[17]

Outside of the *News*, Urban was not a man to regularly mix with anyone outside his social class. He rarely ate in public restaurants, preferring instead the dining rooms of the private clubs to which he belonged. Urban served as president and publisher of the *News* until his retirement on July 1, 1983, and was succeeded by Stanford Lipsey.[18] Urban was the transitional head of the paper, the last publisher during the Butler ownership years and the first following the sale of the enterprise to Buffett in 1977.

Urban served through the tumultuous periods that saw the *Courier-Express* sold and then ultimately go out of business. He was publisher when the *Courier-Express*, following the start of the *Sunday News*, filed its antitrust suit against the *News* and the federal court initially imposed operating restrictions against us. It was a most difficult period in the history of the newspaper and Urban guided the enterprise carefully and conservatively through it all. He scrupulously observed all the court-imposed limitations on the *News* during the period when the new Sunday operation was just getting under way. True to his nature, he sought and followed the counsel of the new ownership and the numerous attorneys involved in the antitrust litigation.

In retrospect, one would have to say that the *News* board of directors made a good decision in 1974 when they appointed Henry Urban publisher and president. His steady, conservative approach to managing the enterprise was what was needed during the nine years of his stewardship.

NOTES

1. *Buffalo News* centennial publication, October 12, 1980, pp. H-6, H-14; *News-News*, *Buffalo News*, September 1974, p. 4.
2. *Buffalo News*, October 12, 1980, p. H-14; *Buffalo News* files.
3. Ibid.
4. Ibid.
5. Ibid.
6. Ibid.; *News-News*, May–June 1983.
7. *Buffalo News*, October 12, 1980, pp. H-6, H-14; *Buffalo News* files.
8. Memo from Henry Z. Urban to Murray B. Light, May 24, 1973.
9. Ibid., October 16, 1974.
10. Ibid., October 6, 1976.
11. Ibid., January 5, 1976.
12. Ibid., August 4, 1977.
13. Ibid., November 1, 1977.
14. Ibid., April 8, 1974.
15. Ibid., January 14, 1974.
16. Ibid., July 10, 1978.
17. *Buffalo News*, October 12, 1980, p. H-14.
18. Ibid., *News-News*, May–June 1983.

16 "He Owns the *Buffalo News*"

For years Kate Butler had repeatedly rejected the advice of her attorneys that she take steps to minimize the tax consequences that would occur upon her death. All told her that it was important that she gift some of her assets before her death. If she failed to do this, she was advised, a "fire sale" of the paper would result to satisfy the estate taxes. She stubbornly refused this advice and when she died in August 1974, the family agreed with the estate executors that the *News* should be put up for sale.[1]

The task of finding a purchaser was given to Vincent T. Manno, one of the country's most respected newspaper brokers. Manno had two papers in mind as possible purchasers. One was the *Washington Post*, which had recently acquired WTIC-TV, in Hartford, Connecticut, and the *Times*, a family-owned newspaper in Trenton, New Jersey.[2] The *Post*, however, had recently undergone two years of union strikes in which the paper emerged the winner. Manno's other choice was the *Chicago Tribune*, which owned two papers in Florida and three television stations in Chicago, New York, and Denver.[3]

Manno initiated talks with executives of the *Washington Post*, hoping to interest them in the *News*. In December 1976 a meeting to

(*From left*) Warren E. Buffett and his "partner" Charles Munger. (Courtesy *Buffalo News*)

discuss the purchase was held among Katherine Graham, publisher of the *Post*; her son, Donald; Mark Meagher, president of the *Post* newspaper division; and Warren E. Buffett, shareholder and member of the *Post*'s board of directors.[4]

Warren Edward Buffett managed an investment partnership that was disbanded in 1969. During the thirteen years it existed, the partnership's assets grew from $100,000 to $100 million. Buffett used his personal share of the partnership, $25 million, to set up a financial network to acquire existing businesses. He used two companies for his investments, Blue Chip Stamps and Berkshire Hathaway, Inc. Charles T. Munger, a Los Angeles lawyer-businessman, was chairman of Blue Chip Stamps. He is a close friend and associate whom Buffett always referred to as his partner.[5]

Buffett told the *Post* people before the meeting that if their decision was not to bid for the *News*, he would have an interest in acquiring it to satisfy a longtime desire to own a major newspaper. In 1971 he had made an unsuccessful bid to purchase the *Cincinnati Enquirer*.

Mrs. Graham decided that the *Post* would not pursue a purchase of the *News*. Among other considerations, she felt that the *News*, with its thirteen unions and Buffalo, a city with a reputation as a strong union town, would not be a welcome environment for the *Post*, which had just crushed an ugly strike at its newspaper.[6] Meanwhile, the Chicago Tribune Company, which had also been approached, made it known that it had decided that it would not make a bid for the *News* because it was an afternoon paper.[7]

Shortly after Manno's meeting with the *Washington Post* people, he received a call from Buffett and a meeting was set up with Buffett and Charles Munger. That meeting led to a formal offer from Buffett for the *News*. Buffett was attracted to the *News* because the paper reached a higher percentage of local households than other big-city dailies in the United States. He was also impressed by the fact that the *News* had almost twice the daily circulation as the *Courier-Express* and 75 percent more advertising revenue. He was aware that the paper was publishing only six days a week, leaving a void in its publishing cycle on Sundays, and knew he would have to move to fill that void quickly.

The sale to Blue Chip Stamps actually was finalized on April 15, 1977; the 1977 Blue Chip annual report said the total price paid for the *News* was $35,509,000 of which $34,076,600 was in cash, with the balance representing assumption of certain pension obligations. At the time, Blue Chip had more free cash than Berkshire Hathaway did. Buffett and Munger, however, controlled Blue Chip, and it later became a majority-controlled subsidiary of Berkshire.[8] Buffett was certain that his investment in the *News* was a good one at the negotiated price, and what he believed was the untapped potential of the newspaper.

The purchase of the *News* was Buffett's biggest investment to that point in his career. Later, as Berkshire continued to expand with major investments, the sum paid for the *News* paled in comparison to his other acquisitions.

News of the sale of the *Buffalo Evening News* to Blue Chip was reported in a front-page story in the *News* on February 17, 1977. The next day a *News* editorial stated that the change in ownership was "the result of the interplay of such complex factors as the inheritance tax laws and the revolutionary changes being experienced all over the country in newspaper production technology." The editorial noted that family-held newspaper properties had the dual problems of inheritance tax laws while retaining sufficient access to investment capital to acquire the new and costly equipment needed to keep pace with the advances in technology.

The *News*, although it had been the dominant media outlet on the Niagara Frontier for many years, was not a big profit center. In fact, when it was put up for sale after Mrs. Butler's death, prospective buyers were amazed how little profit it had made in the prior decade. Additionally, the Buffalo market was not exactly prospering and prospects for its growth were not good. The *News* as an afternoon newspaper was in a publication cycle that was eroding in almost every U.S. market. Significantly in the eyes of prospective purchasers, the paper did not publish a Sunday edition, the fastest-growing sector for newspapers in a period when daily circulation was declining. In 1950 there were 549 Sunday papers, in 1975 there were 639, and by 1999 the number had risen to 905 Sunday publications. "All-day" daily newspaper publication numbers show a declining trend with 1,772 in 1950; 1,756 in 1975; and 1,483 in 1999.[9] Added to all of these negatives was the fact that the *News* workforce of about one thousand was at the time represented by thirteen unions, not something particularly appealing to any prospective bidder for the enterprise.[10]

Numerous books and articles have been written about Buffett's enormously successful business investment ventures as well as his greatly respected personal attributes. *Business Week* magazine's July 5, 1999, cover story on Buffett said he is "world famous as the greatest stock market investor of modern times." It discussed his reputation as "a latter-day Midas." Noting that Buffett from time to time "sends out folksy letters" to the top managers of his numerous enterprises, *Business Week* quoted from one to give an idea of the man's thinking.*

> We can afford to lose money—even a lot of money. We cannot afford to lose reputation—even a shred of reputation.
>
> Look at the business you run as if it were the only asset of your family, one that must be operated for the next fifty years and can never be sold.
>
> All of you do a first-class job in running your operations with

*Reprinted from the July 5, 1999, issue of *Business Week* by special permission, copyright © 1999 by The McGraw-Hill Companies, Inc.

> your own individual styles. We are going to keep it that way. You can talk to me about what is going on as little or as much as you wish. . . .

Andrew Kilpatrick, who has written four definitive books about Buffett, says, "I regard Buffett, as do many people, as an extraordinary human being combining in a single package financial genius, impeccable ethics, and a wonderful sense of humor." Buffett has never cooperated with any of the authors who wrote about him, although he does send letters to friends saying it is up to them to decide on whether to talk to the authors. For years he has been saying that he hopes some day to write his own book and he doesn't want to "give away any of the punch lines."[11]

Kilpatrick describes Buffett as a man with "a fast dry wit, a sunny disposition and a folksy manner; he comes across as a mix between Jack Benny and Will Rogers. When he speaks, his talk comes in a rapid, fully edited form in a Midwestern twang delivered in total intellectual honesty. He has great energy and a zest for life. His immersion in business has done nothing to hamper a great sense of fun and sophisticated sense of humor, whether it be needling himself, Wall Street, or general human conduct. . . . His manner is open and straightforward. Most often it is described as folksy, corn-fed, homespun."[12]

My wife and I can attest to Kilpatrick's remarks about Buffett, having had the advantage of many informal conversations with him in the first few years after his purchase of the *News*. Conversing with Buffett, one would never expect to find some aspects of his personality that emerge in casual conversation. Buffett, for example, loves to gossip about the television and Hollywood personalities he has become acquainted with from his association with Tom Murphy and Capital Cities. He had interesting, behind-the-scenes stories to relate about Rosanne Barr of TV fame. He and I differed on the effectiveness of ABC's Barbara Walters, with Buffett a staunch supporter of her work.

Buffett does have a wonderful sense of humor, which is manifested in many ways, but perhaps, most particularly, in the Christmas cards he sends to friends and business associates. As one of the fortunate recipients, I have looked forward for many years to what Buffett would come up with to bring a chuckle to those who receive his annual greetings. In most, he pokes fun at himself. For example, his

Buffalo News chairman Warren E. Buffett (*right*) and editor Murray B. Light in 1999. (Courtesy *Buffalo News*)

1995 card shows Warren atop a camel, with another camel close at hand. His inscription says, "One of the three wise men—1995 version." In another he is pictured in front of a Christmas tree as Daddy Warbucks, without a single strand of hair on his head. This one is signed "Daddy Warrenbucks."

Buffett gave us insight into the involved work of Congress and the ability of congressmen to add riders to unrelated pending legislation in their unending efforts to advance special interests.

On one occasion, I had informed Buffett that my wife and I were going to be in California to attend a newspaper convention in San Diego and spend some time exploring the state. Warren invited us to use his home in Laguna Beach during that visit and we did. It was interesting to see this casual, extensive ranch-style home so close to the ocean in an exclusive gated environment. Like Buffett himself, there was nothing formal or severe in the home. What was most interesting to me was the very extensive network of telephones and phone lines throughout the sprawling house. The lines were extensive and could cover hundreds of yards. I knew that Buffett spent a great deal of time on the phone for a variety of reasons and this network proved it. He could speak on the phone from any place in a room. His Laguna Beach home has since been extensively remodeled and enhanced.

Shortly after Buffett formally took over ownership of the paper, my wife and I hosted a reception in our home to introduce him to key members of the editorial staff. Buffett was at his best for the lengthy evening, meeting and greeting dozens of staffers in an informal, easy-going manner. He exchanged pleasantries and his newspaper philosophy in a low-key, conversational manner that, based on feedback I later received, impressed all present, including some who previously had doubts about what the new ownership would mean for the paper.

Over the years there have been many who compared the similarities or differences between Buffett and Edward H. Butler Sr. In one respect they were similar, both interested in the profitability of the enterprise. Additionally, both men were not fearful of bucking accepted practices, were risk takers, and above all, were not reluctant to express their opinions. But they did differ in many respects.

Butler Sr. involved himself in every aspect of *News* operations—advertising, circulation, production, promotion, and very definitely the editorial product, including positions the *News* would take on a wide variety of subjects. Buffett, for the most part, has confined his direction to *News* circulation and advertising-rate policies and has refrained from any involvement in its editorial product or policies. He has maintained that hands-off editorial policy steadfastly and fended off numerous opportunities to get involved. These are decisions, he always has said, that can only properly be evaluated and made by the editors of the paper. When readers or advertisers wrote or called Buffett to complain about a *News* story or editorial, he always said these matters were the responsibility of the editor and referred them to me. Not once did he ever get back to me with questions on how I resolved the complaint.

As Berkshire Hathaway expanded through the years, Buffett repeatedly said that his prime areas of control are in capital allocation for all of his holdings and compensation of the top managers of his enterprises. In all other areas, his philosophy has consistently been "hands off," permitting the managers of the individual entities to control policies. He has often said that he might do things differently in some of his properties but did not do so because of his policy of noninterference.

The personal lifestyles of the first and current owners of the *News* differed significantly. Butler was a firm believer that the lifestyle of the *News* owner should reflect the importance of his position as owner of the area's most significant opinion maker. He believed that the way to show the success of the paper was through bricks and mortar. "The people abroad trust much to appearances," he said. "The man who lives in a small house is generally regarded about the size of his house." When Butler purchased the mansion at Delaware and North streets for his residence, he said that he had "the most beautiful home in the country" and that was an important step for the reputation of the *News*.[13]

Along those same lines, Butler took enormous pride in the building that the *News* moved into in 1897. When construction on the structure got under way, Butler's goal was to make it the most beautiful newspaper office in America.[14] Buffett, despite his billionaire status, continues to live in the home in Omaha he bought in 1952 when he was first married and works out of a small office in a modest Omaha office building. Berkshire's five-room suite of offices contains only about four thousand square feet of space. Material possessions have never been of great concern to him.[15]

Buffett is a nondrinker and a nonsmoker. His favorite beverage is Coca-Cola, not surprising since he's a big Coke stockholder. His favorite avocation is playing bridge, and despite his professed aversion to things electronic he spends a good deal of time playing the game via computer with friends and relatives all over the country. Give him a steak and an order of hash-brown potatoes and he's a contented diner.

Butler took great pride in his personal appearance and he was the personification of sartorial splendor whenever he appeared at the *News* office or in public. Buffett, on the other hand, has never had much interest in how he dresses. Some have described his manner of dress as rumpled. The *Wall Street Journal* once reported that he wears $1,500 Italian suits and he does on some rare occasions. His only daughter, Susan, says he won't wear anything that isn't extremely conservative and she notes, "He'll wear clothes until they are threadbare." His buddy Charles Munger, commenting on Buffett's attire, has said,

"Buffett's tailoring has caused a certain amount of amusement in the business world."[16]

Butler and Buffett differed, too, in political allegiance. Butler, after an early streak of political independence, became a dedicated Republican and the *News* for decades reflected that allegiance. Buffett, on the other hand, came from a long line of staunch Republicans but Warren did not follow the family tradition. In October 1993 he told *Forbes* magazine, "I became a Democrat basically because I felt the Democrats were closer by a considerable margin to what I felt in the early 1960s about civil rights. I don't vote the party line but I probably vote for more Democrats than Republicans."[17] Buffett never asked the editors of the *News* to follow his political philosophy. His instructions to its editorial policymakers were to support those candidates the editors felt could be most effective for *News* readers. He has never questioned *News* political endorsements or its opinions on local, national, or international matters.

Buffett was born in Omaha, Nebraska, August 30, 1930. His father was a local stockbroker and Republican congressman. He acquired his first stocks at the age of eleven when he bought three shares of Cities Service Preferred at thirty-eight dollars a share, which he later sold for forty dollars a share, netting five dollars after commissions. He had been reading his father's material about the stock market since he was eight.[18]

His father was elected to the first of his four terms in Congress in 1942 and the family moved to the Washington area. Young Buffett began delivering the *Washington Post* and the *Washington Times-Herald* and at the age of thirteen began paying income tax on the income of $1,000 he earned from the newspaper routes. With his savings from the paper routes, he acquired reconditioned pinball machines for twenty-five dollars each and placed them in local barbershops. He was taking home fifty dollars a week from the seven machines he eventually owned and placed. Ever the entrepreneur, even at this early age, he and a friend bought a 1934 Rolls Royce for $350 and rented it for thirty-five dollars a day. Upon his graduation from high school at sixteen, he had amassed savings of $6,000.[19]

Buffett enrolled at the Wharton School of Business at the University of Pennsylvania following his high-school graduation. He attended the school from 1947 to 1949 and then transferred to the University of Nebraska, earning his undergraduate degree in 1950. After that he applied for admission to Harvard Business School but was rejected. This resulted in his enrolling at the Columbia Business School, from which he graduated in June 1951. It was at Columbia that Buffett studied under Benjamin Graham, whom he emulated in many respects and whose precepts he followed for years in his investment philosophy. Buffett earned his master's in economics from Columbia in June 1951 and returned to Omaha to work in his father's brokerage firm from 1951 to 1954.[20]

Buffett took some time out from his passion for the stock market to wed Susan Thompson of Omaha on April 19, 1952. She and Warren had grown up only blocks away from one another. The couple has three children and since 1977 Susan and Warren have lived apart. She moved to San Francisco and in 1991 was named to Berkshire's board of directors. She and Buffett are still on good terms and see each other on many special occasions. Buffett has lived with Astrid Menks since 1978. She was a hostess at the Omaha café in which Susan had appeared as a singer. The relationship of Warren, Susan, and Astrid has remained cordial through the years.[21]

Buffett organized the Buffett Partnership on May 5, 1956, with seven limited partners who contributed $105,000 but had no say in running the enterprise.[22] Buffett himself put up only one hundred dollars. It was the beginning of a fantastic series of brilliant investments and business strategies over the years and the dedication of a man of great integrity, discipline, and character that made Buffett one of the wealthiest men in the world.[23]

In 1985 Berkshire Hathaway invested $517.5 million to buy three million shares of Capital Cities. In 1986 Capital Cities and ABC, Inc. merged and violated a Federal Communications Commission "cross-ownership" rule. This rule banned a company from owning a newspaper and a TV station in the same town. When discussing this problem with Tom Murphy, Buffett's good friend and chairman of Capital Cities/ABC, Buffett said he was committed to the *Buffalo News* and did not want to sell the paper. "I promised the people there that I would never sell it. I told them when they wrote my obituary it would say, 'He owns the *Buffalo News*.'" The problem was solved when Capital Cities sold Buffalo television station Channel 7 (WKBW).[24]

Buffett's business interests extend far beyond the newspaper field. He is credited by many in the financial world as the greatest stock market investor of modern times. He made his name and his fortune in taking major stock positions in companies such as the *Washington Post*, Coca-Cola, Gillette, American Express, Wells Fargo, Freddie Mac, and numerous others. In recent years he has been buying companies in industries such as aviation, fast food, home furnishings, shoe manufacturing, and flight services. His biggest acquisition ever came in 1998 when he purchased General Re Corporation, the world-renowned reinsurer, for $22 billion.[25]

One of Buffett's more interesting acquisitions came in 1998 when he bought Executive Jet Aviation for $725 million. It is a fast-growing company that sells fractional ownership of business jets. For years Buffett considered corporate ownership of a jet as a wasteful executive perk. But in 1986 I had a phone call from Buffett in which he mentioned that he had purchased a small used jet for Berkshire. Given his previous negative statements on corporate jets, he was going to include mention of it in the Berkshire Hathaway annual report, but the citation would be in the smallest possible type. And that's the way it appeared—in agate. He dubbed the jet "The Indefensible." Despite this, and as his travel needs continued to expand, in 1995 he bought a one-quarter share of a larger jet that he dubbed "The Indispensable."[26]

Buffett's investment vehicle, Berkshire Hathaway, today is a major stockholder in some of the nation's wealthiest corporations and with each passing year owns more and more operating businesses that continue to add to its cash flow. Berkshire's insurance enterprises provide billions of dollars that can be reinvested in ventures that Buffett feels add strength to the corporation and the cushion to sustain major losses such as those experienced by General Re Corporation due to the destruction of the World Trade Center towers on September 11, 2001.[27]

With Berkshire now a multibillion-dollar enterprise and so closely identified with Buffett by its stockholders and the world's financial giants, speculation has been rife about the future of the corporation upon Buffett's death. In the Berkshire Hathaway, Inc. Annual Report for 1999, Buffett said:

> On my death, Berkshire's ownership picture will change but not in a disruptive way. First, only about 1 percent of my stock will have to be sold to take care of bequests and taxes; second, the balance of my stock will go to my wife, Susan, if she survives me, or to a family foundation if she doesn't. In either event, Berkshire will possess a controlling shareholder guided by the same philosophy and objectives that now set our course.
>
> At that juncture, the Buffett family will not be involved in managing the business, only in picking and overseeing the managers who do. Just who those managers will be, of course, depends on the date of my death. But I can anticipate what the management structure will be: Essentially my job will be split into two parts, with one executive becoming responsible for investments and another for operations. If the acquisition of new businesses is in prospect, the two will cooperate in making the decision needed. Both executives will report to a board of directors who will be responsive to the controlling shareholder, whose interests will in turn be aligned with yours.
>
> Were we to need the management structure I have just described on an immediate basis, my family and a few key individuals know whom I would pick to fill both posts. Both currently work for Berkshire and are people in whom I have total confidence.
>
> I will continue to keep my family posted on the succession issue. Since Berkshire stock will make up virtually my entire estate and will account for a similar portion of the assets of either my wife or the foundation for a considerable period after my death, you can be sure that I have thought through the succession question carefully. You can be equally sure that the principles we have employed to date in running Berkshire will continue to guide the managers who succeed me.[28]

The disposition of Buffett's multibillion-dollar estate upon his passing appears to be settled. He has three children but he has stated repeatedly through the years that he would not leave them too much because he feels each has to make his or her own way. Two of the children, Susan and Howard, are directors of Berkshire but are not involved in management of the company. The third, Peter, is not involved in the corporation in any way.[29]

Buffett and his wife, Susan, are by far the largest Berkshire stockholders, owning 38.4 percent of the total. Munger is a major stockholder and Buffett's longtime vice chairman of Berkshire. For many years, Buffett sought out Munger's advice prior to any major stock or business purchase but, while they maintain their friendship, Munger's role has diminished and Buffett says he did not consult Munger prior to his largest acquisition ever, that of Gen Re.[30]

Munger, now in his late seventies, devotes a good deal of his time as chairman of a not-for-profit hospital. A fine attorney who was first in his Harvard Law School graduating class, Munger is dour and taciturn by nature but not without a good sense of humor. Although a totally different personality than Warren, the two enjoyed a wonderful, close relationship for a good many years. Most of Munger's billion-dollar plus net worth is in Berkshire stock.[31]

Asked about Berkshire's outlook after Buffett is gone, Munger says, "It will still be one hell of a business. The one place a death will hurt us is we're not likely to get as good an allocator of capital as Warren in the next CEO."[32]

Notes

1. *Buffalo Evening News* editorial, February 18, 1977.
2. Carol Felsenthal, *Power, Privilege, and the Post* (New York: G. P. Putnam's Sons, 1993), p. 329.
3. Tribune Company, "History," http://www.tribune.com/about/history.html (accessed July 22, 2003).
4. *Buffalo News* sale files.
5. Ralph Dibble, "Warren E. Buffett: Owner Continues Traditions of the *News*," *Buffalo News* centennial publication, October 12, 1980, p. H-11.
6. Roger Lowenstein, *Buffett: The Making of an American Capitalist* (New York: Random House, 1995), pp. 203, 204.
7. Ibid.
8. Ibid.
9. Newspaper Association of America, "Number of U.S. Daily Newspapers," http://www.naa.org/info/facts00/11.html (accessed August 25, 2003).
10. Ibid.

11. Andrew Kilpatrick, *Of Permanent Value: The Story of Warren Buffett* (Birmingham, AL: AKPE, 1994), preface.

12. Ibid., pp. 66–67.

13. Alfred Kirchhofer files, Butler Family Papers, E. H. Butler Library Archives, State University College at Buffalo, box 1; Jerry Goldberg, "Edward H. Butler and the Founding of the *Buffalo Evening News*: The Life and Times of One of the Last Publisher-editors" (master's thesis, State University of New York at Buffalo), p. 88.

14. Kirchhofer files, Butler Family Papers, "History," chap. EHB Sr., p. 6F; Goldberg, "Edward H. Butler," p. 78.

15. Lowenstein, *Buffett*, pp. xvi, xvii.

16. Kilpatrick, *Of Permanent Value*, pp. 64, 65.

17. Ibid., p. 27.

18. Ibid., pp. 17, 18, 28; Robert G. Hagstrom Jr., *The Warren Buffett Way* (New York: John Wiley & Sons, 1994), p. 2.

19. Kilpatrick, *Of Permanent Value*, pp. 30, 31, 33; Hagstrom, *The Warren Buffett Way*, p. 2.

20. Dibble, "Warren E. Buffett."

21. Kilpatrick, *Of Permanent Value*, pp. 38–40.

22. Dibble, "Warren E. Buffett."

23. Hagstrom, *The Warren Buffett Way*, p. 3.

24. Ibid., pp. 174–76.

25. Berkshire Hathaway Inc. Annual Report, 2001, inside cover.

26. Anthony Bianco, "The Warren Buffett You Don't Know," *Business Week*, July 5, 1999, pp. 59, 60.

27. Berkshire Hathaway Inc. Annual Report, 2001, chairman's letter, pp. 6, 7.

28. Ibid. (1999), p. 62.

29. Bianco, "The Warren Buffett You Don't Know," p. 66.

30. Ibid.

31. Ibid.

32. Ibid.

17 Sunday Is Back

A few weeks prior to finalizing the sale of the *News* to Blue Chip, I met with Buffett and Munger in the editorial conference room next to my office. Also at that meeting were *News* publisher Henry Urban and Elwood M. Wardlow, *News* managing editor for administration. Early on in that meeting, Buffett asked my feeling about a Sunday paper, which the *News* had not published since 1915. My response was that I felt very strongly about the need for a Sunday publication, given that every study indicated that the Sunday editions of newspapers were gaining in circulation and advertising and were in effect offsetting the losses in those revenue streams from their daily operations. I said that I had been urging Kate Butler for years to consider starting a Sunday paper but was not successful in changing her mind. She constantly reiterated that she would not "invade the Sunday turf" of the *Courier-Express* and the *Niagara Gazette*.[1]

I also told Buffett that I had been frustrated for a long time in my desire to have the *News* start a weekly arts and entertainment tabloid that could be produced by existing staff and would be a major plus for readers. The idea was rejected by then publisher Henry Urban who was concerned that setting up the presses for another tab would cause

First cover of *Gusto*, the *News* weekly entertainment tabloid, June 3, 1977. (Courtesy *Buffalo News*)

countless logistical problems. Meanwhile, other newspapers throughout the nation were establishing sections along the lines that I had been advocating.

With no hesitation at all, Buffett said, "It sounds like it makes sense. Check out all the angles involved and let's get it done." I was delighted by his response and what was designated as *Gusto* made its debut on June 3, 1977. It has survived and prospered through the years and in 2003 celebrated its twenty-sixth anniversary. I had asked the staff to suggest a name for the publication and received over one hundred nominations. I ended up endorsing my son Jeff's suggestion of *Gusto* because that name embodied the spirit of pleasure and activity I wanted the publication to project.[2]

Buffett listened to my response and while he had immediately given me the go-ahead on an entertainment tabloid, he made no comment on my remarks about the need for a Sunday edition. However, given his facial expressions, I definitely sensed that he agreed with my appraisal. This was affirmed at a reception that I held for newsroom people at my home shortly after the sale of the paper was announced publicly. At that affair, Buffett told the assembled group that "News happens twenty-four hours a day, seven days a week." It was a signal to all of them that the *News* would be getting into Sunday publication.[3]

As Blue Chip reported to its stockholders, the *News* had determined that its failure to publish on Sundays was a "totally obsolete practice" and that the continuing success of the newspaper "depended on changing that obsolete practice." And, the report continued, "The obvious way to change the policy appeared to be to shift the *News* thirty cent weekend edition to Sunday morning from Saturday afternoon and also to follow a national trend by having the *News* publish on Saturdays in the morning."[4]

Munger didn't say too much at that initial meeting but did let it be known that he thought the *News* building was too pretentious for a newspaper. In his inimitable dour manner, he remarked, "I don't know why a newspaper needs a palace to publish in."[5]

At the time of the sale announcement, the *News* was outselling the *Courier-Express* during the week by a significant margin. The *News* circulation was 268,000 daily while the *Courier*'s was 123,000. The *Sunday Courier-Express*, which had no competition in Buffalo, had a circulation of some 270,000. Buffett was aware of newspaper trends and the need for the *News* to start Sunday publication as soon as possible.[6]

He told Urban to immediately set up a task force to study how to implement a Sunday paper. Buffett dubbed the committee, made up of the paper's major department heads, the Blue Chip Committee. Urban assigned William Fallis, his administrative assistant who had been promoted to senior vice president following the sale of the paper, to chair the committee. All the members of the group were told that the group and its function were confidential; all discussions had to be confined to those who were involved in its work.

As managing editor for news at the time, the top editorial position, I represented the newsroom and had to determine what the content of the new Sunday edition would be and how it would be presented. I decided not to appoint a Sunday editor because I wanted to integrate the existing daily staff into the Sunday operation so that we would operate as a unified seven-day operation. The circulation, advertising, and production heads prepared projections on costs, revenues, and production and forwarded these on a regular basis to Buffett in his Omaha office.

Buffett met with the Blue Chip Committee every month or so. I found it fascinating to see my colleagues reach into their jackets to pull out the copies of the reports they had sent to Buffett. When they faltered, he would almost immediately interject and fill in the blanks. He was more conversant with the content of the reports than those who had written them. His analysis of each report and how it would affect *News* operations was insightful and erased the doubts of those who may have questioned his knowledge of the newspaper business. Buffett was knowledgeable and he was totally involved in our process. The confidence in our chances for a successful Sunday launch was enormously enhanced by Buffett's meetings with the Blue Chip Committee.

In 1973 the *Omaha Sun* newspaper, which Buffett owned, was awarded the Pulitzer Prize for special local reporting and the Sigma Delta Chi Distinguished Service Award. Buffett had heard rumors that Boys Town had large stockholdings during the days of the Buffett partnership. He recalls, "Even I was staggered when we found out that the home, which was constantly pleading poverty and caring for less than 700 kids, had accumulated assets of more than $200 million." He passed this information to the *Omaha Sun* people and participated actively in the investigation and story development. He wrote one section of the story that brought the awards to the paper.[7]

Buffett obviously was enjoying the challenge of crafting a Sunday publication for the *News*. He was involved in making determinations about advertising rates, circulation pricing, and even promotional schemes. On the content side, Buffett simply told me to put together the most comprehensive package I could without any major concern about news versus advertising relationships. "We want to be the best the reader can get in Buffalo," he reiterated. "Disregard formulas." A note he wrote to Kay Graham during the process fully expresses his thoughts: "Kay, I'm having so much fun with this it is sinful."[8]

The Blue Chip Committee worked long hours, often seven days and nights a week, and finally, with Buffett's approval, set November 13 as the date for the launch of the *Sunday News*. Executives of the *News* felt this plan for introduction of the Sunday paper was a modest one and less aggressive than that employed by other papers in the past to launch a new product. The prelaunch publicity was kicked off with subscribers informed of the introductory offers and advertisers notified of introductory circulation guarantees. The *News* announced to its readers on September 3, 1977, that its weekend publication schedule would change effective November 12, with the Saturday afternoon weekend edition becoming a morning newspaper and the introduction of the new Sunday newspaper commencing November 13. The period of planning for these changes had been short and was a tribute to the intense effort of the Blue Chip Committee that had been studying the viability of altering the historic publishing pattern of the *News*.[9]

Then, just two weeks before the Sunday paper launch date, the *Courier-Express* filed its antitrust suit against us and asked the federal court to issue a preliminary injunction that would limit the initial launch plans the *News* had reported. The suit charged that the *News* was using its strength during the week to subsidize a money-losing paper on Sunday, seeking to eliminate the *Courier* as a competitor. The suit charged: "Mr. Buffett's *Evening News* is engaged . . . in a concerted effort to use its monopoly power to eliminate the *Courier* as a competitor in Buffalo."[10] The *News* in its response said it would make a profit on its Sunday paper and that it would promote rather than inhibit newspaper competition in Buffalo. The *News* said it had every legal right to publish a Sunday paper.[11]

The *Courier* had retained the services of Frederick Furth of San

Francisco to represent it in its suit against the *News*. A fine attorney with a keen appreciation for public relations, he had the *Courier* launch a campaign painting Buffett as an out-of-town carpetbagger out to ruin the *Courier*. In court he referred to Buffett as "big brother from Omaha."[12]

In a dramatic November 4 court hearing, Furth questioned Buffett and the two highly intelligent, articulate men went at it furiously. Furth was determined to make the case that Buffett had made little effort to learn much about the *News* prior to his purchase and that his principal concern was to acquire it and destroy his competitor, the *Courier-Express*. Buffett patiently and persistently countered Furth's thrust, noting that his purchase was based on information he had dug up and a general knowledge of the newspaper business. Furth reached a point that he obviously felt proved that Buffett's intent in Buffalo was to put the *Courier* out of business. It provided a dramatic point in the court exchange.[13]

Furth read a *Wall Street Journal* article quoting a Buffett friend saying, "Warren likens owning a monopoly or market-dominated newspaper to owning an unregulated toll bridge. You have relative freedom to increase rates when and as much as you want." Furth asked Buffett if he had ever specifically said this. In an exchange of questions and answers, Furth did firmly implant in the court's mind Buffett's feeling about owning a monopoly newspaper. The *New*'s attorneys and executives felt that the exchange following the quote from the *Wall Street Journal* was harmful to the *News* case.[14]

The preliminary injunction issued by Judge Charles Brieant severely limited the ability of the *News* to promote, market, and circulate its Sunday edition. The *Courier-Express*, not unexpectedly, took full advantage of the judge's ruling with stories on his decision and expressions of support for the *Courier*. Included was a major story on the president of the Buffalo AFL-CIO Council calling for a boycott of the *Sunday News*.[15]

The new *Sunday News* was designed to appeal to the widest possible cross section of the area's population. The daily's basic diet of complete local, regional, state, national, and international news was carried through to the Sunday paper, but the new Sunday paper included full ad-free pages of "specialty coverage." With the approval of Buffett, the accepted newspaper formula of 60 percent advertising to 40 percent news was not applied to these pages. The ad-free pages included a neighborhood page, people page, picture page, mini page for children, accent youth and accent maturity pages, and a pause page for puzzle addicts. Additionally it had ten pages of color comics, a new Sunday magazine, and a TV tabloid.

The introduction of the *Sunday News* brought immediate moves by the *Courier* to improve its Sunday paper. In a January 18, 1978, editorial the *News* said, "We readily concede that the *Courier Express* is putting out a lot better paper under the spur of Sunday competition than it ever used to do in its many decades as a comfortable easy going monopoly."

The November 13, 1977, launch edition of the Sunday paper was loaded with advertising. But by the fifth Sunday edition, the *News* carried only 147 inches of ads, compared to more than 500 inches in the *Courier*. The lawsuit and resultant negative publicity about the *News* Sunday startup had taken its toll. The business community and the community at large had bought into the *Courier* campaign that the *News* was trying to drive it out of business. Our ad lineage continued at a woefully low level.[16] There were weeks when the only retail advertiser in the *Sunday News* was General Nutrition. I would call Buffett every Wednesday or Thursday to give him the gloomy report on how much advertising we had in hand for the upcoming Sunday paper.

The result was a $2.9 million pretax loss for the *News* in 1978. Normal operations of the paper continued to be hampered by Judge Brieant's preliminary injunction. His order required us to show a signed customer order authorizing each Sunday delivery. The paperwork involved in carrying out this order was unbelievably time-consuming and restrictive of efforts to stimulate circulation of the Sunday edition.[17]

For example, the court had ordered us to charge fifteen cents for the daily editions and thirty cents for the Sunday or a total of $1.20 for seven-day delivery. On Saturday, December 10, 1977, the *News* became aware that many Sunday edition customers served by independent motor-route operators had made prepayments through

December at the then prevailing rate of $1.05 a week. This involved some sixteen thousand subscribers. In order to comply with the court order, we printed sixteen thousand instruction sheets for these subscribers and bought sixteen thousand pencils to be taped to the instruction sheets. On Sunday, December 11, this material was left in newspaper tubes or mailboxes asking subscribers if they wanted the Sunday paper delivered at the new $1.20 price. That afternoon the motor-route operators retraced their routes and left papers for subscribers who requested them. Preparing these materials for distribution started at 6 PM Saturday and continued throughout the night, with publisher Urban and other executives of the *News* involved in the tedious procedure.

At this time, I attended a law and press seminar in Rochester. For reasons I cannot fathom, my wife and I were seated at a table for dinner with Judge Brieant, another federal judge who was a good friend of his, Doug Turner of the *Courier* and his wife, and a law professor from the University of Buffalo and his wife. During the dinner Brieant surprisingly talked a great deal about the case pending between the *Courier* and the *News*. He made it very clear that he greatly regretted the closing of a paper in his hometown that left the town with one paper. Because of that he intimated that he was out to get the *News* and prevent the *Courier* from closing. I reported this to our attorneys and to Buffett and Munger. They decided that they did not want to take the course of attacking the judge. I, however, have never forgotten the incident and it greatly diminished my opinion of the legal process.

Munger was constantly concerned that an inadvertent action or statement by a *News* executive might bring a contempt citation against the paper for violating the court order. At one point he called me with the news that Buffett was scheduled to give a speech and expressed his concern that Buffett's candid remarks could cause a problem with the judge.[18]

Munger's concern was reflected in the 1978 Blue Chip report to stockholders. He wrote, "Litigation is notoriously time-consuming, inefficient, costly and unpredictable. The ultimate security of the *Buffalo Evening News* remains in doubt, as it will for a very extended period."[19]

Buffett and I would converse by phone once or twice a week to review the competitive situation and see if we could come up with ideas to turn the tide. Our conversations, many of which were of an hour or more duration, basically involved advertising, circulation, and promotion. True to his earlier pledges to me, Buffett rarely initiated conversations about the paper's editorial content. These phone calls came at night, when I had returned from the office, so we could converse without frequent the interruptions that would occur during regular office hours.[20]

One of my favorite Buffett stories confirms that he is a man of his word. In my very first meeting with him he said that editorial policies of the *News* would be established by the editors and not by him. He never deviated from that position in all the years that I served as his editor.

Despite his position on abstaining from news decisions, I thought it was important to give him an opportunity to express his opinion on which candidate the *News* should support for the presidency in the 1980 elections, the first we would experience under his ownership. I asked him to attend a meeting in Buffalo at which I hoped to finalize our decision on the candidate who would receive the *News*'s endorsement. He insisted his attendance wasn't necessary, because in keeping with his earlier pledge, the decision was one in which he would not participate. When I persisted, he finally agreed to attend the meeting.

The meeting in the *News* boardroom in the fall of 1980 was attended by Buffett; myself; editorial page editor Leonard Halpert, who had been named to that position in 1980; publisher Urban; and Bill Fallis, a *News* senior vice president. Halpert and I made our presentations, reporting that the editorial board had unanimously voted to support Democrat Jimmy Carter. Urban and Fallis said the paper should support Ronald Reagan. Buffett listened but did not express an opinion and when pressed said that the editorial board decision was the one that had to be observed. He said that his own opinion could not and would not be voiced in the matter because it was an editorial decision. I never did learn which candidate he favored.

During the troubled period following Judge Brieant's injunction, Buffett frequently came to Buffalo where he and Urban met with the major advertisers and potential advertisers. It was during this time that Buffett turned to Stanford Lipsey, his good friend and publisher of the *Omaha Sun* newspapers. Lipsey was not happy about the thought of moving to Buffalo but did agree to come to Buffalo about once a month to help the advertising and circulation departments in their efforts for the Sunday paper. Later, upon the retirement of Urban on July 1, 1983, Lipsey became publisher and president of the *News*.[21]

NOTES

1. Roger Lowenstein, *Buffett: The Making of an American Capitalist* (New York: Random House, 1995), p. 205.
2. Dale Anderson, "Starting From Scratch," *Buffalo News Gusto*, December 27, 2002, p. 18.
3. Lowenstein, *Buffett*, p. 205.
4. Blue Chip Stamps, Annual Report, 1977, p. 3.
5. Lowenstein, *Buffett*, p. 205.
6. Ibid., p. 206; Blue Chip Stamps, Annual Report, p. 3.
7. Ralph Dibble, "Warren E. Buffett: Owner Continues Traditions of *News*," *Buffalo News* centennial publication, October 12, 1980, p. H-11.
8. Lowenstein, *Buffett*, p. 206.
9. Blue Chip Stamps, Annual Report, p. 4.
10. Ibid.; Lowenstein, *Buffett*, p. 207.
11. Lowenstein, *Buffett*, p. 207.
12. Ibid.
13. Ibid., pp. 208–11.
14. Ibid., pp. 212–13.
15. Ibid., p. 214; Blue Chip Stamps, Annual Report, pp. 4, 5.
16. Lowenstein, *Buffett*, p. 215.
17. Ibid., p. 217.
18. Ibid.
19. Ibid.
20. Ibid., p. 216.
21. "Stanford Lipsey New Addition to Blue Chip Ranks," *Buffalo News*, October 12, 1980, p. H-14.

18 Lipsey Answers the Call

Buffett felt the need to infuse some fresh ideas into the *News* and turned to Stanford Lipsey, asking him to come to Buffalo in late 1977. He had confidence in Lipsey, personally and professionally. Lipsey had been owner of a chain of Omaha weeklies, the *Sun* newspapers, which he sold to Buffett in 1969.[1] After the sale, Buffett kept Lipsey on as president and publisher of the *Sun* papers and the combined efforts of the two resulted in a 1973 Pulitzer Prize for the *Sun* newspapers' story on Boys Town. Given that, it was not surprising that Buffett wanted Lipsey on the Buffalo scene during this critical time.[2]

Although later overturned by an appeals court, federal judge Brieant's preliminary injunction of November 9, 1977, had caused many problems for us and our new Sunday edition. The restrictions laid down by the judge severely hampered the efforts of the advertising director, the circulation director, and the publisher to market the *News*. Each was aware that the *Courier*'s attorneys, who were hoping to find a violation of the court order, were scrutinizing everything they did.[3]

The *News* executives also were aware that the *Courier* had gained

(*From left*) Stanford Lipsey, president and publisher, and Warren E. Buffett, chairman. (Photo by Bill Wippert, courtesy *Buffalo News*)

a major psychological edge, owing to Brieant's ruling that our paper was trying to put the *Courier* out of business. This resulted in a negative impact on circulation and advertising efforts and inevitably caused despair among those charged with improving the *Sunday News*'s bottom line.[4]

In 1978 the *Sunday Courier* was selling some one hundred thousand more copies each week than the *Sunday News*. At year's end the financial picture reflected the problems we were experiencing. It showed a $2.9 million pretax loss and a $1.4 million after-tax operating loss.[5]

Despite their close friendship, Lipsey was not anxious to accede to Buffet's suggestion that he come to Buffalo. Buffett then suggested that Lipsey visit Buffalo once a month to "do whatever you think needs done." For emphasis, he added, "The place will just run better if you're there."[6]

Totally loyal to Buffett, Lipsey began his periodic journeys to Buffalo and the *News*. He spent approximately one week a month here, concentrating his efforts on the circulation and advertising departments. Initially Lipsey was identified as a consultant working with publisher Urban, but in May 1980 he was named vice president of media operations for Blue Chip Stamps, at that time our parent company. On January 1, 1981, he was appointed vice chairman and chief operating officer of the *Buffalo News*. With the retirement of Urban in July 1983, Lipsey assumed the role of publisher and president.[7] He held that dual role until 2001, when he voluntarily gave up the role of president, naming Warren Colville, formerly the advertising director and executive vice president, as president while retaining the title of publisher.[8]

Lipsey had several years earlier purchased a home in California and was spending more and more time there during the winter months while maintaining constant contact with the *News*, and particularly with Colville on matters pertaining to advertising and circulation, and with Jerry Goldberg, editorial page editor, on editorial policies. Ever focused, he was able to maintain constant oversight on the paper from across the continent.[9]

While still in the once-a-month phase of his *News* involvement, Lipsey impressed all of the executives with whom he came in contact. His quick, inventive mind and ability to think problems through carefully and logically won the confidence of everyone. But above all, he was admired for his ability to focus on a subject until a final determination could be made. In all my years of dealing with top executives of western New York companies, I never encountered one with Lipsey's power to focus. Nothing could get him to deviate from a problem or an opportunity that he was considering until he reached a final resolution.

Perhaps Lipsey's most significant achievement during his monthly visits was his creation of *Home Finder*, a *Sunday News* tabloid real estate guide. The *Courier-Express* for decades had dominated the real estate–advertising sector in its Sunday paper. Lipsey targeted that advertising and was determined that the *News* would at a minimum become competitive in securing some of it. *Home Finder*, launched in 1979, became a successful vehicle and still continues to meet the needs of realtors and readers throughout the region.[10]

Lipsey spent a good deal of time in the advertising department, striving to change an environment that was perceived by many as having more "order takers" and relatively few aggressive salespeople soliciting business. This impression had grown during the days when the *News* was running very large papers in the 1960s, particularly on Wednesdays and Thursdays, which were loaded with advertising. Lipsey brought about some turnover in personnel through buyouts and by maintaining steady vigilance over the entire advertising department.[11]

One of his prime objectives was to increase circulation of the Sunday paper and the primary mechanism he employed was the introduction of a game similar to bingo that was dubbed "Jingo." Launched in 1982, it had by July 2001 received over twenty-five million entries and awarded over $5.5 million in prizes. Despite some falloff over the years in weekly entries, it has continued to involve thousands of *News* readers each week, thereby supporting circulation.[12]

Shortly after Lipsey became publisher, he voiced concern about the lack of involvement by the private sector in community affairs. Given my long years at the *News* dealing with most of the top business leaders, Lipsey asked me to join him in a series of breakfasts and luncheons he hosted for dozens of the area's leading executives over a period of many months. At each of these sessions the dialogue involved analyses of what the private sector could do to enhance the economic viability of the Niagara Frontier.[13]

When the extensive list of invitees was finally exhausted, I recused myself from the process while Lipsey made the final determination of those who would form the nucleus of a private-sector group that would attempt to influence the path community endeavors would follow. This became known as the Group of Eighteen, with eighteen founding members.[14]

Through the years some of the original members of the group dropped out and were replaced by other business executives. An informal organization, it had no regular schedule of meetings but initially gathered monthly. It had no slate of officers although Lipsey in effect headed up the enterprise.[15]

Although the Group of Eighteen by design had no desire for publicity and its deliberations were not open to the public, with the passage of time its influence became well known and inevitably it was the target of critics. The group was criticized by some sectors of the community for not having any women or minorities among its membership. Despite these inevitable barbs, the Group of Eighteen has been credited with accomplishments that even its critics would admit could not have been attained without its efforts. Some of the Group of Eighteen's major achievements have been its work on Roswell Park, Buffalo air travel and the Buffalo Niagara International Airport, and the Peace Bridge. It successfully pressured the state legislature and the governor to finance a $241 million physical improvement project for Roswell Park Memorial Institute.[16]

Almost from its inception the group had a deep concern about air service in and out of Buffalo, which was one of the most expensive in the country due to a lack of low-cost carriers. This was a definite negative for the efforts of the city and the area to attract new businesses and retain established ones. After years of badgering the Niagara Frontier Transportation Authority to strengthen its marketing efforts and seek to attract low-cost airlines, results were finally achieved. Air transportation cost in Buffalo went from one of the highest in the nation to seventeenth or eighteenth lowest. The Group of Eighteen also was highly supportive of the NFTA plans for a new terminal to replace the antiquated dual terminals that had been in place for years. The combination of the new, modern terminal and the dramatic lowering of airfares resulted in Buffalo achieving one of the most dramatic increases in airport usage in the nation with the dawning of the twenty-first century.[17]

Members of the group have had numerous meetings with governors of New York State and its U.S. senators and members of Congress, making the case for legislation that could influence the economic development of the Niagara Frontier. The group has been, and continues to be, a significant factor in seeking to enhance the economy of the area.[18]

Lipsey, the sixth publisher in the history of the *News*, brought to the paper a style of management that differed greatly from that of his immediate predecessors. While intense and extremely focused, he also had strong feelings about the need to involve middle-management people in decision making as well as relying on his top management team.

Early on he formed a marketing committee that met weekly to map marketing plans designed to enhance circulation and advertising efforts and project a more positive image of the paper in the community. The committee included members from the marketing department as well as the circulation director, the advertising director, and in a move that later was adopted by many of the nation's newspapers, the editor. An outside perspective was provided by the account executive for the *News* at the paper's advertising agency. This group was joined from time to time by middle managers.[19]

Providing vigorous hands-on leadership for the marketing committee at all times was publisher Lipsey, who encouraged active vocal participation by everyone. The committee was involved in approving all in-paper, radio, and television advertising; reviewing expenditures for public relations activities of the paper; and monitoring the activities of the ad agency on behalf of the *News*. The committee's activities were many but it had no authority over or any involvement in the news product or editorial policies of the paper. [20]

Our labor-management committee, formed as an outgrowth of a brief 1980 labor strike, was a beneficiary, too, of Lipsey's participation. He worked closely with the individual who headed up the union side of the organization, and the committee was kept better informed about the paper's activities that might involve its unions.

Lipsey started a new tradition of company picnics for all employees and their families. Scheduled every few years, they have been hugely successful, attracting a great many attenders from all departments. Planning for the picnics has always involved rank-and-file employees who spend months in arranging the details. Warren Buffett has attended and one year agreed, along with other *News* executives, to allow employees to throw whipped cream pies at them.[21]

Lipsey has expended a great deal of time and energy in his efforts to involve the company's middle managers to an extent never before seen at the *News*. He instituted regular meetings with middle managers from all departments to brief them on decisions of top management and to elicit their suggestions on matters related to their departments specifically and those at the paper in general. He brought in outside consultants to determine the strengths and weaknesses of the middle-management ranks through a series of written and oral exercises.[22]

Department managers have been strongly encouraged to provide training opportunities for their middle managers by attending seminars and conferences. Working with Erie Community College, computer courses have been offered to middle managers and to all other employees to enhance their capabilities.[23]

Lipsey certainly has not overlooked top executives of the *News*. Each year they go off to a resort for a week of golf and other leisure pursuits, but every morning of these retreats is taken up by a full schedule of business meetings presided over by the publisher. Lipsey also hosts a local golf and dinner outing for his top-level executives.[24]

Lipsey's involvement in journalism started early on as a photographer for his school newspaper in Omaha. His interest in and love for photography has continued through the years and he has had successful exhibits of his photographic work. He is particularly proud of the photos he has taken over the years of Buffalo's Forest Lawn Cemetery. Many of these were incorporated in the 1996 volume *Forest Lawn Cemetery—Buffalo History Preserved*. An exhibit of his photos at the Burchfield Penney Art Center in 1985 was highly successful.[25] In 2002 he donated framed photos to Roswell Park Memorial Institute to hang in the Department of Radiation Medicine.

The major project to which Lipsey devoted hundreds of hours has been the restoration of Buffalo's Darwin Martin House, considered to be architect Frank Lloyd Wright's finest creation. Bob Wilmers, Bob Rich, Bob Kresse, and Stan Lipsey secured the millions needed to acquire the property and restore the house. Lipsey received the 1998 Governor's Award for Historic Preservation for his work on behalf of the Martin House Restoration Corp.[26]

A University of Michigan graduate, Lipsey served in the air force during the Korean conflict and was editor of the newspaper for the Strategic Air Command Headquarters at Offutt Air Force Base in Omaha, Nebraska. In 1950 he was employed as an advertising account executive for a Nebaska company that owned two free-circulation weekly newspapers in Omaha. By 1965 he owned a majority of the stock in the Sun Newspapers of Omaha, and from 1965 to 1980 he served as publisher and president of the group of weekly papers that by this time was made up of seven paid and five free weeklies that Lipsey ultimately sold to Buffett. He has served on numerous local boards, including the New York State Business Council, and has been active in the Newspaper Association of America.[27]

Lipsey's philosophy about the role of a newspaper is similar to that of the *News* founder, Edward H. Butler. "As one of society's most important institutions," Lipsey says, "a newspaper must reflect its constituency, while providing independent leadership. That means we must go to the source to be thorough; must cover all sides of a story to assure fairness. Relevant investigative reporting on the institutions in our community is a function with which we are charged. And, if we don't do it in behalf of our readers, I don't know who will."[28] Lipsey is a strong believer that "A paper must be extensive in its content and accurate in its writing. On its editorial page, decisions must be well researched so that positions can be taken to offer readers the benefit of that research in reaching their own decisions."[29] Asked recently what he thought his most important contribution to the *News* has been, Lipsey said, "Well the first thing was to save it. After all, looking back there wasn't going to be two (papers). We never said when we talked that we were going to put the *Courier* out of business but the pattern across the country was clear."[30]

The most traumatic event in Lipsey's tenure as president and publisher of the *News* took place in 1997 with the revelation that a respected officer and major department head had been stealing funds from the newspaper. David W. Perona, circulation director and vice president, was indicted, convicted, and imprisoned after pleading guilty in February 1998 to a felony charge of third-degree grand larceny. Perona had a reputation as a churchgoing individual who had devoted a great deal of time and money to youth activities on Grand Island, where he and his family resided. He was known, too, for his concern for his employees in the circulation department and for his willingness to assist any who had personal problems.

There was nothing in Perona's background that would indicate any problems. He had a fine service record, having earned a Purple

Heart after being wounded in 1965 while with a secret navy squad that infiltrated North Vietnam. A submariner, he served from July 1962 to December 1965. He came to the *News* from the *Seattle Post-Intelligencer* where he had been since January 1979. He also had been employed in the circulation departments of the *San Francisco Chronicle* and the *Oakland Tribune*. He joined the *News* in February 1982 as circulation director and was named a vice president in October 1983.[31]

The *News* suspended Perona on May 24, 1997, after irregularities in the circulation department initially surfaced.[32] The results of the internal investigation were shared with law-enforcement officials and on June 13, 1997, Perona was terminated. On February 5, 1998, he pleaded guilty to grand larceny and agreed to make $65,000 restitution to the *News* for criminal acts committed between February 1989 and May 1997. In his court appearance, Perona stated, "I stole funds or money from the *Buffalo News*." He was one of four *News* circulation department employees dismissed.[33]

Perona, fifty-three, was sentenced on May 14, 1998, to six months in jail and ordered to repay the money he admitted stealing. State Supreme Court Justice Russell P. Buscaglia told Perona that he spared him a longer jail term because he took into consideration Perona's charitable work with children. Perona spent four months in the Erie County Correctional Facility in Alden and was released. The judge had stated that he couldn't place him on probation because his criminal activity involved repeatedly converting revenue to his own use as well as falsifying circulation records to cover the thefts.[34]

Another circulation department employee, Charles Fix, also pleaded guilty in the scheme to drain revenues from the *News*. Fix pleaded guilty on March 27, 1998, to a misdemeanor charge of falsifying business records. A nineteen-year employee of the paper, Fix had served as manager of single-copy sales from stores and honor boxes and testified that from August 1996 through May 1997 he had inflated the number of papers returned to the *News* to hide the thefts. Fix, who was suspended by the paper in May 1997 and fired in December, told the court that he would enter incorrect figures in department records to cover the thefts. He testified that he and other circulation department officials, including Perona, used the money from the honor boxes as a slush fund to buy tickets and other things for all those involved in the theft conspiracy.[35]

In return for getting probation instead of a jail term, Fix agreed to testify in the trial of former *News* circulation driver Thomas Moriarity. Fix was fined $1,155 and ordered to perform one hundred hours of community service. Moriarity had been charged with stealing more than $62,000 from the *News* honor boxes but on May 14 a state supreme court jury was unable to reach a verdict at his trial and a mistrial was declared. The arrest of Moriarity had resulted in the *News* probe that led to the prosecution of Perona and Fix.[36] He was never tried again.

Perona now lives in Colorado. While still incarcerated he wrote a letter to *News* chairman Warren Buffett apologizing for his inexcusable behavior in stealing money from his employer.

A contrite Perona ends his letter saying he filed for bankruptcy and had lost his home and retirement. He promised to pay what the court ordered and regretted the loss of his integrity and career.[37]

Throughout the entire circulation department ordeal, Lipsey never deviated from his determination that all the facts of the malfeasance had to be uncovered and prosecuted. He was ably assisted in the endeavor by Warren Colville and Rod Layton who played major roles in investigating the wrongdoing that finally led to the punishment of those involved.

Notes

1. "Stanford Lipsey New Addition to Blue Chip Ranks," *Buffalo News* centennial publication, October 12, 1980, p. H-14.

2. Ibid., p. H-11.

3. Roger Lowenstein, *The Making of an American Capitalist* (New York: Random House, 1995), p. 214; Blue Chip Stamps Annual Report, 1977, pp. 4, 5.

4. Lowenstein, *The Making of an American Capitalist*, pp. 208–11.

5. Ibid., p. 217; Robert J. Summers, "Blue Chip Stamps Reports Net Loss for the News in '78," *Buffalo News*, March 26, 1979.

6. "Stanford Lipsey New Addition."

7. *News/News*, *Buffalo News*, May–June 1983, p. 1.
8. "The News Promotes Four to New Positions," *Buffalo News*, February 6, 2001.
9. Stanford Lipsey, interview by Murray Light, October 19, 2001.
10. "Stanford Lipsey New Addition."
11. Stanford Lipsey interview.
12. Ibid.
13. Ibid.
14. Ibid.
15. Ibid.
16. Ibid.
17. Ibid.
18. Ibid.
19. Ibid.
20. Ibid.
21. Ibid.
22. Ibid.
23. Ibid.
24. Ibid.
25. Ibid.
26. Ibid.
27. *Buffalo News* files.
28. Stanford Lipsey interview.
29. Ibid.
30. Ibid.
31. *Buffalo News* files.
32. "News Dismisses Circulation Director," *Buffalo News*, June 13, 1997.
33. Matt Gryta, "Ex-executive at the *News* Admits He Stole Funds," *Buffalo News*, February 6, 1998, p. C-1.
34. Matt Gryta, "Ex-*News* Official Gets Jail Term for Thefts," *Buffalo News*, May 14, 1998, p. B-1.
35. Matt Gryta, "Second *News* Official Pleads Guilty to Running Slush Fund," *Buffalo News*, March 28, 1998, p. C-4; Matt Gryta, "Former *News* Circulation Official Fined, Must Do Community Service in Embezzlement Case," *Buffalo News*, June 5, 1998, p. C-5.
36. Ibid.
37. Letter to Warren Buffett from David Perona, June 25, 1998.

19 Good News from the Court

The *News* finally realized a court victory on April 16, 1979, when two years after Blue Chip's purchase of the paper, the U.S. Court of Appeals for the Second Circuit, in a unanimous decision, ruled that the preliminary injunction by Judge Brieant should not have been issued. The three-judge panel found that Judge Brieant "had no sufficient basis for holding that the *Courier* had shown a clear probability" that its arguments would prevail at trial.[1] The tribunal further rejected Judge Brieant's finding that Warren Buffett's purchase of the *News* showed intent to build a monopoly. "We find," said the judicial panel, "simply no evidence that Mr. Buffett acquired the *News* with the idea of putting the *Courier* out of business as distinguished from providing vigorous competition, including the invasion of what had been the *Courier*'s exclusive Sunday market."[2]

Brieant had contended that the *News*'s pretax earnings in a competitive market, $1,659,630 in 1976 and less in the two preceding years, would not justify an investment of $33 million when borrowing would cost $2,557,500.[3] Buffett responded that monopoly newspapers sold for approximately three times gross earnings where the range for nonmonopoly papers was from .6 to 1.6 times gross revenues. Buffett paid .8 of gross revenues for the *News*. Buffett also testified that he purchased the paper on anticipated earnings under new management, not on its past earnings.[4] In Blue Chip Stamps' annual report for 1977 Buffett said, "Our investment was based on the belief that the existing journalistic merit of the *News*, encouraged and nourished, will eventually prosper in the marketplace and that inflation will eventually make a prosperous newspaper company a safer asset than any other company which we could then buy at the price paid for the *News*."

The appeals court, in its devastating reversal of Judge Brieant, also ruled that there was no support for a finding of monopoly intent by Buffett. "All that the record supports is a finding that Mr. Buffett intended to do as well as he could with the *News* and was not lying awake thinking what the effect of its competition on the *Courier* would be," the judges wrote. "This is what the antitrust laws aim to promote, not to discourage. Courts must be on guard against efforts of plaintiffs to use the antitrust laws to insulate themselves from the impact of competition."[5] While noting that it no longer was meaningful because of the passage of time, the appeals tribunal rejected Brieant's ruling that the *News*'s five-week introductory offer was predatory.[6] The court also cited other instances in Brieant's rulings that it found to be in error and specifically stated that he acted "with remarkable speed" in issuing his preliminary injunction on November 9, 1977. The court basically upheld the claims made by the *News* in its January 16 countersuit against the *Courier*.[7]

In the countersuit the *News* charged that the actions of the *Courier* against the *News* were designed to extend the monopoly the *Courier* had on Sunday newspaper sales and to extend that monopoly to the daily operation. The *News* also contended that the *Courier*'s tactics included tying advertising in their Sunday edition to daily papers and selectively reducing advertising rates to special advertisers. Further they charged that the *Courier* and unnamed coconspirators illegally interfered with the *News*'s sale of newspapers and advertising and sought to unreasonably restrain trade by preventing the *News* from selling both newspapers and advertising for its Sunday distribution.[8]

The *News*, in an April 19, 1979, editorial following the ruling by the appeals court, commented that "In wiping out the injunction and the contempt citation based on it, the higher court—from which there could be appeal to the U.S. Supreme Court—upheld virtually every point the *News* has repeatedly sought to make, both in court and to its readers, as to its motives and the economic imperatives which impelled the *News* to enter the Sunday field."

The editorial went on to state: "Now Buffalo's papers publish in the only pattern (seven day printing on each side) which has preserved two competing healthy daily newspapers in any other major city anywhere in the country. We hope to improve our competitive position through comprehensive, interesting, fair, and accurate news coverage. We're sure the *Courier-Express* has similar intentions. And the readers of both should benefit, seven days a week."

The *News* indeed was vindicated in its position and Judge Brieant suffered a major setback. The ruling of the appeals court was, in fact, devastating for a sitting judge. The *Courier*'s attorney had suggested the possibility of pursuing the suit with an appeal to the U.S. Supreme Court but never followed up with this action. The *Courier* suit, however, had taken its emotional toll on publisher Urban and other *News* executives. And although the *News*'s dominance in daily circulation continued, the *Courier* still maintained a significant edge of about one hundred thousand in Sunday circulation.

A new era of *News* relationships with its thirteen unions was signaled in the 1980 Blue Chip report to stockholders with the one sentence that said, "If any extended strike shuts down the *Buffalo Evening News*, it will probably be forced to cease operations and liquidate." Buffett and Munger undoubtedly were sending a message and the Teamsters union tested them, when the union that represented thirty-eight *News* truck drivers went on strike in a dispute over differential pay on December 2, 1980. The dispute leading to the strike centered on a forty-one-dollar weekly differential that was paid in the past to Teamsters who substituted for circulation wholesale distributors. The *News* was computerizing billing and collecting procedures, making it unnecessary for the drivers to perform these tasks. The Teamsters insisted on continuation of the differentials despite not having to perform the duties.[9]

On Monday, December 1, the Teamsters met with Richard Feather, the *News* labor negotiator, and after all-night talks, the Teamsters walked off the job the next day. The *News* did manage to put together a paper and go to press with the December 2 paper and printed ten thousand copies prior to the walkout by the pressmen in sympathy with the drivers.[10]

One humorous event occurred when the *News* executives were in the garage near the overhead doors waiting to see if the drivers would observe the strike. A few of the trucks left and the garage doors were raised to permit their exit. They were immediately closed after a truck departed. At one point the doors were closed and publisher Henry Urban was outside with the strikers and the picketers. There was some concern expressed about his safety but everyone at the *News* respected Henry Urban and he reported later that he exchanged pleasantries with the strikers before returning to the garage to join the other executives.

After an incident with a *News* delivery truck, the pressmen stopped work and the shutdown of the *News* operations was complete. *News* employees then were ordered not to report to work because the paper suspended operations. Talks with management continued and on Wednesday, December 3, the Teamsters approved an agreement and the *News* resumed full publication on December 4. Of the thirty-eight truck drivers the Teamsters represented, fifteen were full time and twenty-three were part time. The drivers previously had rejected a December 1 *News* offer by a twenty-eight to seven vote. They had been without a contract since November 3. The settlement resulted in a 6 percent pay raise, twenty-three dollars a week, for the drivers.[11] The only other strike in *News* history occurred in 1970. It was a four-day walkout by the independent union of hoppers whose job it is to deliver the papers from the delivery truck to the vendor.

Prior to 1980, Buffett had reported to stockholders in the annual report that if the paper failed to publish then he couldn't meet a payroll and would order virtually all employees to leave. And, Buffett added, "the *News* has a limited amount of blood and if it bleeds too much, it will not live anymore. As you know, we are operating at a staggering loss, $4.8 million in the company's most recent year. We simply do not have the ability to pay people if the newspaper doesn't operate."[12]

The Teamsters, under pressure from the other unions at the *News* and particularly from Ray Hill, president of the Newspaper Guild, the paper's largest union, quickly accepted a face-saving concession, and the *News* was back on the streets Thursday, having missed only two days of publication. The *News* did not change its stance on the payment of differentials.

Two pluses emerged from the 1980 strike. It proved to all the unions at the *News* that Buffett did not bluff. Second, it resulted in the formation of a Labor Management Committee that has been functioning ever since and has been a major factor in improving communications between the *News* and its employee organizations.

NOTES

1. Barry Berlin, "A Case Study, The *Buffalo Evening News* Battle," (unpublished data), pp. 6–7.
2. Ibid., p. 12.
3. Ibid.
4. Ibid., p. 13.
5. Ibid.
6. Ibid., p. 7.
7. Ibid., p. 10.
8. "The *News* Files a Countersuit Against *C-E*," *Buffalo Evening News*, January 16, 1978, p. 1; Berlin, "A Case Study," p. 5.
9. Mark Misercola, "*News* Suspends Publication," *Courier-Express*, December 3, 1980, p. 1.
10. "Drivers Union Goes on Strike at the *News*," *Buffalo Evening News*, December 2, 1980, p. 1.
11. Mike Misercola, "*News*, Teamsters Settle Strike; Employees Return," *Courier-Express*, December 4, 1980, p. 1.
12. Internal memo from Warren Buffett to *News* executives, December 2, 1980, "Drivers Union Goes on Strike at the *News*."

20 Rising Losses Bring the End

Another chapter in the history of Buffalo journalism was unveiled on June 24, 1979, with the announcement that the *Buffalo Courier-Express* had been sold to the Minneapolis Star and Tribune Co. It was the second transfer of newspaper ownership in Buffalo in two years, the *News* having been sold in 1977 to Blue Chip Stamps. The *Courier* sale ended the historic ownership of the property by the Conners family of Buffalo. The *News* sale had ended its ownership by the Butler family.[1]

In a front-page message to its readers, the president and publisher of the *Courier*, William J. Conners III, indicated that the sale of the paper was due to the financial condition of the publication. He said, "A strong financial position is necessary to permit the newspaper to continue. The Star & Tribune Company can provide that. . . ." No dollar amount for the transaction was disclosed. The *Courier-Express* publisher's statement for the six-month period ending March 31 reported a daily circulation of 125,163 and a Sunday circulation of 257,219.[2] The sale of the *Courier-Express* set off a chain of events that was to terminate three years later with the demise of that newspaper.

The *Buffalo Courier* was established in 1834 and purchased by

William J. Conners in 1897. A merger in 1926 with the *Express*, founded in 1846, created the *Courier-Express*.[3]

In 1869 Mark Twain was the editor of the *Express* and had a one-third interest in its ownership. His father-in-law helped him obtain the position on the paper and advanced him $12,500, one-half of the buy-in price of $25,000. Twain's father-in-law died in 1870 and Twain's wife, who was pregnant with their first child, was very ill. Their home on Delaware Avenue, which had been a wedding present, was advertised for sale on the front page of the *Express* for six months before it was finally sold for a loss of one thousand dollars. Twain also sold his interest in the *Express* for ten thousand dollars less than he had paid for it. Twain later described this period of his father-in-law's death and his wife's illness as "the blackest, the gloomiest, the most wretched" of his life. He never returned to the city and even refused to honor speaking engagements his agent booked for him in Buffalo.[4]

Although readers were not happy with the merger of the *Courier* and the *Express*, the new paper prospered and a new building was erected at 787 Main Street. William J. Conners Sr. died on October 5, 1929, before the building was completed. He never saw the "Log Cabin" his son had planned for him as a surprise.[5] The "Log Cabin" was a hideaway on the top floor of the building for the *Courier* top executives to entertain outside guests as well as themselves.

The most influential leader of the paper was William J. Conners who was always deeply involved in its progress. The paper was successful for many years but during the 1970s it began to lose money. Buffalo was always a fiercely competitive newspaper town; it became even more so after the *News* was sold in 1977 and both papers were publishing seven days a week.[6]

The sale of the *Courier-Express* to the Minneapolis company in 1979 included the newspaper, Courier Cable, and the Niagara Photo Engraving Co. The announcement in the *Courier-Express* said that a search for a new publisher of the paper would be undertaken and later John Cowles Jr., chairman of the company, named Roger Parkinson president and publisher of the *Courier*. Parkinson previously had been with the *Washington Post*. Parkinson subsequently announced the appointment of Joel R. Kramer, who had been an assistant managing editor at Long

Island's *Newsday*, as the new editor of the *Courier-Express*, succeeding Douglas L. Turner who became the paper's Washington correspondent.[7]

Thirty-six months after its purchase of the *Courier-Express*, the president of Cowles Media Co. announced on September 7, 1982, that it would cease publication on September 19 unless a buyer for the paper could be found. John Cowles Jr. added that this was an unlikely event. Cowles said that the *Courier-Express* had an average pretax loss of $8.6 million annually over the past thirty-five months of his company's ownership. The paper's revenues were at the level of $38 million a year but had not shown significant signs of improving its financial situation, resulting in the decision to sell or close it, Cowles said.[8]

According to Cowles, negotiations with some prospective purchasers had not been successful. Parkinson was quoted in the *Courier* story as saying that some discussions had been held with the *News* about the possibility of a joint operating agreement between the two papers but that the *News* did not have "any practical interest" in any such arrangement. Cowles said that the asking price for the *Courier* was "very modest" but added that a buyer would have to assume the paper's liabilities, which he said were "very substantial" and "in the millions."[9]

The *News* in the same period reported operating losses before taxes of $2.8 million in 1980 and $1.1 million in 1981, down from the $2.9 million loss it sustained in 1978 and a $4.6 million loss in 1979.[10]

Meanwhile, on September 10 the *Courier* reported that Rupert Murdoch, publisher of the *New York Post* and the *Times of London*, had considered buying the *Courier* before Cowles had announced plans to cease publication September 19. A representative of News America Publishing Co., headed up by Murdoch, reported that Cowles officials had held meetings with *Courier* union leaders and with unidentified local people who said they believed the *Courier* could be saved. Otto A. Silha, Cowles Media chairman, also said that he expected talks between News America and the *Courier* would be resumed.[11]

The *News* carried a story on September 14 reporting that if the sale to News America was finalized, the new publisher of the paper would be Robert Page. He was general manager of the *San-Antonio Express-News*, a News America paper, before becoming a vice president for News America. He would become the *Courier-Express* president and publisher and Roger P. Parkinson would join Cowles Media as an executive. Otto A. Silha said News America "would pay nothing for the *Courier-Express* assets but would assume most of the paper's liabilities." He predicted that the *Courier-Express* under Mr. Murdoch "would be a very lively newspaper, vigorously managed."[12]

Bob Page and I had known each other for years and I had high regard for him and his abilities as a newspaperman. In fact, I thought he had the potential to lead the embattled United Press International successfully out of its problems and was disappointed when he left the wire service to join News America.

Negotiations between the Murdoch people and the *Courier* union representatives continued with News America setting September 16 as a deadline for reaching agreement on conditions it set out for buying the paper. News America would cut the newsroom staff from 151 to 100. News America also said that it alone would determine which newsroom employees it wanted to retain, bypassing guild contract guarantees of layoffs by seniority. This, it later was learned, was the major guild objection.[13]

News America also said it would have to cut composing-room employment from 126 to 60, needed job cuts in other departments of the paper, and wanted elimination of all minimum manning requirements outlined in various union contracts. Lifetime job guarantees in force for the printers would be eliminated under the News America proposal.[14]

When the News America demands were made public, Stanford Lipsey, then vice chairman of the *News*, told *News* members of the Newspaper Guild at a meeting September 13 that if Murdoch got the concessions he wanted, the *News* would be forced to seek the same cutbacks in order to survive.[15]

Negotiations between News America and the nine unions of the *Courier-Express* broke off the night of September 16, three hours before the deadline. The president of the guild said his union's prime objection was the proposal on layoffs for guild members by company choice rather than by seniority. The president of the Council of Newspaper Unions, a *Courier* pressman, said the other unions were not close to agreement on issues affecting their membership. The next day, September 17, some three hundred members of the guild overwhelmingly voted to reject Murdoch's terms for takeover of the

Courier. About twenty members voted for approval of the Murdoch concessions. This vote sealed the fate of the *Courier* and the conditional sale of the paper to News America was canceled.[16]

Following the collapse of Murdoch's efforts to acquire the *Courier*, I received a call from Page inviting me to have lunch with Murdoch and himself in New York City. I joined him for an interesting three-hour-long lunch. Unfortunately, Murdoch had to cancel because of illness in the family. That was disappointing because I had looked forward to meeting him.

During the course of the luncheon, Page surprised me with the revelation that he told Murdoch that he wanted to remain in Buffalo as publisher for a period of only six months. Following that, he said, he had told Murdoch that he was certain he could convince me to leave the *News* to take over as editor and publisher of the *Courier*. Murdoch, he said, approved the scenario despite the fact that he had never met me. I asked Page what made him so certain that I would entertain that idea. He responded, "Murdoch would make you an offer you wouldn't be able to refuse. Money always talks."

I have often thought of that conversation with Page. I'd say it's extremely doubtful I would have entertained an offer from Rupert Murdoch. I would not have considered leaving the *News* to compete with the paper that had been my home for so many years. I felt a strong sense of loyalty to Warren Buffett and Stan Lipsey as well as to my staff. I was, however, sincerely flattered by Bob Page's offer but while money is important, it is not the ultimate refuge.

Representatives of the *Courier* unions at the same time met with an unidentified group of local investor representatives who were pursuing the possibility of purchasing the *Courier*. Nothing materialized from these meetings.

With the announcement by the *Courier* ownership of its plans to cease publication on September 19 if a buyer for the paper could not be found, the *News* had to consider a plan of action if that did occur. Warren Buffett, Stan Lipsey, and I met in the *Washington Post* offices shortly after the *Courier* announcement. After a thorough discussion of various scenarios, the decision was made that if the *Courier* were not sold and halted publication, the *News* would start a morning edition Monday through

Friday to fill the void. No announcement of our intentions was made until September 15, when Lipsey disclosed that if the *Courier* did close and the *News* launched a morning edition it would hire *Courier-Express* employees needed for this expansion of its editions.[17]

On Sunday, September 18, the *Buffalo News* announced in a front-page story that the new morning edition of the *News* would be available the next morning. It would be easily recognizable, the story said, because it would carry a dominant "Sunrise" designation at the top of page one. It noted that the sunrise edition would have a different look and feature package from the afternoon editions.

The announcement did emphasize that Sunrise would be prepared by the same editorial staff that produced the *Buffalo Evening News* weekdays and the *Buffalo News* on Saturdays and Sundays. This was in line with a decision I had made not to designate a particular segment of the staff as the Sunrise staff just as I had earlier decided that we would not have a separate *Sunday News* staff. I felt strongly that a unified staff that could service our afternoon editions, our morning editions, and our Sunday editions as needed would be in the best interest of producing the best products for all *News* readers.

As Lipsey had pledged earlier, we did augment existing staff in the newsroom with the talent available from the *Courier*, adding those we felt would contribute most and would be compatible with members of the *News* staff. Other departments of the *News* fleshed out their ranks with former *Courier* people, basically utilizing the same standards for selection as the newsroom. To the credit of all involved the integration of staffers worked well for everyone.

Publishing in the morning cycle created a good many logistical problems. Setting up work schedules was difficult and many employees initially were less than happy with their new shifts. Despite the addition of new personnel from the old *Courier-Express*, establishing the priorities of coverage was not easy and adjustments had to be made as time went on.

Always cognizant of its responsibilities to vent diverse opinions, the regular viewpoints page facing the editorial page was cleared of all advertising so that more opinions could be printed. This page remained the same for all afternoon as well as morning editions.

Many of the syndicated columns that formerly appeared in the *Courier* were added to the regular *News* roster.

With the addition of the sunrise edition, the *News* necessarily had to change its name from the *Buffalo Evening News* to the *Buffalo News*. It could not publish a morning paper under the designation of "Evening." Surprisingly, the decision to make this change engendered significant debate among *News* executives, many of whom were reluctant to give up the traditional name. Finally, however, good sense prevailed and the change was made.

The metamorphosis of the *News* from a six-day afternoon daily was now complete. We had become a seven-day, all-day publication with morning and afternoon editions and a successful Sunday publication. As Warren Buffett said during the antitrust suit, news does not know the barriers of publication times. It continues day and night, seven days a week. And now the *Buffalo News* was able to report on this without interruption. And, there was plenty to report on.

The death of the *Buffalo Courier-Express* reflects the competitive newspaper situation throughout the United States. It differs only in that the *Courier* was Buffalo's morning paper and in the vast majority of cases in other parts of the country it was the afternoon paper that disappeared.

Afternoon papers were fast becoming a thing of the past due mainly to distribution problems. In many cities the hours the paper had to be distributed were "high traffic" times and traffic congestion led to inordinate delays in delivering the papers. These are problems that TV and cable did not have and they could transmit the day's breaking news events as they happened. This meant the PM paper was no longer significantly timely.

In cities where two papers still exist it is the result, in most cases, of joint operating agreements between the two papers. The Newspaper Preservation Act in 1970 exempted newspapers from antitrust laws, and sanctioned existing and prospective joint operating agreements. Daily rivals could combine their business and printing operations while maintaining independent editorial functions. Competitive independently owned newspapers today exist only in six major markets: New York, Boston, Chicago, Denver, Los Angeles, and Washington, DC. Eight smaller markets continue to have two competing daily papers.[18]

NOTES

1. "Family Owned Buyer Renowned for Leadership," *Courier-Express*, June 24, 1979, p. A-1.

2. Ibid.

3. Alfred Kirchhofer files, Butler Family Papers, E. H. Butler Library Archives, State University College at Buffalo, box 2; Rich Scheinin, "Cowles Blames Rising Losses," *Courier-Express*, September 8, 1982, p. A-6; Margaret Sullivan, "Rise and Fall of *Courier Express* Wrote Colorful Chapter in Buffalo History," *Buffalo Evening News*, September 20, 1982, p. B-1.

4. Joseph B. McCullough and Janice McIntire-Strasburg, eds., *Mark Twain at the Buffalo Express* (DeKalb: Northern Illinois University Press, 1999), pp. xix, xxiv.

5. A. Gordon Bennett, *Buffalo Newspapers since 1870*, Adventures in Western New York History, vol. 21 (Buffalo, NY: Buffalo News and Erie County Historical Society, 1974), p. 8.

6. Sullivan, "Rise and Fall of *Courier-Express*."

7. *Buffalo News* files.

8. Scheinin, "Cowles Blames Rising Losses," p. A-1; Michael Beebe, "Civic Leadership Mourning the Fate of *Courier-Express*," *Buffalo Evening News*, September 8, 1982, p. A-10.

9. Ibid.

10. *Buffalo News* files.

11. "Publisher of *N.Y. Post* Renewing His Interest in *Courier*; Visit Expected," *Buffalo Evening News*, September 10, 1982, p. A-1.

12. "Unions at *Courier* Weigh Cutbacks in Murdoch Plan," *Buffalo Evening News*, September 14, 1982, pp. A-1, A-5.

13. Ibid.

14. Ibid.

15. Ibid., p. A-1.

16. Celia Viggo, "After Heated Debate, Guild Votes Down Murdoch's Cuts," *Courier-Express*, September 18, 1982, p. A-1; "Courier Unit Rejects Murdoch Proposals," *Buffalo Evening News*, September 18, 1982, p. 2-A.

17. "The News Will Publish a Morning Edition if *Courier* Shuts Down," *Buffalo Evening News*, September 15, 1982, p. 1.

18. Paul Farhi, "The Death of the JOA," *American Journalism Review* (September 1999): 50–53.

21 Doing What I Loved Best

After assuming the role of managing editor in 1969, I refrained from issuing any sweeping manifestos to the senior editors and department heads. But over a relatively short period of time I informed each how I wanted our operation to function. The key was to let them know that they would be given a lot of liberty to manage their operations in exchange for holding them responsible for the work their departments were producing on a daily basis. I stressed that micromanaging their areas was not something I wanted to do and would not do unless forced by circumstances, which could only be brought about by their failure.

I also emphasized to all the editors that it was their responsibility to alert me to any "sensitive" stories being produced by their people. I did not want any surprises, and as the editor, I could only do my job if they gave me the opportunity to review politically sensitive stories, those that involved major controversies in the community, and any stories involving the *News* and/or its owners.

While I relaxed many of the rigid and what by then were unreasonable rules from the Kirchhofer-era stylebook, I informed the editors that the *News* still felt strongly about being a family newspaper and that certain standards of language and content had to be maintained. I told them we would not be taking the route of many cable television stations; so if they had questions about the propriety of any material, it would be in their interest to alert me and let me make the final judgment.

While I was working with editors and staffers, Elwood M. Wardlow was pursuing his administrative duties and in particular spending a great deal of time with the Newspaper Guild, which represented the vast majority of the newsroom staffers. He had the patience to listen and respond in detail to all of their complaints. The guild, aware they had his attention at all times, took advantage of the situation and even at one time complained at length about the quality of the toilet tissue in the newsroom restrooms.

Wardlow also capably coped with the numerous administrative details that arose with a staff of more than two hundred people. Included were vacation schedules, overtime monitoring, requests for work-shift changes, complaints about bulletin-board postings, and countless other matters, small and occasionally big. He spent a good bit of his time meeting with the staff about their personal or family problems, something I felt that *News* management should best stay out of. And I also recall Wardlow relating that he staked out the home of a newsroom employee whose repeated absences for "sickness" were cause for suspicion. This was not the only time he had done this and fortunately the Newspaper Guild was unaware of this practice. Inevitably it would have resulted in the filing of a grievance.

A function I thoroughly enjoyed as managing editor and later as editor was my role on the editorial board. In naming me managing editor, publisher James Righter said he wanted me to be a participating member of the board that set *News* policy on its editorial page. I had made a determination early on that my role on the editorial board would not in any way undermine that of the editorial page editor. I met with the board daily but made no attempt to preside at its meetings. I contributed to the dialogue and debate in what I felt were important issues but basically was silent on those that I felt were not significant. If the majority of the board did not join with my opinion on these lesser issues, I made no attempt to overrule them. I believe that the editorial page editors I had the privilege of working with appreciated my stance. There were some occasions on which I met privately with the editorial page editor to fully explore differing positions on significant policies. In all of these instances, compromises resulted in satisfactory solutions that ultimately became news policy.

Newspapers, and the *Buffalo News* is no exception, are much different in looks, content, and tone than they were when I was first put in a position in 1969 to have a significant role in the future direction of the *News*. Papers now carry longer stories, and many have lengthier leads. More stories are continued on inside pages. Most newspapers carry more local stories on their front pages. Readers traditionally have complained about stories that jump from the front page to an inside page but these complaints while heard have not been heeded. In the 1960s very few stories jumped to an inside page, but twenty years later it was common practice to jump front-page stories.

The biggest change in newspapers since the decade of the 1960s has been in appearance. The papers of yesteryear were loaded with short stories. To accommodate Kirchhofer's insistence on story count, I used to load up page one with so-called late-news bulletins, each a single paragraph. Many were not really worthy of page-one exposure but they satisfied his desire for a multistory page.

Newspapers now carry many more features than those of earlier days and they also carry many more local and syndicated columns expressing opinions. These opinions frequently conflict with those on the newspaper's editorial page, confusing readers who can't determine where the newspaper stands on a particular issue. No matter how many times the paper informs its readers that only its editorial page represents the position of the paper, readers tend to ignore these statements.

The newspapers of today are loaded with market-driven special sections created to attract advertising although frequently publicized as reader-friendly material. Better newspapers candidly inform their readers that their advertising or marketing departments produce these sections and make no attempt to pass them off as legitimate news. The *Buffalo News* follows this procedure when special sections such as the restaurant guide, the Erie County Fair section, the annual auto review, or many more throughout the year are included with the paper.

On the positive side, most newspapers are better written, better organized, and better looking than they were in the1960s and before. They carry more material to appeal to younger readers, and more sports, business news, and features. They also carry much more material, in small type known as agate, particularly in the sports and business sections, providing readers with useful information.

On the negative side of the ledger, as television channels and Web sites have proliferated, many newspapers have taken steps to meet the competition that really undermines their credibility. Chief among these are the use of overly large headlines, particularly on page one, on stories that in past years would not even have been placed out front. These efforts have created ever-increasing distortions in news values.

In 1969 the circulation of the *News* in Erie County was 251,410, a lead of 17,926 over the Sunday *Courier-Express.* Total *News* circulation was 284,454 daily and 300,166 for its weekend edition. The *Courier* daily total circulation that year was 155,911 and its Sunday circulation was 311,798.[1] The population of Buffalo that year was some 460,000 but there were disturbing trends developing and by 1980 it had dropped significantly to 357,000. One of the problems that economists looked at was the increasing negative impact of the St. Lawrence Seaway, which opened in the summer of 1959. The seaway provided a direct inland water route between the Great Lakes and the Atlantic Ocean, completely bypassing Buffalo. By diverting shipping from Buffalo, it undermined the city's economy. As a result, for example, by the mid-1960s, Buffalo's grain business started to feel the effects and by 1966 five flourmills had been shut down.[2]

The *News*, fearful of what would happen, had conducted an all-encompassing, although losing, campaign against the construction of the seaway. At the same time, Canada enlarged the small Welland Canal to a depth of twenty-seven feet, and with the completion of the seaway most of the warnings about negative economic consequences raised by the *News* were realized.[3]

The *Buffalo News* has never aspired to be a national newspaper. From its very beginning as a Sunday-only newspaper in 1873, its more than a century as a six-day afternoon publication, and now as a seven-day all-day publication, we have prided ourselves on being the strongest possible regional newspaper. To attain and then to maintain this status, the *News* has been committed to having a large staff dedicated to reporting on local events in its circulation area of western New York. But unlike many of the nation's regional newspapers, the *News* has never neglected to report on national and international news. The editors have always believed that readers of the *News* should be fully informed about all major news events anywhere without any dependence on other media outlets.

Here are some examples of local stories that captured the nation's attention and became major national stories. One occurred in 1971, another in 1977, and still another in 1978. More recently the murder of Dr. Barnett A. Slepian, a gynecologist who performed abortions, became a major national story on October 23, 1998. Coverage locally involved large numbers of newsroom reporters and editors and close cooperation with the production and circulation departments as deadlines were stretched to cope with ever-breaking late developments.

The 1971 story was the rioting in Attica State Prison that started on September 9 and continued through September 13, ultimately resulting in forty-three deaths of prisoners and corrections officers. *News* story and photo coverage was comprehensive and accurate to a remarkable degree given the conflicting stories of prisoners, corrections officers, and politicians who became involved. I felt our coverage of the Attica rioting was worthy of a Pulitzer Prize and I later learned that the prize was awarded to a Rochester paper for its coverage in a very close call. The *News* from September 9 through September 17 printed eighty-two stories, countless pictures, and numerous editorials on the Attica uprising and its aftermath.

The initial story on September 9, 1971, reported that Attica inmates had seized four cellblocks, and that eleven guards were injured and others were being held hostage. These stories were written by Bob Buyer, first on the scene, and Ray Hill, one of the top reporters on staff.

The next day, September 10, the *News* carried nine stories on the Attica riot, an editorial, and a full page of pictures taken at the prison. And on September 11 we had nine stories on the prison situation and another full page of pictures.

The extent of *News* coverage the following week increased. On Monday, September 13, there were seven stories and a page of pictures. But on Tuesday, September 14, when the number of dead at Attica had reached forty, the *News* published fifteen stories, a page of pictures, a Bruce Shanks editorial page cartoon, and two Attica editorials. On the following day, our menu on Attica included fourteen stories, an editorial, and a page of pictures. On September 16 there were ten Attica-related stories, another editorial, and a Shanks cartoon. And on Friday, September 17, as things were wrapping up at the prison, the *News* published fifteen Attica stories and still another editorial.

The saturation coverage of the Attica rioting and its aftermath involved dozens of reporters, photographers, editors, and editorial writers. It was a Pulitzer Prize–winning effort, although that certainly was not the motivating factor in allocating all of those resources to the effort. The work of the staffers involved was excellent under conditions that were difficult at best. All of those involved will never forget the experience. Years later the *News* carried numerous stories on the trials stemming from the riots and the lawsuits resulting from the uprising.

The 1977 story that warranted extensive national media coverage was the blizzard that started on January 28, but the cumulative effect of the area's snowfall before that day really made it into a horrendous experience. The October preceding the actual date of the blizzard recorded a foot of snow. Two more feet of snow fell on November 28 and 29. And even more fell on January 1, 2, 7, 10, 15, and 17. Thirty-four inches had accumulated before the blizzard struck on January 28, resulting in seven deaths and countless hardships. Winds that day gusted up to sixty-nine mph and wind-chill temperatures dropped to fifty degrees below zero. Federal troops were called in to help the region dig out after days of emergency driving bans.[4]

The Love Canal situation that became a milestone in the national environmental movement actually got started in 1894 when William T. Love envisioned the establishment of a new city with industries powered by water dropping through a canal, bypassing Niagara Falls. He got the project started and had 3,200 feet of canal dug before he ran out of money and financial backing and had to abandon his ambitious plan. By the 1920s and 1930s, the city and industries in the Nia-

A scene showing prisoners and hostages during the Attica Prison uprising September 9–17, 1971. (Photo by Barney Kerr, courtesy *Buffalo News*)

gara Falls area needed a place to dump wastes and they used the canal as a dumpsite.[5]

The Hooker Chemical Company estimates that from 1942 to 1953 it buried 21,800 tons of chemical residues in Love Canal, a perfectly legal action at that time. The buried residue was walled and capped with earth, procedures that were considered safe two decades earlier. Hooker also confirmed that it buried some 200 tons of dioxin in the canal. As the result of corroded steel drums of chemicals; years of heavy rains; and the invasion of the cap by roads, utility lines, and buildings—including a school—the earthen "bathtub" began to overflow and by the mid-1970s the chemicals were pooling on the surface. Black ooze and white suds were bubbling through cracks in basements and driveways of nearby buildings.[6]

The story of Love Canal came to light in 1978. The *News* ran a story about the concerns of area residents on August 2, 1978, the first of countless articles produced as the situation developed. Our lead writer on Love Canal was our longtime environmental reporter, Paul

MacClennan. An interesting sidelight that gives some insight to newsroom reactions was the initial somewhat negative response at the *News* to the material being produced by MacClennan. Because he was known as an ardent champion of environmentalists, many of the editors expressed doubts about the seriousness of the Love Canal situation, feeling that MacClennan was going too far in his concern about the developing story. In fact, MacClennan was right on target.

It was the grassroots movement led by housewife Lois Gibbs and other neighborhood residents that finally caught the attention of the community and of the nation. Gibbs was in the forefront, demanding that the government order the evacuation of the Love Canal area and full remediation of the site.[7]

A fast-breaking and continuing series of events heightened awareness and concern about Love Canal. It was not until August 7, 1978, that Love Canal was declared an emergency by edict of President Jimmy Carter. Two months later the state began building a drainage system to collect the poisons coming from the canal. In May 1980, upset by reports that some inhabitants had chromosome damage, residents held two federal officials hostage. On May 21, 1980, President Carter declared a second federal emergency, clearing the way to relocate 728 families.[8]

Meanwhile, more and more voices were expressing concern. For example, Dr. Beverly Paigen of Roswell Park Memorial Institute called for evacuation of the area and sounded a very strong warning about health risks and the possibility of birth defects. Adding to the clamor for remediation was confirmation by the state in 1979 of the presence on the canal site of dioxin, the deadliest chemical synthesized by man.[9]

All of these happenings and many dozens more were reported fully in the *News* on a daily basis. The *Buffalo Courier-Express* and the *Niagara Gazette* were also doing a good job in keeping up with the fast-breaking story and forcing *News* editors to remain on their toes to keep up with or stay ahead of the print competition.

Love Canal triggered action to set up a special state and federal Superfund for environmental remediation projects. The reports of chemical industrial wastes buried under a school and leaching into adjacent neighborhoods shocked the nation. As a result, Love Canal came to symbolize nationally the need to protect public health by cleaning up the environmental mistakes of the past. The news media played a key role in defining the Love Canal disaster and maintaining a steady drumbeat of reporting and commentary that gripped the interest of the nation. Lois Gibbs was the fiery, determined, passionate spokesperson for Love Canal action, but her warnings might not have been heeded had it not been for the media listening to her and eventually getting the ear of state and federal officials.[10]

Another major local story during my period as managing editor was the April 30, 1976, decision by Federal judge John T. Curtin in the desegregation suit that had been tried one and a half years earlier. Curtin ruled that the Buffalo Board of Education was guilty of "creating, maintaining, permitting, condoning and perpetuating racially segregated schools. . . ." It was a blockbuster decision. Curtin's ruling was only the first of many steps that took place in succeeding years to come up with a desegregation plan that satisfied the plaintiffs and the court. It's been an ongoing story for years and *News* staffers have covered every facet of it in literally hundreds of stories.

Throughout this decade there were, of course, countless major stories on national and international fronts. All were given the full coverage *News* readers expected. The resignation of Vice President Spiro Agnew in October 1973, and more importantly the resignation of President Richard Nixon on August 9, 1974, and all the events leading up to it commanded a great deal of attention in the *News*.

Notes

1. *Buffalo News* marketing-research files.

2. Mark Goldman, *City on the Lake: The Challenge of Change in Buffalo, New York* (Amherst, NY: Prometheus Books, 1990), pp. 169–70.

3. Alfred Kirchhofer files, Butler Family Papers, E. H. Butler Library Archives, State University College at Buffalo, box 4.

4. Goldman, *City on the Lake*, pp. 151–55.

5. "Tale of the Century," *Buffalo News* special section, January 1, 2000, p. B-8.

6. Ibid.

7. Ibid.

8. Mike Vogel, “A Tragic Symbol Still Scars Land,” *Buffalo News*, August 2, 1988, p. 1-A.

9. Ibid.

10. Ibid

22 Wonderful Years

In 1978 I made a move that was applauded by many but at the same time aroused the ire of some staffers who felt the background of the individual involved would be a problem. It was the appointment of Richard D. McCarthy, better known as Max McCarthy, to our Washington bureau. McCarthy had been a reporter, a public relations executive, a congressman, a diplomat, a White House aide, a college teacher, and an aide to a Buffalo mayor. The political orientation of much of his career was a matter of concern to the staffers who challenged my judgment in hiring him. I had confidence in McCarthy's integrity and was convinced that his past experiences would be a plus for the *News*. In fact, it proved to be the case.[1]

McCarthy first came to our attention in 1952 when he was in the army, stationed in Japan. He sent his accounts of military life to the *News*, which published many of them. When discharged from service, he was hired as a reporter and continued in that role for three years before he resigned to become public relations director for the National Gypsum Company, then located in Buffalo. He kept that position until 1964 when he was elected to the House of Representatives at the age of thirty-six. He remained in the House until he made an unsuccessful run for the U.S. Senate in 1970, which cost him the House seat that he had held for three terms.[2]

Following the election loss, McCarthy served as community development director for a Buffalo company and then was named a Harvard fellow, lecturing at the Kennedy School of Government. In 1972 McCarthy ran again for Congress but lost the race. Soon thereafter he reentered academia as a visiting professor at Canisius College in Buffalo and at Niagara University, to the north. McCarthy's odyssey continued in 1973 when he joined Buffalo mayor Stanley Makowski's administration to help form a city Department of Human Resources. Following that short-lived venture, he received an appointment by President Gerald Ford to the U.S. Information Agency and during the next two years he served as press attaché at the U.S. Embassy in Iran.[3]

In 1976 President Jimmy Carter appointed McCarthy to his staff in a role involving domestic legislative affairs. In 1978 I invited him to join the Washington bureau of the *News*. He accepted, and three months later I appointed him bureau chief when Lucian Warren retired after ten years as head of the bureau. McCarthy in due time was elected to the prestigious Gridiron Club, continuing the paper's tradition of membership in that organization. He was the sixth member of the *News* to be elected to Gridiron.[4]

A graduate of Canisius College, McCarthy was the author of two well-received books. *The Ultimate Folly* was an exposé of the evils of chemical-biological warfare, and the 1972 *Elections for Sale* was one of the first books ever produced on political fundraising and spending. *The Ultimate Folly* was published in 1969 and resulted in congressional hearings and a national policy review that brought about the canceling of a plan to dump nerve gases into the sea.[5]

McCarthy frequently appeared on national television and was in great demand as a speaker.[6] He enjoyed these roles enormously and used all these opportunities to sing the praises of Buffalo. His family's roots in the city went back to the 1850s and he was fiercely loyal and protective of his city.[7]

McCarthy's background in politics served him well as our Washington correspondent. Although a lifelong Democrat, he was always aware of the need to strive for an evenhanded approach in his reporting. Without question his Saturday Viewpoints column did for the most part reflect his partisan bias. An eternal optimist, he was a joy to work with and his loyalty to his community, country, friends, and newspaper endeared him to friend and foe alike.[8] He was the Washington bureau chief until he officially retired in 1989, after falling victim to Lou Gehrig's disease, although he continued to write a weekly column for the *News*. The disease affects the body but not the mind, and McCarthy would dictate his column to a friend who would transmit it to the *News*. It was a heroic effort and continued until his death on May 5, 1995, at the age of sixty-seven.[9]

Warren Buffett, consistent with his pledge to me at our initial meeting, did not make any suggestions about moves that might be made in the newsroom. However, one major development did take place in November 1979 when Wardlow retired from the *News*. In June he had informed Urban and me that he planned to leave. Our initial reaction was one of complete surprise. We urged him to consider the consequences of such a move after twenty-seven years at the paper and, frankly, both Urban and I did not think he would carry through with his plans. On his last day at the *News*, I was gratified to receive a note from him that said in part,

> It's been a deep satisfaction to work with you in the *News*room over the past twenty-seven years . . . and most of all in a special relationship over the past ten. I feel particularly pleased that in a time of corporate turbulence and difficulty, Editorial never faltered. It ended up in better shape and doing a better job. I leave with the sure knowledge that in many of its most important areas, the paper is in fine hands.[10]

With Wardlow's retirement, Buffett promoted me on October 29, 1979, to editor and vice president and four years later to senior vice president. I in turn promoted Foster Spencer to managing editor[11] and Ed Cuddihy to assistant managing editor.[12] Both were longtime employees who had proven their worth and their loyalty to me, a necessary ingredient in putting together an effective team. The managing editor was needed to make the edition-to-edition decisions in the editor's absence and to perform some of the housekeeping duties that Wardlow had done for so many years. My next major appointment as editor of the paper came with the retirement of Millard Browne on January 1, 1980, as editorial page editor. Browne had joined the *News* in 1944 as an editorial writer and became chief editorial writer in 1953, following the death of William Meldrum, who had held the job for twenty years.[13] In my tribute to Browne upon his retirement, I wrote in my column that "His keen intellect, amazing ability to get to the hub of a problem quickly, fine analytical mind and beautiful writing style have made Browne one of the *News*'s most vital assets since his arrival here. We have seen him undergoing great mental anguish in arriving at many difficult decisions, deeply conscious always of his responsibilities to the *News* and its readers."[14] Millard Browne died July 17, 1996.

I had no problem in selecting Browne's successor. Leonard Halpert was eminently qualified to fill the position. He had become a *News* staff reporter in September of 1948 and made an immediate positive impression. In August 1950 he left the *News* to join the *Washington Times Herald* staff as an editorial writer. But in March 1951 he returned to the *News* as an editorial writer because he found that "conscience and a sense of ethics are too strong within me" to remain on a paper that espoused many policies with which he disagreed.[15]

My appointment of Halpert as editorial page editor was effective January 1980. Working with Halpert was a pleasurable experience. He was a fine editor, totally dedicated to his job. He had an absolute passion for fairness and accuracy in all editorials and disdained what I called the sledgehammer approach to any subject. He was always thoroughly prepared for editorial board meetings with supporters or opponents of local, national, or international subjects. He never failed to do his homework.[16]

Halpert had a well-deserved reputation for his sartorial habits. While others over the years had relaxed their manner of dress somewhat, Halpert, right up until the day of his retirement, always came to the office dressed in suit, tie, and long-sleeved shirt. Unlike others who deviated somewhat and in some cases dramatically from their usual office attire on Saturdays, Sundays, holidays, or during night hours, Halpert was steadfast. He was more conservative in dress than he was in philosophy. He was somewhat to the right of Browne, but still a liberal with many of the same concerns as those of his predecessor. Halpert was greatly respected by his staff and by publisher Lipsey. From the time he took over the job until he retired in July 1989, Halpert maintained the integrity and high standards of the editorial page. He was always thoroughly prepared to handle the daily editorial board meetings and would amaze public officials who met with the board with his knowledge of the subjects that came up at these meetings. He was a credit to the *News*.[17]

In a retirement tribute to him I wrote in a July 25, 1989, column that he was "A man of great intellectual capacity and in-depth knowledge of an infinite number of issues. His contributions to the development of an effective editorial page are too numerous to tabulate."

Named to succeed Halpert was Barbara Ireland, the first woman editorial page editor in the history of the paper. An editorial writer since January 1985, her educational and life-experience background and her above-average intelligence put her far ahead of other candidates for the job. Ireland had joined the *News* staff in October 1977 as a copyeditor and served as editor of the *Sunday* magazine from 1980 to 1984. In 1985 she became the first woman ever to serve on the editorial board. Her newspaper career started in 1973 as a reporter on the Auburn, New York, newspaper and after four years there she moved on to Albany's *Knickerbocker News* as a copyeditor.[18]

Under Ireland, the pendulum of *News* editorials moved farther to the liberal side. She, as could be expected, was very strong on issues of importance to women, but she also was thoroughly schooled on economic matters and foreign affairs. It was fascinating to watch Ireland grow in the job, starting somewhat tentatively but getting progressively stronger in her relationships with staff and asserting herself when she sought to win over board members to her way of thinking.[19]

Ireland was the recipient of a John S. Knight Fellowship at Stanford University and spent the period from October 1988 to June 1989 at the California campus. She returned to the *News* with greater confidence in her ability to pursue the course she had set for herself to "produce an editorial page that is informed, thoughtful, and fair and to encourage a lively and balanced discussion in our letters column and on our Viewpoints Page." She fulfilled these pledges well before resigning in 1998 to assume an editor's position at the *New York Times*.[20]

The unanticipated departure of Ireland resulted in a review of the entire *News* staff, including all of the editorial writers, for a potential successor. Candidates from many other newspapers also were interviewed, but in the final analysis, Gerald Goldberg, a *News* staffer since November 1977, was selected to succeed Ireland. Goldberg had come to the *News* from his reporting position with the *St. Louis Globe-Democrat*. Prior to that he had worked at the *Annapolis Capital* and the *Rochester Democrat and Chronicle*.[21] He joined the *News* as a reporter and later asked for reassignment to the copydesk and from that point on advanced through the ranks as assistant news editor, news editor, and assistant managing editor before being named editorial page editor.[22] During the interview process, Goldberg had told me that philosophically he was somewhat to the right of Barbara Ireland. I had no problem with that since I had felt for some time that Ireland was far too liberal in some areas and I had to constantly strive to move her toward a more moderate stance.

Goldberg is an intelligent man with an outgoing personality. He has a proclivity for occasionally losing his temper but is quick to calm down. His claim to be "somewhat to the right" of Barbara Ireland didn't materialize as I had expected. As I told him dozens of times after he took over the job, he was much more than "somewhat to the right" of her. And while I formerly spent time moving Ireland toward the middle of the road, I had to spend time moving Goldberg somewhat to the left. To his credit, however, Goldberg is flexible and we were always able to work out our differences quite readily. He and his staff now produce some editorials that I, as the retired editor, don't always agree with but likely are more in line with the thinking of today's middle-of-the-road readers.[23]

With the closing of the *Courier-Express* on September 19, 1982, and our decision to add a morning edition to the *News* publication schedule, the new staffers added were, whenever feasible, from the ranks of the *Courier*. I started my recruitment process with that in mind and, given my familiarity with the *Courier*, I had targeted in advance those I wanted to invite to join our staff. I particularly felt it was important to acquire the services of editorial cartoonist Tom Toles and former executive editor Doug Turner, whose career at the *Courier* ended at the paper's Washington bureau.

I made no secret of my intentions and both men were interviewed in my office and seen by *News* staffers. When word got out, as I knew it would, there was a very positive reaction to the prospect of Toles joining the staff but Turner brought negative responses. Given the long competition between the two newspapers and the *Courier* antitrust suit filed against us when we announced the *Sunday News* startup, the negative feeling against Turner didn't surprise me. However, the depth of that feeling certainly did. I was presented with a petition signed by a good many staffers urgently requesting that I not hire Turner. This staff petition was almost immediately followed up with similar petitions from the community. These, I was able to ascertain, originated from politicians and others who had run-ins with Turner during his years as *Courier-Express* editor.

Despite these petitions, I was convinced that Turner would be a fine choice for our Washington bureau to replace Roland Powell, whose resignation created an opening at the bureau. My meetings with Turner leading up to his hiring went very well and after a brief orientation in the Buffalo office he started his work in Washington,

Having been an investigative reporter at the *Courier* prior to his elevation as editor, Turner served the *News* well as McCarthy's number-two man in the bureau. He was well acquainted with the political leaders of the Buffalo area and very knowledgeable about Buffalo's economy and the problems facing the city and the area. He was a natural choice to replace McCarthy when he retired.

Turner always had been somewhat controversial as editor of the *Courier*. He was never known to be bashful about expressing his opinions on a great variety of subjects and, in fact, he and Max McCarthy went through some difficult periods when their personalities clashed. Turner was not the easiest man to get along with but his professional attributes were many. An exceptionally bright man, Turner often rubbed people the wrong way, resulting in complaints to the editor's office. But the stories Turner had written for the *Courier* while he was in its Washington bureau indicated that he had retained his reporting and writing skills. I have never regretted my decision to hire him.

With McCarthy's retirement in 1989, Turner became bureau chief and in addition to his daily reporting duties he initiated a weekly commentary column for the Sunday viewpoints section. It provided an outlet for his opinions, some along liberal lines, others that were much more conservative. As one area congressman told me, the Turner columns perplexed him; he never knew which side of a controversy Turner would come down on. He certainly was not predictable and that, I felt, was a definite strength.[24]

Assigned to the Washington bureau, as Turner's number-two man, was one of our finest young reporters, Jerry Zremski. He has proven to be a very valuable asset in the bureau because of his aptitude for in-depth analyses of situations and a fine work ethic. He also adapted well to working with the sometimes volatile Turner.

Turner, like his predecessors in our Washington bureau, was elected to membership in the Gridiron Club several years after joining the *News*. Membership in Gridiron had become a *News* tradition that was coveted by its publishers and editors. Tickets for attendance at the annual Gridiron dinner are very difficult to come by, and distribution for the most part is limited to members. Celebration of Gridiron weekend for many years had become a tradition at the *News*. The paper most years had five dinner tickets and utilized them for the publisher, the editor, and early on for friends of the publisher from the Buffalo community. Later, the publisher and the editor were accompanied to the dinner by leading advertisers of the *News*.

The Gridiron weekend tradition for years started on Friday night with an elaborate reception at the F Street Club, one of Washington, DC's most exclusive private dining clubs. Hosting the reception was the publisher of the *News* and the chief of the Washington bureau. Invited were a host of news sources utilized through the year by the bureau, and area congressmen and the senators from New York State. Following the F Street Club affair, our publisher hosted a dinner at one of Washington's finer restaurants for the Gridiron guests of our paper and their spouses and members of the Washington bureau and their spouses.

The Gridiron dinner always has been a Saturday night affair. While the men attended the dinner, their spouses were guests of the *News* at a Washington restaurant followed by attendance at one of Washington's theaters. Later that evening, the *News* party would gather in our hotel suite and then attend one or more of the many receptions held that night in the Hotel Statler, site of the Gridiron dinner for many years.

Another tradition of the weekend that continued until the 1980s was an excursion to a Washington-area restaurant for Sunday brunch by all of those making up the *News* party. The weekend was capped Sunday evening when all were invited to a repeat of the Gridiron show, which only the men had seen on Saturday night.

The Washington bureau of the *News* has been a major strength of the paper for all the years since Alfred H. Kirchhofer opened it in 1921.[25] Its performance always has depended, as could be expected, on the bureau chief. Some expanded the parameters of the bureau's coverage; others maintained a more limited but still valuable role. The bureau through most of its history has been manned by the chief and another reporter from the staff in Buffalo. These included stalwarts such as Frank Fortune, Irv Foos, Roland Powell, Ron Maselka, and most recently Jerry Zremski. During one period, the bureau was made up of the chief and two other reporters as well as a full-time secretary, Joan Kiser.[26] Doug Turner initiated a program that utilized the services of an intern for a good part of the school year, recruited from a Buffalo college. These internships have proven valuable for the *News* and for the young people chosen as well.

* * *

My determination to recruit Tom Toles was a sensitive endeavor. Editorial cartoonists are creative people and in my negotiations with Toles a great many areas had to be reviewed and agreed upon. I had no desire to retain the services of a talent who would be a recurring problem, but I did want someone for the job who would be controversial but not outlandish. I certainly did not want a cartoonist whose work would be bland or lack stimulating elements.

Tom Toles, winner of the 1990 Pulitzer Prize for his First Amendment cartoon series on a constitutional amendment banning flag burning. (Photo by Robert Kirkham, courtesy *Buffalo News*)

I assured Toles that his work would not be censored and that he did not have to be in concert with *News* editorial policy as expressed in its editorials or with the personal opinions of the editor. I stressed that I would reject his work only for what I considered to be in poor taste or possible libel. Toles and I reached a final agreement and he joined our staff in October 1982, serving us well until July 2002 when the *Washington Post* retained his services.[27] His departure was something that I had long anticipated would occur when the *Post*'s editorial cartoonist's position became available. It was a great opportunity for Toles and nobody could begrudge his seizing the opportunity, one he well deserved.

Toles, a native of Hamburg, a town in western New York's southern tier, is the son of the former financial editor of the old *Buffalo Times*. He was hired by the *Courier* as a graphic artist in 1973 following his stint as a staff artist at the University of Buffalo student publication, the *Spectrum*, during his undergraduate days. During the latter days of the *Courier*'s existence, he had been drawing editorial cartoons from time to time.[28]

Basically a shy and somewhat withdrawn man, Toles came to the *News* office early every morning and started his day by pacing around the newsroom deep in thought. He would bounce his ideas for cartoons off a select group of staffers whose judgment he respected. He would then retire to his cubicle adjacent to the space occupied by the editorial writers, rough out several cartoons, and present them to the editorial page editor for his review. They jointly selected the cartoon that he was to complete for use in the next day's paper. On rare occasions, when Toles and the editorial page editor did not reach agreement or there was a question of taste or potential libel, I was called upon to be the final arbiter. Toles enjoyed the freedom he had to express his views and I, as editor, relished his outstanding and challenging creations.

Confirming our confidence in Toles's outstanding performance, the Pulitzer Prize jury in 1990 awarded him a Pulitzer for a series of his editorial cartoons published in 1989. He competed against 129 other entries in the editorial cartooning category. The Pulitzer jurors particularly cited his First Amendment cartoon that dealt with the ramifications of a constitutional amendment prohibiting flag burning.[29]

In tribute to Toles following his Pulitzer award, I wrote in my editor's column that he is "a singular talent and his work is hard-hitting and provocative. His sense of outrage at assault on the environment or military spending at the expense of social programs and his strong opinions on education and waterfront access are manifested regularly in his work." I added, "the bite, the hyperbole, the vision of Toles cartoons are what elevate his work to the level of the truly fine editorial cartoonists in America."[30]

Toles was the second *News* editorial page cartoonist to win a Pulitzer. The first was Bruce Shanks who won the coveted prize in 1957 for his cartoon "The Thinker."[31]

I served as a Pulitzer Prize juror in 1990 and again in 1991. It was a fascinating, difficult, and exhausting experience—one that is far from perfect in its execution. The Pulitzer board, which is made up of members who serve for an extended period of time and ultimately make the final decisions on prizewinners, approves a list of journalists who are invited to serve as Pulitzer jurors. The secretary of the board invites the journalists to participate in the process that takes place at the Columbia University Journalism School in New York City in March. All jurors have to pay for their own expenses for what generally is a three-day affair.

In 1990 sixty-four professional journalists with hundreds of years of accumulated experience accepted the coveted invitations. They came from all parts of the country and from newspapers large and small. The sixty-four were assigned to jury panels in fourteen journalism categories: public service, general news reporting, investigative reporting, explanatory journalism, specialized reporting, national reporting, international reporting, feature writing, commentary, criticism, editorial cartooning, spot news photography, and feature photography. Most of these categories still exist today but changes have been made through the years, adding some and dropping others.

In 1990 I was assigned to the Pulitzer commentary category jury, which had two hundred seventeen entries to be judged. The following year I was assigned to the jury considering editorial writing, which had fewer than one hundred entries. The jurors can't express a preference for a specific panel. If an entry from their newspaper is before the jury on which they are serving, they have to recuse themselves from any consideration or even conversation about that entry.

The 1990 panel on which I served was made up of five jurors. Each had to read every one of the 217 entries at least once and there were dozens that we all read at least six times as we struggled to reach final determinations and a consensus. Each of the entries had up to ten samples of the entrant's work. Fortunately, in many instances reading each of the samples wasn't necessary. Given time constraints, each of us quickly realized there was no need to read them all if the first few turned us off.

Unfortunately, the environment in which the panel worked was not conducive to the absolute concentration such an important endeavor deserved. The rooms were hot and poorly ventilated and the jurors didn't have ideal lighting conditions or particularly comfortable chairs. Despite this, the judges worked assiduously on the selection process for three days, and from conversations with jurors on other panels we learned that conditions under which they operated were not much better than ours.

The jurors in each of the categories had the responsibility of culling from all of the entries before them the three that they agreed were the best and sending these to the Pulitzer board whose members would select the Pulitzer Prize winner in each category. The jurors do not rank their three finalists. The Pulitzer board has the sole responsibility for the final choice and has been known to reject all three of a jury's selections and move an entry from one category into another one and declare it a prizewinner.

We had been told at the outset that some Pulitzer juries have extreme difficulty in arriving at a determination of which three entries to recommend to the board. In fact, the panel on which I served in 1990 found itself in just that situation and despite the fact that the five of us had airline flight reservations for what should have been the day the judging process ended, we debated vigorously over one entry that held up our final determination for many hours. We were still debating while all the other panels had completed their work. Several of us had to reschedule our flights out of New York. It was heartening to be involved in that final debate. Even though we all knew that it likely would result in inconveniences for us—as it did—the primary consideration of the entire panel was to send to the Pulitzer board the very best of the work we had reviewed.[32]

Many editors like to boast to the readers of their newspaper about stories that have been nominated for the Pulitzer Prize, failing to take note that some editors make nominations that they know don't have a chance to win. My policy was very restrictive, nominating only those stories that I truly felt were worthy of meeting the challenge presented by the Pulitzers.

Our coverage of the 1971 Attica prison riot and its aftermath was one I believed was worthy of such consideration. The paper's objective coverage had received the plaudits of journalism observers and law-enforcement officials throughout the nation. I heard through the grapevine that the the panel judging the submissions, in which our Attica entry had been placed, had selected the *News* submission. Much to my great disappointment and that of the staff, the prize for Attica coverage was awarded by the Pulitzer board to the Rochester paper. We later learned that the board gave the edge to Rochester because as a morning paper it was able to break one key Attica story earlier in the day than the *News* had. Our overall coverage, we felt, was more comprehensive and insightful.

The efforts of *Buffalo News* staffers have been rewarded countless times over the years with commendations from the State Society of Editors and the New York State Publishers Association. These awards have gone to reporters, editors, photographers, and staff artists in competition with other major newspapers in New York State. Various foundations and professional organizations in many different fields also have frequently cited our staff. The *News* has never endorsed staff entries in competitions sponsored by commercial enterprises that tend to be self-serving, seeking only to enhance their image.

* * *

I have always believed that two of the most important functions of the editor are the hiring of staff and the allocation of human resources in the newsroom. For example, in July 1985, I hired Stan Evans, the city editor of the *Syracuse Herald Journal* and the *Sunday Herald American* since 1983. He had a fine reputation as an editor and staff manager. He joined the *News* as a copyeditor and was promoted in November to assistant city editor. A newspaperman since 1974 with New York's *Hornell Tribune*, he was highly respected for working well with staffers on in-depth stories and projects.[33]

In February 1987 I promoted Evans to assistant managing editor with responsibilities for operations of the city desk, the cityside reporting staff, and the suburban and outlying news bureaus. Assistant Managing Editor Ed Cuddihy, who had previously filled that role, had been spending more and more time on newsroom computer-systems operations and was assigned also to direct a guidance program for newsroom personnel interested in advancing their careers. He also continued his role in newsroom management functions. Dan MacDonald, who had been functioning as city editor since 1983, continued in that role, reporting directly to Evans.[34]

In December1987, I promoted Cuddihy and Bill Malley from assistant managing editors to deputy managing editors in recognition of their continuing major contributions to newsroom operations and also to further strengthen the senior newsroom management team. At the same time, Jerry Goldberg, who had been a news editor, was advanced to a management position as an assistant managing editor.[35]

Given our longtime major emphasis on reporting the local political scene, I faced an important decision when George Borrelli decided to retire in 1992 after twenty-four years at the paper. He had long filled a highly sensitive and vitally important reporting position.[36]

With the departure of Borrelli, I gave the political beat to Robert McCarthy, a move that surprised a great many on the staff. McCarthy was a respected reporter and *News* staffer since 1982, coming from a five-year stint at the *Olean Times Herald*. He had done some political reporting but few, if any, anticipated he would be named to replace Borrelli because he and I had an acrimonious exchange at an earlier arbitration hearing. McCarthy had represented the Newspaper Guild and the verbal exchange between us at one point became very heated. Frankly, I was really angry.

In evaluating the staff following Borrelli's departure, I determined that the staffer who could best represent the *News* in this very important beat was Robert McCarthy. I set aside personal considerations and named him to the job, a decision I have never regretted. McCarthy has been a worthy successor to Borrelli and in addition to his daily reporting of the political scene he has consistently written an excellent Sunday commentary piece for the viewpoints section. The column has given *News* readers interesting and important insights into the political scene without compromising his position as an objective reporter. This is a difficult path that many in the past have not been able to successfully travel. McCarthy has been cited, by qualified observers in the state, as one of the finest political writers in New York.

Another key element in our political coverage has been the Albany bureau. Following Jerry Allan's retirement in March 1982, I filled the vacancy with Dave Ernst who assumed the role in July 1982.[37] A totally different personality than the somewhat flamboyant Allan, Ernst was laid-back and a quiet, unassuming man but very definitely a fine journalist. When Allan advised us that he was going to retire, Ernst worked with him for a period during a tryout/transitional stage. Asked for his appraisal of Ernst, Allan praised his ability to get the job done and added, "Dave's not as bellicose and grumpy as I am on occasion." He was right on both counts.[38] Ernst did a creditable job for the *News* until he decided in the summer of 1989 to resign and join the state Department of Transportation in a public relations role, ending his twenty-one-year career at the paper.[39]

We hired Jon Sorensen, who had been chief of the *Ottaway News Service* in Albany for the previous six years. He had applied for our Albany post and his credentials were too good to ignore. Just months before, in May 1989, he was selected by former Capitol reporters as the top Albany correspondent for 1988–1989 in an unprecedented unanimous decision. Sorensen had been a finalist for this same distinction the year before. He had previously worked for several newspapers in New York State: the *Watertown Times*, the *Oneida Daily Dispatch*, the *Schenectady Gazette*, and the *Troy Record*. While with *Ottaway* he covered state government and politics for five *Ottoway* newspapers. Sorensen proved to be a competent reporter with good sources in Albany, but as his past employment record indicated he was ambitious and always looking to improve his lot. He left the *News* after a relatively short period of time.[40]

With Sorensen's departure, we hired Tom Precious from the *Knickerbocker News.* A knowledgeable observer of the state legislature and the governor's office, he has proven to be a fine choice as our Albany correspondent.[41]

One of the ugliest incidents an editor is unfortunate enough to face is to learn that a member of his staff has been guilty of the cardinal journalistic sin—writing about happenings on his beat in exchange for receiving monetary considerations from his sources. We were faced with this in March 1992 when the reporter's immediate supervisor learned that he was demanding and getting payments from his source to distort his reporting. The reporter had been a longtime member of the sports department and his actions, as our careful inquiry confirmed, definitely amounted to extortion.

When confronted with the findings of our inquiry, the staffer could not deny the allegations. The proof of what he had been doing for some time was overwhelming and there was no way he could remain in the employ of the *News* despite his many years of service and his shamefaced admission of what he did and why he did it. It was my first experience with this kind of malfeasance and while I had known the staffer for many years, I had no qualms at all about terminating his employment. In a March 31, 1992, column, I wrote about the incident. I did not use the reporter's name nor will I now, but I did say,

> A newspaper reporter's integrity, once shattered, destroys his value to his employer and places a cloud over all of his colleagues. Those with whom he makes regular contact must wonder if other *News* staffers conduct their business in the same unethical manner. We can categorically state that we know of no other such dereliction on the part of any remaining members of our staff and if any were to come to light dismissal would be immediate.

Fortunately in my remaining years as editor of the paper, no other such incidents came to my attention. Reporters and editors must be above reproach in their conduct while on the job. Staffers have to scrupulously avoid even the slightest indication that they can be influenced by monetary or other considerations. This experience was the most distasteful in my thirty years of newsroom oversight.

The *Buffalo News*, to my knowledge, has never experienced a scandal such as the *New York Times* recently underwent with Jayson Blair. Blair was fired in May 2003 for fabricating stories, plagiarizing, and generally violating accepted ethical standards for reporters. In the wake of this revelation, the executive editor and the managing editor were asked to resign their positions by the *Times* publisher. With this deplorable situation in mind, I reviewed the notes and memos of my predecessors at the *News* and could find no mention of any such incidents at the paper.

The *Times* problem resulted from a lack of communication between department heads, and despite assurances to the contrary, a willingness to tolerate Blair's record of errors because he was a minority. The result was a major embarrassment for the nation's finest newspaper, the end of Blair's journalism career, and a setback for newspaper staff integration efforts throughout the industry.

Notes

1. *Buffalo News* obituary, May 6, 1995, p. A-2.
2. Ibid.; *Buffalo News* personnel files.
3. Ibid.; Marjorie Hunter, "The Press, the House, Then Back," *New York Times*, February 2, 1985, p. 5.
4. Ibid.
5. Ibid.
6. Murray B. Light, "The News—Your Newspaper," *Buffalo News*, March 4, 1980, second front page.
7. Ibid.
8. Ibid.
9. Ibid.
10. Letter from Elwood M. Wardlow, November 28, 1979. Quoted by permission.
11. *Buffalo News* obituary, March 28, 1997.
12. Murray B. Light, "Your Newspaper," *Buffalo News*, December 8, 1987, second front page.
13. Ralph Dibble, "The *Buffalo Evening News* Is Born," *Buffalo News* centennial publication, October 12, 1980, p. H-6.
14. Murray B. Light, "The News—Your Newpaper," *Buffalo News*, January 7, 1980, second front page.
15. *Buffalo News* personnel files.
16. Dibble, "The *Buffalo Evening News* Is Born," p. H-7.
17. Light, "The News—Your Newspaper," *Buffalo News*, July 25, 1989, second front page; Len Halpert, interview by Murray B. Light, August 2002; Kirchhofer files, Butler Family Papers, box 4.
18. Ibid.
19. Light, "The News—Your Newspaper," *Buffalo News*, July 25, 1989.
20. Ibid.

21. "Goldberg Named Editor of Editorial Page," *Buffalo News*, May 27, 1998.

22. Light, "Your Newspaper," *Buffalo News*, December 8, 1989, second front page.

23. "Goldberg Named Editor of Editorial Page."

24. Light, "Your Newspaper," *Buffalo News*, October 3, 1989, second front page.

25. Alfred Kirchhofer files, Butler Family Papers, E. H. Butler Library Archives, State University College at Buffalo, box 11; Alfred H. Kirchhofer Papers, Buffalo and Erie County Historical Society Archives, box 11.

26. *Buffalo News* personnel files.

27. Light, "Your Newspaper," *Buffalo News*, April 17, 1990, second front page.

28. Ibid.; *Buffalo News* personnel files.

29. Ibid.

30. Ibid.

31. "Array of Honors for the News Includes Coveted Pulitzers," *Buffalo News*, October 12, 1980, p. H-9.

32. Light, "Your Newspaper," *Buffalo News*, March 27, 1990, second front page.

33. Ibid., February 10, 1987.

34. Ibid.

35. Ibid., December 8, 1989.

36. Ibid., June 23, 1992.

37. Ibid., March 16, 1982.

38. Ibid., April 6, 1982.

39. Ibid., July 4, 1989.

40. Ibid., August 15, 1989.

41. *Buffalo News* personnel files.

23 A Wealth of Talent

A local columnist who has a large and loyal following is an important circulation factor for any newspaper. We're talking about someone who becomes a "must-read" for a great many people and whose columns become conversation pieces for many in the community because of their general subject matter, emotional appeal, or controversial content. In my fifty years at the *News*, I worked with many talented reporters, editors, photographers, and artists whose combined efforts have enhanced the reputation of the paper as one of the nation's outstanding regional publications.

When I first joined the paper in 1949, reporters for the most part worked anonymously. A bylined story was a rarity. That changed over the years and today most stories carry the byline of the reporter. There's a plus and a minus factor in this development. Readers now readily associate certain bylines with particular types of stories and have more confidence in a story if it carries the byline of a reporter they have come to respect for the knowledge he or she brings to each new story on the subject. That's the plus factor. On the negative side, too many stories of a routine, humdrum nature carry bylines. Just as familiarity can breed contempt, too many bylines on less than important or specialized types of stories tend to undermine the value of the bylined story.

For many years the *News* was fortunate to have a greatly respected and popular columnist in Ray Hill. He was a law-and-order man whose reputation in western New York was first established in his role as one of our investigative reporters for years.[1] He broke stories about corruption of some officials in Lackawanna that led to many reforms there. He hammered away at city street-paving irregularities, the city police-garage scandal, and crime in the city and the state. He also criticized judges for lenient sentencing. His 1973 series with John Hanchette on the "License to Kill" highlighted drunk driving and the disparities in sentencing for those convicted of that offense. The series infuriated many judges who were not happy about seeing their records in reducing charges paraded before the public. His 1978 series with Dick Haynes on arson was cited by the National Firefighters' Association as the best in the nation on the subject. Although judges in various jurisdictions often were targets of Hill's barbs for being too lenient with defendants, the Judges and Police Conference in 1986 gave him its outstanding citizen award.[2]

Shortly after the *Buffalo Courier-Express* closed its doors in 1982, the *News* sought permission from a *Courier* officer to continue that paper's annual charity drive. Without citing a reason, our request was rejected. Hearing this, Hill approached *News* publisher Stan Lipsey with an idea for an annual *News* drive to assist the needy of the community during the Christmas holiday season. Lipsey approved the idea and the paper's Neediest Fund was created, kicking off its first annual drive on November 21, 1982. The annual appeal, with its efforts concentrated primarily on donations from individuals, has, since its inception, raised millions of dollars in cash, foodstuffs, clothing, and toys.[3]

For many years Hill was the principal figure guiding the Neediest Fund. He wrote hundreds of deeply touching stories about the effort and those who were recipients of the appeal's largesse. He was the guiding spirit of the fund, virtually directing all of its efforts, including collection and distribution of the dollars, food, toys, and clothing. After a period of years, the *News* invited the United Way to join with it in the venture, which had grown beyond anything originally envisioned.[4]

Hill, who had a special feeling for the needy and particularly for children, turned his attention to another worthy endeavor that had been launched but had not received much publicity. Hill adopted Camp Good Days and Special Times as a special project. He spotlighted this facility for children with cancer by writing countless stories about its role and the beneficiaries of the Camp Good Days experience. Much like his efforts with the *News* Neediest Fund, Hill was enormously successful in increasing the fundraising efforts for Camp Good Days. He was named its Man of the Year in 1985. He had raised its profile enormously in all of western New York and sparked countless donations from individuals, corporations, and foundations.[5]

In addition to his writing duties, Hill for years served as chairman of the *News* unit of the Newspaper Guild, which represented and continues to do so, newsroom, circulation, and bookkeeping department employees. A responsible union leader, he came up with the idea that led to the establishment of our Labor Management Committee after a brief strike in 1980.[6]

An incident in 1979 exemplifies the high regard management and the unions had for Hill. It occurred on November 10 when the *Courier* had publicly acknowledged its financial problems and the possibility that it could close its doors. Hill approached me that day to report that Richard Roth, the *Courier* guild unit chairman, had asked him to pass along to the *News* a request by Jim Schaeffer, the acting publisher. Schaeffer was interested in an expression from the *News*, through the auspices of the guild, of possibly increasing the circulation price of both newspapers so those guild members at both papers could benefit. Schaeffer felt that the increased revenue of both papers would enable them to enhance the salary structure.

I immediately raised the specter of antitrust considerations but Hill said it would not be a factor because the guild would be the go-between and both papers would act simultaneously on a good-faith basis once the guild had the word that both papers would honor such an arrangement. I transmitted this request the next day to Buffett and Munger, both of whom rejected the idea flatly, saying that it would instantly raise antitrust problems. They asked me to transmit that rejection to Hill, while thanking him and the guild for their concern. The *News*, they said, would have no interest in any such arrangement.

Hill served many times as a member of the guild negotiation team as the Buffalo Newspaper Guild contract came up for renewal. He was a tough, knowledgeable negotiator but was always aware of his responsibilities to be fair to his members and his employers and not press persistently for contract provisions that he knew the paper could not responsibly approve. He and Thomas McMahon, guild counsel for years before he was appointed a court of claims judge, were a fine negotiating team involved in the guild's bargaining with the *News*.

Ray Hill enjoyed enormous popularity with *News* readers and for good reason. His compassion, concern, and sensitivity came through in every column he wrote about the underdog, the victims of circumstance, the ill, the handicapped, and the injured. When Hill wrote, the people of western New York reacted. The response his columns engendered was remarkable. Readers said that what they particularly liked about Hill was that he could get tough and mighty mean when writing about those he believed were wronging the little guy. He didn't pull any punches when he felt criticism was warranted. Interestingly enough, in his long career as an investigative reporter and his twelve years as a columnist, not a single libel suit was filed against Hill.[7]

A native of Hamilton, Ontario, Hill's first newspaper job was with the *Toronto Star*, then the *Daily News* in Hamilton, followed by nine years with the *Toronto Telegram* as a city hall reporter and political columnist before joining the *News* in November 1964. He died on August 20, 1997, at the age of sixty-six, several years after his retirement.[8] Ray Hill was a legend to those whose lives he touched. His many crusades for the needy and the underdog were legendary and he was without question the most popular columnist the *News* ever employed.

* * *

Readers associate most reporters with one specialty but there are exceptions such as Jeff Simon. Three decades of *News* readers have come to respect Simon for his extensive knowledge of movies, television, books, and music—particularly jazz. Through the years, his colleagues at the *News* have expressed their enormous admiration for the extent of Simon's knowledge in all of these areas.

A Buffalo native who attended the Nichols School, Syracuse University, and the University at Buffalo, Simon started as a copy aide at the *News* in 1964 and in 1969 was hired as a general assignment reporter. He started writing the television-radio column in 1975 and after that stint was completed he continued to write a television commentary column in *TV Topics* every Sunday.[9]

Simon is well known for his lengthy—and at times overly lengthy—interviews with luminaries in the film and television fields. He is proudest of his interview with Robert Redford while *The Natural* was being filmed in Buffalo. Redford was not generally available for interviews, but he spent a good deal of time with Simon, resulting in an interview that ultimately was carried by the *New York Times* Syndicate and was widely reprinted in Sweden, Finland, France, and a great many U.S. newspapers.[10]

Simon has an uncanny ability to get leaders in their fields who are usually reluctant to talk to the press to agree to meet with him. He has conducted interviews with Paul Newman, Jane Fonda, Madonna, Paul McCartney, Steven Spielberg, John Cage, Anthony Burgess, and many others. Simon has written hundreds of movie reviews for the *News* since his stint as a TV columnist ended. Although he still hasn't abandoned his love affair with film, he now says he derives the most satisfaction from writing book reviews and overseeing the selection of reviews for the *Sunday News* book pages.[11]

A unique talent, Simon is readily identified by our readers as an experienced and highly qualified observer in his areas of interest. Readers learn the kinds of movies, books, and TV shows that win Simon's plaudits and those that turn him off. They have learned over the years to either agree or disagree with his appraisals but most importantly he has become a barometer for them.

In my more than thirty years of reading Simon's reviews, I never changed his copy to reflect my opinions, although they frequently were at odds with his. I did, however, exercise my editor's prerogatives to alter some of his language. Simon, not infrequently, would use words that I had not heard of and which I thought our readers would be equally unfamiliar with. His copy often resulted in my consulting the dictionary to see if this or that word he used actually was in the

English language. There were occasions when my suspicion that Simon enjoyed manufacturing new words proved to be valid. Much to his chagrin, these nonwords would be exorcised from his review. Having said this, however, I have to say he has an excellent—and most unusual—command of the English language.

Another *News* columnist with a large and dedicated following is Donn Esmonde, who came to the paper in January 1982 and was on the sports staff until April 1989 when I assigned him to write a column with a local orientation. While in the Sports Department, he clearly manifested his significant skills as a talented writer. In speaking of his work I often would refer to him as our "beautiful writer." He earned his promotion as the prime local columnist because of his writing ability, his obvious intelligence, and his dedication to Buffalo.[12]

Esmonde has become a spokesperson and champion of the area's underclass and a strident critic of political leaders who, in his mind, have not done enough to enhance the area's economy. He also has championed the cause of regionalism, the combination of city and town government and services. There are those who have expressed the hope that Esmonde would ease up on occasion and write about some lighter subjects, but he is a dedicated reformer and so it is unlikely that he will soften his approach any time soon. He has become a spokesperson for Buffalo's preservationists. He consistently opposes proposals for demolition of downtown buildings that have been abandoned for years to make way for parking lots. Esmonde, the purist, tends to overlook the realities of today's world, insisting that downtown parking is not needed to attract business. People, he says, can walk from a distant parking spot to the place where they work. He doesn't face that problem because our large parking lot is immediately adjacent to the *News* building. Reading Esmonde regularly I wonder why I created this column opportunity for a writer with whom I so often disagree. He does, however, generate comment and controversy, which is the hallmark of an outstanding local columnist.

Given the dominant role that television plays in the lives of the vast majority of Americans, a newspaper's television critic is a major factor in its product mix. That critic has to know the medium well, have the ability to relate his personal feelings plainly to his readers, and consistently stay abreast of all developments in a medium that is constantly changing.

When I first came to the *News* in 1949, the paper was ahead of many others in the nation in its regular coverage of television and radio news and commentary. It also published a listing of the few television stations in the market. Many newspapers, concerned about the competitive impact of television, barely acknowledged the subject. Our TV-radio column at that time really was nothing more than a public relations outlet for the newspaper's television station and its AM and FM radio stations. The paper's principal editor, Alfred H. Kirchhofer, also had primary responsibility for its electronic media and used the column to hype the stations.

By the time I became managing editor in 1969, the situation had changed and Gary Deeb was writing the television column. Deeb was a very bright, highly articulate writer and the TV column changed dramatically from its early days. In fact, Deeb developed into an extremely tough critic who used a hammer approach when commenting on television programming. He was not subtle in his criticism. In fact, one got the impression that somebody was standing beside him yelling, "Hit 'em again, harder, harder."

I tried unsuccessfully to get Deeb to tone down his approach somewhat and look for some positives instead of continually accentuating the negative. It didn't work and finally, in frustration, I suggested to Deeb that Buffalo was not a good market for his overly strong approach and that it would be best if he looked for the opportunity to relocate. He agreed and remained on the *News* payroll until he was offered a wonderful opportunity to work as the television critic of the *Chicago Tribune*. He did very well there and was syndicated nationally, with his columns appearing in many newspapers throughout the country. His success was no surprise, given his writing talent. His approach was made to order for a major market such as Chicago.[13]

Hal Crowther next stepped into the role of television columnist and did a highly credible job for several years before he opted to move to a university setting in the South that offered him the opportunity to express himself more fully and satisfy his intellectual pursuits.

Crowther was a good critic who was not timid about expressing his opinions. He could come down hard on some programming but did not employ Deeb's sledgehammer approach. However, he was the only TV columnist whose work resulted in a libel suit against the *News*. The lawsuit involved columns written over a period of a year criticizing a local radio station for cutting back on its local news staff. The owner of the station, who had never complained about the columns, filed a libel suit against us. He denied the allegation that his station had cut back on local news coverage. The suit went to trial and the presiding judge threw out several of the charges and the jury found the *News* innocent of the rest. Crowther resigned in 1979 to take advantage of a position in North Carolina.[14] He had been a fine critic with a good touch and we were sorry to see him leave.

Replacing Crowther was Mary Ann Lauricella, a delightful person who was well liked by all. She was also a good reporter and fine writer. Unfortunately, the former *Courier-Express* reporter just could not bring herself to criticize anything or anyone. I had made a mistake in naming her to a critic's role because she was just too good a person and it went against her nature to criticize programs or personalities when they did not live up to certain standards. After a time Lauricella returned to reporting duties and ultimately left the *News* and later established her own local public relations agency.[15]

Alan Pergament, a Syracuse University graduate who joined the staff in 1970 and moved into the Sports Department as a reporter in 1973, was appointed our television critic in February 1982 and has filled that role with distinction ever since.[16] Prior to that, he had been writing a Saturday sports television column for three years. When I named Pergament to the TV columnist role I informed him that his progress would be reviewed each year and that his status on staff could change if I was not satisfied with his work. This was the result of my less than happy experience with prior TV columnists.

Pergament has set a record for longevity in the job. His greatest asset has been his ability to remain a fine reporter while also in the role of columnist. He's a dedicated newspaperman who works the phones constantly; watches more television than any person should have to endure; meets frequently with television executives, anchor persons, and personalities; keeps abreast of all the trends in local and national television; and always informs readers on the latest TV trends.

Pergament clearly explains why he likes or dislikes a program. His writing style is simple and straightforward, an approach that is easy to comprehend. Unlike some of his predecessors, he is not overly harsh in his negative critiques, but when he doesn't like something he says it without equivocation. He has been a highly successful critic in almost every respect.

* * *

Bob Buyer reported to work for the *News* on August 1, 1951, and by the time he retired in June 1998, he had written 1,080 weekly farm columns, starting in 1977. This from a man who was born, bred, and educated in New York City, not exactly farm country. Eight months after coming to the paper from the regional *Jamestown Sun*, he was assigned to what was then known as the western New York beat. This launched his love affair with the smaller communities in our area and developed his interest in agricultural subjects and his dedication to writing about the problems and interests of farmers.[17]

Although most *News* readers invariably associate his name with reporting on agricultural matters, Buyer also had a special knack with "people stories" and he wrote hundreds of those to warm the hearts of our readers. He thoroughly enjoyed traveling around western New York's rural areas, unearthing unusual and mostly heartwarming stories about people and their pursuits, not necessarily people holding public office or important business positions.[18]

The highlight of his reporting career, however, was his role in our coverage of the 1971 Attica Prison riots. He was a key member of the paper's team from beginning to end. On the morning of September 9, 1971, our Attica correspondent called in to report that the prison whistle was blowing, signaling a problem. Buyer was sent to the scene because he had been there a half dozen times on assignments. He had the contacts to get into the prison. He spent part of the first day and night inside the prison with the inmates, covering for the *News* and acting as a pool reporter for all the media. Buyer played a major role in the intensive coverage by numerous staffers during the uprising and later he covered many of the court trials resulting from the lawsuits brought by riot survivors and kin of those killed or injured.[19] In the aftermath of the Attica rioting, Buyer said, "The whole Attica affair, a blotch of history, represents a breakdown of the social order. Too many things went wrong for too many people. People are all flawed and at Attica too many of those flaws converged at once. There's blame enough all around for what happened."[20]

In the fifteen years prior to his retirement, Buyer became a dedicated writer on the Summer Harvest of the Food Bank of Western New York that dispenses food to the needy through its network of pantries. It was a cause that he believed in and after getting the initial assignment, he requested that he be assigned to cover it each summer. His stories were responsible for raising more than $1 million dollars for this important charitable endeavor. The Food Bank people repeatedly said that the drive never could have achieved its results without Buyer's efforts.[21]

Buyer had a reputation as a frugal man and his expense accounts reflected that characteristic. In the years that I reviewed staff expense accounts, I always was amazed at the ones submitted by Buyer. He, without doubt, spent less on out-of-town assignments than any other staffer. At the other end of the spectrum was Larry Felser, the sports editor and columnist, whose expense accounts were on the high end, although he always had receipts to verify the validity of his expenditures. Larry, when questioned about his spending, would respond that he represented the *News* when he was out of town and he didn't want any of the sportswriters from other newspapers to get the idea that we wanted to do things "on the cheap."

Buyer and his wife, Sue, a former *News* reporter, have lived for decades in Williamsville. The most convenient access to his home from the *News* office is the New York State Thruway. In all his years at the paper Buyer rarely used the Thruway to get to the office or to return home. He preferred to use the local, nontoll streets.

Buyer was a fine reporter who always did his job well. When we announced in the paper that he was retiring, we received numerous letters and phone calls from readers who said they would miss his work. As a result we asked him to continue writing the farm column after his retirement and he did so for a time before finally calling an end to his fine newspaper career.

Everything sooner or later comes to an end and newspaper features are no exception. "NewsPower" was introduced in 1967 as an action-line feature responding to readers' consumer-oriented questions and problems with companies large and small. The column was finally discontinued twenty-four years later as more and more governmental and nonprofit agencies were created to deal with the same kind of consumer problems. NewsPower, which had been an effective medium for unhappy consumers, was no longer the primary outlet for solving their problems. It was discontinued in June 1991 after a long, highly successful run helping thousands of people through the years. The same fate befell action-line columns in the many other newspapers that had been running them.

After four years of rotating the writing and researching of the NewsPower column among different staffers, the assignment was given on a permanent basis to reporter Dick Christian. He thoroughly enjoyed the job and unlike others who had previously been involved, Christian understood its potential to become an important and popular feature. He had the uncanny ability to solve readers' problems without alienating the businesses with which he had to work to satisfy the complainants.[22]

Christian's best newsroom buddy was Ray Hill. The two had desks in the rear of the cityside sector of the newsroom and were known to imbibe back there from time to time. I was aware of the practice but tolerated it because it never caused a disturbance and both performed their duties well.

Christian, now retired and living in Arizona, has been divorced and remarried. His first wife used to enjoy baking Christmas cookies every year for Warren Buffett. She also wrote to him regularly. Warren enjoyed both the cookies and the letters.

Working with Christian for many years was a very capable part-time assistant, Marcia Harasack. Her duties included the handling of the great volume of NewsPower mail, pursuing the consumer avenues for Christian to follow in settling reader problems, and a host of other matters that on other newspapers occupied three or four full-time employees.[23]

One particular sector of news coverage that troubled me for years was religious reporting by the paper. A strong believer in the separation of church and state, I also questioned the validity of a secular newspaper getting involved in coverage of religion, and its ability to do so without seeming to favor one religion. In fact, one of the first moves I made as managing editor back in 1969 was to eliminate the use of the Reverend Billy Graham's column that the paper had been publishing once a week for a considerable time.

The Buffalo area population is predominantly Catholic, and in recognition of that fact the paper for years published a long list of contributors to Catholic Charities, but did not do the same for those who gave to other religious drives. I ultimately bit the bullet and discontinued this practice after explaining my rationale to the bishop of the Catholic diocese. The move was accepted with good grace by the bishop and the paper's relationship with the diocese continued to be good, perhaps because the paper reported regularly on the Catholic Charities drive and its progress.

The *News*'s religion coverage, outside of the special things it did for the Catholic Church, consisted for the most part of what I categorized as the "bulletin board approach." We would run short items on special services, speakers, dinners, and other routine items on church activity. The coverage rarely, if ever, included analysis of what was transpiring in the various religions and why. These were the questions I thought needed to be explored and the issues that should be explained. We were not doing the job.

Finally, in July 1985 I was convinced we had a religion reporter who had the experience and the expertise to make our religion coverage meaningful. I had hired David Briggs, who had years of reporting experience at the *New Haven (CT) Journal-Courier*, and had graduated from a special two-year course at Yale University's Divinity School that prepared its students for specialization in religion reporting. Briggs, indeed, provided what I had long sought. I was aware of the need for meaningful reporting on religion and up to this point had not gotten it. Briggs brought a thoughtful approach to our religion reporting with analyses of trends, and the reasons for what was occurring. Unfortunately for us, his work attracted the Associated

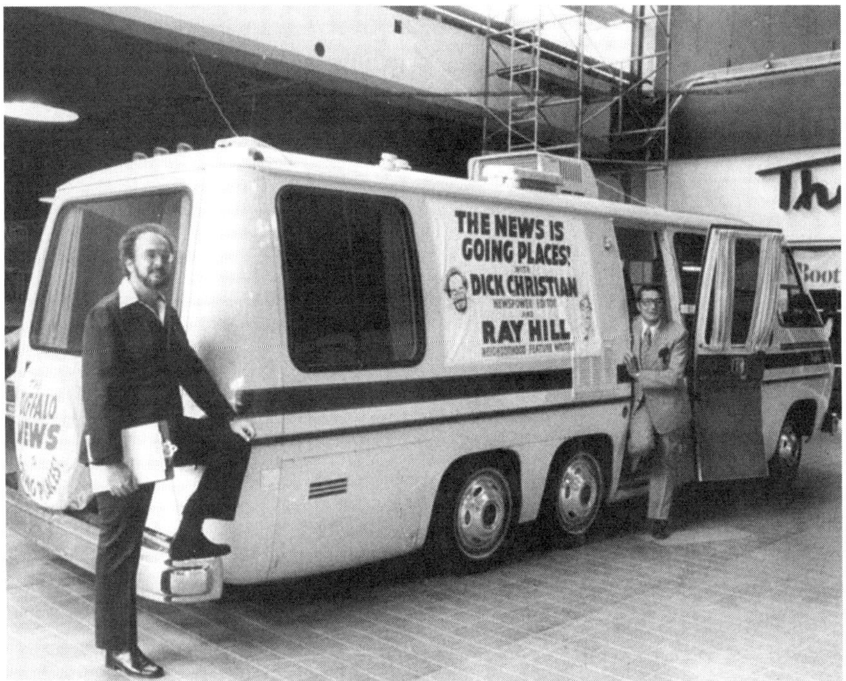

Two popular *News* reporters, Dick Christian (*left*) and Ray Hill, undertook a 1971 tour of western New York communities to spread the word about the *News*. (Courtesy *Buffalo News*)

Press whose longtime religion reporter decided to retire. They hired Briggs in his place and we lost his expertise much too quickly.

Briggs's successor on the religion beat was competent but most certainly did not have the background of his predecessor. I had to constantly remind him and his editors that he was giving too much attention to the Catholic Church and for the most part not covering the activities of the other religions.

In 2000 Susan LoTempio, an assistant managing editor, made a significant move to upgrade the paper's religion coverage, devoting the lead page of the Saturday features section to the subject. This page, and at times the following page, includes messages from leaders in the local religious community and their philosophies. From my personal perspective, I feel LoTempio has done a good job in upgrading the paper's coverage of religion but I still have serious reservations about the approach, and most particularly the headlines on the articles, which definitely are not objective, but are instead reflective of the particular bias presented in the article. That's a direction that I strongly believe would be fine in religious publications but not in the secular press.

Notes

1. *The Buffalo News* obituary, August 20, 1997; Murray B. Light, "Your Newspaper," *Buffalo News*, August 13, 1991, second front page; *Buffalo News* personnel files.
2. Ibid.
3. Ibid.
4. Ibid.
5. Ibid.
6. Ibid.
7. Ibid.
8. Ibid.
9. Jeff Simon, interview by Murray B. Light, December 19, 2001; *Buffalo News* personnel files; Light, "Your Newspaper," *Buffalo News*, September 3, 1991, second front page.
10. Ibid.
11. Ibid.
12. Light, "Your Newspaper," *Buffalo News*, April 4, 1989, second front page.
13. *Buffalo News* personnel files.
14. Ibid.
15. Murray B. Light, "The News—Your Newspaper," *Buffalo Evening News*, November 13, 1979, second front page.
16. *Buffalo News* personnel files.
17. Light, "Your Newspaper," *Buffalo News*, June 26, 1998, second front page.
18. Ibid.
19. Light, "The News—Your Newspaper," *Buffalo Evening News*, January 15, 1980, second front page.
20. Ibid.
21. Light, "Your Newspaper," June 26, 1998.
22. *Buffalo News* personnel files.
23. Ibid.

24 A Breaking Story

Although columnists are important to any paper, the real backbone of a newspaper organization consists of the reporters and editors who produce and edit the hard news day after day. I am going to take you through a day in the newsroom and show you how the Three Mile Island story developed in 1979 and how the staff responded to breaking developments.

Friday, March 30, started as a routine day in the newsroom of the *Buffalo Evening News*. At the 8:30 morning meeting *News* editors reviewed the events of Thursday night and early Friday morning.

The word from the Three Mile Island nuclear plant near Harrisburg, Pennsylvania, where an accident had occurred at four in the morning, is that the situation is stable. The story has no elements of fresh news. The page-one story is allocated a spot on an inside page of Friday's state edition.

By 8:45 AM the decision is made—the lead story in the state edition would be on a U.S. inspection team and its visits to the problem dumpsites in Niagara Falls. The Love Canal controversy was still in its infancy.

At 9:10 AM a bulletin flashes on the wire-service machines, kicking off seventeen hours of frenetic activity in the newsroom that continued through the Friday afternoon editions and subsided only when Saturday morning's final edition went to press. The message that started it all said a new uncontrolled release of radiation had taken place at the Three Mile Island nuclear installation.

Instantaneously alerted by wire editor Bob Meister, news editor Gene Harasack, although past his state edition copy deadline, reorders all the priorities set at the earlier news meeting and shifts the lead story in the state edition. "Radiation Spews from Nuclear Plant" becomes the eight-column headline at the top of page one.

Within a matter of minutes, a torrent of copy gushes from wire-service machines in the newsroom. The situation is confusing. Contradictory statements come from local, state, and federal authorities on the scene. But the gravity of the situation is obvious. The possibility exists that the greatest peacetime nuclear tragedy has just been unleashed.

Although wire-service copy is flowing into the *News* at the rate of 1,200 words a minute, the decision is made at 9:30 AM that a staff reporter should be sent to the scene. To some this might seem ludicrous. With all the resources of the Associated Press and United Press International, why would the *News* feel that its own reporter could add a dimension of importance to its readers?

The answer is basic: with its own man on the scene, *News* editors can specifically order stories they feel the wire services are overlooking or are being handled inadequately in their rush to serve thousands of news organizations around the world.

In this case, too, we know we have an ideal man for this type of "extra" coverage. David Shribman is an excellent writer who can dig out the human stories behind the factual material. But getting him to Harrisburg isn't easy. More than a dozen calls to commercial airlines prove fruitless. Flight times are not satisfactory, flights are filled, and connections won't work out no matter what circuitous hookups are explored.

Finally, Elliot Shapiro, assistant city editor, contacts Prior Aviation and arranges for a charter aircraft to fly Shribman to the site. But more problems arise as Prior is refused clearance to land at Harrisburg or at any of several neighboring airports. Finally, the Harrisburg clearance comes.

Rental cars are reserved at various airports so that our reporter will have wheels when and where he finally lands at around 2 PM. These arrangements and others are being made to ensure the coverage we want for Saturday's paper. But in the meantime four more editions of Friday's *News* are in the making. And the appearance and content of page one in each edition changes as reports from Three Mile Island come in. The changes are dictated by myself, as editor, in consultation with the managing and news editors. The rapidly changing situation and the difficulty in shaping conflicting reports about what was occurring into comprehensive and clear stories that eliminate as much confusion as possible for readers keeps editors constantly on the move, fighting the additional pressures of copy deadlines.

Fortunately, the adrenaline flows in the newsroom and the production departments during tense, breaking-news situations such as this. Everybody involved digs deeper to achieve their common goal of getting the paper on the presses in time. At the *News*, we've always been blessed with a harmony of reaction. When the newsroom has a major story, the production people respond in kind and kick in that extra gear to get the job done. Such is the case in Friday's nuclear accident situation.

The story is still changing as Friday's final edition comes off the press at 4:30 PM and the handoff starts from the editorial crew responsible for Friday's papers to those arriving to shape Saturday morning's *News* editions. Just about this hour the startling word comes that the nuclear plant might face a meltdown, the most serious possible nuclear accident.

Quickly the decisions are made to give our Saturday readers every aspect of the story—the spot news, the human interest, the statistics, the questions and possible answers, the pictures, the graphics, the backgrounder. Under the overall supervision of Foster Spencer, assistant managing editor at the time, the Saturday morning *News* is skillfully put together. The report on the nuclear accident totals sixteen stories, nine pictures, and two graphic illustrations.

It is a package put together with care and dedication to the principle that *News* readers expect and deserve the best we can possibly give them. And it is done without sacrificing coverage of local or wire news. It is a package in which all involved can take immense pride, totally overshadowing our Saturday morning competition.

The seventeen hours of hectic but orderly activity finally end when the last person leaves the newsroom at 2 AM Saturday. Eight hours later, at 10 AM, newsroom activity starts up again, gearing up to get the job done once more for the *Sunday News*, increasing in tempo as the hours move on, shifting into second gear about 4 PM and into high gear as the evening approaches.

The results in Sunday's *News* and Monday's and Tuesday's *News* are the same—topflight coverage, a thorough job. The most spectacular nuclear story since Hiroshima, the story bound to be one of the top domestic events in 1979, has been covered for *News* readers in line with the newspaper's ninety-nine-year tradition.[1]

Shribman, one of the key *News* reporters covering the Three Mile Island story, winner of the Pulitzer Prize in 1995 for his coverage of American politics, was named executive editor of the *Pittsburgh Post-Gazette* in December 2002.[2] He started his journalism career at the *Buffalo News*, where he was a summer intern. He later became the Washington bureau chief of the *Boston Globe* while continuing to write a nationally syndicated column on national politics. Shribman was a fine choice for the top Pittsburgh editorial post. He's a highly intelligent, laid-back person with excellent news judgment who's always been admired and respected by his colleagues at the *Buffalo News*, the *New York Times*, the *Washington Star*, the *Wall St. Journal*, and the *Boston Globe*.

NOTES

1. Murray B. Light, "The News—Your Newspaper," *Buffalo Evening News*, April 3, 1979, second front page.
2. *Buffalo News*, December 12, 2002, business section.

25 The Feminine Side

Women today are part of every department in the newsroom at the *News* and in most American newspapers. Some of the nation's journalism schools now have more women students than men. Desk jobs in newsrooms are no longer the exclusive province of male journalists. Men no longer fill all the reporting and editing roles in sports and business departments. And most importantly, the top management jobs in newsrooms are no longer off limits to women.

Edward H. Butler, founder of the paper, would have been very pleased to read the announcement that Margaret Sullivan was tapped to succeed me as the editor.[1] Butler, who served as the paper's first editor and publisher, never had any hesitation about hiring women for his staff. As with so many things he did, Butler was ahead of his time and his success can be traced in large measure to his willingness to be different, to initiate new approaches.

Butler would have been particularly gratified by the choice of Sullivan as editor because her path to the top newsroom position started at the *News* and every level of her advancement was attained there. Sullivan was initially hired as a reporter intern in the summer of 1980, coming out of the Medill School of Journalism at Northwestern Uni-

Margaret M. Sullivan succeeded Murray B. Light as editor of the *News* in 1999. (Photo by Derek Gee, courtesy *Buffalo News*)

versity. She showed so much promise that with the completion of her internship she was retained as a regular, full-time staffer in the fall of that year. Sullivan was assigned to the financial staff, performed very well there, and in 1982 was shifted to the cityside reporting staff on the education beat. Starting in August 1984, she wrote a weekly downtown column in addition to her reporting duties and in September 1987 was named an assistant city editor.[2]

Sullivan went on maternity leave in August 1988 and returned to work in February 1989 as an assistant managing editor responsible for the Lifestyles and Feature department, directing the activities of twenty-seven staffers. I had made the decision to promote her while she was on leave, and had met with her about the details of what I wanted her to accomplish in her new role. She had achieved senior editor status faster than anybody in the history of the *News*. In making the appointment, I particularly cited her interpersonal-relationship skills as well as her proven record as a top-notch reporter. She was charged with the responsibility of welding a large group of talented professionals into a unified entity, something that had not been achieved up to that time.[3]

Hers was a difficult assignment, given the very high ego quotient of many involved in Lifestyles and Features, but she achieved results with a minimum of anticipated obstacles. Her administrative strengths were now proven and when my retirement date had been set for September 1999, Sullivan was named managing editor in 1998 with the anticipation that she would succeed me when I stepped down if she performed well at that interim management level. That did indeed occur.[4] In 2001 she took on the additional title of vice president.[5]

In the last decade of the 1800s, very few women were on the reporting staffs of America's newspapers and the handful who were found themselves assigned primarily to reporting on social events. The journalism schools had an insignificant number of women enrolled. Journalism, most particularly in the larger metropolitan papers, was a man's world. Despite this, Butler in the early 1890s added Marion DeForest to the staff of the *Buffalo Evening News* and although she did write some social news she also was a general assignment reporter and at times even reported on murder trials.[6]

One of Butler's favorite female reporters for many years, and one to whom he gave special consideration at all times, was Esther Davenport. He hired her as society editor of the *News* in the early 1890s and she held the job for nearly fifty years, working until just a few days before her death at the age of ninety-seven on September 3, 1940. Davenport wrote her Social Chronicle column in longhand and for years the secretary to the managing editor was assigned to type her copy each day. For the Saturday editions Davenport wrote a column called "As I Went Home Last Night" that became one of the most popular features of the *Saturday News*. On Butler's orders, her columns reportedly were never altered in any way.[7]

News readers for generations loved the Lucy Lincoln column. The *News* founder got the idea for the column while en route to Europe, and when his ship arrived in France, he fired off a cable to Ina Russelle Warren asking her to write a column that was to be dedicated to women readers, answering questions on home, health, and etiquette problems. A native of England, Warren had been an editor of the *Magazine of Poetry* in New York City before joining the *News* and before starting to write the column had been handling the material for the daily Everybody's Column on the editorial page. She and Butler came up with the idea of calling her column Lucy Lincoln although there's no record of why they ultimately settled on that name after rejecting many other suggestions. It was the first newspaper column in the country exclusively dedicated to matters of interest to women, and from its start in 1912 it was enormously popular. Just a few weeks after it got under way, the Lucy Lincoln column was receiving nearly 250 phone calls and upwards of six hundred letters each week.[8]

Warren died on April 18, 1951, as the result of injuries she sustained after being struck by a taxi. Because of its enormous popularity, Edward H. Butler Jr., then the publisher, decided that publication of the column was to continue under the name of Lucy Lincoln. The identity of the column's author was never made known. With the proliferation of material of interest to women in all sectors of the paper, the usefulness of the Lucy Lincoln column eventually diminished, as did its popularity with readers, leading to its disappearance from the pages of the *News* some sixty years after it was launched.[9]

Another woman staffer who successfully advanced to department head status was Rachel Cain, who joined the *News* in 1936 and was assigned to what was then designated as the society page. In 1958 she was named society editor and served in that role until her retirement in 1979. Cain was eminently successful at this position because she refused to deviate from established rules for those seeking to have their engagement or wedding pictures published and because she also was diplomatic in dealing with those who were disappointed by the rules she had laid down over the years. Her rules dealt primarily with the type of photo to be submitted, and when information had to be received by the paper. Pat Swift, another tough-minded woman who refused to bend the rules, an attribute that the job demanded, succeeded Cain.[10]

Three women reporters of earlier years stand out in the minds of many *News* readers. All made their mark with excellent contributions to our editorial product for long periods of time. A woman staffer who covered every conceivable type of story in the 1920s and 1930s was Mary Nash. But for the last couple of decades of her career, Molly, as she was known to all, concentrated on movie and drama reviews. It was a specialty that she thoroughly enjoyed and it showed in her work. In those days the *News* didn't utilize many freelance reviewers and as a result the reviews of Nash set a consistent standard by which *News* readers were able to judge a film or a stage presentation.[11]

Another reviewer during these early years developed the same kind of rapport with readers. Theodolinda Boris, like Nash, initially covered all sorts of events with a concentration on stories about the Buffalo area's ethnic groups. But in the last two decades before her death in 1956, she was the paper's music critic, covering concerts of the Buffalo Philharmonic as well as a host of other musical events in the community. She was knowledgeable and therefore credible but, unlike many music critics, her reviews never became too technical for readers to enjoy. She wrote honest reviews, telling the readers if she liked or disliked a performance, but didn't single out any particular lapse by a particular musician, as some critics did.[12]

Mildred Spencer for many years was a general assignment reporter who covered every type of story, from police to politics. She later concentrated on reporting medical news in the Buffalo area and, in fact, became one of the earliest reporters in the nation to make that her specialty. Spencer gained the trust of the medical community, including physicians and hospital administrators, and over the years her byline over medical news stories was a very important facet of the paper's daily output. The medical beat was one Spencer developed, nurtured, and thoroughly enjoyed.[13]

One can't discuss women who contributed to the *News* output over the years without citing the work of Ellen Taussig. Talented and charismatic, Taussig for decades was the talk of the newsroom and perhaps of the town. Coming to Buffalo from the *Philadelphia Bulletin*, Taussig was known for her courtly manners, her distinctive hats, and her ever-present white gloves. She was rarely seen without a hat or gloves, even in the newsroom itself. A gracious person with an ever-present smile, Taussig was universally admired. She loved her profession, and even after retiring to Cape May, New Jersey, she still wrote a column for a weekly at the age of ninety-two. Taussig was a great admirer of royalty and covered many events in Canada and Great Britain involving the royal family. Her writing had a particular flair that was not typical of newspaper verbiage. When she had a problem coming up with a lead for her story, she would inevitably begin with a bit of poetry or an elaborate quote. Beloved and respected, Ellen Taussig will forever be remembered by staffers and readers alike.[14]

A strong-minded woman who served the paper admirably for many years in an administrative role was Joan Danzig, the Living Section editor who changed the thrust of that well-read section from its emphasis on news "for women only" to an overall emphasis on lifestyle trends. A highly competitive woman who was a tough and demanding editor, she did her job well despite differences with some of the editors and her staff from time to time. She ultimately left the *News* in 1989 to take a job with the public relations department of the University of Buffalo.[15]

Two outstanding, longtime women reporters who are now retired are Margaret Hammersley and Karen Brady. They were both staff stalwarts for decades and joined the *News* when there were not too many women on the staff. In many respects they paved the way for others who followed them as key members of the newsroom.

Hammersley started her *News* career in 1946 as a general assignment reporter and through the years covered the schools, county hall, federal court, and the Lackawanna area. She tackled all of her assignments with zest, including those she did not particularly relish. In every one of the beats to which she was assigned, Hammersley went beyond surface reporting to uncover material that made her work somewhat controversial but undoubtedly of more value to *News* readers. She was a fine, thorough, dedicated reporter for fifty-five years. She retired in 2001.[16]

Karen Brady's retirement in 2002 after some forty years at the *News* marked the end of a fine career as a reporter and many years as the popular columnist of Karen's Korner since 1969. Most of her columns reflected her involvement in cultural matters, endeavors involving women in various community roles, area history, and her experiences as a mother. Karen's Korner reflected her personality as a serious, caring individual. Each was a product of thought and concern, making them intensely personal. Brady, at one point in her career, had some serious health problems, but to her enormous credit she fought through them and continued her work. When her endeavors as a columnist ended she continued as a productive reporter, particularly in reporting on area colleges.[17]

Another milestone for women in the *News* newsroom was achieved in June 1981 with the appointment of Stephanie Christopher as an assistant city editor. She was the first woman in the history of the paper to serve on that all-important desk through which all local copy must pass.[18]

A woman who worked in the payroll department for four decades prior to her retirement in January 1984 was very familiar to newsroom employees who called on her regularly when they had questions on their pay and benefits. Alice Lankes, known to countless *News* employees as Little Alice, was the *News* payroll manager who was trusted to be scrupulously fair in interpreting union contracts between management and its many unions. The *News*/Newspaper Guild contract had numerous provisions involving pay differentials, automatic pay increases because of service time, and vacation credits that often befuddled newsroom employees and managers. Fortunately, all had total faith in Lankes' ability to wade through contract verbiage and assign the proper compensation to the right employees. She was an invaluable aid to the editorial department and all other departments at the paper.[19]

The roster of women who contributed greatly to the editorial output of the *News* is too lengthy to detail. In addition to Sullivan, one who played a significant policy role for many years was Barbara Ireland. I believe she left the *News* in 1998 possibly because she was disappointed at not being promoted as managing editor. Ireland had been given strong consideration for that role, which ultimately went to Sullivan because she had previously manifested such important administrative skills. The departure of Ireland from the newsroom staff was a significant loss. Over a period of time she had consistently grown in her responsibilities, and under her leadership the editorial page of the *News* grew in stature and increased its readership.[20]

Susan LoTempio, another strong-minded personality, came to the *News* in 1986 as a copyeditor for the Features Department copydesk. She had been feature editor at the *Niagara Gazette* and at the *Valley Times* in Pleasanton, California, and chief of the features' copydesk at the *Oakland California Tribune*. At the *News* she was named Lifestyle assignment editor in 1989 and in 1995 also assumed the duties as editor of *Next*. LoTempio was a key person in the origination and formulations of the tabloid *Next* section aimed at teen readership. A regular Wednesday section of the *News*, it generates almost no advertising revenue but is popular with young *News* readers. LoTempio's promotion to assistant managing editor for features was one of the first moves made by Sullivan when she became editor.[21]

Three women reporters who have performed very well and whose careers have blossomed with the passage of time are Susan Shulman, Sharon Linstedt, and Paula Voell. Each has the ability and the desire to be productive staffers for many more years.

Schulman is an intense woman who started at the *News* as a general assignment reporter, was shifted to the Northtowns bureau, and then appointed bureau head. In that role she has proven her administrative ability and still continues to contribute as a fine reporter who is able to discern trends.[22]

Linstedt has had an interesting *News* career. She did well as a general assignment cityside reporter but was disappointing in terms of productivity on the county hall beat. Reassigned to the financial department in October 1993, her career took off. She was a splendid and highly productive addition to the department. She enjoyed the assignment and that enthusiasm was reflected in her work. When cityside staff needed some bolstering in 2001, she returned to that side of the newsroom and has become one of the most productive reporters there.[23]

Paula Voell is a low-key, highly productive Lifestyle department reporter whose talent any editor would relish having on his or her staff. She willingly undertakes any assignment and is particularly adept at human-interest stories. She is a regular contributor to the weekly religion news page and has been writing a volunteerism column for years.[24]

The *News* has been fortunate to have so many outstanding women reporters through the years, but the paper has been dominated for the most part by male editors, reporters, and columnists in the past. This has been particularly true in the management positions of the paper. There is now a woman holding the top position in the newsroom and that is a definite sign of progress.

Notes

1. Michael Beebe, "Sullivan Is Named Editor of the *News*," *Buffalo News*, August 11, 1999, business section.
2. *Buffalo News* personnel files.

3. Ibid.

4. Ibid.

5. "The *News* Promotes Four to New Positions," *Buffalo News*, February 6, 2001, business section.

6. Ralph Dibble, "The *Buffalo Evening News* Is Born," *Buffalo News* centennial publication, October 12, 1980, p. H-3.

7. Ibid., p. H-4.

8. Ibid., p. H-6.

9. Ibid.

10. Ibid., p. H-9; *Buffalo News* personnel files.

11. Ibid.

12. Ibid.

13. Ibid.

14. Ibid., p. H-9; *Buffalo News* personnel files.

15. Ibid., p. H-9; Murray B. Light, "The News—Your Newspaper," *Buffalo News*, March 11, 1980, second front page; *Buffalo News* personnel files.

16. *Buffalo News* personnel files.

17. Ibid.

18. Light, "The News—Your Newspaper," *Buffalo News*, June 2, 1981, second front page.

19. Light, "The News—Your Newspaper," *Buffalo News*, January 31, 1984, second front page.

20. Ibid. (July 25, 1989; May 28, 1998).

21. Information supplied by Susan LoTempio, July 17, 2002.

22. Ibid.

23. Ibid.

24. Ibid.

26 A TOUGH STORY TO COVER

Abortion has been and continues to be a highly emotional issue that has plagued this country for many years. Buffalo is certainly no exception and, in fact, because of its religious makeup the Buffalo metropolitan area has always had a particularly large contingent of pro-life supporters. Reporting on demonstrations for and against abortion, as a result, has been particularly sensitive for the *Buffalo News.*

Our editorial page position has been consistently in favor of pro-choice for many years and the *News* has stated and restated that position countless times. Each editorial has resulted in numerous letters to Everybody's Column condemning our position and each time we printed countless letters condemning our pro-choice stance. The editorial page position on this sensitive issue made it extremely important that our reporting on the abortion and related issues had to be handled with responsibility and evenhandedness. This became an abiding principle for the reporting staff and was rigidly enforced.

The initial antiabortion demonstrations of any consequence occurred in the Buffalo area in 1990: one in November in the northern suburb of Amherst followed by another in an area near downtown Buffalo in December. As a result of these, U.S. District Judge Richard Arcara issued orders restraining the conduct of pro-life protests in western New York. His order prohibited demonstrators from positioning themselves less than fifteen feet from abortion clinic property, from blocking anyone entering the clinics, and from continuing to speak with clinic clients after they had been told to leave them alone.[1]

The 1990 demonstrations were not massive, and reporting on them and their consequences did not pose particularly unusual or difficult problems. But the situation changed in 1992 when abortion foes announced in January that the national pro-life group known as Operation Rescue would be coming to Buffalo some time between April 20 and May 16. Rescue Leader Randall Terry said that Buffalo would be the focus of a massive pro-life demonstration that would rival one that his organization had held in Wichita, Kansas, which resulted in more than two thousand arrests. Terry said that pro-life groups from across the country would be invited to join in the Buffalo demonstration and said he was encouraged by support for the effort by Buffalo mayor Jimmy Griffin.[2]

The announcement by Terry resulted in numerous news stories giving the positions favoring and opposing the promised massive demonstration. Months before the scheduled event passions quickly heated up. Given all the advance publicity and numerous inquiries from both sides of the issue on how the *News* would report the event, I wrote a column outlining our position. The column served the dual function of informing our readers and sending signals to *News* staffers. It said in part,

> We here at the *News*, after a good deal of thought, have made the decision to refrain from an ongoing stream of stories on the April event, which we wish were not going to take place. We will assiduously seek to avoid being "used" by proponents of the pro-life or the pro-choice positions in the period leading up to April 20.
>
> Media hype tends to give credibility to an event whose value is questioned by many on both sides of the abortion issue and will undoubtedly increase anxieties of all in the community as the time for the demonstrations nears.

> The *News*, of course, does have the responsibility of reporting on actual related news stories leading up to April 20, if, in our judgment, they are legitimate news events and not artificial contrivances to bestir the populace. We fully realize that these judgments will be difficult to make, and it is possible that mistakes will be made. But we will tend to be conservative in our judgments of what is legitimate news and what is hype. The *News* will not be influenced in any way in its decisions on Project Rescue coverage by what is broadcast on area radio or television stations. . . .
>
> We frankly are not looking forward to the period immediately following Easter. It is a given that our reporting of Project Rescue must resolutely aim at total objectivity. We will do all we can to achieve it on an issue of such extreme volatility. Those who will be reporting on Project Rescue will be carefully selected with the objective of choosing those who we believe can best set aside their own personal feelings on the abortion issue. . . .We shortly will be distributing a set of guidelines to any on the newsroom staff who might have any involvement in the *News* presentation of Project Rescue. . . .These guidelines will seek to assure fairness and objectivity in our coverage and to outline steps to minimize erroneous perceptions by readers. . . .The *News* has received requests for and agreed to meetings with those representing differing sides of the abortion issue. . . .[3]

The Project Rescue leaders set a definite date of April 20 for the start of their demonstrations and rejected pleas from the community's religious leadership to cancel their plans. As the date neared, I distributed a memo to the entire editorial staff, which stated in part:

> Project Rescue . . . will be a difficult time for all of us. Experience here and elsewhere has shown that the media is always the fall guy in situations such as this. No matter what we do, we will not satisfy the pro-life or the pro-choice advocates. Despite this, we must strive throughout to be totally objective.
>
> It is incumbent upon all to remember that we are professionals. We must shed our own personal feelings . . . so that those beliefs do not in any manner color our presentation of what transpires in Project Rescue. This cuts across every element of our coverage—words, pictures, headlines, and story play. Editors must constantly be alert

> to every nuance that might be construed to compromise objectivity. Avoid the use of adjectives in stories, headlines, and cutlines involving Rescue. Adjectives are subjective. For example: don't write, "angry words were exchanged." Instead, quote what those on both sides say. Let the readers decide if the words were angry or whatever. Be extremely careful in the use of verbs. For example, we have seen pictures of Rescue people crawling to block an abortion entrance while the accompanying story used the words "stormed" and "rushing" to describe the approach. That's a sure way to cause problems.
>
> Don't try to dramatize what is occurring. We must not go beyond what is actually taking place. If force is used . . . describe the actions accurately, precisely. . . . Do not fall victim to reporting rumors originating from any faction. There undoubtedly will be efforts made to steer us into certain stories. We will decide what is news, not the participants in the demonstrations. . . . Be extremely careful about crowd estimates. . . . It's an area that always causes problems. All crowd estimates must quote a responsible law-enforcement official heading up the contingent on the scene. Pin the estimate directly to that individual. . . .
>
> It is our expectation that any and all persons on the newsroom staff who might reasonably expect to be called upon to participate in coverage will avoid any direct or indirect participation in Project Rescue demonstrations. . . . If you have any doubt about your ability to be objective on this issue and are called upon to participate in coverage, please notify your supervising editor so that assignments can be reassessed. . . . We seek to give *News* readers complete, fair, unbiased coverage. Editorializing will be confined to the editorial page. We do not want to sensationalize; we do not want to inflame. We will not take cues from other media. We will do our jobs in the professional manner I am confident we can all achieve.[4]

The *News* staff performed professionally throughout that difficult period. A few asked to be recused from a Rescue assignment. Their requests were granted and there were no resulting recriminations.

Operation Rescue's Spring of Life protest started as planned April 20 and continued through May 2. It attracted an estimated one thousand outside pro-life activists and resulted in 625 arrests. Police and resulting court expenses came to more than $500,000.[5]

Operation Rescue's Spring of Life protests produced the expected confrontations between pro-life and pro-choice advocates but fortunately did not result in any serious physical incidents. There were numerous verbal exchanges and angry confrontations, as well as spitting and pushing incidents, but the police did a masterful job of separating the protestors and avoiding life-threatening attacks from either camp. The number of demonstrators at the sites varied from dozens to hundreds and name-calling and insults filled the air. Nevertheless, overall the eight days of protests proved to be less strident than many had feared.

One rally of pro-life supporters attracted some 1,500 participants. As part of the protest, antiabortion leaders aired a radio commercial directly aimed at five local doctors, accusing them of performing abortions. One of the physicians targeted in the ad was Dr. Barnett Slepian, an obstetrician and gynecologist who also performed abortions, and who later fell victim to a sniper's bullet and brought the whole abortion issue to a new phase in the public arena.[6]

The *News* reporting of the eight days of demonstrations and their related public relations efforts continued to be straightforward and consistent with my memo. Both sides seemed to be content with the coverage, given the relatively few complaints to the office of the editor and in letters to Everybody's Column.

There were numerous letters and complaints from pro-lifers aimed at U.S. District Judge Arcara who was still making decisions resulting from demonstrations. In one action, Arcara leveled a $20,000 fine against a pro-life minister and a $10,000 fine against another for harassing Dr. Barnett Slepian by lying in front of his car as he pulled into a Main Street clinic parking lot in September 1991, and abusing him by screaming insults, thereby violating the judge's restraining order. Arcara's rulings in these cases were the latest in a series of decisions in which he criticized the Buffalo Project Rescue organization. In a two-month period from July 24 to September 1992, Arcara had fined seven individuals and the Project Rescue organization a total of $137,543.[7]

Given events that followed, it is interesting to note that the Rev. Paul Schenck, who had been the recipient of Arcara's $20,000 fine, had called Dr. Slepian a "pig and a murderer." Arcara had said in his ruling that Schenck berated Slepian with a constant barrage of accusations and name-calling.[8]

After a long period of relative calm, a tragic event occurred that brought the pro-life, pro-choice controversy back into the headlines locally, nationally, and internationally. On October 23, 1998, Dr. Barnett Slepian of Amherst was killed by a sniper's bullet while he was in his kitchen with his wife and four sons just a few feet away. Given the verbal attacks on him in the past and his role as the primary doctor for Buffalo's lone abortion clinic, the ensuing search for the killer of the prominent obstetrician-gynecologist focused on known antiabortion zealots.[9]

The nationwide search for the killer later became an international search. In addition to local law-enforcement officials, the FBI became involved and the story of the assassination was reported by radio, television, and newspapers throughout the world.[10]

Glenn E. Murray, a pro-choice lawyer, expressed what many felt was the reason for the killing of Dr. Slepian. "This assassination was not just perpetrated to eliminate a provider but to terrorize others who provide abortion, to show them that unless they abandon safe and legal abortion, they and their families are not safe in their own houses."[11]

After a long, intensive investigation, law-enforcement officials became convinced that the killer was James Kopp, forty-four, of Vermont, a well-known antiabortion activist. He was indicted while still at large, and was added to the FBI's Most Wanted List. Kopp was linked to violent antiabortion groups, tracked to Ireland, and then finally tracked down and arrested in France. More than one million dollars in reward money had been posted for his apprehension.[12] U.S. authorities had to guarantee French officials that Kopp, if returned to the United States, would not face the death penalty. Without such assurance, France would not have considered granting extradition.[13]

Any doubt about Kopp's role in the slaying of Dr. Slepian ended on November 2, 2002, when Kopp in a jailhouse interview confessed to *Buffalo News* reporters Lou Michel and Dan Herbeck that he was Dr. Slepian's killer. Kopp, in this exclusive interview, insisted that he did not intend to kill Dr. Slepian. He said he only wanted to injure him to keep him from performing abortions.[14]

Shortly after Slepian's murder, pro-life forces announced that an event billed as Operation Save America would be held in Buffalo April 18–25, 1999. Unlike the 1992 Spring of Life demonstrations, the 1999 event resulted in no arrests, no fines, no jailing, and in reality made no news.[15] The demonstrations, small as they were, were held outside a dozen high schools, three bookstores, two abortion clinics, and several hospitals and doctor's offices. Police estimated that no more than a couple hundred pro-lifers took part in the demonstrations although the sponsors had predicted that more than three times that many would be attracted. The agenda of Operation Save America was broader than that of the 1992 affair. It focused on pornography, teen sex, and homosexuality as well as abortion. The prevailing feeling was that many pro-lifers did not necessarily sympathize with all of these feelings. The event also coincided with the six-month anniversary of Dr. Slepian's assassination and with his birthday. There was conjecture that many decided not to participate in Operation Save America out of respect for the slain physician.[16]

The national media did not give much attention to this Buffalo antiabortion happening. The *New York Times* said, "There has been little difference between Operation Save America and peaceful demonstrations in other cities on more mundane subjects, with people holding homemade signs, talking among their ideological brethren and waving to honking drivers. . . ."[17] Long Island's *Newsday* wrote that "Except for callers to talk-show radio, residents of this windy city seem to be taking little notice of the abortion protestors who have fanned out across town . . . quoting scripture and waving posters of bloody fetuses."[18] The *Buffalo News* did not disagree with the *Times* or *Newsday*. Although some of the protestors tried to stimulate more interest by the *News*, they were unsuccessful. We carried stories but they were not lengthy or prominently displayed.[19]

In the aftermath of the Slepian slaying and the indictment of James Kopp in the case, the New York State Legislature passed and the governor in November 1999 signed a measure that mirrors the earlier ruling of Judge Arcara and a federal law. The state law makes it illegal for protesters to block women desiring to enter an abortion clinic or to harass or intimidate healthcare workers at abortion facilities. It makes it a responsibility of state and local police to enforce these protections and simplifies the legal steps needed to form buffer zones around clinics during protests.[20]

Notes

1. Dan Herbeck, "Pro-Life Twin Ministers Fined $10,000 Apiece," *Buffalo News*, September 14, 1992, p. A-1.

2. Jan Kwiatkowski, "Abortion Foes Target Buffalo," *Buffalo News*, January 4, 1992, p. A-1.

3. Murray B. Light, "Your Newspaper," *Buffalo News*, March 3, 1992, second front page.

4. *Buffalo News* staff memo, April 13, 1992.

5. Jerry Zremski, "Delay by Supreme Court Stalls 13 Abortion Protest Cases," *Buffalo News*, June 9, 1992, p. B-4.

6. Kwiatkowski, "Abortion Foes," *Buffalo News*, January 4, 1992, p. A-1; David Montgomery, "The Unlikely Extremist," *Buffalo News*, March 1, 1992, p. E-1; Dan Herbeck, "Children's Seeks Rein on Pro-Life Rally," *Buffalo News*, April 3, 1992; P. Split; Dan Herbeck, "Marshals Sought to Help Arrest Protestors," *Buffalo News*, April 11, 1992, p. TRK; David Condren, "Church Group Asks End to Plan for Massive Pro-Life Protests," *Buffalo News*, April 17, 1992, p. C-4; "Abortion Restriction Predicted by Meese," *Buffalo News*, sunrise edition, April 22, 1992, p. A-5.

7. Dan Herbeck, "Pro-Life Twin Ministers," *Buffalo News*, September 14, 1992; Dan Herbeck, "Robert Schenck Lashes Out," *Buffalo News*, September 29, 1992, p. TRK.

8. Ibid.

9. Phil Fairbanks, "Slepian's Murder: A Year After," *Buffalo News*, October 17, 1999.

10. Ibid.

11. Ibid.

12. Dan Herbeck and Lou Michel, "Evidence Near Home of Slepian Is Tested," *Buffalo News*, November 29, 1998.

13. Jerry Zremski, "U.S. Applauds French Move to Extradite Kopp," *Buffalo News*, June 29, 2001, p. C-1.

14. Dan Herbeck and Lou Michel, "Kopp Confesses," *Buffalo News*, November 20, 2002, p. A-1.

15. Gene Warner, "Little Impact Seen as Protest Ends Run," *Buffalo News*, April 25, 1999.

16. Ibid.

17. Ibid.

18. Ibid.

19. Ibid.

20. Tom Precious, "Law Enacted to Protect Clinic Workers, Clients," *Buffalo News*, November 23, 1999.

27 The Ever-Expanding Sports and Business News

Sports are of major interest to Buffalo-area residents, and the *News* has consistently produced an outstanding sports section to meet the demands and satisfy the interest of the many thousands who seemingly can't get enough news and trivia about the teams representing the area, particularly the Buffalo Bills football team and the Buffalo Sabres hockey team.

The *News* coverage of sports started slowly. In fact, the first issue of the daily in 1880 contained not a single sports item. Things picked up on the second day of publication with a grandiose total of six sports briefs occupying a total of three inches of space. General assignment reporters wrote the sports stories carried by the *News*; there was no separate sports staff.[1]

By 1889 the *Sunday News* was carrying up to six columns of sports content each week, and then in 1896 the *News* launched its first regular daily section dedicated to sports under the direction of Charles Griffiths. Not much has been recorded about Griffiths but he was succeeded by James Parke Jr. who built a following with a column he started in 1914 under the heading "Karpe's Comment." That effort initiated a practice for years of the sports editor writing a column on a regular basis, either weekly or daily.[2]

Bob Stedler, who served in the role of sports editor until 1953, succeeded Parke in 1928. In addition to building the sports staff and expanding the coverage of sports to include high-school and amateur events, Stedler wrote the very popular Sports Comment column. The *News* sports coverage grew significantly during the twenty-five years that Stedler was at the helm. With no major-league teams representing Buffalo during his years as sports editor, Stedler dedicated a great deal of sports page space to the coverage of amateur athletics in the area. The *Buffalo Evening News* suburban baseball leagues and the American Legion leagues were extensively covered with game stories and box scores. Stedler became a well-known figure in the community, making many speeches filled with interesting anecdotal material about Buffalo sports figures.[3]

With Stedler's departure in 1953, Charley Young took over the helm of the sports department, a post he retained until his retirement in 1977. A *News* staffer for sixteen years prior to his designation as sports editor, he was well prepared for the job and was a dominant editor, giving strong direction to the ever-growing sports staff as major-league sports teams entered the Buffalo picture. The Buffalo Braves were awarded a franchise in the National Basketball Association in 1970 during Young's tenure. The team played here through 1977. The Buffalo Bills of the National Football League and the Buffalo Sabres of the National Hockey League also became part of the Buffalo sports scene during Young's time as sports editor. With the arrival of major-league sports in Buffalo, the coverage emphasis in the *News* sports pages shifted dramatically. Despite ever more space being dedicated to sports, coverage of area amateur events fell off.[4]

Young recruited top-notch talent to his sports staff and inspired his reporters and editors with his own hard work and dedication to the job. In addition to straight reporting of sports events, Young encouraged his staffers to do analytical and commentary pieces about the teams they covered. From time to time he also produced some hard-hitting sports commentary columns that became very popular with readers.

Serving for many years as assistant sports editor under Young was Al Cohen. In addition to his editing duties he wrote the very popular

Benny the Bookie pieces. These were colorful, humorous articles that added a special element to the sports pages when they appeared from time to time through the year. "Benny" did not offer his readers any wagering advice but did provide a light touch that readers enjoyed. Allie, as he was called by his colleagues, was himself a colorful figure, short in physical stature, and rarely ever seen without an oversize cigar in his mouth. Cohen was a horseracing fan and covered the track for many years until his retirement in the late 1970s. In more recent times, Bob Summers covered flat and harness racing but did not revive Benny the Bookie. He did, however, add to *News* coverage of racing with in-depth pieces on problems of area tracks and analyses of the horses that raced.

With Young's retirement, Milton Joffe became the *News* sports editor in 1978. Joffe had been the paper's chief copyeditor and had been doing a superb job in that demanding role. Joffe was an avid sports fan and was interested in making a career switch by taking over the sports job. But despite producing a fine sports section, Joffe found that he missed his old job and returned to his role as copydesk chief in 1981.[5]

With the closing of the *Washington Star*, that paper's deputy sports editor, Howard Smith, became available and I hired him to succeed Joffe. Smith had been deputy sports editor of the Associated Press prior to joining the *Star*.[6] He quickly made his mark as a fine administrator of a department that is one of the most difficult to manage because of the constant need to juggle the schedules of staffers to meet the demands of a schedule of sports contests. Postseason play, when a Buffalo team is in the playoffs, makes it more difficult to meet the demands of a changing schedule. Smith was particularly adroit at meeting this challenge while minimizing overtime and keeping staff content.

Smith also had to cope with the rapidly expanding sports scene in Buffalo. Coverage of women's involvement in college sports, sparked by congressional passage of Title Nine legislation, grew with each passing year. The minimum coverage of past years no longer was acceptable. Additionally, three new professional sports teams entered the Buffalo picture and needed coverage. These were the Buffalo Bandits, the indoor lacrosse team; the Buffalo Blizzard, the soccer league entry; and the Destroyers, an arena football team.

Smith's expertise in handling staff and producing a fine product was particularly manifested in the four successive years that the Buffalo Bills appeared in the Super Bowl. It was a remarkable achievement by the Bills and a major challenge for a sports editor.

The first Bills appearance was in Super Bowl XXV in Tampa on January 27, 1991. The *News* contingent, managed by Smith in Tampa, was made up of sixteen staffers, with seven from sports, three from cityside staff, three photographers, and three from the features staff. The Bills on January 26, 1992, made it to Super Bowl XXVI in Minneapolis. On January 31, 1993, the Bills played in Super Bowl XXVII in Pasadena, California, and then on January 30, 1994, the Bills did it again, making it to Super Bowl XXVIII in Atlanta.

Smith orchestrated the coverage of all four of these bowl appearances with staff from various sectors of the newsroom and numbering from sixteen to eighteen people. In addition, he was responsible for the preparation of special Super Bowl sections before each of these games as well as postgame special sections. While at the Super Bowl sites, he coordinated sports coverage with his editors in Buffalo and was involved in solving a great many logistical problems at the game sites and back in the Buffalo newsroom.[7]

The Bills feat in making it to the Super Bowl in four successive years has never been duplicated and the likelihood of it ever happening again to any team is considered remote. Unfortunately, the Bills were not victors in any of the four appearances but came closest to a victory in their first appearance in Tampa in 1991. A missed field goal in the final seconds of the game is still recalled vividly by Bills fans after all these years. Bills kicker Scott Norwood, who had had a highly successful career, failed to make the field goal by a few inches. It spelled defeat for the Bills and marked the end of Norwood's football career.

Marv Levy was the Bills coach during these highly successful seasons and following his retirement from coaching he was named to the Football Hall of Fame. He continued his contact with the National Football League as an analyst with the sports network ESPN.

The enormously popular Larry Felser, the sports impresario. (Photo by Robert L. Smith, courtesy *Buffalo News*)

The roster of outstanding reporters on the *News* sports staff through the years has been remarkable, but few would question the designation of Larry Felser as the brightest star of all. The people of Buffalo had a love affair with the Buffalo Bills and to vast numbers of them Felser was the voice of the Bills who called the shots, pro and con, candidly for many years, first as the prime *News* reporter assigned to Bills coverage and then for some twenty-three years as the *News* sports columnist. Our circulation on the day after a Bills game frequently went up about ten thousand despite the fact the results of the game were well known to all. *News* studies showed that the fans wanted to read Felser's commentary on the game; they trusted his judgment, his calling the shots as he saw them. Despite all the postgame analyses and commentary on television, Bills fans wanted to know what Felser had to say. His ability to attract readers to the paper during the football season was unique. The *News* had many other popular bylined staffers during Felser's time but none had his drawing power.

Felser started in the news business as a copyboy at the *Buffalo Courier-Express* in 1951. His reporting job there was on the police beat, but the former football player for Canisius High School jumped at the opportunity to transfer to the *Courier* sports department when an opening occurred in 1953. When the Bills were formed in 1960 and became part of the American Football League, Felser was assigned to cover them, starting a long relationship that brought him local and national recognition.[8]

In 1963 Paul Neville, then editor of the *News*, recognized Felser's talent and convinced him to move down the street and join our sports staff. His prime assignment was coverage of the Bills and off-season he enjoyed reporting on local college basketball. When the infamous Blizzard of '77 struck Buffalo and sports columnist Steve Weller decided that it was time to enjoy a better climate and resigned to join a Fort Lauderdale newspaper, Felser got the nod to take over the sports column. Weller had been a very popular columnist with a fine sense of humor but he had been having health problems and reluctantly decided that it was best to move on. [9]

Felser had been writing an occasional column, mostly about the National Football League and particularly the Bills. As the full-time columnist he was able to comment on a wide range of sports topics and his column quickly became the cornerstone of our sports coverage. He thoroughly enjoyed the wide-ranging role the column afforded him. Reporter Milt Northrop covered the Bills for the sport pages while Felser's column gave full dimension to the football coverage.[10]

In addition to his work at the *News*, Felser wrote a column for the national publication the *Sporting News* for twenty-four years and many of his articles have appeared in *Sports Illustrated*, *Reader's Digest*, and other publications. He is only one of eight sportswriters in the country who covered all of the first thirty-five Super Bowls and served two terms as president of the Pro Football Writers of America. In 1983 he was named the winner of the Dick McCann Award and entered the Pro Football Hall of Fame.[11]

As our sports columnist, Felser covered many of the major sporting events in the nation. Among the many events he witnessed was the historic U.S. win over the Soviets in hockey at the 1980 Olympic Games in Lake Placid. In recognition of his outstanding reputation, Felser was named sports editor of the *News*, reporting to the executive sports editor, Howard Smith.[12] Felser remained our much-admired sports editor until his retirement in February 2001.

Felser was not the only sports luminary at the *News*. In 1993 Jim Kelley, principal hockey writer who covered the Buffalo Sabres of the National Hockey League for many years, was elected president of the Professional Hockey Writers Association. Kelley joined the *News* in 1968 as a copy aide and was assigned as a sportswriter in 1977. He remained in the department until he resigned in 2000 to take a post with the national publication of the NHL. He also appears regularly on a sports television station offering informed commentary on the sport.[13]

Still another sports department member, Vic Carucci, was elected president of the Professional Football Writers of America in January 1993. He had covered the Bills for the *News* since 1982 and resigned in 2000 to take a position with an NFL publication. He, too, now appears regularly on television with comments on the NFL.[14]

Despite the loss of three top writers in one year—Felser, Kelley, and Carucci—Smith has been able to sustain the high level of expertise among his staff. As of this writing, Mark Gaughan and Allen Wilson do a splendid job in covering the Bills; Bucky Gleason and Tim Graham team up to cover the Sabres; and Mike Harrington and Amy Moritz follow the Bisons. Harrington, Moritz, and Wilson also cover college sports while Keith McShea and Mary Jo Monin do a thorough job in reporting on high-school contests.[15]

Sports department staffing has continued to expand through the years as the sports scene has grown locally. It now is made up of thirty-two full-time employees, including five clericals and three photographers. These numbers do not include the numerous stringers Smith utilizes for coverage of areas such as tennis, autos, and outdoor activities, and it does not include the interns who join the staff during the summer vacation period. The staff that was all male for decades now includes six women: one copyeditor, two reporters, and three who handle the all-important clerical duties in a department that produces a large volume of daily agate material.[16]

The amount of space allocated to sports has continued to expand with the passage of time. In 2002 its daily space allotment was between twenty-eight and thirty-four columns. When the high schools are in session, sports are assigned an additional twelve columns on Tuesdays to accommodate the high-school section. This occurs about thirty weeks each year. Sports also receive an additional full page of space on Thursdays for coverage of the auto-racing scene locally and nationally. The *Sunday News* allocates a whopping sixty-six columns of space to sports and, in addition to that, another eighteen columns is included for National Football League coverage during its season.[17]

Smith and his top assistants, including Deputy Sports Editor Steve Jones as well as Scott Johnston and Dennis Danheiser, assistant sports editors, produce a great many special sections each year, the number varying depending on the success of Buffalo's major-league teams. Smith and his staff put together highly informative, interesting special sections that *News* readers have come to anticipate and always appreciate.[18]

Among the many names familiar to *News* sports page readers in years gone by are Cy Kritzer, Frank Wakefield, Mike Dodd, Jack Horrigan, and Dick Johnston. Kritzer was best known for his coverage of the baseball Bisons, Wakefield for his expertise on boxing, Dodd and Horrigan for football, and Johnston for hockey. Each was involved for many years in coverage, particularly of their special areas, and developed a large and loyal following.[19]

* * *

Another section of the *News* that has been continually upgraded through the years is that devoted to business and financial news. The greatest growth in the allocation of space and staff in that area occurred in the first decade of the 1980s as the readership, which had been mostly male, expanded greatly and attracted many women as well as an expanded male base.

Long before that period, in the early 1920s, the *News* was the first newspaper in the state west of New York City to compile and print stock market quotations. This preceded the age of computers, so all the work was done manually by "board markers." The stock market crash of 1929 resulted in increased business coverage that only began to flourish during the past two decades.[20]

The Financial Department enjoyed good leadership over the years with Hilton Hornaday, Jim Collins, Mike McKeating, and for more than two decades starting in 1980 under Bill Flynn, now the paper's city editor. The amount of space dedicated to stock tables and business/financial news continued to expand with each passing year.

A major expansion got under way in the fall of 1992 when the weekly space allotment was upgraded from 182 columns to two hundred columns. Later, six more columns were added to the Saturday space allocation for business news and tables as well as more space several days a week.

Changes have been made from time to time in the various stock tables to keep up with Wall Street trends. For example, the American Stock Exchange table has been cut back considerably as its activity has decreased, but the over-the-counter (OTC) table has grown considerably and constantly as have the mutual funds listings.

As could be anticipated, the financial editor often received complaints from business executives who were unhappy about coverage of their enterprises. When complaints at that level did not result in satisfaction, many took their concerns to the publisher, the chairman of the board, or the editor. All of these invariably, but politely, would stand firmly behind the financial editor's decisions.

One annual business section story almost always brought complaints. It was a listing of total compensation for the corporate executive of a local enterprise. When years of complaints failed to deter the *News* from running this list, the cries of anguish from unhappy corporate executives gradually diminished. As in all other newsroom departments, the *News* policy of fairness and standing behind its staff—when justified—paid off and the annual compensation listing continues to be published each year.

NOTES

1. Ralph Dibble, "Amid Much Excitement," *Buffalo News* centennial publication, October 12, 1980, p. H-8.
2. Ibid.
3. Ibid.
4. Ibid.
5. *Buffalo News* personnel files; Murray B. Light, "Your Newspaper," *Buffalo News*, August 18, 1981, second front page.
6. Ibid.
7. Ibid., January 22, 1991.
8. Larry Felser, "Larry Legend at a Glance," *Buffalo News*, February 14, 2001, p. C-16.
9. Ibid.

10. Light, "Your Newspaper," *Buffalo News*, September 1, 1981, second front page.

11. Felser, "Larry Legend," *Buffalo News*, February 14, 2001, p. C-16.

12. Ibid.

13. *Buffalo News* personnel files.

14. Ibid.

15. Information supplied by Howard Smith, sports editor, July 15, 2002.

16. Ibid.

17. Ibid.

18. Ibid.

19. *Buffalo News* personnel files.

20. Ralph Dibble, "The *Buffalo Evening News* Is Born," *Buffalo News*, October 12, 1980, p. H-9.

28 Free Press–Fair Trial

Free press–fair trial opinion panels have engaged in dialogue for decades in most jurisdictions of the nation. They are exercises enjoyed by editors, attorneys, and judges, providing them the opportunities to vent their views on a subject that has long been a bone of contention. Both sides ultimately agree that the courts and the press have their respective responsibilities—the courts assure fair trials, while the press informs the public by reporting fairly and objectively on trials. Disagreement comes over how each faction functions to protect their role in the courtroom.[1]

The late Supreme Court Justice Hugo Black many years ago said that free speech and fair trials are two of the most cherished policies of our civilization. His remarks, however, would not be accepted as basic principles in England, where far less is permitted the press in the courtroom than in the United States. British judges are much more likely to impose restrictions on the press than are their American counterparts.[2]

We at the *News* learned firsthand about the limitations placed on the press by our Canadian neighbors, whose system of justice more closely resembles the British system than ours.

When news of the arrest of Karla Homolka in a sensational Canadian rape/murder case first broke, we at the *News* had absolutely no idea of the subsequent free press–fair trial implications the case would involve for our newspaper and the enormous interest it would arouse in the United States and abroad. It was difficult for any *News* executive to believe, but for the first time in the more than a century of publication the *Buffalo News* was told that the Canadian government was challenging its entry into Canada to cover the sensational murder trial. The time was November 1993 and an order by a Canadian court threatened the historic friendly relationship that had never in any way impeded a free exchange of American and Canadian newspapers across our common border.

The problem arose from the most horrific murder case in Canadian history. It ultimately involved the *Buffalo News* in a controversy over press freedom that captured the interest of the media in the United States, Canada, and many European nations. The fallout resulted from three sex and torture killings by a handsome young middle-class Canadian couple. As a result, in the period between Thanksgiving Day and December 2, 1993, I, as editor of the *News*, was bombarded with interview requests from print and electronic media from both home and abroad. Despite ducking dozens of such requests, I actually did talk to some 130 media reps on what had happened and the actions taken by the *Buffalo News*. The avalanche of interest astounded us. The *Wall Street Journal*, aware of the unbelievable reaction, asked me to do an article on the series of events that led to our involvement. Published on December 8, 1993, it tells much of the story and since it was written when all the details were fresh in my mind, it's best to reprint much of it here.* What follows is the bulk of the *Journal* piece.

> The setting was a quiet day last July in the Ontario city of St. Catharines, a community of some 130,000 located about forty miles from Buffalo. Violent crime rarely intruded in the lives of residents in the Garden City.
>
> Behind the closed doors of his courtroom this July 5 Ontario Justice Francis Kovacs imposed a rigid gag order on the proceedings

---

*Reprinted with permission of the *Wall Street Journal* © 1993 Dow Jones & Company, Inc.

> of the trial of Karla Homolka, accused in the deaths of two local teenage schoolgirls. The judge said his order was intended to insure a fair trial later for Homolka's estranged husband, Paul Teale, who is charged with the same deaths as well as a multitude of rapes. . . .
>
> It is ironic, most observers agree, that had the gag order not been issued, interest in the case would have slowly withered away. . . . But forbidden fruit sows seeds of heightened curiosity. Now it is the judge's ban rather than the sensational murder case that is in the spotlight.
>
> The *Washington Post* on November 23 published a detailed account of the series of sex and torture killings allegedly committed by Homolka and Teale. . . . The story recounted many but certainly not all of the lurid details that were heard by the fifty or sixty persons in the St. Catharines' court during the trial.

(I did not mention in the *Wall Street Journal* article that the *Washington Post* article contained one startling new detail—that there had been a third victim of the couple. Homolka's sister, Tammy, fourteen, was knocked unconscious with an animal tranquilizer on December 23, 1990, and Paul and Karla each had sex with her before she eventually choked to death on her own vomit.) [3]

The *Journal* article continued:

> The publication by the *Post* . . . did not stir much interest in the U.S. or Canada. But all that changed on November 28 when the *Buffalo News*, the *Detroit News* and the *Detroit Free Press* published the *Post* story. All of these border newspapers have some circulation in Canada.
>
> The *Buffalo News* was contacted Saturday, November 27, by Canadian officials who had gotten wind of the fact that it was planning to reprint the *Post* story. They outlined to *News* circulation officials the possible legal ramifications to our Canadian distributors and others in distribution of our papers in Canada.
>
> Given this development, the decision was made to eliminate the *Post* story from the Sunday papers destined for Canada. The concentration of Canadian authorities at the bridge entrances to Canada Sunday morning proved the decision to be the right one. *News* trucks were stopped, every bundle of papers was checked. When the *Post* story was not found, entry into Canada was permitted.
>
> But Canadian authorities could not legally stop Canadians throughout the day from crossing over into the Buffalo area and

purchasing copies of the *News* with the *Post* story. . . . And cross the border they did in great numbers.[4]

Up until this day, computer bulletin boards and data networks in Southern Ontario spread the rumors about the case that had been rapidly multiplying since the judge's information ban had been imposed. News travels fast, rumors even more rapidly. Given the opportunity to learn the solid facts in a news story, Canadians were quick to respond.

Niagara regional police permitted persons returning to Canada to take in only one copy of the *Buffalo News*. Other copies were seized and 61 persons were arrested and temporarily detained for having multiple copies of the *News*.

The events of Sunday the 28 became the spark for the media barrage that followed. . . . The *Toronto Globe & Mail* said editorially December 1 "when a law is so widely flouted, and forces the authorities to such lengths to enforce it, is sometimes a signal that it was misconceived to begin with."

Given today's sophisticated communications networks, it is difficult to believe that any Canadian interested in the case had been prevented from learning some of the facts.

Imposition of censorship deprives the citizenry of the right to know in a timely manner what transpires in their courts. Was the twelve-year sentence for Homolka too lenient for the crimes committed? Interestingly enough, the attorney for Teale opposed the *News* blackout. It was only the prosecution, Homolka's attorney and the judge who approved of it. Were they concerned about citizen reaction to what most expect was a plea bargain struck for Homolka? How can intelligent, rational public discussion of the sentence be carried out without knowledge of what transpired?

A *Buffalo News* editorial said, "closed trials breed problems. Secrecy stirs suspicions of deals and cover-ups. It also belies a certain judicial arrogance that distrusts the ability of citizens to know the facts, evaluate them, and reach fair conclusions."

Blacking out television signals from the United States and banning newspapers with "offending" stories serves only to infuriate the citizenry and generate disdain for a system that forces such odious, antidemocratic procedures. . . . The power of the courts in Canada to close proceedings to public and press must be modified. It is counterproductive and unworkable in this age of sophisticated telecommunications; it breeds suspicion and rumors and has no place in a democratic society.[5]

Under terms of the court ban, Canadian journalists who were permitted to attend the trial could report only the sentence. They could not report basic facts, such as how Homolka pleaded or whether a plea bargain had been struck. American journalists were not even permitted in the courtroom. The *Buffalo News* had printed much of the material that came out in the trial in pretrial stories written by staffers who had spoken to those familiar with many of the details of the grisly affair. The judge's publication ban, of course, could not cover the American media. It applied only in Canada and what was aired or appeared in print form in Canada. Canadian news sources maintained a nearly perfect blackout despite the misgivings of some. Canadian journalists were faced with possible jail terms and penalties for the stations or newspapers involved if the judge's gag order was violated.

Many Canadian journalists regretted their attendance at the trial. They felt bound by the court ban but say they could have reported more details from what they already knew had they not attended the trial.

Canada's Charter of Rights and Freedoms, adopted in 1982, upholds "freedom of thought, belief, opinion and expression, including freedom of the press." However, in Canada, as in Great Britain, judges have more discretion than in the United States to muzzle the press when it comes to potential conflict with an individual's right to a fair trial. In the Homolka case, Justice Kovacs said he imposed his ban to ensure that Teale would get a fair trial when his case came up. He specifically forbade publication of the circumstances of the deaths of any person disclosed at the Homolka trial. The judge paid no heed to Teale's attorneys who opposed the gag order. They contended that full disclosure would help their client.

As I wrote in an article for the January 1994 issue of *Presstime*, the publication of the American Newspaper Publisher's Association, "When you boil it all down the controversy is a perennial one. It is a fair-trial/free press matter. American editors, judges, and attorneys have engaged in this debate for decades, and the conflicts between First Amendment and Sixth Amendment guarantees are unlikely to ever be resolved satisfactorily." These guarantees don't apply to Canada.

What the infamous Homolka case did prove, however, is that in this age of electronic bulletin boards and personal computers, no gag order can really be effective in cases that have great public interest. Canada's cable operators blocked access to reports and rumors about the Homolka case but could do nothing to prevent news reports from being beamed down to dishes from satellites. Students plugged into the Internet computer network to get their information and in an effort to block this information outlet, three Canadian universities shut down students' access to that Internet bulletin board. But these students could go off campus and get the access they no longer could get on campus. No democratic society can wall itself off entirely. In the United States judges can ban the media from pretrial hearings under certain circumstances but journalists are basically free to report all they see or hear in open court. And U.S. judges have rigid criteria they must meet to justify the imposition of a media ban at the pretrial stage.[6]

Notes

1. Louis M. Lyons, ed., *Reporting the News, Selections from Nieman Reports*; Simon E. Sobeloff, "Free Press and Fair Trial" (Boston: Belknap Press of Harvard University Press, 1965), p. 76.

2. Ibid., pp. 78–79.

3. Anne Swardson (*Washington Post*), "Grisly Detail in Ontario Case Defy Gag Order," *Buffalo News*, November 28, 1993, p. A-1.

4. The *News* sold four thousand more papers at the border crossing than they usually do on any given Sunday.

5. Murray B. Light, "Rule of Law," *Wall Street Journal*, Wednesday, December 8, 1993, p. A-15.

6. Stories related to the Karla Homolka-Paul Teale kidnap-rape-homicide case appeared in the following publications: *Buffalo News*, November 28, 1993, November 29, 1993, November 30, 1993, December 1, 1993, and December 2, 1993; *Globe and Mail*, November 30, 1993, December 1, 1993, December 6, 1993; *Toronto Star*, December 3, 1993, May 4, 1994; *USA Today*, November 30, 1993; *New York Times*, November 30, 1993, December 2, 1993, December 10, 1993; *Wall Street Journal*, December 8, 1993; *Independent* (London), December 2, 1993; Associated Press, December 2, 1993; *Calgary Herald*, December 5, 1993; *Washington Post*, November 23, 1993, December 7, 1993; *Newsweek*, November 29, 1993; *Time*, December 13, 1993; *Presstime*, January, 1994.

29 How I See It

On January 3, 1979, I started a dialogue with *News* readers in a column that I hoped would give them better insight into what we are, why we do what we do, and what we hope to accomplish. The idea for the column originated with Warren E. Buffett and reader response to it has been positive through the years. My successor, Margaret Sullivan, has continued the tradition of communicating with readers of the *News* through a special column.

In 1979 not too many newspaper editors were reaching their readers in this way, but over the years it has become somewhat more common. We found it to be an effective means of relating to readers and "The News—Your Newspaper" was a feature I continued until my retirement. The many hundreds of columns I wrote covered a wide range of humdrum topics as well as serious observations on the basic philosophy of the editor on controversial issues.

Those who preceded me as editor of the *News*—Edward H. Butler Sr., Edward H. Butler Jr., Alfred H. Kirchhofer, and Paul Neville—expressed their philosophies on the role of newspapers in general and the *News* in particular in speeches and in articles for journalism publications. But the average *News* reader did not have the opportunity to become aware of their thoughts. I found the editor's column to be the ideal communication tool to reach the many thousands of *News* readers. I was always surprised and gratified at reader response generated by these columns.

A newspaper editor sets the tone and determines the content of the paper he or she edits, so I will quote various parts of a limited number of the columns I wrote through the years. Each involves a subject that has always aroused significant interest among readers.

My predecessors as editors of the *News* may not have agreed with all of my thoughts, nor might my successors. But given my extensive reading about the founder of the *News*, E. H. Butler Sr.—most particularly his memos to the staff and his public statements—I am surprisingly confident that I have been pretty much on the same wavelength as he was more than a century ago. I was not aware of this until I undertook this history of the *News.*

A common thread of complaints about the *News* through the years has been the concern that its stories about problems in Buffalo are hurting the city and will result in its further decline. These complaints accelerated as economic conditions in the city worsened and reached a peak in 1996. They prompted this column published on March 21, 1996.

> One letter, typical of many, landed on my desk the other morning and in a few sentences seems to summarize what others are saying, "The articles read as if the *News* is encouraging people to leave the city in droves, running for the safety and superior schools and neighborhoods of the suburbs. . . . I wonder how many people who were indecisive about leaving the city read these articles and become convinced they should leave. Maybe the *News* should change its name to the Suburban News. . . ."
>
> Are we doing these stories to hurt the city? The answer is emphatically in the negative. We feel it is a major obligation of the *News* to continue to point out the city's problems in stories and editorials so that all in the area are aware of what they are and in the hopes that we can stimulate action to gain support for the city that is so vital to the ultimate strength of all its suburbs and even rural neighbors.
>
> The *News* is dedicated to the city. Unlike many, we are not

> willing to give up on it or despair of its ability to make a comeback. We are located downtown and have been for more than 100 years. The publisher, the editor, the editorial page editor and the managing editor all live in the city, as do many of the newsroom staff and employees in other departments of the *News*.
>
> We are proud of being a Buffalo newspaper. Many American newspapers have dropped the name of their central city from their name. We have never given that move any consideration. Behind the scenes, the *News* publisher and editor continue to work with others in the community to seek out solutions to the problems plaguing the city and to identify opportunities.
>
> Putting on blinders and ignoring problems is not the way to assist Buffalo. . . . We have to acknowledge that the "self-fulfilling prophecy" theory might have a certain amount of validity. That result, if it does occur, certainly goes counter to our goal of aiding the city. But we firmly believe that we have no choice other than to continue to strive to alert the citizenry and public officials of the county, the state and the federal government to the immediate needs of the City of Buffalo.

The "good news" versus the "bad news" syndrome has been with us for many decades. A 1979 study showed that readers throughout the country felt that newspapers are biased in favor of so-called bad news because, they feel, newspapers are convinced that "bad news" sells more newspapers. Here is my response, in a May 1979 column:

> Unfortunately, for those who feel we are the purveyors of gloom and doom, it's almost always the "bad news" that in the final analysis people really want to read, even though they complain about it. News, by definition, is the unusual, the unexpected, that which takes an event out of the commonplace. A newspaper reporting the usual would serve no useful function.
>
> In the *News* we do make a conscious effort to print the good things that people or organizations do. We try to soften the impact of the hard news on our display pages . . . with the human pieces, the stories of outstanding achievers, the success stories. . . .
>
> Another complaint nationwide is that readers feel their hometowns are better than their newspapers portray them to be. Hometown pride is admirable and important. Newspapers should do as

> much as possible to encourage this community spirit. But we can't gloss over the problems of our area—we can't always accentuate the positive. . . .
>
> Sometimes in our editorial pages and news columns we may tend to sound too much like the common scold. But the squeaky wheel theory has always been an effective method of achieving results. And the watchdog role of the press has been its historic function. . . .
>
> We at the *News* never have been bashful about extolling the virtues of our community when and where deserved because we have a great sense of pride in Buffalo and western New York.

Columns that explained the paper's policy in matters that did not have approval of many readers were difficult to undertake, but we thought it was important to inform our readers about policies that were controversial. One of those was the use of negative material in obituaries, a policy that invariably inflamed many readers. Many of the nation's newspapers avoided controversy in this area by eliminating any reference to negative events in the life of the deceased. It certainly is the easy way out. We at the *News* took the tack of the *New York Times* and many other major newspapers and did not ignore the negatives of a person's career in obituaries. In a column on September 24, 1980, I talked to *News* readers about our policy on this and why we pursued it. The policy was controversial, as was the column about it. But it was important to clarify where the *News* stood and why. The following is a portion of the editor's column on the matter.

> Maintaining the integrity of its news report is vital if a newspaper is to sustain a reputation for quality and evenhandedness. It is always easier to compromise, to take the non-controversial road, most particularly in the preparation of local stories that have a more direct impact on readers.
>
> But the path of compromise inevitably leads to a lessening of respect for the newspaper by those who are aware that the less-than-candid report has been published. There is no question that yielding to the easy way out can make life more comfortable for the editors responsible in such cases. It is in those areas where compromise can occur readily that the greatest protest often arises.

A typical example is if major negative incidents in the deceased's life are to be used in an obituary. If a local person has had an unfortunate but celebrated incident in his life and you omit mention of it in his obituary, an editor rarely will get negative reaction.

However, *News* policy is that such major negative incidents are to be used in obituaries. We are not speaking of unimportant, minor scrapes with the law. These are easily forgotten and should not be revived upon a person's death.

Recently a former state assemblyman from this area died. Two years after leaving the legislature he became a key and celebrated prosecution witness in the police garage trial of a South Buffalo realtor. Although not indicted, the former legislator had been named as a co-conspirator in the case. The investigation, the report of the grand jury, and the trial itself were major news in Buffalo for many months, dominating the headlines and the airwaves.

The *News* obituary of the former assemblyman carried one long paragraph summarizing his involvement in the police garage scandal. This brought several phone calls and indignant letters, all with the same basic refrain—why bring the matter up after the man's death and add to the grief of a distraught family?

We sympathize with the feeling of friends and family but firmly believe *News* policy is fundamentally correct. We cannot relinquish our responsibility to report the *News* factually.

In reporting the deaths of famous or infamous persons not from the Buffalo area, readers would be surprised if similar well-known negative material were omitted from their obituaries. When it comes closer to home, the same rules must be followed.

There are other instances where hard-line policies trouble some readers. Several years ago an extremely prominent area resident committed suicide, using a gun. The *News*, in its comprehensive obituary, reported how the individual died. Most of the other media yielded to entreaties made in calls from prominent persons in the community urging—almost demanding—that no mention be made of the cause of death.

It would have been easier for the *News* to yield to the pressure. But it would have been unethical to do so in this case when we regularly report other deaths by suicide.

Tough discipline is necessary to maintain rigid standards we feel are absolutely necessary. It usually is expedient to take the easy course,

> but that is not the responsible path. Compromise your ethical standards once and it becomes difficult not to do so again and again.

A 1980 column dealt with a subject that is as controversial today as it was then. A letter protesting a headline that said a teacher had been arrested for drunk driving prompted it. The thrust of the letter was that it is unfair to single out the teaching profession in the headline of a negative story. My column comment offered the following point:

> A teacher by his calling, as do other professionals, carries a certain level of respect in the community. When such persons are charged with a breach of the law or other deviations from the customary standards of society, they sometimes pay the price of being singled out by profession in headlines or identification in stories. . . .
>
> In the purist, textbook approach to journalism, one does not treat a doctor or lawyer or teacher differently in news pages than one treats a production worker, a laborer, a clerk, or any other occupation.
>
> But in the daily exercise of our craft this rationale would place everything on an equal scale, wiping out one of the essential elements upon which all stories are judged. The "who" in an incident frequently makes the difference between a story and a non-story. Certain people, by their calling in life, achieve a stature that elevates them in the eye of the average man above others.
>
> In the particular instance of the teacher arrested on a drunken-driving count, we cannot overlook the fact that . . . teachers are expected to be role figures for their students, setting examples by their behavior. . . .
>
> Let's pursue the point a step further. If a minister, for example, were arrested for drunken driving, the *News* definitely would run a story on that arrest. . . . His action in driving while intoxicated is out of the expected character and therefore news. The arrest of a man working in an office on that same charge might not necessarily be worthy of a story unless it involved personal injury or physical damage. The key words are "people in positions of public trust." . . .
>
> The *News* policy in this area involves judgment. But we feel it is part of our responsibility to make these judgments, difficult as they may be. They are not made to sensationalize, to sell newspapers or because of a bias against a segment of society. . . .

> If we, on occasion, incur the wrath of a group of readers because of this policy, it is the price we must pay because of our firm convictions.

The policy enunciated in that column is controversial and was not, in fact, one favored by many staffers, as they informed me after the column appeared. Many readers, too, reacted negatively to this policy, saying it unfairly targeted some segments of society. But it was a policy that I felt was in the best interest of a newspaper in performing its watchdog role.

Editors are constantly making judgments. The chief editor of a newspaper is selected by the publisher and is responsible to him. If the publisher does not agree with his judgments, among other criteria, he replaces the editor. The value judgments editors make are often difficult and the need to set aside personal biases in making these judgments is paramount.

Many of the toughest judgment calls come in the selection of photographs. I set out *News* policy many years ago in a July 1, 1980, column that in effect followed the policy laid out by my predecessors but was often challenged by my own editors.

> The general rule followed by the *News* is not to print pictures showing charred or mangled bodies, the victims of fire, accidents or crime. Experience has proven to us that readers generally find these photos repulsive and vigorously object to seeing them in their family newspaper.
>
> The *News* will at times run pictures of accident victims, but these are reviewed to be certain that they are not gruesome, would not cause a sense of loathing. In line with this thinking, we refrain from using pictures displaying an inordinate amount of blood. . . .
>
> There is the feeling among most newspaper editors that reader reaction frequently depends upon how close to home the pictures strike. Tough pictures recording events from far away generally will generate less criticism than those from the area basically displaying the same type of subject matter will. We would agree with that consensus. . . .
>
> We constantly keep in mind the sensibilities of our reading public and often discard a top-grade wire service picture if we feel it is too harsh. There always are exceptions to every rule. A striking

example occurred on April 28 when the Associated Press moved a series of pictures showing the burned bodies of American servicemen who died in the efforts to rescue the hostages in Tehran.

Several of these pictures were really tough to take. Two showed a charred serviceman's body next to airplane wreckage. We used one of the photos showing a burned body and several others showing the wreckage. The decision was made to use them on the Picture Page rather than on Page One—a nuance experience has proven to us is important. Use of that picture out front would have, we are certain, brought much greater negative reaction than did its placement on the Picture Page. . . .

The key question remains why did we decide to use the very harsh picture of the charred body? The decision, made by a group of top editors, was not unanimous. However, the overriding factor was that the aborted rescue attempt that ended in tragedy for eight American servicemen was an event of historical importance. The aftermath could not be projected at the time of decision to publish a picture that normal policy would mandate be rejected.

The event could possibly have been the start of another war. Not to record it in our pages was unthinkable, although in making the decision all agreed we would get negative reader reaction. As it turned out, we were wrong in our appraisal of how *News* readers would react. The picture brought only two complaints by mail and two by phone. . . .

In checking later with the Associated Press, we found that its survey indicated that most metropolitan newspapers published the pictures, generally on Page One. The *Boston Globe* received more than 200 negative calls. . . . Editors generally apply a rule to pictures that "if it's a big story and the picture tells it, print it." When you get down to the basic reason for our deciding to use the charred body photo that really was it.

This is in no way inconsistent with our policy as it applies to pictures of an accident victim, a fire victim or a crime victim. . . .These are not really big stories. So on these we practice the rule of good taste and respect for human dignity.

In reviewing the file of hundreds of "Your Newspaper" columns I wrote over the years, I turned up quite a few explaining the role of local columnists and critics and most particularly how they differ from staff reporters in the freedom they have in expressing their views. Probably the biggest verbal beatings editors take come from readers who object to a columnist's or critic's opinions and feel the editor should have stifled these opinions. The columns I've written have tried to clarify the status of these special staffers. I've selected portions of a 1986 column on the role of the local critic and some from a 1990 column on the role of local columnists to explain the paper's policy in handling the material generated by these staffers.

First, the August 1990 piece:

> Local columnists are important elements of a good newspaper. But because good columnists are not bashful about expressing opinions on subjects familiar to readers, their work inevitably results in more complaints than of the hundreds of news stories we publish each week.
>
> The "heat" from offended readers generally is applied to the editor and in some cases to the publisher. Life would be much easier if we carried no local columnists but the *News* certainly would be a much duller product.
>
> Columnists are not instructed to deliberately be offensive, to be critical, to swing an ax. They are aware, however, that to be effective they can't studiously forestall controversy by avoiding critical commentary. They are columnists, not feature writers. . . .
>
> What all of the columnists have in common is the right to express their opinions. They are not limited, as are our regular news reporters, to straight factual reporting of events. They introduce their thoughts, their personalities into their work. That is basically the difference between a columnist and a reporter.
>
> While the editor is still responsible for all that is printed in the *News*, he must give his columnists the right to express views. We do not necessarily agree with all they write. We do not tell them what to write. Essentially they are similar to editorial writers and Tom Toles, our political cartoonist.
>
> Unlike general assignment and beat reporters, they have the latitude to choose subjects they are familiar with or with which they are comfortable. We certainly have the responsibility to see that our columnists are not defaming people, are maintaining the newspaper's standards of good taste, and are not using their columns for personal gain or goals.
>
> It is very important to note that columnists cannot base their

> opinions on material that is not factual. There is no question that this is a tricky area. The Supreme Court in a 7-2 ruling stated that statements of opinion are only immune to claims of libel if they do not contain provably false factual connotations. . . .
>
> Most expressions of opinion, however, still will have constitutional protection. Chief Justice William Renquist in the majority opinion wrote that those who file libel suits against the media must be able to prove that the disputed statements were wrong, and, he noted, it is difficult if not impossible to prove that statements that are clearly opinion are wrong.

I really can't evaluate too well the effect columns such as this have on the reading public. No matter how many times it's been stated, readers still hold the editor, and at times the publisher, responsible for the opinions of the columnists. And on a related topic, I addressed the subject of critics in a January 1986 column, again reiterating what I had alluded to several times in the past. This column was published four years after the *Courier-Express* closed its doors, but theater directors and producers were still insistent that this sad event should change the role of *News* critics. The column put forth our thoughts:

> Does the fact that the *Buffalo News* now has no major print competition make a difference in how its critics evaluate a performance? Strangely enough, many involved in various cultural pursuits at many different levels truly believe that that should become an influential factor.
>
> We totally disagree with such appraisals. It is abhorrent to our way of thinking. A good critic cannot and should not permit outside factors to influence critical judgment. There are too many today who believe it is the basic responsibility of *News* critics to encourage audience participation, through attendance and/or contributions, in the arts. This is nonsense.
>
> Critics should be fair in their evaluations. . . . Critics are not supposed to be cheerleaders. Nor are they arms of the Chamber of Commerce. The critic is charged with the responsibility of making honest appraisals. The "honest" I speak about is a personal factor, not subjected to outside forces. Given this, how can the reviews change because the *News* is the only voice in town? They definitely should not and we hope that they do not. . . .

> A good critic should never lower the sights of the community. It is important for the critic to point out what others are doing better, if such is the case, and how and why we should aspire to achieve that level. . . . There is today too much of a tendency among those in arts organizations to reach for the cloak of protection they feel is afforded them by the absence of two major newspapers. They cite the "fairness" factor in attempting to stifle or diminish critical evaluation.
>
> It won't work here. Fairness is not an issue if you have honest professional reviewers. If we did not think ours were in this category, we would remove them from reviewing roles. . . .
>
> . . . It matters not if there are one or two or more print media in town involved in reviewing. The key is that standards remain constant, they do not deviate because of circumstances.

A newspaper that doesn't have the flexibility to adapt its practices to the changing world would quickly become dated and out of touch with reality. An editor must constantly review standards of the past to be sure that his newspaper continues to reflect what is happening around it. But in doing so he has to consider the path his paper has followed in the past and not deviate too drastically. That was the situation that prompted a column in May 1987.

> The media, including the *News*, in recent months have carried an unusually high number of stories about subjects that not too many years ago would have been shocking to most readers throughout the country.
>
> When the enormity of the AIDS situation surfaced, the word "condom" appeared in our pages in editorials, news stories, and headlines. While there is nothing wrong with the word, in the past it rarely was one used with any degree of frequency in a family newspaper.
>
> Leonard Halpert, (retired) editorial page editor, some weeks ago remarked that we had two editorials in one week mentioning condoms. Having said that, he added: "In my more than thirty-five years at the *News*, I can't remember once using the word in a story or editorial. And now twice in one week."
>
> In the past few weeks we've had numerous stories about the alleged sexual exploits of the Rev. Jim Bakker, including charges of infidelity, wife swapping, homosexuality and involvement with prostitutes. These stories have been given prominent exposure. . . .

> We raise the issue because of my concern that readers might get the idea that the *News* is taking a new tack and becoming a "sensationalized" newspaper. That is not the case now, nor do we plan on such an odious course in the future. The truth of the matter is, however, that part of our job is to mirror what's occurring in the community, the nation, and the world. We cannot ignore events and situations that affect the lives of many. Times change, and what in the past was hidden away today often becomes public knowledge and subject to public purview and discussion.
>
> Many would argue that these changes are not always for the good and that society would be better off if certain matters remained private. We would not totally disagree with the feeling. . . . On the other hand; we could make the argument for a full airing of some issues that were verboten in the past because of sexual connotations.
>
> We are fully aware that there are stories we carry today that are distasteful to a percentage of our readers. We exercise caution in use of language, selection of photographs, and the headlines on such material. We are, however, to a large extent driven by events. Many of the stories coming to us through the wire services are not published because of their tawdry nature and the fact that they have little significance. Those that do have impact in one way or another cannot be ignored. . . .
>
> On occasion material has been used that we would have preferred not to see in the *News*. This most frequently occurs in some of our syndicated columns. This calls to mind a meeting we had about a dozen years ago with columnist Ann Landers. She severely chastised us for permitting editors to eliminate so many items from her columns. We replied that we felt some of the material she was writing was too suggestive for a family newspaper. In retrospect, we realize how tame the column items were by today's standards.

While the *News* has a definite policy on publishing corrections when it has printed an article containing incorrect information, I utilized the editor's column on June 2, 1987, to correct what I felt was a gross injustice to Senator Daniel Patrick Moynihan. I felt so strongly about the erroneous impression given by a May 23 story that I felt a correction using this method, although most unusual, was called for. The portion of the column pertaining to the apology stated:

> On Saturday, May 23, the *Buffalo News* published a page one story about a tax-exempt foundation that Sen. Patrick Moynihan set up to handle his charitable contributions. The thrust of the story was to report on the establishment of the trust and to note that the senator had neglected to list himself as a trustee of the foundation on his Senate financial-disclosure form as required by law.
>
> Unfortunately, the headline appearing over the story was misleading and unfair to Moynihan, giving the erroneous impression that the senator had kept the funds destined for charity. The story itself was one that needed to be written and the material it contained needed to be made public.
>
> While the *News* and all of its editorial employees strive constantly for accuracy and fairness, we, too, are subject to human error. In this particular instance, a misunderstanding of the story resulted in an incorrect headline. . . . The incorrect impression conveyed to *News* readers by the headline was dismaying. I personally have apologized to the senator and his wife. But this public apology and explanation are also important to set the record straight.
>
> We are aware that readers frequently look only at a headline and in this case could be left with a lasting impression that would be unfair to Moynihan. The senator has since filed an amended disclosure report to put himself into compliance with the law.

Moynihan, to his credit, responded to the column with a letter to Everybody's Column, said the story was "untrue, a falsehood. I have never come upon as open, full and heartfelt acknowledgement of a mistake as that by Murray Light, editor of the *Buffalo News*, in his Tuesday column. The *Buffalo News* is his ship and he takes responsibility for the way it is sailed. He is a man of real integrity and of courage yet more rare. Murray Light behaved not just in dignity but with valor. All honor to him."

The column in this instance served to right an injustice to a most honorable public official and gave me the opportunity to right a wrong in a forum that could attract more than customary attention.

Setting standards for the staff is an important function of a newspaper editor. The person so positioned is responsible for its tone and content. With the easing of standards by the television industry, and particularly cable TV, the staffers are tempted to use language previously barred in the *News*. Early in 1991 we had published some things that even with somewhat relaxed standards made me uncomfortable. As a result I addressed the issue in a column published February 12, 1991. Most readers who commented on it were pleased but more than a few thought it was time for the *News* to "lighten up and get with it in today's world." The column, which was aimed at readers, offered these thoughts:

> The stylebook and policy manual of the *News* clearly states that "the use of profanity, obscenity and blasphemy is generally unacceptable" in *News* editorial matter.
>
> As we moved through the 1960s, '70s and '80s, many newspapers relaxed their prohibitions in these areas—some, in my opinion, shockingly so. The *News*, too, eased up somewhat in language restrictions but far less than many newspapers and periodicals.

The column goes on to cite three instances of material that I felt should not have been published in the paper. I categorized them as "aberrations that should not have occurred." It then goes on,

> The *News* does not intend to relax its standards on language usage. The policy manual, which guides our staff and is definitely still in force, states, "The main question to be addressed in any decision on questionable language is this: What purpose is served by the use of such language? We do not resort to the use of colorful language merely to entertain some of our readers: we can be certain that it will offend an even larger number of them."
>
> There are, of course, exceptions to these rules and one came into play not too many weeks ago. President Bush used a vulgarism in describing what U.S. forces would do to the Iraqis [during the first Gulf war]. We printed his exact words because the public use of such language is unusual for a president and the words he used expressed his strong feelings about the subject. Not using the exact quote would have failed to transmit the depth of the president's emotions.
>
> The newsroom policy manual, in discussing the issue of language, further states: "it is true that society's attitudes are changing. We are freer, more open, more frank, less reserved in our use of

> harsh language. But we must take the greatest care to avoid becoming more tolerant than our audience as a whole."
>
> We still live by that standard. There is occasional slippage, which is not sanctioned by the top editors who manage newsroom operations. . . . There are times when decisions are made on publication that you know will justifiably upset some readers. You have to weigh this expected negative reaction against the need to inform readers about an incident or subject that is likely to result in future actions or comments.

Many of the "Your Newspaper" columns were prompted by national stories that stirred up great interest and/or debate. One of these occurred on March 30, 1991, prompting a great many reader requests for a statement on *News* policy on the naming of rape victims. These requests came from individuals but also from a significant number of women's organizations. The column discussing the matter was published May 7, 1991, and resulted in a significant phone and mail response, some agreeing or disagreeing with parts of the column, others (but not many) totally in agreement with what was said, and a significant number who thought our explanation made no sense at all.

The event that sparked this outpouring was an alleged rape by a member of the Kennedy family at the family compound in Palm Beach, Florida. The debate was kicked off by the publication in a supermarket tabloid of the name of the woman who claimed she had been raped. Much to the surprise of most observers, NBC and the *New York Times* also used the woman's name. My comment on the incident read, in part,

> We have had numerous requests for a statement on *Buffalo News* policy relative to the naming of rape victims. The *News* stylebook addresses the issue: "We never identify the victims of a rape or other sexual assault unless extraordinary circumstances call for it and then only with express prior approval of a senior editor." Although the stylebook dates to 1985, the policy on rape victims has been in existence at the *News* for decades. . . .
>
> The policy does not categorically state that the *News* will never publish the name of a rape complainant. A loophole of "extraordinary circumstances" does exist. . . . If we had a local story with the

> type of conditions existing in the Palm Beach situation we might have authorized use of the alleged rape victim's name.
>
> An extremely public family was involved. The prime suspect, although not charged with a crime, was publicly named by officials. The suspect had never had a single brush with the law. Day after day his name was published throughout the country. The Palm Beach police were not forthcoming with details and appeared to be dragging their feet in pursuing the investigation.
>
> Was it fair to constantly point the finger at the suspect and not name the alleged victim so that those with information about her or the incident might come forward?
>
> Some, including women, say they favor naming all rape victims as well as suspects. We can't go along with that. Such a policy inevitably would result in an even greater number of rapes than now go unreported. If we had a case here where a prominent public officeholder or business leader was accused of rape and became the focus of great negative publicity but was not charged with the crime over an extended period of time, we would give serious consideration to naming the alleged victim. This would open other avenues of investigation and public input that could prove valuable in bringing the case to some type of conclusion. . . .
>
> The *News* would have no problem in publishing the name of a rape victim if that individual voluntarily came forward and offered to have her name cited in stories we publish on the incident or to state that she once was a rape victim and wanted to comment for publication on rape and its ramifications. Before accepting such an offer we would seek to determine the woman's motivation for going public and to be certain she was aware of the possible problems that it might entail for her. . . .

An area of constant irritation for many readers—and for editors as well—is utilizing information in stories from "anonymous sources." In a May 3, 1988, column I discussed the matter in terms of national news. Reading it again many years later, I find the column wanting in that it failed to discuss our situation at the *News* in the use of that phrase. In actuality, the rule we utilized here for years mandated that if a story quoted an "anonymous source" and the editor had reason to wonder who that source was in order to determine if there was any validity to the quote, the reporter was obligated when requested to identify that source to the editor. The column confined itself to State Department rules on dealing with the media, and while it was interesting, it was not as pertinent as it should have been. The column stated,

> During the Watergate investigations we were inundated with letters from readers who protested the numerous stories quoting "anonymous sources" or using the phrase "sources said." The majority of these protesters were convinced that there were no such sources and the words were just those of reporters with an ax to grind against the Nixon administration. Similar complaints were registered during the Iran-Contra investigation. Undoubtedly they will be voiced any time the press is put in the position of being forced to protect the identity of a news source or forfeit the information that the individual can disclose.
>
> We certainly prefer to identify all sources of information in our news stories and constantly urge staffers to avoid, whenever possible, use of anonymous sources. But in many cases it is not possible to attain the ideal.

The column then quoted an article by Chuck Lewis, Washington bureau chief for the Associated Press, published in the March 1988 *American Society of Newspaper Editors Bulletin*. Lewis disclosed a U.S. State Department memo titled "Guidelines for Talking with the Press." The memo outlined four courses of action for the department's personnel in dealing with the media. In addition to "on the record," which all reporters prefer, the department discusses "backgrounders" which prohibits the use of direct quotes and direct identification of the official who gave the information. "Deep backgrounders" are those stories that say "it is understood that" or "it has been learned." Then there's the "off the record" category in which the newsperson can't use anything he's been told except for planning purposes.

The State Department, however, is aware that many of these categories are not honored and warns that "nothing substantive ever stays off the record." The fact is that, as the column stated, "any experienced newsman knows that an official will not give him important information 'off the record' and expect it to remain unpublished. You go under the premise that nothing substantive ever stays off the record." This applies to talks with local officials and politicians as well as State Department chieftains.

"Our own government," the column concludes, "forces reporters into a type of reporting that results in credibility loss for the media."

Every year the *News* hires a host of young people to serve as summer interns in the newsroom. These college students are important to us during the heavy vacation period when so many staffers are away from the newsroom. Their internships involve hands-on reporting and editing and a weekly orientation session conducted by Newsroom Department heads as well as representatives from some of the other *News* departments.

As editor, I generally kicked off the series of weekly meetings, and year after year I started by talking about the "newspaper business." This invariably surprised the young people who thought it somewhat demeaning for me to describe our enterprise as a business. I then differentiated between newspapering as a whole, which is definitely a business that must be profitable, and the newsroom environment, which is a professional one. The dialogue with the interns prompted a column about the goals of a newspaper, which in the minds of some seem to be in conflict. It basically repeats what I often tell the interns as well as visitors to the *News*.

> To accomplish our multiple goals we must report aggressively, invariably bringing us into conflict with different sectors of the community. There are stories that must be written that bring us into conflict with our own business interests, good advertising customers of the *News*. And yet these stories are written and published.
>
> When the *New York Times* or the *Wall Street Journal* reports on the problems of a major Buffalo business, readers in our area don't get too upset. When the *News* does the same, readers react differently, wondering why the *News* would print a negative story about a local enterprise. Those of us in the newsroom don't look at it as a betrayal of a local business if we report the facts accurately and objectively.
>
> On the other hand, the editors of the *News* at times are accused of boosterism when we praise the successes of local businesses of communities. We view the plus as being legitimate news also.

In addition to providing information that is important or interesting, a newspaper must also provide entertainment through its comics, puzzles, and feature columns. Is the entertainment factor in conflict with the information goal? We don't believe that. One can't be expected to plunge into a product that is concerned only with the economic, political, and social problems of the community.

Then, of course, we come to advertising. Without it, no newspaper can survive. Some purists still say that advertising is in conflict with a newspaper's other purposes. That is not true. Reader surveys always show advertising to be among the best read material in a newspaper.

None of the multiple goals of a newspaper have to be at cross-purposes. An editor's role is to guide the newspaper into the proper channels so that the primary goals are never forgotten or deterred. More importantly, he must not let them be thwarted by forces out of sync with the newspaper's purposes.

30 The Community Gains

The *News*'s involvement with the community it serves has been extensive for generations and has grown with the passage of time. As stated in our report to readers on our community activities: "We believe that being a good newspaper also requires being a good citizen. For that reason, we either initiate or are asked to help support many causes throughout western New York each year. We respond with cash contributions, promotional support, printed materials, equipment, and volunteers—using our resources to make western New York an even better place to live."[1]

This credo is not of recent vintage. Our founder, Edward H. Butler Sr., was a firm believer in the newspaper's need to involve itself with the community, and this heritage has continued and grown through the years. There's been one major change in the paper's approach to community involvement. For many decades the *News* did little to inform the community of its civic endeavors. Its approach was definitely not to "blow its own horn." The prevailing ethic of *News* leadership was to do the good things because they should be done but to trumpet them was not in good taste. As a result, the *News* did not get credit for the many things it was doing to assist organizations and individuals in need.

This laid-back approach to its public spiritedness changed with the arrival of Stanford Lipsey and his appointment as president and publisher. Lipsey understood the need to inform the public about the paper's community involvement and he initiated a program to do this on a continuing basis, always aware of the need to do it tastefully. In addition, Lipsey also undertook an immediate campaign to extend our involvement in community action.

One of the key steps Lipsey took to implement his community involvement campaign was the hiring in December 1996 of Dottie Gallagher-Cohen as manager of promotion and public affairs. She previously had twenty years of experience in public relations and marketing and had developed numerous successful campaigns in the community. Her initial role at the *News* involved corporate marketing and oversight of all promotional activities. Her value to the *News* continued to grow as she assumed more responsibilities, including directing the important Newspapers in Education program.[2]

In recognition of her fine work, Gallagher-Cohen was promoted to vice president of news media and integrated marketing in 2001. She has responsibility for promotion, corporate marketing, educational services, and Internet ventures such as Buffalo.com, Buffalocar.com, Buffalonews.com, and Buffaloapartments.com.[3] Her strong leadership qualities and outgoing personality have made Gallagher-Cohen a valuable member of the *News* executive management team. Her innovations greatly expanded our presence in community affairs.

As part of Lipsey's program the *News* publishes periodic reports to readers of the newspaper's numerous outreach programs. The following is culled from the report for 2001:

NEWS NEEDIEST FUND—Launched in 1982 at the suggestion of columnist Ray Hill following the closing of the *Courier Express*, the fund solicited food, clothing, and toys for needy families in western New York. The *News* each year has paid for all expenses involved in the effort, with every dollar collected going directly to the needy. With the growth of the endeavor through the years, the paper solicited and received the assistance of the United Way in its effort. In 2001, a total of 11,625 families received food, clothing, and toys from the Neediest Fund. For years, Ray Hill was the voice of the fund, writing all the stories that attracted the contributions and to a great extent organizing the entire effort.[4]

KIDS DAY—An enormously successful endeavor that other newspapers have tried to imitate without success. The *News* launched its annual Kids Day in 1983. It involves thousands of volunteers who raise many thousands of dollars for the Variety Club of Buffalo, all of which go to Children's Hospital and the Robert Warner Rehabilitation Center. The special Kids Day edition of the *News* is sold on the streets of communities throughout western New York on a morning in February for $1 a copy. In 2001 some six thousand volunteers braved the frigid weather to hawk the Kids Day edition and raised a total of $154,000. In its initial year of 1983, the effort raised $85,000; the following year the total increased to $92,000 and has steadily increased in each succeeding year. The *News* uses three full-time employees for three months each year to meet the enormous logistical requirements of this fundraising endeavor. Various unions at the *News*, particularly in the production and circulation departments, voluntarily donate their time to produce and distribute the Kids Day edition. The *News* newsprint suppliers traditionally have been involved in the effort, contributing the tons of newsprint used for the Kids Day edition. After nineteen years, Kids Day has become an important part of the fabric of the *News*. It is a highly respected tradition internally and externally, with area radio and television stations joining in the effort to alert the community about Kids Day.[5]

KIDS VOTING WESTERN NEW YORK—The *News* has played a major role in an endeavor designed to introduce schoolchildren to the fundamentals of democracy. Publisher Stan Lipsey was the key individual behind the formation of the western New York affiliate of Kids Voting USA, a voter education program designed to encourage young people from kindergarten through high school to get involved in voting. The youngsters learn about the election process and then on Election Day are encouraged to cast their ballots in a mock election for local, state, and national candidates.

Kids Voting in Western New York has grown with each passing year. In 2001 a total of 323 public, parochial, and private schools were involved in the program with a total of some 35,000 students casting their ballots in the polling sites. Additionally, the effort involved more than 5,000 adults who staffed Kids Voting polling sites on Election Day.

In addition to bringing Kids Voting to western New York, the *News* has supported the program with full-page ads and countless stories to encourage involvement by the students and adults as well. The *News* also provides office space for the paid administrator of the effort as well as supplies. It's an effort that has won plaudits from all involved as it encourages a habit so fundamental to a democracy.[6] It has not been possible to ascertain if participants in the program become regular voters when reaching adulthood.

CLASSROOM CONNECTION—In 1994 the *News* launched a program in western New York utilizing the technology that could never have been envisioned when the paper was first established. An interactive voice response service, Classroom Connection has logged an amazing five million or more calls since its startup. As the link between more than 4,000 teachers and thousands of parents interested in the classroom welfare of their children, it likely would win the popularity poll among western New York adults as the best of all the services the *News* provides. Without the cooperation of the teachers, this program could not survive. The teachers involved constantly update a voicemail message for students and their parents; it gives the parents the opportunity to be aware of what is going on in the classroom and share in the learning experience of their children every day, not just at scheduled parent-teacher conferences. Countless numbers of parents have expressed their appreciation of the service that is available without charge and is made available by the *News* with the cooperation of Tops Markets, a local supermarket chain, and Independent Health, a health maintenance agency in the Buffalo area. Classroom Connection really links, possibly for the first time, the parents into the learning process of their children.[7]

CRADLE BEACH—The *News* in 1946 joined hands with the Rotary Club of Buffalo to support the operation of Cradle Beach on Buffalo's lakeshore. For many years the paper's fundraising efforts for the camp was its prime community endeavor. Every contribution to the camp fund, no matter how small, was reported in the *News*, encouraging others to get involved. The camp had special appeal as a site where disabled and disadvantaged youngsters could spend some summer days at a facility equipped to care for their needs. In 2001, the fifty-fifth year of our involvement, Cradle Beach played host to nine hundred young people. While the role of the paper has changed over the years, it continues to assist in the fundraising efforts of this most worthwhile endeavor.[8]

NEWSPAPER IN EDUCATION—A long-standing involvement of the *News* has been its newspaper in education program. Its fundamental premise is to establish in young people the habit of reading newspapers. Teachers receive the sunrise edition of the *News* and a curriculum with activities that align with the New York State learning standards. The *News* offers school subscriptions at a reduced rate and makes available guided tours of our editorial and production facilities.

The Newspaper in Education supervisor for the paper provides teachers with materials needed to enhance the program and involves them in workshops and seminars. Local businesses have supplemented our effort with funds to support those classes in need of dollars.[9]

NEWS BOOKS FOR KIDS—This relatively new outreach endeavor, initiated at the suggestion of then staffer Rose Ciotta, was launched in 1994 and has succeeded in providing needy youngsters with books to stimulate their interest and expand the love of learning. In 2001 the effort distributed a total of 177,456 books with individual children receiving nearly 85 percent of them. The program has achieved its goals, thanks in great measure to the work of our partners, Buffalo State College, and Project Flight. They have been instrumental in implementing the proper distribution of the collected books, with each volume carefully matched to the individual youngster.

In addition to allocating books to individuals, the program gave 27,491 books to some 100 community lending libraries in the year 2001, and collected more than $10,000 for the purchase of Braille and large-print books.

The community has responded generously to this endeavor to get books into the hands of young people whose families cannot afford to purchase books for them. The three partners involved in the collection and distribution of the books have dedicated long hours to the effort and have been gratified by the response of the hundreds of book donors. This endeavor has exceeded the expectations of its originator, Rose Ciotta.[10]

THE *NEWS* AND MUSIC—Although many *News*-sponsored activities are designed, understandably, to encourage reading, we have also undertaken two major efforts in the musical world. The *News* has been sponsoring the Buffalo Philharmonic Orchestra New Attitudes Series designed to attract new audiences to Buffalo's fine orchestra. The music in this series is described as "funky, jazzy, folksy, and groovy"; a dramatic departure from the orchestra's usual menu. Attendance at these Friday night ventures indicates they have been fulfilling a need.

Another *News* musical involvement has a much longer history, having gotten under way in 1982. Stan Lipsey, a dedicated jazz buff, initiated a series of free concerts on the steps of the Albright-Knox Art Gallery bordering Delaware Park's Hoyt Lake. These concerts entertain thousands each summer. The Buffalo Jazz Workshop and other musical artists are showcased Sunday afternoons in July and August. These free concerts have become a Buffalo tradition.[11]

ANNUAL SPELLING BEE—The granddaddy of all *News* promotions, launched in 1927 and still going strong, is the annual spelling bee. The event involves more than 300 schools and 50,000 western New York youngsters. And as has been done every year since its inception, the top speller receives a trip to Washington, DC, to participate in the national spelling bee final.

In addition to the numerous *News*-sponsored events, the paper lends its name and support to dozens of worthwhile causes each year. Some, like the Summer Harvest Drive of the Food Bank of Western New York, are annual events that depend upon the *News* to promote participation by the community. Others are one-time only or even one-day events that seek and receive support from the *News*, primarily with stories publicizing the activity. Decisions on lending support to one-time endeavors are made by Gallagher-Cohen or the editor. Long-term commitments generally are made by the publisher.

Notes

1. "We Deliver More Than Just Newspapers," *Buffalo News*, January 29, 2002, pp. B-6, 7.
2. Information supplied by Dottie Gallagher-Cohen, July 22, 2002.
3. Ibid.
4. "More Than Just Newspapers."
5. Ibid.
6. Ibid.
7. Ibid.
8. Ibid.
9. Ibid.
10. Ibid.
11. Ibid.

31 Coverage and Content

A review of the *News* since its inception in 1880 as a daily shows the extent of its coverage of national and international news events. These reports were culled from the numerous wire services we subscribed to over the years to provide readers with complete coverage. The services were utilized for national and international news coverage and for specialized news such as religion and science. The services have their own staff of reporters and editors and they derive their income from selling their reports to the media. Among them, some no longer in existence, were the Associated Press, United Press, International News Service, Reuters, North American News Alliance, Chicago Tribune News Service, Chicago Daily News Service, Science Service, and Religious News Service. In addition, the *News* has always utilized the services of freelance writers and its own staffers to provide the supplemental coverage that its editors felt was needed.

Although the paper budgets more than a million dollars a year for these wire services, it has always kept in mind that its primary mission as a regional paper is its coverage of local news, including extensive reporting of the local sports scene and business and financial news from the western New York area.

The *News* established and maintained Albany and Washington bureaus to keep abreast of news pertaining to the Buffalo area long before it set up a network of local bureaus to report on suburban news as the outward migration from the central city of Buffalo continued to increase.

The earliest suburban bureau was set up in Amherst in the late 1960s and was staffed for almost three decades by Dick Dawson, a competent reporter who witnessed and wrote about the enormous growth of that town. As the village of Williamsville and the neighboring town of Clarence continued to grow, part-time stringers were utilized to assist Dawson in his coverage.

In 1978 a bureau was opened in Niagara County, coinciding with a Circulation Department decision to concentrate efforts on developing more readers in that area. The bureau is responsible for covering the entire county. It was the first bureau to have editorial and circulation department people in the same offices. The Niagara bureau has always been staffed by at least three full-time reporters whose work has been supplemented by many part-time correspondents covering the numerous town and village boards in the county as well as local news stories. The bulk of the copy for the *News* Niagara edition, which was established in May 1979 to help us compete with the dailies in the northern cities of Niagara Falls and Lockport, comes from those two communities. Circulation gains in Niagara County have always been difficult to achieve and have never reached our expectations. Polls taken by the *News* have indicated great loyalty to the Lockport paper, which does a particularly fine job in providing coverage of sports activities in the schools and communities.

Over the years the *News* also established bureaus in our communities in Tonawanda, Cheektowaga, and the Southtowns. In April 1997, taking the cue from the *Orange County Register* in California, which had consolidated many of its bureaus, the *News* did the same after a survey of its suburban reporters and editors indicated they felt they could be more effective if they were in one location rather than being scattered in a series of small bureaus. The *News* consolidated its Amherst, Tonawanda, and Cheektowaga bureaus into one bureau and located it on Main Street in Snyder. The office was equipped with police scanners, new computers, and software to enhance their reporting capabilities. The staffing of this combined bureau was upgraded, almost doubling the number of reporters and editors involved prior to the consolidation.

The Southtowns bureau had not been involved in the consolidation move but near the end of 1997, three part-time reporters were hired to supplement the work of the two full-time members there. The move was motivated by the population trend that indicated continuing growth in the suburbs south of the city. The three part-timers hired later became full-time *News* staff reporters in various roles.

All of the paper's bureaus in the various suburbs and outlying areas report on the activities and news events that are important to those residing or doing business there. Many of these items appear only in the edition distributed in that particular area or community. These are what are designated as zoned editions. For example, one goes primarily to the Southtowns, another only to the northern towns, one to outlying areas, and another is distributed only in the city of Buffalo. Some of the more important or interesting material generated in the bureaus is published in all editions, particularly if the material has ramifications that go beyond a particular zone. Many of the communities in which the *News* has a bureau have their own local paper and we do compete with them for news and subscribers. Most of these publications are intensely local and provide coverage of minor events that we don't provide. It's their particular niche and not the role of a metropolitan daily.

* * *

Unlike many newspapers that started charging for publication of wedding and engagement pictures in the 1970s, the *News* has continued to offer that service free of charge to its readers. We also publish, as a reader service, pictures of couples celebrating their fiftieth wedding anniversaries. And the *News* is well known in the industry for publishing in agate type the record of births in the area, bankruptcies, incorporations, and judgments. Many years ago, before the proliferation of crimes of all kinds, the Daily News Summary also included the entire police blotter for the city of Buffalo.

A random list of major stories reported in the *News* starting in 1881 gives a good overview of local, national, and international stories as viewed by the editors of the paper. It is not an all-inclusive list, but is an indicator of the vast array of events and issues that the *News* traditionally has highlighted on its front page. The *News* has long been respected for giving its readers more national and international news than the majority of regional newspapers.

1881—The President [Garfield] Shot in Washington!
1901—The Exposition [Pan-American] Dedicated!
1901—President M'Kinley [McKinley] Shot!
1901—President McKinley Dies!
1906—Earthquake Kills Hundreds in City of San Francisco
1907—McKinley Monument Dedicated with Imposing Ceremonies
1911—Probing the [New York City] Fire Horror
1915—1500 Lose Lives on *Lusitania*. Famous Roycrofter Elbert Hubbard Aboard.
1917—Nation Is Now at War. [World War I]
1918—Huns Give Up! Armistice Signed by the Enemy
1938—Falls Bridge Plunges into Gorge; Workmen Narrowly Escape Crash
1939—Nazis Attack Poland; Planes Bomb Warsaw
1941—Japanese Bomb Pearl Harbor
1945—Full Nazi Surrender Ends War in Europe
1945—Saddened by Roosevelt Death, Nation Unites Behind Truman
1945—Atomic Bomb Used on Japs; Equals 20,000 Tons of TNT
1950—Truman Orders Air, Sea Units into Action on Korea, Formosa
1950—Frank Lloyd Wright's Larkin Building Is Destroyed
1950–1960—Buffalo's Famous Elm Trees Start Disappearing
1951—Collision of the Freighter *Penobscot* and Gas Barge *Morania* in Buffalo Harbor Starts Three Day Fire Resulting in 11 Deaths
1953—Signing of Korean Truce Ends Warfare

1954—11 Pupils Killed, 19 Hurt in Explosion and Fire in School at Cleveland Hill
1954—M'Carthy Rebuked on Second Count
1956—Schoellkopf Plant Loss $100 Million; Flooding Threatens Part Remaining
1960—Boy Survives Plunge Over Falls
1963—Kennedy Dead, Shot by Sniper in Texas
1968—Rocky [Gov. Nelson A. Rockefeller] Breaks Ground at New UB
1968—Dr. King's Killer Sought; U.S. Mourns
1968—Sen. Kennedy Survives Surgery; in Extremely Critical Condition
1969—We Walk on the Moon: "A Leap for Mankind"; *News* follows up with special section: Our Men on the Moon.
1970—Militants Blockade Building at the University of Buffalo
1970—Student Protests Continue. 32 arrested at Buffalo State College
1971—Attica Inmates Seize Five Cellblocks; 7 Guards Hurt, Others Held Hostage
1971—Appeals Court Unanimous in Dome [Stadium] Ruling
1973—High Court Eases Abortion Law
1973—Ceremony in Paris Ends Vietnam War
1973—Watergate Figures Get Stiff Terms
1973—Agnew Resigns Post, Pleads No Contest to Tax Evasion
1973—Bills Play First Game in Orchard Park Stadium
1974—Supreme Court Orders Nixon to Surrender Tapes
1974—President [Nixon] Is Resigning; to Address Nation at 9
1974—Pardon for Nixon Stirs Furor
1976—U.S. Funds Light Rail Rapid Transit for Buffalo. Federal Aid Set at $269 Billion.
1977—Blizzard Paralyzes WNY, Kills 7, Strands Thousands. Blizzard special section published
1977—Griffin Triumphs in Record Voting; GOP Captures County Legislature
1978—$4 Million Aid Sought for Love Canal
1978—Heart Attack Fatal to Pope John Paul

1981—Hostages Free
1981—Joseph Christopher, 22 Caliber Killer
1981—Reagan Shot in Chest in D.C., Is Stable; Aide [Press Secretary James Brady] Is Wounded
1983—Six Dead in Tragic Blast; Six Firemen Killed [One of most serious fires in history of Buffalo]
1983—[Downtown] Mall Plan Draws Future from the Past
1983—Steelmaking Ends in Steel City [Lackawanna]
1988—Pilot Field Puts City in Spotlight
1991—Massive Air Offensive Pounding Iraq Targets
1991—Terry Anderson Free [from Iran]
1991—Key, M&T Banks Buy Goldome [Bank]
1991—Gulf War Ends
1993—Assault Launched on Waco Cult
1994—The Last of the Buffalo Bills Four Successive Appearances in the Super Bowl Ends in Loss as Did the Previous Three
1995—16 page Section to Launch Series on Buffalo Schools
1995—O. J. Not Guilty
1995—Explosion in Oklahoma Kills19
1996—Marine Midland Arena: Latest Jewel in Buffalo Sparkles at Opening Gala
1996—Jumbotron in Downtown Sports Arena Falls
1997—Gala Welcoming Greets First Passengers as Operations Take Off at New Airport Terminal
1997—Crash Kills Princess Di
1997—Timothy McVeigh of Pendleton Sentenced to Death
1998—Inferno on Buffalo's I-90, Killing Six in Massive Chain Reaction Crash
1998—Buffalo Bills Reach $11 Million Seat Sale Goal
1998—U.S. Air Strikes Against Iraq
1999—President Clinton Impeachment. House Impeaches President December 20, 1998. Senate Vote, as Expected, Falls Well Short of Convicting Clinton of Perjury, Obstruction of Justice
1999—Hope fades for JFK Jr.
1999—Littleton, Col. School Disaster. Two Students Kill 14 and Themselves[1]

In the 1800s and into the early years of the 1900s, the *News* front page carried dozens of stories each day. This included numerous short local items that in later years were run on inside pages and in many instances would never have been included in the *News* at all. In the mid-1990s and thereafter, fewer and fewer stories appeared on page one, and for the most part the front page "menu" contained only five stories, the index, and a column of briefs referring to stories carried on the inside pages.

Severely limiting the number of page-one stories was part of a nationwide trend. It contrasted vividly with the philosophy espoused for years by A. H. Kirchhofer. For many years he was adamant in insisting that the final edition of the day, the only one of the day's editions that had street sales only (no home delivery), carry a minimum of thirty-two front-page items. These included the index, any promotional boxes, and even one-paragraph stories, but if the total didn't reach thirty-two, the editor in charge of that edition had to listen to a stern lecture from AHK. The word was that thirty-two items in the final had become a religion with Kirchhofer. That mandate quickly disappeared when he retired. His practice actually was a good one, offering readers of the final edition a taste of all they might hear on the six o'clock news when they got home from their jobs.

When Edward H. Butler Sr. founded the *News* as a Sunday-only paper, he targeted what he thought to be wrongdoing in the community in the pages of his publication. He struck forcefully and repeatedly in news stories and editorials, making the *News* an effective force for reform in the community. That thrust continued, but to a somewhat lesser degree in the *Buffalo Evening News* when it was established. And as the years rolled by, the paper, although never known as a muckraking newspaper, continued to target what it considered to be malfeasance by officeholders, civic waste, and unequal administration of justice at various levels.[2] For many years, under the editorship of Kirchhofer, the *News* targeted Communism and Communists, more so than most of the American media.[3]

Two Buffalo mayors were also continuing targets of *News* attacks in news stories and editorials. The *News* did not hesitate to use its front page to highlight attacks against Mayor Frank Sedita and, years later, Mayor Jimmy Griffin. Strong editorials were utilized in these campaigns. The paper differed with Sedita and Griffin on many issues of importance to the community. Both of these mayors were not shy about firing back at the paper when they were criticized in its editorials.

Notes

1. Parts of listing from *Headlines & History* (Buffalo, NY: Buffalo News, 1999).

2. Jerry Goldberg, "Edward H. Butler and the Founding of the *Buffalo Evening News*: The Life and Times of One of the Last Publisher-editors" (master's thesis, State University of New York at Buffalo), pp. 59–67.

3. Alfred H. Kirchhofer Papers, Buffalo and Erie County Historical Society Archives, C67-6, box 24.

32 Grab a Six-Pack

The *News* has constantly put the spotlight on elected leaders of the city and the county, regardless of party affiliation. Edward H. Butler Sr. felt it was the responsibility of the paper to the communities it serves to ensure that political leaders fulfill their roles. In chapter 10, I told the story of Mayor Frank Sedita and his long, bitter exchange, which started in 1959, with Kirchhofer and the *News*. Passions were high but the coverage of Jimmy Griffin engendered the most heat, the most mixed emotions among readers, of all the politicians the paper has covered in its history.

Jimmy Griffin was elected mayor of Buffalo in 1977, reelected in 1981 and again in 1985,[1] and 1989. In his sixteen years as mayor he made hundreds of speeches and was interviewed countless times, but a statement he made during the Blizzard of 1985 is the one most people still recall. The mayor counseled the citizens of Buffalo to "stay inside, grab a six-pack, and watch a good football game."[2]

In retrospect, it might have been the smartest bit of advice the mayor could offer, but it certainly was not what one would expect from the chief executive of a city. Community leaders and people expected to hear him express compassion for the ill and elderly who were undergoing hardships due to the storm, advice on following restrictions imposed on vehicle use, and information on what to do in emergencies arising from the blizzard. Griffin personally directed cleanup of the snow after the storm, which although not as severe as the Blizzard of 1977, did close down the city for a week.

However, those who knew the street-smart, intuitive mayor were not surprised by his words. He always prided himself on saying what he felt would appeal to the "average Joe Blow" on the streets of Buffalo. He governed by instinct and let the chips fall where they may.[3]

One of his basic instincts was to categorize people as "with us or against us." There was no in-between for Jimmy Griffin. For example, in the years he was constantly feuding with the *News*, he felt his one true friend at the paper was the very popular columnist Ray Hill. But one day Hill wrote a column that criticized the mayor and that marked the end of the honeymoon between the two. Griffin called Hill to his office and told him, "You can be with us or against us and it's obvious you're now against us." The mayor didn't care about all the good things Hill had written about him and his administration. One negative wiped it all out.

The relationship the *News* had with Mayor Griffin was relatively good, up to a point, but it really started deteriorating during his second term. I had made a determination that we would not respond in editorials or columns to his negative remarks about the paper and its staff but had to deviate from this in 1983 as the mayor and his ardent supporters became more open in their attacks on us. Finally, on May 31, 1983, in my editor's column, I wrote in part:

> Through circumstance and not by design, this newspaper has been making a series of revelations about situations in Buffalo's City Hall that are troublesome from the standpoint of morality, ethics, and possible illegality.
>
> The series of stories on different subjects centering on City Hall have given the false impression to many of a contrived vendetta by the *News*. The events and circumstances dictated the timing of the stories. There has been no "grand design."
>
> We have, in a continuing series of stories, investigations, and editorials, disclosed the executive branch's interference in the elec-

> tion of an independent school board, the practice of selling tickets to political fund-raisers in a manner seemingly inconsistent with state law, the mayor's acceptance of a monetary gift from City Hall employees for a Florida vacation, and the failure of city housing inspectors to perform a day's work for a day's pay. . . .
>
> The reaction from the executive chamber in City Hall has been a series of unfair attacks on members of the *News* reportorial staff, including a challenge to fisticuffs, and a refusal to talk to staffers who have been involved in the reporting of City Hall stories.[4]
>
> This seeming intolerance of criticism will not deter the *News* from its reporting of news of interest, nor will it alter our determination to provide fair and unbiased coverage of what is transpiring in City Hall.
>
> Editorially, this newspaper has been supportive of the city's chief executive on many issues and ventures. We also have been critical of some of his undertakings. This policy of calling the shots as we see them will not be affected by the mayor's use of the airwaves and public forums to castigate the *News* and its employees.
>
> The *News* is not interested in petty quarrels with government officials. Nor will it countenance unfair reporting. But we will continue to explore events and issues and report them as we find them.[5]

Given the ever-increasing exchange between friends and foes of Griffin, the *News* early on in 1988 decided to start work on a major series of stories about the mayor and his administration. Margaret Sullivan, then an assistant city editor, headed up a team of eight reporters and five editors involved in putting together the eight-part series that was published in May of 1988.[6] Sullivan, aware of the strong feelings about Griffin, said, "In putting together the Griffin series, the reporting and editing team really felt a strong obligation to be scrupulously fair to the mayor."

Not unexpectedly, given his past relationship with reporters, Griffin refused to talk to any of the participants in the project. The series, titled "Griffin: A Decade of Power," was received as we had anticipated, eliciting praise as well as howls of outrage. The team, I felt, presented a fair and balanced picture.

The series very properly noted that Griffin had a definite distaste for urban planning and Buffalo suffered as a result. It also noted that the city's neighborhoods had not fared well during his stewardship up to that point. But it gave the mayor credit for his efforts in downtown development and particularly attracting the Hyatt and Hilton hotels, developing the theater district, and coming up with the concept for Pilot Field.

I had not told the Sullivan team the role the *News* played in the construction of Pilot Field, for our minor-league Bisons. The idea for a downtown baseball facility originated with Mayor Griffin. He said it would aid in downtown development and should be funded by the state. I never publicly acknowledged the paper's involvement in fulfilling the mayor's dream, not wanting to be in a position of appearing to undermine his role. There's no question that he originated the idea, which proved to be a good one for downtown Buffalo, although it never resulted in any significant economic activity in the area of the stadium.

Shortly after Griffin went public with his hope for a baseball facility I received a phone call from then governor Mario Cuomo. He wanted to know if the *News* believed a downtown stadium for baseball could really be an economic generator. I said that we hadn't had discussion on that as yet but offhand would suggest it might be doubtful. The governor asked me to give it some thought so we could discuss it more fully.

About a week later Governor Cuomo called again and I reported that those with whom I had discussed the baseball facility were somewhat dubious about the benefits it could bring to the downtown sector. The governor said he had the same doubts and then asked me to give some thought to any other downtown project the state could fund that could prove more beneficial. Another week or so passed and the governor called again. I reported to him that nobody could come up with a better project at the funding level projected for a small baseball stadium and that all things considered it likely would have some economic benefit. The final call from the governor on the subject came not too long after and he reported that he was going to support Mayor Griffin's plan and pledge the state funding needed.

Although the relationship between the *News* and the Griffin administration continued to be rocky at the best through the years, it really turned totally sour in the latter part of 1989 and early 1990. The *News* had been publishing a series of stories about corruption in the City Parks Department and Parks Commissioner Robert Delano in particular. The stories cited numerous examples of Delano utilizing city materials and manpower for personal profit. They noted his activity over a period of years to distribute city-owned swimming pool chlorine to private citizens. One allegation revealed in *News* stories that infuriated much of the citizenry was Delano's dumping of chemicals in Delaware Park Lake, polluting the lake. *News* stories also pointed up Delano's use of city employees to perform services such as tree cutting and paving parking lots for private citizens and churches. There were also stories about Delano using city employees on city-paid time to remove trees from the police commissioner's property and other such incidents. Among the *News* revelations was the work performed by city employees on the mayor's car and supplying materials for a privately owned and operated tennis center on Elmwood Avenue.[7]

The *News* stories on the activities of the Griffin administration and its utilizing of city funds were the talk of the town. They were picked up by television and radio commentators and were the constant theme of the radio talk shows. The mayor repeatedly charged that the *News* was getting its information from governmental sources that should not have been feeding the media. I finally felt it was time for me as the editor of the *News* to reply and I did so in a column published February 13, 1990. In part, it said:

> In the bars, bowling alleys, and barbershops of Buffalo, the No. One topic of conversation these days is the continuing saga of Parks Commissioner Robert Delano. There's no doubt that reports by the *News* and electronic media are intriguing many.
>
> But there are some misconceptions about the *News* stories of the investigation by a federal grand jury and the local office of the FBI into allegations of corruption involving the Parks Department and Delano. These are the facts:
>
> Neither the office of U.S. Attorney Dennis Vacco nor the staff of G. Robert Langford, special agent in charge of the FBI's Buffalo office, is providing the team of reporters working on the Delano sto-

> ries with any information or tips. These federal officials are doing their jobs, and the *News* reporters are doing theirs independently.
>
> Phone and mail tips have provided the bulk of the material that our reporters have tracked down and developed into the numerous stories on the alleged activities of Delano and some parks employees. . . . Much of the material provided to *News* reporters has come from current and former employees of the Parks Department. . . . We know their names, background, biases and credibility. . . .
>
> Despite the contention of some, the *News* did not set out to "get" Delano or his associates or to embarrass the City Hall leadership. When we printed the first story about alleged Parks Department corruption activity we had no idea that it would be the first of many. But as has happened in the past in other situations, the first story brought phone calls and letters that, when followed up, resulted in additional stories. I can't recall, however, any story in years that has resulted in as many phone tips to the *News* that has proved to be fruitful.
>
> Our role is, and always has been, the traditional one of a news organization in a free society: to investigate allegations of misuse of power and/or taxpayer dollars. . . . [8]

A week after publication of that column, I had to come back with another one on February 20 to comment on a lengthy Griffin news conference that bitterly attacked the *News* and was so bombastic it created an unbelievable amount of comment in all the electronic media. It was a Griffin performance that topped all his previous public appearances.[9]

I started the column by stating that I had been tempted to forgo any further comment "but fearing that silence on the subject by the editor of the *News* might be misinterpreted by some as the result of mayoral intimidation." The column tells the story and it follows in part:

> Wipe out all the bombast, the mud slinging against the media, the attempts to attract sympathy by relating his personal history. Wipe out, in fact, most of the 100 minutes of the mayoral performance, and one thing emerges—the mayor admitted that the basic thrust of the numerous stories about the Parks Department in the *News* and on television was not media fantasy.
>
> The mayor also reported that he finally was going to do some-

thing about Parks Commissioner Robert Delano. But in the heat of his tirade against the media he contradicted himself on exactly what he was going to do. That's strange, given that the news conference was convened to announce his decision on Delano.

Initially, he said he was going to put Delano on leave of absence and ask the Common Council to continue his salary. If the Council turned down this request, he said, Delano would be out as parks commissioner. But later he hedged on that, saying that if the Council refused his request for the paid leave he would have to decide what Delano's future in city government would be. Given that the Council is unlikely to accede to the mayor's request, we'll have to wait to learn Delano's fate.

Amid all the noise, the mayor repeatedly evaded questions about why he was putting Delano on leave at the same time that he vigorously endorsed the job Delano had been doing as commissioner. Finally, and quite lamely, he said it was because that's what the commissioner wants.

The credibility of the mayor's statements throughout the news conference suffered enormously, in my view, because he was so far off base in areas he touched upon in which I was directly involved.

In trying to impugn the integrity of the *News* he stated that he understood the *News* paid $800,000 to a city building inspector mentioned in a series of 1983 stories. The figure he cited is an extraordinary exaggeration. Unfortunately we cannot report the actual amount because, by agreement and by order of State Supreme Court Justice Norman J. Wolf Jr., the terms of disposition (of the libel suit) were to remain a private matter between the parties. I sincerely wish we were at liberty to detail the agreement.

In another matter, the mayor alludes to attempts by the *News* to review the financial records of three development companies controlled by the administration. . . . Turned down in our attempts to get the records through normal channels, the *News* filed legal action to get access. The mayor said, "the *News* lost and they won't pay their lawyers. Here's what you call a crybaby. They lost in court. Why don't you pay the lawyers?"

This is outrageous and untrue. The *News* certainly paid its attorneys as it pays all of its obligations. The *News* did not lose its court action. Two filings were rejected by the courts on technicalities involved in filing dates. . . .

> The mayor also came up with a conspiratorial theory involving two of the finest *News* reporters, George Borrelli and Ray Hill, saying they met with the mayor's political enemies in a downtown health club to plot against the mayor. Hill and Borrelli do belong to the club and do work out there. Conspire against the mayor? Both reporters vigorously deny any such activity, and knowing their integrity and dedication to the principles of journalism I have every reason to believe them and to scoff at the mayor's allegation.
>
> Personal attacks against staffers and mudslinging against the *News* will have no effect on our continuing efforts to disclose what we feel is important for people to know. Nor will the mayor's admission that he sees nothing wrong in spending taxpayer dollars to aid private parties and religious entities deter us from reporting such activities when and if they come to our attention and are verified.[10]

Delano was indicted on six felonies in March 1991.The Delano trial lasted more than three months and he was found guilty on October 23, 1992, on five of ten counts and sentenced to four years and one month imprisonment. He was basically charged with using city materials and manpower for personal profit, ending a three-year federal investigation. He was acquitted on a charge of polluting Delaware Park Lake and stealing city swimming pool chemicals. He was found guilty on a count of racketeering that involved extorting city employees to perform services on private property. He also was found guilty of fraud for misapplying federal funds given to the city and of violating the Hobbs Act by forcing city employees to remove trees from the police commissioner's property.[11]

The mayor, after Delano's conviction, called him a good friend and a good boss. In May 1995 the Second Circuit Court of Appeals overturned the most serious Delano convictions for racketeering and racketeering conspiracy but let stand the other three felony convictions. Delano was released from prison in March 1996, having served over two years.[12]

At his trial, the story on Delano's Delaware Park incident, which had puzzled many, came out. It seems that he ordered the dumping of anti-icing chemicals into the lake because the Common Council had forced him to shut down a refreshment stand in the park casino that was run by members of the Parks Department social club. The chemicals prevented the lake from freezing sufficiently to permit ice skating.[13]

Jimmy Griffin's sixteen years as mayor came to an end with the completion of his fourth term in office. His first bid for public office came in the early 1960s when he made an unsuccessful attempt to win a seat on the county's old Board of Supervisors. He was elected to the Common Council to represent the Ellicott District and held that seat from 1961 to 1965. In 1965 he ran for councilman-at-large but was defeated. Elected to the state senate in 1967, he served for ten years representing south Buffalo, Lackawanna, and part of West Seneca.[14]

Griffin without question was the most controversial mayor in Buffalo's long history. He demanded and received loyalty from his aides, all of whom were named to key administrative posts regardless of education or work experience. City hall was filled with his south Buffalo supporters. There were competent persons among them, others had no business being employed by the city, except that they were friends of the mayor. Griffin worked by instinct and many of his instincts were good. He was stubborn, opinionated, and outspoken. He never did understand the role of the media and couldn't countenance criticism from them.[15]

The *News* through the years was fortunate in having fine reporters covering city hall. The efforts of John Boccio and Bud Zubler in the period from the 1940s and 1950s come quickly to mind. They were well-respected reporters. But the time they and their predecessors covered city government couldn't even begin to approach the twenty-six and a half years George Gates had been involved in the cauldron-like political environment of Buffalo's city hall.[16]

Gates covered the mayoral administrations of Chester Kowal, Frank Sedita, Stanley Makowski, and Jimmy Griffin. Thoroughness, impartiality, and the ability to report on government in language all could comprehend marked his coverage. The years that Griffin was mayor were particularly difficult for Gates, given the mayor's refusal to talk to *News* reporters. Even though the relations between the *News* and Griffin were always strained, Gates, being the pro that he was, never permitted that tension to color his stories about the mayor's office. It was the ultimate test and Gates passed it with flying colors.[17]

Most city hall observers and long-term councilmen considered Gates the most knowledgeable person in all of western New York on the workings of Buffalo's government, past and present. He was highly regarded by both Democrats and Republicans for his even-handed coverage and his ability to distance his coverage from the paper's opinions about the political personages in city government.[18]

When a spot on the *News* editorial board opened up in August 1989, Gates was named to fill the opening. Although he had not complained about his many years of covering city hall, the feeling was that his expertise on city government would be a major plus for an editorial writer. Until his retirement in November 1998, he wrote almost every editorial involving city government. The anonymity of an editorial writer didn't faze Gates although those in city hall still called him with praise or complaints, knowing that if an editorial was about city government, he almost certainly had to have been the author.[19]

Gates also wrote numerous editorials on regionalism and the need to control urban sprawl, subjects he felt strongly about. An avid baseball fan and a dedicated college basketball follower, Gates wrote many sports editorials in his nine-year stint on the editorial board.[20]

Gates graduated from Amherst College in Massachusetts, and came to western New York in November 1956 to a job as a Niagara Falls *Gazette* reporter. In the spring of 1961 he joined the staff of the *News*. George Gates retired from the *News* after thirty-seven years on staff. His was a distinguished career and his performance was above reproach.[21]

Notes

1. "Griffin, A Decade of Power," *Buffalo News*, May 15, 16, 17, 18, 19, 20, 21, 22, 1988.

2. Ibid.

3. Ibid.

4. Griffin encountered Ray Hill and George Borrelli, *News* political writer, in the Buffalo Athletic Club, made some nasty remarks to them about *News* disclosures, and then challenged them to fight. They wisely walked away from him.

5. Murray B. Light, "Your Newspaper," *Buffalo Evening News*, May 31, 1983, second front page.

6. "Griffin, A Decade of Power," *Buffalo News*, May 15, 16, 17, 18, 19, 20, 21, 22, 1988.

7. "The Parks Scandal: The Federal Case Against Robert E. Delano," *Buffalo News*, March 8, 1991, editorial page.

8. Light, "Your Newspaper," *Buffalo Evening News*, February 13, 1990, second front page.

9. George Borrelli, "In Bizarre Spectacle Mayor Evades Queries, Ridicules Press," *Buffalo News*, February 14, 1990, *News* library.

10. Light, "Your Newspaper," *Buffalo Evening News*, February 20, 1990, second front page.

11. Editorial, "Delano Verdict Gives Justice for a Pattern of Outrages, Parks Head Robbed Taxpayers; Now He Pays," *Buffalo News*, October 23, 1992.

12. Dan Herbeck, "2 Delano Convictions Overturned; Three Other Felonies to Stand," *Buffalo News*, May 17, 1995, p. 1.

13. Michael Beebe and Mike Vogel, "Prosecutor Hits Delano Credibility, Urges Common Sense in Deliberations," *Buffalo News*, October 13, 1992, p. 1.

14. "Griffin, A Decade of Power."

15. Ibid.

16. Light, "Your Newspaper," *Buffalo Evening News*, August 1, 1989, second front page.

17. Ibid.

18. Ibid. (October 29, 1998).

19. Ibid.

20. Ibid.

21. Ibid.

33 —30—

All mature corporations reach a stage where they have to start thinking, planning, and conceptualizing what lies ahead for them. They have to put into effect personnel moves and capital expenditures that will keep their institutions viable in their marketplaces for many years in the future. A newspaper such as the *Buffalo News* is no exception to this rule. Publisher Stanford Lipsey has taken the steps needed to ensure the future of the *News* as the major media outlet on the Niagara Frontier.

The process of change at the top started with my decision in the latter part of 1998 to retire on September 19, 1999, after fifty years of service. While I still enjoyed coming to the office each morning, I realized that it was time for me to make way for that fresh thinking in the newsroom that would be beneficial to the newspaper. I could not agree with the direction newspapers were taking. For example I did not like the use of large headlines for insignificant stories and displaying those stories on the front page, when in my judgment they did not belong there. It was a trend I could not support, since to my mind it created distortions that I did not believe were good for a newspaper or its readers. Too many so-called soft stories were displayed in a manner that indicated they were really important, when in fact they were not.

(*From left*) Murray B. Light and Stanford Lipsey having fun for a change. (Courtesy *Buffalo News*)

My career at the *News* started in 1949 when in August of that year I was interviewed by Alfred H. Kirchhofer, following the completion of my master's degree from the Medill School of Journalism at Northwestern University. He informed me that he wanted to talk to me, as a prospective employee, but that there were no job openings at the time. Two days later I was interviewed by the editor of the *New York Telegram*, was hired immediately, and started to work the next day as a copyeditor. Some six or so weeks later, I received a telegram from Kirchhofer informing me that a job had opened and inviting me to join his staff as a reporter. I accepted the invitation and joined the *News* at fifty dollars a week, twenty-five dollars less than I had been receiving from the *Telegram.* I accepted Kirchhofer's offer despite the salary difference because I wanted the reporting experience.

For years I was the benefactor of what I always said were "fortuitous circumstances." My path of advances through the newsroom hierarchy certainly involved a modicum of talent and drive but it was also a result of being at the right place at the right time. For years, the word around the newsroom was "if Light is your backup, be aware that something will propel him into your position." That did indeed occur through the years and ultimately resulted in my elevation in 1979 to the post of editor of the *News.* I moved through a series of positions in the newsroom as those I was assisting suffered through heart attacks, Meniere's disease, strokes, and other disabilities, providing me with opportunities to advance. Occasionally, the editor I was backing up just wasn't up to his job and I was advanced as his replacement. My path to the top culminated in 1969 when editor Paul Neville had a stroke at his desk and died two days later at the age of forty-nine after only three years as head of editorial operations.

Having made the difficult decision that it was time for me to retire, I met with Stan Lipsey, with whom I always had an excellent and cooperative relationship, and informed him that I wanted to stay on until September 19, 1999, giving the *News* about a year to identify a possible successor, and to have the individual ultimately selected serve in a "break in" period while I was still on board. Lipsey agreed that this was an approach that would serve the *News* well.

Lipsey invited Warren Colville, then executive vice president, to join him and me in the process of finding a successor to the editor's job. I had identified several incumbent members of the *News* department whom I felt should be given an opportunity to compete for the newsroom's top job. In addition to these people, we made it well known throughout the newspaper industry that the *News* was in the market for a new editor. We were encouraged and gratified by the number of inquiries we received, including some from major newspapers throughout the country. Each inquiry was carefully followed up directly or indirectly. The process was time consuming but fortunately we were under no tight deadline pressure.

Ultimately, after a lengthy period of review, we had eliminated all of the nonstaffers from consideration for a variety of reasons and had narrowed our search to two incumbent members of the newsroom staff. Lipsey, Colville, and I spent many hours reviewing the advantages and disadvantages of the two finalists and decided that Margaret Sullivan would best serve the paper as editor.

With this determination made, Sullivan was promoted to managing editor with the understanding that if she performed as we anticipated, she would be advanced to the editor's chair when I departed.

After a period of time, Lipsey asked me to let Sullivan make all the newsroom decisions subject to my review. I was to counsel with her, evaluate what she did and why, and brief her on why certain things were done and others were not. I also was to initiate her into the mysteries of the vast amount of paperwork that every editor would prefer not to have, but necessarily has to review and process almost daily. I wanted to prepare her as best I could for all facets of the editor's job, some of which are readily apparent but also a good many that are known only to those who have actually filled the editor's role.

The orientation period for Sullivan was a difficult one for me. After decades of calling the shots on the *News* side, I really didn't relish sitting on the sidelines and second-guessing another editor's decisions, but I agreed it was a wise course of action to prepare her for the top newsroom job. Sullivan was a quick learner and did so well that Lipsey, Colville, and I had no doubt that we had made the right choice. She was named editor upon my retirement and two years later, in February 2001, she was appointed a vice president, the first woman in the history of the paper to hold that title.[1] Sullivan designated Ed Cuddihy and Steve Bell as her managing editors and Gerald Goldberg continued to serve as editorial page editor, a position he had attained in May 1998.

Two years after the selection of Sullivan, Lipsey promoted four *News* executives, in effect establishing the leadership of the newspaper for years to come. The most important move involved Lipsey himself. He voluntarily gave up his role as president, promoting Warren T. Colville to that position.[2] Lipsey retained his role as publisher, and Colville, who had been executive vice president since 1997, continued to report to Lipsey. It's interesting to note that Lipsey's move was similar to one made by Edward H. Butler, founder of the *News*, who had been editor and publisher and in 1914 voluntarily gave the title of publisher to his son while retaining the editor's role for himself.

Colville joined the *News* in 1988 as vice president and advertising director. He previously had been ad director at the *Sarasota Herald Tribune* in Florida and at New Jersey's *Newark Star Ledger*. As president, he supervises the advertising and circulation departments, and also runs other parts of the day-to-day operation of the paper.[3] As publisher,

Lipsey continues direct supervision of news operations, with Sullivan and Goldberg reporting to him. Although Lipsey now spends several winter months at his California home, he is in daily contact with the Buffalo office by phone, e-mail, and fax and is kept fully informed on all *News* affairs.

Warren T. Colville became *News* president in 2001. (Photo by Mike Groll, courtesy *Buffalo News*)

Colville is well qualified to fulfill his obligations as president and he is a likely candidate to be named publisher when Lipsey decides to retire. He is totally familiar with the operations and personnel of the Advertising Department and has had significant involvement in the Circulation Department. He and Comptroller Rod Layton played key roles in ascertaining and ultimately bringing to a conclusion the malfeasance in that department that had been festering for so long under then circulation director David Perona.

Colville is not timid about making tough decisions concerning personnel changes when needed, yet he has always manifested a deft touch in managing the people who work for him as well as winning the approbation and confidence of advertisers. The big issue that could potentially influence Colville's future is his political orientation. He is a conservative and while he has had little or no opportunity to influence editorial policy in his past roles, the question remains what his orientation should be at some time he becomes publisher. The *News* departed from its Republican orientation with the sale of the paper to Warren E. Buffett and has endorsed Democrats as well as Republicans, leaning more toward Democrats during my thirty years as the leading editorial voice of the paper. Buffett himself is liberal on social issues and tends to be more conservative on economic matters.

However, he has never dictated editorial positions since assuming ownership of the paper but it is doubtful he would want his newspaper to revert to its previous position as a dedicated Republican organ.

Lipsey also promoted Robert J. Casell, a senior vice president since 1996, to executive vice president responsible for production, transportation, operations, and information systems. Casell joined the *News* in 1993 as vice president of production. He had previously been pressroom manager at the *Fort Lauderdale Sun-Sentinel* and production director for the Fort Wayne newspapers in Indiana.[4] As an innovative production director, he has been willing to try many of the things that his predecessors had rejected as too difficult for our facilities to handle properly, and for the most part he was able to make good on his promises for increased performance in our production facilities. Highly intelligent, a quick study, and always ready to meet challenges in the area of his expertise, Casell revolutionized our thinking about what the outdated letterpress presses at the *News* were capable of doing. At the same time, for years he continued his campaign for new presses. His persistence finally paid off when Buffett approved a multimillion-dollar expenditure for new presses. Casell had never hesitated to push for new presses despite knowing that Buffett had consistently rejected all suggestions toward such a shift in production.

Casell had succeeded longtime production director Al Wainwright but wisely retained his predecessor's services as his key aide. The two worked well together for years until Wainwright took retirement in 2001, ending decades of dedicated service to the paper.

Lipsey also acknowledged the ever-increasing role of Rodney E. Layton by naming him vice president and chief financial officer. Layton joined the paper in 1989 as treasurer and comptroller, having been audit manager at Berkshire Hathaway.[5] Layton's duties have increased with each passing year as Lipsey requested and received much more sophisticated financial data than any of Layton's predecessors had provided. Department heads received financial reports about their operations that previously were not available, making it easier for them to track their expenses.

Another senior executive position was filled some time later with the promotion of Philip T. Catanese to vice president and advertising director. He joined the *News* in November 2000 as director of sales after many years as sales director at Fleming Company and general manager of Peter J. Schmitt Company, a major grocery concern, where he had worked for eighteen years.[6] Colville had become acquainted with Catanese during his years as advertising director and had been impressed with both his drive and his fine relationship with the employees and customers at Schmitt. Cantanese quickly stepped in and contributed significantly to the Advertising Department.

Paul Glaeser, who had been hired in June 1998 from the *San Francisco Chronicle & Examiner*, continued in his role as vice president and circulation director.[7] He had taken over a department that had been rocked by the Dave Perona scandal and the malfeasance of others in the department. His quiet, unassuming manner helped steer the ship back on course. Morale in the department, which had deteriorated to an all-time low, improved considerably under Glaeser's direction. He and his key aides put into motion various measures to halt the declining circulation of the *News* daily and Sunday. Circulation losses had been occurring in most of the nation's newspapers for a variety of reasons, and for a number of years the *News* had been experiencing the same downturn.

Daniel Farberman joined the *News* as vice president for human resources shortly before Lipsey's reorganization began. He replaced Joe Saeli. Saeli served for a short time, replacing Ralph Wray, the successor to Dick Feather, a long-term senior vice president and director of industrial relations for the *News*. Unlike those who came after him, Feather had been at the paper since 1950 before retiring in June 1988. Human Resources has always been a very important department and is even more so today. It is responsible for monitoring benefits including health insurance and retirement for over a thousand full-time employees. It negotiates with the representatives of the many unions to renew contracts and meets year-round with them to interpret the contracts, which always present conflicts.

Another top executive, Dottie Gallagher Cohen, continued as vice president for new media and integrated marketing. She has performed her many challenging duties well since joining the paper in December

1996. These various promotions, Lipsey said, would "position the *News* to face a changing future with strong leadership."[8]

Notes

1. "The News Promotes Four to New Positions," *Buffalo News*, February 6, 2001, business section.
2. Ibid.
3. Ibid.
4. Ibid.
5. Ibid.
6. *Buffalo News* personnel files.
7. Ibid.
8. "Gallagher-Cohen Named a *News* Vice President," *Buffalo News*, August 4, 2001, business section.

34 The New Face of Newspapers

Newspapers throughout the nation have been undergoing changes due to a multiplicity of circumstances. In the 1960s there were approximately 1,750 daily papers published but by 2001 the number dropped to 1,480. Between 1950 and 1995, twenty-seven dailies with circulation of over two hundred thousand went out of business.[1] The number of family-owned newspapers continues to decline also. In 1910 there were 2,100 independently owned newspapers. This dropped to 700 in 1980 and in 1998 the number stood at only 250 to 300 out of 1,500 daily papers, the numbers varying depending on the source used. The primary reason for this decline in independent papers, the experts say, is the estate tax, which prevents the continuation of a family business.[2] This was certainly true with the *Buffalo Evening News* after the death of Kate Butler. Independent papers accounted for 69 percent of annual newspaper circulation sales in the 1980s but are in the single digits today. Ten companies now own more than 51 percent of the nation's weekday circulation. As recently as 1999, the top ten held under 46 percent of weekday circulation. Gannett holds its position as the nation's largest circulation company with ownership of ninety-nine dailies, including *USA Today*.[3]

Although the number of newspapers has declined, competition for readers and advertising has actually increased with the enormous proliferation of cable television and Internet Web sites. Other factors are involved as well to account for a pattern of considerable circulation losses of dailies throughout the country with the exception of the high-growth areas of the Southwest and Florida.

Changing lifestyles definitely have become a major factor in the United States as more and more women have entered the job market. With husbands and wives working and then returning home to do all the chores involved in maintaining a household and raising a family, there is significantly less time available in most homes for reading a newspaper. Children of all ages are creatures of the electronic age and spend significantly less time reading and more sitting in front of the TV set or the computer screen.

The continuing outflow of people from the central cities is another major factor in circulation losses. An ever-increasing number of those leaving the cities are settling in rural areas, further removed from the suburbs where major metropolitan dailies still have a good chance of retaining many of their former subscribers. However, long before this trend developed, the loss of population in Buffalo (for a variety of reasons) caused significant circulation losses for the *Buffalo News*.

In 1950 Buffalo was the fifteenth-largest city in the nation with a population of 580,132. By 1960 it was the twentieth-largest; by 1970 it was twenty-ninth in population; and by 1980 it had fallen to the thirty-sixth position.[4] Today its population has plummeted to 292,648 with fifty-eight other cities in the country having greater numbers of residents than Buffalo. Only St. Louis and Pittsburgh have lost a greater percentage of their populations in the past fifty years.

It's difficult to draw a direct correlation between the city's population loss and the circulation decline of the *News*. Our peak circulation came in the twelve months ending September 30, 1993, when the daily six-day average was 302,357 and Sunday circulation had reached 383,393. Why it peaked in that year is hard to explain. The *Courier* had halted publication in 1982 and as a result circulation at the *News* in 1983 had a six-day average of 312,779 and a Sunday circulation of 364,230. These numbers did not hold up for too long, however. Compare these figures with the ABC audit figures for the twelve months ending June 30, 2001, which showed a daily circulation of 224,490 and Sunday at 307,505. The publisher's statement for the six months ending March 31, 2002, showed the downward trend continuing with daily circulation at 220,345 and Sunday circulation at 302,400.[5]

One factor that cannot be overlooked in reviewing circulation numbers at the *News* is the increasing cost of the newspaper. In addition to the continuing 12 percent annual decline in circulation was the high percentage of those remaining in the city who had incomes at the poverty level or below. Most of those who had left the city were the more affluent and were more likely to subscribe to a newspaper. Those at or near the poverty level could not afford to subscribe to the *News* even if they had a desire to do so. An expenditure of more than $200 a year is a significant amount of money for these families.

The *News* under Buffett's ownership has had a policy of adjusting circulation pricing annually. These increases have been relatively small and have been in line with his thinking that small annual increments are more consumer friendly than imposing rather large rate increases from time to time. He suggested that I inform *News* readers in my weekly column that they could expect regular, rather small circulation price increases.

The nature of the newspaper business mandates continuing review of circulation and advertising pricing. Newspapers are labor intensive and annual wage increases for employees are more the norm than the exception. Additionally, the price of newsprint, the basic raw material utilized in production of a newspaper, can fluctuate wildly from year to year, depending upon supply and demand factors. And like any business, a newspaper has the usual expenses for utilities, supplies, and countless other items.

I do recall a speech I gave in the early 1980s to a large group of businessmen in which I expressed my concern even back then that the day would come when newspapers would price themselves out of the market for a good many people. Unfortunately, that prediction has become today's reality.

In a time when newspapers throughout the country were contracting rather than expanding and delaying or calling a halt to major

View of four Wood presses used since 1956 at the *News*, the last major newspaper in the United States to print with letterpress. (Courtesy *Buffalo News*)

capital expenditures because of declining circulation and diminishing advertising revenue, the *News* in June 2001 announced a major capital expenditure that will benefit its readers and advertisers for at least thirty years.

Publisher Lipsey announced that the *News* had signed an agreement with a German press manufacturer to purchase two state-of-the-art printing presses at a cost of $24.25 million. The total cost of the press project has been put at $40 million, which includes the $1.5 million to raise the pressroom roof to accommodate the new presses that are sixty-five feet tall. The remainder of the costs is to be allocated for other equipment and necessary modifications to the press building.[6]

Installation of the KBA Colora presses ends the letterpress-printing era for the *News*, which was the last large newspaper in the country still utilizing the letterpress. The *News* had been utilizing Wood letterpress since 1956. Parts for these Wood presses were no longer available anywhere and for years our machinists had to fabri-

(*Above and below*) Two new KBA Colora presses purchased by the *News* as part of a $40 million project. The new offset presses can produce 75,000 newspapers an hour. (Courtesy *Buffalo News*)

cate whatever parts were needed. Letterpress is a method of printing from raised surfaces, now obsolete in the computer age.

Not too many months after Buffett bought the *News* in 1977, he and I had a phone conversation during which we discussed the progress of our new Sunday paper. During our talk I took the opportunity to say that we could not produce a truly good-looking product with our outmoded presses. Buffett patiently listened to my presentation and then responded, "Murray, we will continue to use our present presses as long as Johnson & Johnson continues to make Band-Aids." That was the end of any further conversation about presses, and Lipsey, obviously aware of Buffett's feelings about the matter, did not encourage conversation about new presses for the paper. However, when Bob Casell joined the paper as production director in 1993, he initiated talk about the need for new presses and continued his campaign until Buffett finally approved the purchase of the two new offset presses. On hearing that news, I reminded the owner of his Johnson & Johnson quote many years earlier. He smiled and simply retorted, "I do remember saying that but there comes a time when things change."

Casell is in charge of the entire project. He says the paper's printing operations will "go from the 1950s into the twenty-first century." Casell had reviewed the possibility of purchasing offset presses from other newspapers but in each instance there were reasons why such a purchase did not make good economic sense for us.[7]

News readers will be the prime beneficiaries of the new era of presses. Once in operation, the presses will have the capability to reproduce more color photos because each of the two presses will be able to print up to twenty-four pages of four-color art. But it is in two other areas that readers will discern the greatest advantage. First, there is every expectation that the *News* will achieve significantly improved reproduction of pictures. The days of "muddy" pictures should be at an end. Photos will be reproduced with significantly greater detail than has been possible in the past. And one of the greatest complaints of readers should end, as ink rub-off on readers' hands will be minimal. Low-rub ink will be used in the new system and the automated ink-control system will ensure a more consistent application of ink on each page, doing away with the problem of some pages that are difficult to read because of poor ink distribution.[8]

The entire multimillion-dollar press project is scheduled for completion in March 2004, and when that occurs the two new presses will be producing 75,000 newspapers an hour. Currently, the presses can produce 45,000 newspapers an hour.[9]

The significant investment in new presses and improvements in the forty-three-year-old press building is a strong affirmation of commitment that the *News* has to downtown Buffalo and particularly to the lower Main Street area, which has been home to our operations for more than 120 years.[10]

Shortly after the huge press project got under way, the *News* Circulation Department launched another major initiative that publisher Lipsey said, "demonstrates our belief that the *Buffalo News* will be here for a very long time." While this undertaking will cost only in the neighborhood of $1 million, it will give the Circulation Department, under the direction of Vice President for Circulation Director Glaeser a new, fully integrated circulation system. It is the largest circulation project ever undertaken in the paper's history and it received the go-ahead signal from Lipsey even in a time of increasing competition and decreasing readership. The new computer hardware and software will replace a 1980s system and a 1990s customer service system. "It's a huge investment that shows the importance of the circulation division and how important it is to have the right tools as we move ahead," Lipsey said in announcing the project.[11]

After a slow start, the *News* has been a highly profitable enterprise under Buffett's ownership. In the first five full years, from 1978 through 1982, the paper sustained millions of dollars in losses, principally as a result of startup costs for the Sunday paper and major legal expenses resulting from the *Courier-Express* antitrust suit. But the financial picture brightened considerably starting in 1983 and has continued since. The September 12, 1998, edition of *Editor & Publisher* reported that "over the past five years, the *News* has boasted the best profit margins in the business, out-performing all other publicly reported papers in the U.S."

The *News* peak operating profit before taxes was achieved in 1997 when it reported a $55.9 million profit and its profit level before taxes remained above the $50 million level, except for 1995 when it dropped some to $46.8 million. These numbers were achieved despite a continuing loss of major advertisers as many retail and grocery chains closed. Since Buffett became owner, the list of *News* advertisers who have gone out of business includes well-known department stores, banks, supermarkets, clothing stores, and discount stores in the Buffalo area. Just prior to the change in ownership, the paper sustained major advertising losses with the closing of many more major advertisers.

The loss of many millions of dollars in advertising revenues has been offset to a degree by annual advertising rate adjustments, a substantial increase in part-run advertising that appears only in editions aimed at specific distribution centers, new products to attract advertising dollars, greater emphasis on securing classified advertising, and publishing more special sections throughout the year that attract focused advertisers.

Special sections are also public service projects designed to serve our readers and the community. One of the most significant was the five-part series on Buffalo schools by reporter Jim Heaney. The series was one of the most comprehensive published in the history of the paper. It was launched in March 1995, with a sixteen-page section on the state of the city schools. The entire series contained more than 120,000 words and resulted from fourteen months of research and writing by Heaney. He evaluated the city's entire seventy-two schools operating at that time. Another major special effort by the paper was a six-part series by Arthur Page, advising readers on steps that they could take to quit smoking. Written in February 1987, it created significant interest, and in response to requests, the *News* published the articles in a booklet that was distributed to thousands of readers.

In 1980, the year of the paper's centennial, we published six consecutive Sunday sections, starting January 27, covering virtually every aspect of the city's business and cultural activities over the one-hundred-year period. These are only a few of the extra efforts taken by the paper. Many other special sections were produced over the years of the *News*'s publication. All have been prime examples of good journalism totally independent of commercial efforts to attract advertising.

The retail and national advertising staffs have undergone extensive changes in personnel from top to bottom with major reforms in marketing approaches and much more aggressive, personal contact in sales efforts. Publisher Lipsey and president Colville have been particularly effective in making the changes that have produced positive results in a market that has sustained losses in population and the consumer outlets that serve them.

The *News*, meanwhile, had undertaken its first steps into the new world of Web sites and all the opportunities that these make available. Under the initial impetus from Colville, who threaded his way through all the technical difficulties and with the aid of Ed Cuddihy who adroitly overcame the problems of jurisdiction raised by the Newspaper Guild, our Web site Buffalo.com was born. By December 2001, more people visited Buffalo.com than any other local Web site in the area. It powered HomeFinder Extra.com and other avenues produced by the *News*.

The *News* Web site did not produce any profits but did position the paper for future development that could lead to commercial success and helped to maintain our position as the prime provider of news and information of all kinds on the Niagara Frontier.

Lipsey today believes that his major contribution to the *News* was saving it from extinction. "Looking back," he said recently, "there wasn't going to be two newspapers in the Buffalo market. We never said when we talked that we were going to put the *Courier* out of business but the pattern across the country was clear. The Newspaper Preservation Act for joint operations hadn't worked out either. [This act established joint operating agreements, which allowed papers to combine business functions in areas that could no longer support two competing dailies.] I dedicated myself to saving the paper. The *News* product was always there but circulation and advertising was a problem in terms of the attitude people had.[12]

"I remember Charley Sands [former advertising director] saying to me that as soon as you get the circulation better than the *Courier* I'll be able to get the ads. Well, you can't do that. I tried to get advertising to go up like that but it didn't work. So then we would take segments and the first nail in the *Courier*'s coffin was the establishment of

HomeFinder on Sunday March 4, 1979. We took most of the real estate advertising away from them. That got people reading our paper. We put it in the Sunday paper to build up the Sunday circulation. Instead of just getting ads we put out HomeFinder Extra all around the city. We took it to all major companies so if someone was hired they had a place to look for a home."[13]

Lipsey's initiative and his drive to be a winner was evident from the first days he started coming to the *News* in 1977 as a consultant to the advertising and circulation departments. It has not diminished with the passage of time and it has made the *News* a winner. Now he has set the stage for a new and challenging future for the *Buffalo News*.

The *News* is somewhat of an anomaly in today's newspaper world. Unlike the great majority of large and small papers today, the *News* is not owned by any of the numerous media giants, the chain operations that purchase papers and proceed to take steps that endanger the quality but enhance the prospects of greater profitability.

Chain ownership of newspapers is not of recent vintage. It actually started in the 1900s with E. W. Scripps and his papers.[14] Today there are fewer than fifty cities with more than one paper, and in sixteen of these cities the same company owns the papers.[15] The *News* is owned by one of the world's wealthiest men, a person who, fortunately, also feels a strong obligation to produce a newspaper dedicated to fairness and to objectivity. Warren E. Buffett, and his principal representative in Buffalo, publisher Stanford Lipsey, owe no allegiance to any political party, or to any present or potential advertiser. The *Buffalo News* from every standpoint is truly an independent newspaper. Buffett's wealth and his conscience guarantee the independence that chain operations and their obligations to stockholders do not have.

When the *Courier-Express* closed its doors in 1982, Buffett emphasized the increased importance of the *News*'s obligation to present all sides of controversial issues, local and national. He stressed that syndicated columns on the opposite editorial page had to reflect these divergent views, and even suggested the possibility of publishing two op-ed pages each day. As editor at that time, I rejected this idea since it could potentially confuse readers.

The *News*, in its primary and secondary circulation areas, faces competition for readers and advertising from a great many smaller daily and weekly papers. While the paper always strives to compete, never have we made any determination to put any competitor out of business. In fact, the *News* thrives on healthy competition whether it be presenting the news or in advertising. Lipsey, since his arrival in Buffalo, has devoted a good deal of his time in efforts to stimulate business activity in Buffalo, and to involve private enterprise in this effort to a greater extent than ever before. On another level, Lipsey has been involved with the publishers of the Rochester, Albany, and Syracuse papers to share ideas for expansion of the state's economy.

The paper also has been very active in promoting community development ventures. Although its success has been limited, the need has been even more important during times of economic downturn. The *News*, historically, has been a leader in greater support for education, and more recently, for development of the city's waterfront. The *Buffalo News*, in fact, since Butler founded it in 1873, has been a responsible and responsive newspaper, always endeavoring to promote the Buffalo area. Fortunately, the change in ownership in 1977 maintained this stance.

When Edward H. Butler decided to alter his publishing schedule in 1880 from a Sunday-only to daily publication, he was an optimistic, energetic young man ready to meet new challenges. The outlook was good, with a growing city and its enormous potential for economic development. His optimism was validated: the *Buffalo Evening News* ultimately became the city's leading daily. Now, some 125 years later, the *News* is still the leading communications vehicle in the Buffalo-Niagara region. The current path to success, however, is more difficult than the one young Butler had to tread. The *News* still faces competition from daily and weekly publications in the western New York area; from network and cable television, which serves a larger geographic area than the newspaper; and also from the emergence of the immediate news-responsive Web sites. The challenges facing publisher Lipsey and president Colville are difficult ones in this highly competitive world of communications. They must continue to strive for the advertising revenue needed to sustain an outstanding news product.

Warren E. Buffett strives to limit his involvement to capital allocation and compensation for the top executives of his holdings. In the case of the *Buffalo News*, he also establishes the basic rate structure for subscribers and advertisers. Otherwise he has always given the managers of his enterprises the freedom to run their own show. In Warren's own words, "If they need my help to manage the enterprise, we're probably both in trouble."[16]

Notes

1. "The Day the Papers Died," *Columbia Journalism Review* (November/December 2001): 61.

2. Seattle Times, "The Death Tax Is Killing Family Owned Businesses," http://www.deathtax.com/deathtax/news498.html (accessed August 26, 2003).

3. David Asher, "Who Owns What (As The Year Turns)," *Newspaper Association of America, Inc. Presstime* (January 2001): 46.

4. Mike Vogel, "Then and Now," *Buffalo News*, May 2, 1982, p. Sesqui 13.

5. *Buffalo News* circulation department.

6. "Presses: Publisher Says the *News* Never Considered Moving to Suburbs," *Buffalo News/Sunday*, June 10, 2001, p. A-1.

7. Ibid., p. A-10.

8. Ibid.

9. Ibid.

10. Ibid.

11. *News-News* (September/October 2001): 2.

12. Stanford Lipsey, interview by Murray B. Light, October 19, 2001.

13. Ibid.

14. Frank Luther Mott, *American Journalism, 1690–1940* (New York: Macmillan Company, 1941), p. 648.

15. "The Day the Papers Died."

16. Janet Lowe, *Warren Buffett Speaks* (New York: John Wiley & Sons, Inc., 1997), p. 80.

Selected Bibliography

Published Sources

Asher, David. "Who Owns What (As The Year Turns)." *Newspaper Association of America, Inc. Presstime* (January 2001): 46.

Bennett, A. Gordon. *Buffalo Newspapers since 1870*, vol. 26. Adventures in Western New York History. Buffalo, NY: Buffalo News and Erie County Historical Society, 1974.

Bianco, Anthony. "The Warren Buffett You Don't Know." *Business Week*, July 5, 1999, pp. 54–66.

Buffalo Architecture: A Guide. Cambridge, MA: MIT Press, 1996.

"The Buffalo News: One Hundred Years," centennial publication. *Buffalo News*, October 12, 1980, pp. H1–H20.

Condon, George E. *Stars in the Water: The Story of the Erie Canal.* New York: Doubleday & Company, 1974.

Dillon, Michael J. "From Populist to Patrician: Edward H. Butler's *Buffalo News* and the Crisis of Labor, 1877–1892." *American Journalism* 16, no. 1 (1999): 41–58.

Dolan, William H., compiler. *Our Police and Our City: The Official History of the Buffalo Police Department and a History of the City of Buffalo.* Edited by Mark S. Hubbell. Buffalo, NY: Bensler & Wesley, 1893.

Farhi, Paul. "The Death of the JOA." *American Journalism Review* (September 1999): 50–53.

Goldman, Mark. *City on the Lake: The Challenge of Change in Buffalo, New York*. Amherst, NY: Prometheus Books, 1990.

———. *High Hopes: The Rise and Decline of Buffalo, New York*. Albany, NY: State University of New York Press, 1983.

Hagstrom, Robert G., Jr. *The Warren Buffet Way*. New York: John Wiley & Sons, 1994.

Harriman, Lewis G. *Buffalo Evening News and Its Courageous Leader Edward H. Butler*. Buffalo, NY: Newcomen Society in North America, 1955.

Headlines & History, Buffalo News. Buffalo, NY: Buffalo News, 1999.

A History of the City of Buffalo, Its Men and Institutions. Buffalo, NY: Buffalo Evening News, 1908.

Kilpatrick, Andrew. *Of Permanent Value: The Story of Warren Buffet*. Birmingham, AL: AKPE, 1994; revised edition, 1998.

Larned, J. N. *A History of Buffalo*, vol. 1. *Delineating the Evolution of the City*. New York: Progress of the Empire State Company, 1911.

Lowenstein, Roger. *Buffett: The Making of an American Capitalist*. New York: Random House, 1995.

Lyons, Louis M. *Reporting the News: Selections from Nieman Reports*, Simon E. Sibeloff, "Free Press And Fair Trial." Cambridge, Massachusetts: The Belknap Press of Harvard University Press, 1965.

McCullough, Joseph B., and Janice McIntire-Strasburg, eds. *Mark Twain at the Buffalo Express: Articles and Sketches by America's Favorite Humorist, Mark Twain*. DeKalb: Northern Illinois University Press, 1999.

Mott, Frank Luther. *American Journalism, 1690–1940*. New York: Macmillan, 1941.

Rundell, Edwin F. *Buffalo: Your City*. Revised by Charles W. Stein. Buffalo, NY: Henry Stewart, 1962.

Unpublished Papers

Barry Berlin. "A Case Study: The Buffalo Newspaper Legal Battle," presented to the Law Division Open Paper Competition, Association for Education in Journalism Convention, Boston, Massachusetts, August 1980.

Buffalo and Erie County Historical Society Archives, C67-6. Alfred H. Kirchhofer Papers, a collection of Kirchhofer papers documenting his career with the *Buffalo Evening News* and political and civic activities.

E. H. Butler Library Archives, State University College at Buffalo, Buffalo, New York. Butler Family Papers, a collection of business and personal papers of the E. H. Butler family and *Buffalo News*.
E. H. Butler Jr. Collection
E. H. Butler Sr. Collection
Kate R. Butler, Butler Family Papers
A. Kirchhofer Papers including "History of the *Buffalo Evening News*."

Dillon, Michael J. "Private Life and Public Identity: Two Nineteenth Century Publishers Confront Scandal." Paper presented at the Mid-Atlantic Popular Culture Association/American Culture Association, November 5, 1993.

———. "Anatomy of a Crusade: Reform, Independent Politics and the *Buffalo Evening News'* Polish Crusade of 1881." Paper presented at the Mid-Atlantic Popular Culture Association/American Culture Association, October 28, 1994.

Goldberg, Jerry. "Edward H. Butler and the Founding of the *Buffalo Evening News*: The Life and Times of One of the Last Publisher-editors." Master's thesis, State University of New York at Buffalo, 1997.

INDEX

Page numbers in *italics* refer to illustrations